Atlantic Virginia

Atlantic Virginia

Intercolonial Relations in the Seventeenth Century

April Lee Hatfield

PENN

University of Pennsylvania Press
Philadelphia

10   9   8   7   6   5   4   3   2   1

First paperback edition 2007

Published by
University of Pennsylvania Press
Philadelphia, Pennsylvania 19104-4112

Library of Congress Cataloging-in-Publication Data

Hatfield, April Lee.
    Atlantic Virginia : intercolonial relations in the seventeenth century / April Lee Hatfield.
        p.   cm.
    Includes bibliographical references (p.   ) and index.
    ISBN-13: 978-0-8122-1997-5 (pbk. : alk. paper)
    ISBN-10: 0-8122-1997-X (pbk. : alk. paper)
    1. Virginia—History—Colonial period, ca. 1600–1775.   2. Virginia—Commerce—History—17th
century.   3. America—History—To 1810.   4. America—Ethnic relations.   5. Intercultural
communication—America—History—17th century.   6. America—Commerce—History—17th
century.   7. Great Britain—Colonies—America—History—17th century.   8. Spain—Colonies—
America—History—17th century.   9. France—Colonies—America—History—17th century.
I. Title.

F229.H274 2004
975.5'02—dc22

                                                                                        2003061646

For Jon

Contents

Introduction

Seventeenth-century Virginians lived in an Atlantic world held together by a web of connections linking the Chesapeake to England and Africa, to Dutch and other English colonies, and (more by their acute awareness than by direct experience) to French and Spanish colonies. Access to the Atlantic world pervaded seventeenth-century Virginia. Most of Virginia's seventeenth-century colonial population lived along navigable rivers and creeks, giving residents direct and personal connection to the Atlantic world and its inhabitants. Algonquians in the Chesapeake coastal plain and Siouans in the piedmont also lived in a world defined by long-distance contacts, using networks of trails and rivers to trade and travel widely in North America. Indian and European trade and travel networks intersected immediately upon contact and altered one another over the course of the century. By the 1690s, overland Indian travel influenced Virginia's relations with England and with other mainland colonies.

The Atlantic world emerged around the movement of goods but then provided routes as important for moving people and information. Intercolonial information had particular value for such aspects of colonization as relations with the metropole, negotiations with Indians, and the development of labor systems using African slaves, for which little or no English precedent existed. Recent work of Alison Games and Cynthia Van Zandt (and earlier work by Bernard Bailyn, Richard Pares, and Frederick Tolles) demonstrates the presence of vital intercolonial migration and communication lines during the seventeenth century, and Ian K. Steele describes an "English Atlantic" spanning the the seventeenth and eighteenth centuries.[1] Nonetheless, much seventeenth-century historiography still embodies the unspoken assumption that each colony operated as a largely self-contained entity that interacted with other colonies only indirectly, through England.[2] In fact, the intercolonial, international, and transatlantic connections that constituted the Atlantic world had a more significant impact on the development of individual colonies such as Virginia in the seventeenth century than in the eighteenth because a greater sense of experimentation prevailed in English colonies during the seventeenth century.[3] Intercolonial networks, the principal focus of this study, expanded and strengthened during the eighteenth century, but they were very much present during the seventeenth century, existing alongside and intertwining with older colonial communication lines to England so well documented by James Horn and David Cressy.[4] As colonists and officials shaped colonial institutions and societies, they looked to other colonies for both positive and negative examples. Early in the century when the only successful American colonies were Spanish and Portuguese, those models informed Virginia planners', officials', and colonists' expectations about America, especially regarding the roles of Indians and Africans in colonial American societies. Spanish and French colonies continued to hold an important place in the minds of Virginia colonists, especially during times of actual or feared war with Indians, but the later seventeenth-century Atlantic world that most Virginians experienced directly involved mostly English and Dutch colonies.

While early Americanists have increasingly realized that an Atlantic world of trade and communication grew during the early modern period, many have not yet incorporated this understanding into their treatment of events in individual colonies, still writing seventeenth-century histories as if colonies existed alongside, but not within, the Atlantic world. By examining the Atlantic world's impact on one colony, *Atlantic Virginia* argues that such approaches are incomplete. While my primary concern is to explore Virginia's connections with other parts of mainland North America and the Caribbean, these intercolonial contacts took place within a context that included Virginia's much better understood transatlantic ties. I have tried to provide a broad picture of the Atlantic world in which Virginia developed, hoping to make clear that seventeenth-century colonies can be fully understood only within their entire Atlantic (transatlantic and intercolonial and international) context.

Far more than the historians who have studied them, seventeenth-century Virginians understood that they lived in a world much larger than the Chesapeake. Neglecting or underestimating the firm links between colonies, their impact on Virginia's history, and their relevance for understanding seventeenth-century English colonists' perceptions of their world, most historians have framed colonial history largely within political boundaries. They have, moreover, often drawn a further distinction between mainland and Caribbean colonies, as if the sea constituted an effective barrier between these maritime societies, though in fact, as we have long known, it linked and exposed them to each other.[5] Such approaches fail to capture a dimension of colonial experience that was mobile, that crossed and recrossed the Atlantic Ocean and colonies' political boundaries, that entailed the adoption of a transatlantic and transnational sense of geography among colonial "adventurers," that faced outward toward seas and ships at least as intently as it looked toward westward and interior expansion, and that took for granted the circulation of people from diverse ethnic and national points of origin and the ideas and information they brought with them as they traveled. The work that follows here reconsiders the nature of these political and geographic boundaries in light of evidence that colonists moved frequently and easily across them. It also considers the impact of boundary permeability on the spread of ideas and information that affected Virginia's political, social, cultural, and economic development.

I believe I could have undertaken this project using any mainland or Caribbean colony, but it seems to me that Virginia provides a particularly useful example of the significance of an Atlantic context. Virginia's historiography has been even less mindful than average of colonial residents' relations with the inhabitants of other colonies. Indeed, historians and the American public have often understood Virginia as the beginning of a new English American world, created by repeated waves of Englishmen who, through a process of trial and error, gradually learned to survive in an isolated Chesapeake. However, Virginia was not invented by Englishmen from scratch. It was, rather, embedded in an indigenous world, looking back to Spanish models and out to other colonies. It is my hope that a persuasive case for the importance of Virginia's Atlantic context should provide historians with considerable incentive to attend to the impact of intercolonial relations on other colonies.[6]

The first three chapters of *Atlantic Virginia* describe two separate but linked intercolonial networks and explain how they functioned not only to permit the travel of goods and people but also to facilitate the movement of information. Chapter 1 examines Indians' precontact overland travels and interaction networks within and beyond the Chesapeake that shaped English colonists' perceptions of their colony, its boundaries, and its place in North America. Those overland travel routes continued to be used primarily by Indians during the seventeenth century, although those Europeans and Africans who sought to evade notice of colonial officials (Quakers and runaway servants and slaves) used them as well. The second chapter explores a different kind of long distance network, one that followed shipping routes across the Atlantic and between European colonies along the Atlantic seaboard and in the Caribbean. Because for European colonists water travel was easier, faster, and more common than overland travel, and because Barbados was the primary English colony in the second half of the seventeenth century, Virginia's seventeenth-century economic and social connections with the Caribbean were as important as its contact with other mainland colonies. Chapter 3 explains how the Chesapeake's unusual geography and dispersed trade facili-

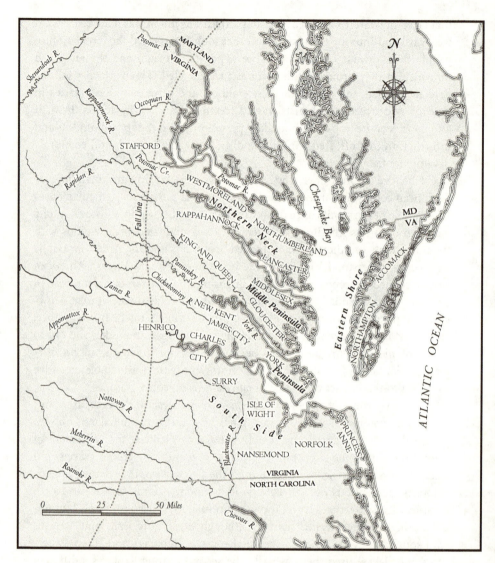

Map 1. Seventeenth-Century Virginia

tated significant communication between mariners and colonists, broadening the worlds of even the most stationary settlers. Trade patterns shaped both maritime and overland interaction patterns. The desire to move goods from one location to another thus encouraged both Indians and Europeans to form economic links that both allowed and shaped social, cultural, and political interactions. While such trade connected all Virginia colonists to the Atlantic world, the nature of those connections varied regionally within the Chesapeake. Because intercolonial trade mattered most to the Eastern Shore and the counties south of the James River, mariner-settler interaction and maritime trade routes connected those areas more firmly to other colonies in North America and the Caribbean. Maritime trade tied areas producing better tobacco (the Peninsula and Middle Peninsula) more firmly to England.[7]

Chapters 4, 5, and 6 deal with the social and cultural ramifications of Atlantic interactions that evolved around European coastal trade routes connecting mainland and Caribbean colonies to one another and linking colonies to Europe. The markets and trade opportunities that determined the configuration of these maritime trade routes subsequently shaped communication and social networks. These middle three chapters of the book suggest three different ways in which intercolonial connections mattered to colonial Virginians and to Virginia's development. Chapter 4 explores how migration and social networks evolved along intercolonial trade routes. Such interactions allowed colonists to maintain familial and social networks and shaped their sense of themselves as residents of the Atlantic world. The regional patterns of Virginia's transatlantic and intercolonial trade affected the colony's religious map, the subject of Chapter 5. Those counties most closely tied economically to New England, New Netherland, and Barbados harbored significantly larger numbers of Puritans and Quakers than did those counties more tightly tied by tobacco production to England. Chapter 6 argues that such intercolonial networks also facilitated a flow of information that shaped the development of Chesapeake slavery. Caribbean slavery and intercolonial trade provided Virginia planters access to enslaved laborers and to legal and cultural precedent for the development of a colonial American society dependent on that labor. The presence of slaves in Virginia before the 1670s depended largely on Virginia's connections to the English Caribbean and to Dutch merchants, many of them based in New Netherland. In the final quarter of the century, laws regulating the lives of slaves tightened and European colonists' belief in racial distinction began to harden throughout the English Atlantic, in patterns reflecting intercolonial communication and emulation.

Though in the background after Chapter 1, the overland movements of Indians remained a powerful part of English conceptions of Chesapeake (and indeed, North American) geography. Chapters 7 and 8 illustrate how, over the course of the century, the two kinds of networks became intertwined. Criminals and runaway servants and slaves used precontact overland routes as well as maritime routes in their attempts to flee one colony for another. Europeans who traded with Indians for beaver furs and deerskins increasingly traveled along Indians' overland trade routes, and Indians, of course, also continued to use such routes to travel for trade, hunting, migration, visiting, or warfare. Late in the seventeenth century, the establishment of England's Restoration colonies, English conquest of New Netherland, and English defeat of coastal Algonquians in several colonies encouraged English officials to believe they could use the coastal networks built up over the decades to control the overland movements of traders, Quakers, criminals, runaway servants and slaves, and most importantly, long-distance Indian travelers: all those who used such routes and who, for various reasons, attracted the censure of English officials. The meanings that intercolonial boundaries acquired in this process represented, in part, officials' reaction to the very permeability that maritime and overland interaction networks allowed. In negotiating who could travel using what methods, officials' efforts dovetailed with late-seventeenth-century English Crown attempts to control its colonies and its colonists' trade more fully. The process altered how England's North American and Caribbean colonies responded to one another and to a growing English vision of empire.

In other words, not only did intercolonial interactions allow transfers of information and people that helped define Virginia, but in addition, Virginia officials' efforts to delimit that permeability also helped define Virginia and its place within the Atlantic world. In a process that strengthened their own intercolonial ties and broadened their own colonial perspectives, seventeenth-century officials responded to intercolonial movements they deemed undesirable by trying to determine whether political boundaries between colonies would carry cultural, ethnic, and religious significance, and if so, for whom.

This book is not intended to contradict the conclusions of Darrett Rutman, Anita Rutman, and others that daily face-to-face contact on a local level created geographically limited communities. But I do suggest that we reevaluate their conclusion that in "any early American locale" members "for the most part look[ed] 'inward toward the community itself, their activities and their contemplations confined, localized,' but with a few here and there 'whose activities and thoughts' went beyond the locale."[8] Rather, I argue that an Atlantic orientation and attention to Indian travel routes; heavy reliance on transatlantic and intercolonial trade; continued transatlantic, intercolonial, and intracolonial migrations into and out of each county and parish; and frequent and intensive integration of mariners into local Chesapeake worlds all worked to enmesh such communities fully within an Atlantic context.

Part of the inward-looking nature of Virginia's historiography may derive from the colony's primacy. As England's first permanent American colony, Virginia could not rely on substantial intercolonial material support, as subsequent English colonies did. However, the colony of Virginia did begin as part of a broadly American English vision, not as a singular project divorced from other American plans. Early promoters understood Virginia to be one piece of a larger English project to challenge Spain in the Americas. Early Virginia promoters also expected that Virginia and future English colonies would together further England's international goals, contributing differently based on varied climates and strategic locations. Many of the same investors therefore contributed to the Virginia, Somers Island (Bermuda), Massachusetts Bay, and Providence Island companies.

Their hopes of challenging Spain's American dominance meant that Virginia's early promoters initially saw Virginia very much in relation to Spanish colonial America. Atlantic currents and prevailing winds took ships traveling from England to the Chesapeake first to the Caribbean, where those vessels short on supplies stopped for fresh water and food. Before the founding of English Caribbean colonies in the 1620s, English vessels bound for Virginia stopped in the Spanish Caribbean, where they took on not only supplies needed to complete their voyages but also crops, such as sugar cane, that they hoped would grow in their own colony as they did in many of Spain's. While in the Spanish Caribbean, many English migrants to Virginia received their first vision of American colonization, reinforcing their perception that they were entering a world to be understood largely by Spanish American histories. While there was much about Spanish America that Virginians did not want to emulate, Spanish successes provided enviable models for English American colonies, and Virginia's promoters looked there rather than to English failures in Roanoke or Guiana in order to predict their own opportunities. Such an international intercolonial perspective, in which Virginia could hope to rival Spanish colonies on their own terms, gave way by the 1620s to Chesapeake realities that afforded no minerals, tropical crops, or large sedentary Indian populations of potential laborers. In the same decade, the settling of Dutch and other English colonies further redirected Virginia's intercolonial focus. But before those shifts in the 1620s, the English Virginians' persistent efforts to see their own colonial project in a Spanish American context directed their own early behavior in the Chesapeake, most notably their interactions with its Powhatan natives.

Chapter 1

Indian and English Geographies

Before the Virginia Company's first ships sailed for the Chesapeake in 1606, promoters likely knew that a relatively strong and well-organized group of Indians inhabited the lower Chesapeake. Roanoke colonists had reported a powerful kingdom centered on the Chesapeake Bay.[1] That knowledge would have made the location attractive to Virginia Company officials hoping to find (as the Spanish had) an indigenous population organized in such a way to allow them to profit from trade or indigenous labor. The English knew that for over a century, Spanish colonists had adapted preexisting tribute systems in the Caribbean, Mexico, and Peru to their own benefit, using Indian labor to extract minerals and to produce food and commercial crops. Given such knowledge, the presence of a settled population made the Chesapeake more, not less, attractive as a region for colonization. Virginia Company promoters understood their efforts in light of the Spanish before them. Thus, Virginia's Atlantic world context, at a time when the Spanish dominated the Atlantic world, suggested to many Virginia Company promoters that Spanish American experience best predicted Virginia's prospects. Those expectations pointed them to the Chesapeake in the first place and suggested that they pay careful attention to the economic and political organization of the indigenous world they found there.

When the English arrived, they hoped to establish hegemony over the Chesapeake and impose their own meaning on its geographic features. Most importantly, they assumed the region would develop a new focus around its connections to Europe. However, they did not intend to establish the colony independent of its existing human geographies, nor could they have succeeded in doing so if they had tried.[2] By using the plural term geographies, I mean to suggest that there was no one way of understanding the Chesapeake geographically during the seventeenth century. Communication and conflict between Indians and Europeans created multiple but usually related ways of understanding the relationship between the physical characteristics of the Chesapeake's land and waterways, and the human relationships that added political, economic, social, or cultural meaning (geographies) to those physical spaces.

English understandings of how their exploitation of physical and human geographies would work in Virginia remained vague. They chartered a colony whose boundaries extended two hundred miles north and south of Point Comfort, and made plans to look for gold and routes to the South Sea, and to grow Spanish American tropical crops such as sugar. None of those plans panned out, and within two decades Virginia colonists abandoned most of their plans that had been based on Spanish colonization literature. However, their attention to indigenous political and economic geography, also initially derived in part from Spanish American examples, did have a lasting impact on Virginia's own political and economic geography.[3]

While the English in Virginia proved unable to profit from indigenous labor as the Spanish had, they nonetheless found that patterns of settlement, trade, and warfare provided them with opportunities to take over existing cleared land and travel routes and also placed geographic limits on their ability to explore, trade, and plant. English settlers in the Chesapeake worked within an existing Powhatan world. Preexisting exchange patterns provided them with one mechanism for moving from a situation in which they struggled to understand Indian modes of reckoning space in the Chesapeake to one in which they commanded part of that space themselves. Other factors—most importantly the demands of the tobacco trade—also shaped their settlement and drew the focus of most Anglo-Virginians eastward toward the Atlantic and Europe. However, the lasting impression of Indian geographies reinforced features of the physical geography, such as the fall line that marked both the navigable limits of the rivers and a precontact political border. While the English succeeded in renaming many important geographic features in the areas they appropriated first, making the Powhatan River the James and the Pamunkey River the York, for example, they were more likely to fail in their renaming efforts where Indian control over the geography lasted longest. They were unable to rename the Rappahannock River the Queens or the Potomac the Elizabeth, and do not appear to have even tried to rename the Appalachian Mountains or Shenandoah Valley, places they could not even explore, much less attempt to possess, for decades.[4]

Rather than representing an obliteration of Indian political and economic geographies, English colonization instead used Indian geography along with their own Atlantic orientation (supplying endless settlers and elastic tobacco markets) to establish dominance in the region. Because the English used Powhatan trade networks that connected the coastal plain to Powhatan partners and avoided Powhatan enemies, Virginia retained geographic legacies of the alliances and enmities of its weakened indigenous inhabitants. Furthermore, while the English controlled the Chesapeake coastal plain by the end of the seventeenth century and regarded its geography as wholly English, Indians remained paramount beyond the coastal plain, and Virginia colonists knew it. When European traders did travel into the piedmont and the Appalachian Mountains, precontact paths determined the routes they took. Even as European traders and travelers increasingly entered the precontact trail system in the final decades of the century, they did not take it over. Indians continued to use the trail system for trade and travel in far greater numbers than did Europeans. Thus, while the Chesapeake coastal plain became English over the course of the seventeenth century, the path system that connected it to other parts of eastern North America remained primarily Indian. That path system, which had evolved and acquired its shape because it conformed to Indians' political and economic needs, retained that shape as the trade along it increasingly met the demands of Euro-Indian trade. As Europeans established colonies along the Eastern Seaboard and drew borders between them, long-established trails crossed new political boundaries. Travel along the historical path system therefore acquired new political meanings in the colonial period—meanings that the governments of Virginia and other European colonies tried to control.

At the start of the seventeenth century, the Algonquian-speaking Powhatans inhabited the Chesapeake coastal plain south of the Potomac River. The Algonquian-speaking Piscataways and other Algonquian speakers lived in the coastal plain north of the Potomac, and Iroquoian-speaking Susquehannocks at the head of the Chesapeake Bay and on the Susquehanna River. Those Indians' political, economic, and cultural geographies contributed to a developing English colonial understanding of the Chesapeake and its relation to other parts of North America. The Powhatans, within whose territory Virginia colonists settled, most affected English Virginians' sense of the colony's boundaries, but the Susquehannocks and Potomac River Algonquians, with whom Virginia merchants traded, affected colonists' sense of their relationship to other regions and people. After the 1634 founding of Maryland limited Virginians' interactions with Indians north of the Potomac River, Powhatan connections beyond the Chesapeake determined English Virginians' opportunities for overland travel. Powhatans provided English explorers, traders, and colonists with guides and interpreters, established path systems, and verbal descriptions and drawn maps of the region. Because the English settled in Powhatan core areas, Powhatan boundaries and hostilities with other Indians limited English movements. But even after Maryland's establishment shifted Virginia fur traders' attention to the southwest, long-distance travel routes originating in Maryland continued to affect Virginia. Indians and a few Europeans traveled from other regions of North America to Virginia via these northern Chesapeake routes well into the eighteenth century. So even though Virginia traders found themselves unable to profit from trade routes north of the Potomac, Virginians remained highly aware that those paths tied them to Iroquoia, to England's northern colonies, and ultimately to French Canada. Colonists' sense of Virginia's geographical relationship to other regions of North America and to other mainland colonies developed from a combination of knowledge gained via ocean navigation and their growing understanding of Indian travel routes and political geographics.

Map 2. The Powhatans' World. After Helen C. Rountree, frontispiece and Figure 3.1, in Rountree, ed., *Powhatan Foreign Relations: 1500–1722* (Charlottesville, Va., 1993), 77.

When the English established Jamestown in 1607, Powhatan Algonquians occupied the Chesapeake coastal plain from the south bank of the James (Powhatan) River to the south bank of the Potomac River, a territory they called Tsenacommacah. The paramount chief Powhatan had taken his name from the name of his birth town at the falls of the Powhatan River. He in turn gave that name (at least in English records) to the thirty-odd Algonquian-speaking communities he governed.[5] Powhatan had inherited the power he held over six communities on the upper James and York River tributaries, which remained the core of his territory.[6] He had conquered the rest and maintained his control over them through links of exchange and alliance. A lesser chief, called a *werowance*, governed each of these communities. Algonquians on the south bank of the Potomac River, such as the Patawomecks, were only loosely bound to Powhatan, and retained more independence than Tsenacommacah's chiefdoms farther south.[7] Tsenacommacah was bounded on the west by the fall line that divides the flat coastal plain from the hillier Appalachian piedmont. The fall line runs from the northeast to the southwest crossing the major rivers at their falls, whose rocky rapids mark the point above which the rivers are not navigable by oceangoing ships. To the west of the fall line, in the piedmont, lived the Powhatans' Siouan-speaking enemies the Monacans and Mannahoacs: Monacans up the James River from Powhatan core settlements; Mannahoacs above the fall line of the Rappahannock.[8] A relatively uninhabited area was maintained between the coastal plain and the piedmont, from present-day Richmond west to about twenty miles above the falls of the James.[9] John Smith's 1612 map of Virginia, depicting information learned from the Powhatans during his 1608 exploration of the Chesapeake, showed a clearly defined zone separating westernmost Powhatan settlements from Monacans and Mannahoacs.[10] Iroquois hunting and war parties from the Five Nations (whom the Powhatans called Massawomecks) traveled southwest along the Appalachian mountains and Shenandoah Valley to the Chesapeake and to regions farther south.[11] Their seasonal raids on the Powhatans reinforced the fall line as a boundary between Algonquian land and western enemy land. The Monacans also regarded the Massawomecks as important enemies.[12] In the coastal plain north of the Potomac in what became Maryland, and south of the James in what became North Carolina, lived Algonquian-speaking Indians culturally and linguistically similar to the Powhatans, and who had occasional and generally friendly contact with the Powhatans. The Piscataway and Patuxent chiefdoms encompassed much of the coastal plain north of the Potomac.[13] To Tsenacommacah's southwest and south were long-time Powhatan trading partners: Siouan-speaking Occaneechees and Iroquoian-speaking Nottoways, Meherrins, and Tuscaroras.[14] Tsenacommacah's southern and western borders may have originated in physical geography (the fall line and the Great Dismal Swamp). The northern Potomac boundary did not. Rivers were a means of transportation, facilitating communication, not impeding it. The Potomac, therefore, was not a natural boundary, a fact illustrated by the cultural and linguistic continuity of Algonquians to the north and south of the river.

Indians traveled throughout eastern North America using a network of paths and streams. Many trails followed waterways so that travelers could walk upstream and canoe downstream. They traveled for trade, war, diplomacy, and social visits and to spread news. The longest journeys, for war, trade, or diplomacy, could cover distances as great as five thousand miles.[15] Women and children, as well as men, made short- and long-distance trips. Messengers brought news of Indians and Europeans from the lower Mississippi Valley to the Great Lakes and Canada. In the early seventeenth century Powhatan reportedly sent men overland every year to "West India" (likely the Gulf of Mexico), Newfoundland, and other regions "to bring back word of what is going on."[16]

The "Great Indian Warpath" was one of the main paths running northeast-southwest from the Gulf of Mexico to Iroquoia, with connections to Canada. One branch of it followed the Shenandoah Valley—a route later used by U.S. Highway 11 and Interstate 81—and connected with paths that penetrated the Appalachian Mountains to the Chesapeake piedmont and coastal plain. From this branched other trails and river routes that connected all Eastern woodland Indians to Lake Superior's copper sites and the Atlantic and Gulf Coasts. Chesapeake Algonquians' primary trade routes ran east-west. Shell beads (roanoke and peake) from the eastern mainland and the Chesapeake's Eastern Shore and copper and the red root dye puccoon from the west were the primary trade goods flowing into the Chesapeake coastal plain. Powhatan also received furs from some of his western trading partners and probably collected corn (which he exported) as tribute from Tsenacommacah's lesser chiefdoms.[17] There were two central points in the Virginia path networks that connected the coastal plain to the Great Indian Warpath and other trails. The first was at the falls of the upper James River Powhatan settlements (near the fall line of the James and Appomattox Rivers) to the south and southwest, crossing the Appalachians in Carolina to connect to the Great Indian Warpath. The Powhatan tribes on the James River just below the falls (Appamattucks, Arrohatecks, Powhatans, and Weyanocks) had the best access to this route and the most contact with Iroquoians to the south and southwest. Though Siouan Monacans and Mannahoacs in the piedmont to the west and northwest had access to copper (found in Michigan's Upper Peninsula and in the Blue Ridge Mountains), warfare between Powhatans and these groups had precluded

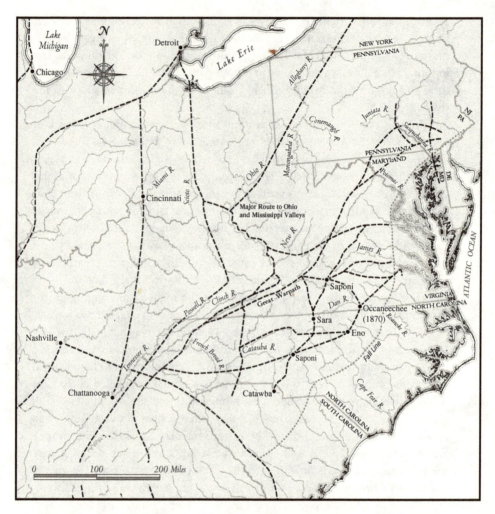

Map 3. Precontact Path Systems. After Helen C. Rountree, Figure 1.3., *Powhatan Foreign Relations*, 34, and Helen Hornbeck Tanner, frontispiece, in Peter H. Wood, Gregory A. Waselkov, and M. Thomas Hatley, eds., *Powhatan's Mantle: Indians in the Colonial Southeast* (Lincoln, Nebr., 1989).

trade directly west for decades and perhaps centuries.[18] Because Powhatan's inherited core towns on the upper York and James River tributaries straddled the trade routes connecting the Chesapeake's southeastern coastal plain to the mountains, he could therefore get western copper and puccoon without crossing the piedmont to his west, a situation that reduced any incentive to try and therefore over time probably strengthened that boundary. Because Powhatan's geographical position allowed him to exercise control over the exchange of copper and shell beads between the coastal and mountain regions, it provided economic advantages that likely enabled him to create Tsenacommacah.

The second nexus of paths lay at the falls of the Potomac River. Trails led up the Potomac to what is now Harpers Ferry and connected to the Great Indian Warpath and other northeast-southwest Indian trails at the confluence of the Potomac and Shenandoah Rivers.[19] Through this route the Patawomecks near the falls of the Potomac River had access to long-distance contacts independent of Powhatan's southwest contacts. Indeed, the name Patawomeck itself means "a landing place for goods," suggesting the importance of their access to western trade routes. Powhatan's weaker control over the northernmost chiefdoms in Tsenacommacah and his northern boundary at the Potomac (despite cultural and linguistic continuity across the river) probably resulted from the existence of an alternative copper and shell bead trade route on the north shore of the Potomac that provided Potomac River Algonquians with their own access to western goods and therefore the ability to resist Powhatan expansion.[20] Their travels provided them with goods and knowledge from as far away as Spanish settlements on the Gulf Coast. Sometime before 1621 an English explorer in a Patawomeck town saw a "Boxe or Casket" made of palmetto and lined with blue taffeta "after the China or East India fashion." The Patawomeck chief said that it had been a gift from mountain people living to the southwest, who had gotten it from farther people who lived a total of thirty days' journey from Patawomeck and only four days from the ocean, on a river into which "Ships come."[21]

To the northeast, at the head of the Chesapeake Bay, lived the Susquehannocks. They were Iroquoian speakers living on the Susquehanna River, which connected via canoe routes to the Great Lakes and Ohio River tributaries. This was an important trade route connecting the Chesapeake to other parts of North America, a route to which Powhatans did not have access. Though the Powhatans and Susquehannocks knew of one another, they had little direct contact. The Susquehannocks, like the Powhatans, were enemies of the Iroquois Five Nations and impeded Iroquois travel to the Chesapeake via the Susquehanna River route.[22]

When the English arrived and settled near the core of Powhatan's Tsenacommacah, they planned to make use of Indian exchange routes. They not only hoped that Chesapeake Indians would trade animal pelts and food (and gold and silver) for European copper and manufactured goods, but they also hoped to extract tribute payments from Powhatans. This hope derived from English familiarity with Spanish colonization literature. The Spanish in the Caribbean, Mesoamerica, and Peru had appropriated indigenous systems for funneling goods and labor to political elites. Spanish American colonists had benefitted by leaving the structures of indigenous political and economic hierarchies in place, while intensifying them and altering their purpose. They thereby provided themselves with food, gold and silver, and labor and created colonies whose geographic shape reflected those of the indigenous polities they had replaced. Some Virginia promoters and colonists wished to do the same in their colony. John Smith was perhaps most explicitly interested in following a Spanish model.[23] He later reported that while in Virginia he had argued that the colonists should have "forced the treacherous and rebellious Infidels to doe all manner of drudgery worke and slavery for them, themselves living like Souldiers upon the fruits of their labours." Had they done so, according to Smith, they could have avoided their starving time. The context for the quotation makes clear Smith's expectations that his readers would know the Spanish texts and interpret English opportunities in their light: "The manner how to suppresse them is so often related and approved, I omit it here: And you have twenty examples of the Spaniards how they got the West-Indies, and forced the treacherous and rebellious Infidels to doe all manner of drudgery worke and slavery for them."[24]

While Powhatan collected some tribute from his lesser chiefdoms, the scale and organization level of Tsenacommacah's tribute system did not approach those of the Caribbean, Mesoamerica, and Peru, so even if the English had gained firm control of Powhatan himself and Tsenacommacah's core (which they could not for years), they would not have been able to use that control to feed themselves or to channel significant wealth. Nevertheless, the stubborn belief of some colonists and promoters that English colonists could insinuate themselves into a preexisting Chesapeake system for concentrating wealth provided English Virginians with great incentive to study Powhatan exchange networks, and increased their tendency to see Virginia and Tsenacommacah as synonymous. John Smith's map of Virginia (first drawn in 1608 and published in 1612) encompassed a territory that corresponded to Tsenacommacah but not to Virginia's much more extensive charter boundaries or to the much less extensive scope of English settlement, limited to a few hundred people on the lower James River. Smith chose Powhatan political borders, rather than Virginia's official or functional boundaries, to define Virginia visually. He, who hoped so strongly to imitate Spanish conquests, had paid careful attention to Tsenacommacah's political geography when Powhatans described it to him. Smith's placement of the letters "Powhatan" across his Virginia further suggested his identification of the two polities with one another.[25]

As the most important (though not only) translators of the region to the

Map 4. John Smith's Map of Virginia. Courtesy Newberry Library, Chicago.

English, the Powhatans imparted a sense of both the region's borders and its relations with Indians beyond those borders. The English learned quickly that the fall line defined the political geography of the Chesapeake Indian world as finitely as it limited European ability to navigate the region's rivers.[26] In the first years of English settlement, the Powhatans staged a graphic illustration of that political geography for the English. To demonstrate their fighting skills to the newcomers, the Powhatans divided themselves into war companies of "Powhatans" and "Monacans," established war terms (the losers' wives and children to go as prizes to the winners), sang war songs, shouted, and pretended to fight.[27] The English clearly absorbed the Powhatans' geography lesson. William Strachey and John Smith both filled their accounts with references to the enmity between the Powhatans and the Indians beyond the falls.

During the first years of English presence in the Chesapeake, including the First Anglo-Powhatan War from 1609 to 1614, Powhatans and English both attempted to force one another into a subject position. The English tried to create a tribute situation whereby Powhatans would feed them, and Powhatan tried to make Jamestown a lesser chiefdom whose primary role would be to supply him with copper, thereby bolstering his position vis-à-vis his own lesser werowances and other Indians in the region. In 1613 the English did succeed in collecting corn that had previously gone to Powhatan from Eastern Shore and Potomac River chiefdoms.[28] However, any English hopes of secure food or revenue sources from tributary Powhatans and any hopes among the Powhatans of forcing the English colony into a role as a subsidiary lesser chiefdom ended with the decade-long Second Anglo-Powhatan War that began in 1622. English colonists' earlier hopes of a Spanish-style exploitation of Indian labor, requiring an integration of European and Native American worlds, gave way to English plans to separate themselves from the Powhatans and wage war, raiding corn to feed themselves and weakening the Powhatans in the process.[29] But fifteen years spent trying to appropriate Tsenacommacah in Spanish style left their mark on English colonists' and promoters' perception of Chesapeake geography. In 1622, Englishman John Martin wrote that "That parte of Virginia wthin wch wee are seated and fitt to be settled on for many hundred yeares: is wth in the Territories of Opichankano [Powhatan's successor] . . . whoe Commaundeth from the Southemost parte of the first River [the James] to the Southermost parte of the fourth River called Patomeck. . . . In longitude it extendeth to the Monakins Countrie . . . west and west by North."[30] Martin, like Smith, saw Virginia as Tsenacommacah, despite a charter that extended the colony's boundaries two hundred miles north and south of Point Comfort, and settlement limited to the James River and the southwestern Eastern Shore.[31] While some English merchants traded in the northern Chesapeake, the boundaries Martin described remained Virginia's functional borders until the end of the century, well after increased population and land speculation had put considerable pressure on colonists to expand beyond Tsenacommacah.

Chesapeake Indians' exchange routes within and outside Tsenacommacah likewise shaped English perceptions of the region and their opportunities in it. When the English began their explorations within Tsenacommacah, they relied heavily on the guidance of Powhatans who knew who had what to trade, knew the routes to and from their trading partners, and could travel more safely in some directions than in others, based on their cultural, political, and economic relations with surrounding and more distant Native American nations.[32] Before John Smith began his discoveries of the Chesapeake Bay, Powhatan told him what to expect and drew "plots upon the ground (according to his discourse) of all those regions," relaying his knowledge both visually and verbally.[33] In 1608 chief Powhatan showed Smith some canoes and told him (as Smith understood it) "how hee sent [his people] over the Baye, for tribute Beads, and also what Countries paide him Beades, Copper or Skins." In June of that year as Smith began to explore the Chesapeake Bay (in part to look for fur trading locations), he already knew the best place to trade for furs and for shell beads, information he could only have gotten from Indians.[34] The English asked for Powhatan guides when traveling and frequently relied on Indians to direct them to towns and to explain to them what lay ahead. While they also received descriptions of geography from non-Powhatan Algonquians and at least one Monacan guide, their initial Powhatan introduction to the region and their settlement focus on areas overlapping with Tsenacommacah's core led them to see Powhatans as normative and their perspective on the region as primary.[35] The rapids at the rivers' falls and Powhatan hostilities with piedmont Siouans limited Virginians' opportunities to move beyond Tsenacommacah's western borders, despite their interest. On an exploratory voyage up the James River, John Smith's Powhatan guide took him as far as the falls, but "further he would not goe" so they turned around and Smith had to settle for Powhatan descriptions of the Indians and landscape beyond.[36] Referring readers to his 1612 map of Virginia, Smith noted that "as far as you see the little Crosses on rivers, mountaines, or other places have beene discovered; the rest was had by information of the Savages, and are set downe, according to their instructions."[37] Those crosses appear at the fall lines of the rivers.

Powhatan consciously labored to make the Powhatan boundary meaningful for the English as well as for the Powhatans, recognizing the potential threat that English contact with his enemies could pose and trying to keep them apart.[38] Strachey reported that "it hath bene Powhatan[']s great care, to keepe us by all meanes from the acquaintaunce of those nations that bordure and Confront him, for besides his knowledge how easely and willingly his enemyes wilbe drawne upon him by the least Countenance and encouragement from us, he doth by keeping us from trading with them monopolize all the Copper brought into Virginia by the English."[39] If Powhatan could monopolize English trade, that trade would provide yet another means of increasing his strength.

The English quickly recognized the Susquehannocks as potentially important trading partners. Their access to northern trade routes gave them better furs. John Smith placed them at the edge of his map of Virginia, but his use of a large human figure to represent them suggested their importance to the region and the colony. The Massawomecks/Iroquois represented trading opportunities and reinforced the western political border. John Smith noted that "Beyond the mountaines from whence is the head of the river Patawo-meke, the Savages report inhabit their most mortall enimies, the Massawo-mekes upon a great salt water, which by all likelyhood is either some part of Cannada some great lake, or some inlet of some sea that falleth into the South sea. These Massawomekes are a great nation and very populous." But Smith then explained that seven boats of Massawomecks met English explorers at the head of the Chesapeake Bay. Their "Targets, Baskets, Swords, Tobacco pipes, Platters, Bowes and Arrowes, and every thing shewed, they much exceeded them of our parts, and their dexteritie in their small boats made of the barkes of trees sowed with barke and well luted with gumme, argueth that they are seated upon some great water."[40] Smith understood that the Massawomeck/Iroquois could travel to the Chesapeake both by boat to head of the Chesa-peake bay and overland through the mountains and down the Potomac. Their appearance at Tsenacommacah's western borders and at the head of the bay therefore suggested to the English at least two routes by which Virginia was connected to Iroquoia. They represented trading opportunities and potential danger to Virginia. Indian alliances, trade routes, and antipathies thus sug-gested parameters for English Virginians' trade and exploration, at times rein-forcing physical geographic boundaries such as the fall line separating the coastal plain from the piedmont. Although traditional enemies such as the Powhatans and the Monacans sometimes allied with one another in response to English invasions, the long-established path systems and the patterns of interaction these made possible continued to reflect and reinforce historic hos-tilities.[41]

Even after the English defeated the Powhatans in the Second Anglo-Powhatan War during the 1620s, Virginia colonists continued to learn geogra-phy from Chesapeake Indians. Learning about people and places beyond Tsen-acommacah from maps that Powhatans and Potomac River Algonquians drew (like the "plots upon the ground" that Powhatan drew for Smith), the English incorporated information about physical and social and political geographies into their own drawn maps.[42] The way Indians visually portrayed their political geography to the English emphasized that overland routes connected the Chesapeake to other regions of North America. Indians drew many of their maps with circles to represent tribes or nations, with lines drawn to represent routes (either waterways or overland paths) that linked them, rather than attempting to represent entire geographic spaces as European maps did.[43] The blank spaces between circles on Indian maps emphasized both the connections that did exist (if lines traveled through those spaces) and the difficulty of travel where they did not. Even Indian maps that provided more representations of topography nonetheless simplified the landscape to emphasize those aspects

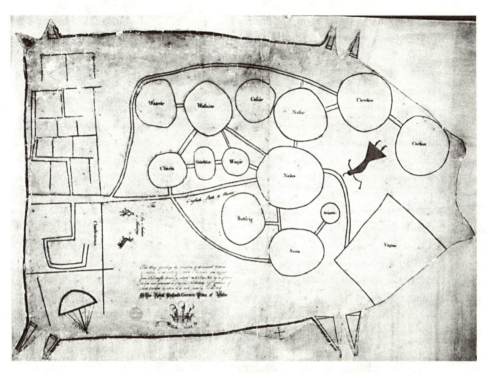

Map 5. Deerskin Map. Courtesy British Library, London.

that facilitated travel (trails and rivers) or impeded it (mountains or dead-end trails).[44] The English relied on these maps for knowledge of the interior. Their own maps, which sought to provide detailed accounts of the coastlines for shipping and represent space either settled or available for settlement, stood in stark contrast to Indian maps emphasizing routes between peoples. Indians throughout eastern North America did not edge their maps with a frame or border, preferring to draw them on the ground, which extended out in all directions beyond the drawing, rather than on a piece of paper, which possessed edges and therefore created visual endpoints to the geography portrayed by the map.[45] The lack of borders on Indian maps further emphasized to European viewers that despite the existence of Indian political boundaries, the routes crossing those borders and connecting nations far distant from one another were a salient feature of North American Indian geography.

Moreover, precontact interaction patterns determined English travel opportunities. Existing paths dictated where travel was possible, and though the English found many paths well worn and easy to follow, they needed Indian guides who knew which led where and how to get food along the way, and who could introduce them to other Indians and serve as interpreters.[46] Thus, Powhatan contacts and Powhatan boundaries not only shaped English perceptions of the boundaries of Virginia but also determined their own trade and travel options. Though the English Virginians had no interest in either the puccoon or the Great Lakes copper that made precontact trade routes valuable to Chesapeake coastal plain Algonquians, these same routes nevertheless determined the course of their fur, deerskin, and slave trade and their exploration to the west and south from Virginia.[47] European involvement in Chesapeake long-distance trade began when westernmost Powhatans (those involved in copper and puccoon trades), Potomac River Algonquians, and Susquehannocks brought furs, skins, and war captives to English ships in the James or Potomac Rivers or at the head of the bay, all points near the three paths leading out of the Chesapeake. While this method dominated in the northern Chesapeake, in the southern Chesapeake Powhatans began to bring goods to English settlements and occasional English traders traveled to Powhatan towns until exchange then moved to trading posts at the falls of the rivers. English traders there met non-Powhatan traders who brought pelts and slaves to the places where they had for centuries traded western copper for Algonquian shell beads.

Henry Fleet's experiences trading in the Potomac during the 1620s and 1630s provide particularly good evidence of Chesapeake Indians' long-distance connections and the opportunities these provided for English traders. Fleet's trade also illustrates how antagonistic Algonquian relations with Indians in the piedmont and beyond limited English trade with those people, bounding English interaction patterns at the falls. In the 1620s as a captive of the Anacostans, Fleet jointed his captors on several long-distance overland trips. The Anacostans were Algonquian speakers who lived on the north bank of the Potomac River just below the falls and maintained wary but usually peaceful contacts with both the Algonquian-speaking Piscataway chiefdom in the Maryland coastal plain and with the Iroquoian Massawomecks/Five Nations who traveled to the Potomac, though the Piscataways and Massawomecks were enemies.[48] Fleet reported that the Piscataway tayac (paramount chief) feared the Anacostans "because they are protected by the Massomacks of Canyda Indians, who have used to convey all such English truck as cometh into the river to the Massomacks."[49] After Fleet's escape he used his language skills and knowledge of Potomac River Indians to become an active trader in the area, exchanging a variety of English goods for beaver skins destined for England and corn for New England.

In May 1632 Fleet arrived in the Potomac to find that other English traders had circulated rumors that he had died in a storm, in order to preempt his trade with the Piscataways. Fearing that the Piscataways would trade away all their beaver skins before he arrived, Fleet went ashore as soon as he reached the mouth of the river and sent messengers overland to the Piscataways, a three-day journey toward the falls, instructing them "not to miss an Indian town and to certify them of my arrival." But rival trader Charles Harman had already gotten the beaver from both sides of the river as far as the Piscataway town where the tayac lived. The tayac came aboard, apologized for trading with Harman, and gave Fleet 114 beaver skins as a gift. Upriver, Fleet managed to trade for "800 weight" of beaver at the Anacostans' town.[50]

Not wanting to leave without a full cargo, Fleet remained in the Potomac and in June learned from an Indian interpreter recently returned from the Massawomecks that they possessed an "infinite store of beaver." Fleet considered traveling to Massawomeck territory, but found his "neighbor Indians" strongly opposed to his plan. The Piscataways said they had recently lost a thousand people in a Massawomeck attack and wanted no friend of theirs trading with their enemies. The Massawomecks, however, came to the Potomac in birch bark canoes and lobbied for Fleet to change his alliance. The third group of Indian actors, Fleet's former captors the Anacostans, tried to prevent him from trading directly with the Massawomecks because it would jeopardize the precarious position they enjoyed as middlemen between the Iroquois and the English in the Potomac River. Fleet's desire for the Massawomecks' beaver trumped any loyalty he may have felt toward his Piscataway and Anacostan partners. He sent two "trusty Indians" and his brother "who could travel well" to the Massawomecks with gifts for each of the reported Massawomeck chiefs and a message for the Massawomecks to come to the falls of the Potomac, where he would wait with his ship. When his brother and the two Indians returned in early July, they confirmed the reports of populous towns and abundant beaver, reporting that 110 Indians laden with pelts had accompanied them half way. Those Indians had been chosen "by the whole nation, to see what we were, what was our intent, and whether friends or foes, and what commodities we had." The Anacostans, however, stopped them, relying on duplicity, a tactic open to them as middlemen who could communicate better with both Englishmen and Massawomecks than either could with the other. They told the Massawomecks that the English planned to destroy them to avenge the thousand Piscataways that the Massawomecks had recently killed. According to the Anacostans' story, the 114 beaver skins that the Piscataways had given Fleet as apology for trading his promised skins to Charles Harman actually constituted payment with which they hired Fleet to kill the Massawomecks.[51] When Fleet confronted the Anacostans with their lie, they responded by offering to bring the Massawomeck traders to the Potomac to do business

if Fleet promised to make "a firm league with" the Anacostans, an arrange-
ment that would preserve their position as middlemen. Fleet, still hoping to
trade directly with the Massawomecks, refused the offer, but Indian rivalries
and Anacostan interceptions of traders continued to plague his efforts to
establish direct trade, and he later wished he had continued to trade through
the Anacostans.[52] Thus, the Anacostans, for a time, successfully preserved the
fall line boundary and their own unique position as boundary crossers by
using the Piscataway-Iroquois rivalry and the known English affiliation with
Chesapeake Algonquians.

English Virginians like Fleet initially found northern trade on the Potomac and at the head of the Bay most attractive because northern furs were
thicker and more highly valued on European markets, but by the end of the
1630s, the establishment of Maryland ended Virginians' efforts to trade with
Potomac River Algonquians and with the Susquehannocks.[53] Thereafter, Virginia fur traders' aspirations focused on Powhatan trade routes that lead from
the falls of the James and its tributaries to the southwest. Through the 1640s,
English traders depended on Powhatan middlemen, but the English defeat of
the Powhatans in the Third Anglo-Powhatan War of 1644–46 encouraged
English exploration attempts in the following decades. An English effort to
explore and trade along the southwestern trade route in 1643, before the defeat
of the Powhatans in the 1644–46 war, left no record of success (and in fact
may have provided additional incentive to the Powhatans to challenge English
Virginia the following year).[54]

The Second Anglo-Powhatan War of the 1620s had established Virginia as
dominant over Tsenacommacah. Their victory in that war allowed the English
to stop thinking of the region in explicitly Powhatan terms, the way Martin had
done in 1622 when he described Virginia as "wth in the Territories of Opichankano." But while such associations of Virginia and Tsenacommacah were no
longer explicit after the 1620s, English Virginians continued to think of their
colony's boundaries as those that had been Powhatan's. The Third Anglo-
Powhatan War in the 1640s marked the end of the process whereby Virginia
appropriated the region and established it as their own. By midcentury, then,
Virginia no longer represented an invasion within Tsenacommacah but, rather,
an effective supplanting of the now-defunct Powhatan polity. The 1646 treaty
ending the war culminated the decades-long English attempt to conquer Tsenacommacah. It forced Powhatans to pay twenty beaver skins a year to the
English, politically significant though economically unimportant tribute. The
treaty also kept the Powhatans out of their former core area between the York
and James Rivers.[55] During the war, in 1645, the General Assembly ordered forts
built at the falls of the James and Appomattox Rivers, on the Pamunkey and

the "ridge" of Chickahominy, and on the Rappahannock, despite a treaty that preserved both sides of the Rappahannock for the Powhatans. By establishing most of their forts at fall line boundaries of Tsenacommacah—where Smith had drawn his crosses—the English colonists transformed his symbolic appropriation into a more concrete one. While their wartime purpose was to protect the English from the Powhatans whom they had driven beyond Tsenacommacah, after the war those forts at the falls of the James and Appomattox marked the boundary (formerly Tsenacommacah's) now delineating the division between the English colony and the Indians beyond the falls, some of them historic Powhatan enemies. These antagonists now became more dangerous because the English had weakened the Powhatans and assumed Tsenacommacah's western border. This process would continue as the English built forts at the falls of other rivers over the course of the century, an activity they deemed necessary only because falls marked a political, as well as geographic, boundary.[56]

Although the Powhatans lost much of their political power within the Chesapeake by 1646, their historic political geographies remained important to the English at and beyond its perimeters. Their newly defined tributary status included an alliance in which the English revealed their perceptions of Powhatans as subjects, as familiar, and as buffers against "stranger" Indians. The English use of Powhatans as a buffer against Indians beyond the falls was clear by the 1650s. In 1655 or 1656 six to seven hundred Richahecrians (Monacans) moved from the west to settle near the falls of the James, perhaps having been forced there by the Iroquois/Massawomecks. The Weyanock werowance told the English that the "Massahocks" (probably Massawomecks) had come "to fight the Rickahockans." Virginia sent Edward Hill and Totopotomoi (werowance of the Pamunkeys) with one hundred men each to drive the Siouans west. In defeating the combined English-Powhatan forces, the Siouans killed Totopotomoi and nearly all the Powhatan soldiers. In 1657 another militia force seems, in turn, to have defeated the Siouans.[57]

Continued Siouan presence in the piedmont and continued—perhaps heightened—Iroquois travel meant that historic Powhatan alliances and enmities remained crucial to the Virginia colony and especially to European traders. Thus, when colonists traveled beyond Tsenacommacah's borders in the second half of the seventeenth century, they had little choice but to journey along Powhatan routes to trade with Powhatan partners. However, while precontact paths determined the direction and precise routes of European traders' travel, those traders entered the path systems with some distinct advantages: they brought European trade goods that Indians had begun to depend on.[58] So while Indian disagreements about who controlled what aspects of trade hindered and sometimes endangered English traders, the increasing dependence of southeastern Indians on English weapons and alcohol ensured a growing market for their goods that increasingly gave the English an upper hand in the situation. Moreover, burgeoning English populations made Indian resistance increasingly difficult. Nonetheless, their resistance to direct English participation in trade beyond the falls persisted in the second half of the seventeenth century, frustrating traders to the point of helping to precipitate a civil war—Bacon's Rebellion—in the colony.

During the second half of the seventeenth century, several explorers followed the most important Powhatan trade paths, those that led from southern Virginia to the south and southwest.[59] European explorers pursued trade, routes to the Pacific, and mining possibilities. They exchanged cloth and guns from England and rum from the Caribbean for furs and deerskins for European markets and slaves for the Caribbean.[60] The Powhatans' loss of power limited their ability to prevent incursions from other Indians on their middleman role in English-Indian trade, and in 1662 the Virginia Assembly worried that "Northern Indians" prevented Virginia's tributary Indians from the trading that many of them depended on for survival.[61] But despite the Powhatans' much weakened position in the Chesapeake, English traders depended on them for translation and introductions, because while the English had achieved dominance in the Chesapeake coastal plain, they had not done so beyond Tsenacommacah's borders. They used the now weakened but useful Powhatans to negotiate Indian economic and political geographies beyond the fall line borders that were now Virginia's, using paths established by years of Powhatan trade. Although furbearing animals lived throughout the Appalachians, English Virginians after the 1640s had access only to those captured by Indians connected with Powhatan by precontact trade networks. Thus, increased English trading activity represented not a blazing of new trails but rather European traders' gradual ability to encroach on preexisting trade routes. While their increasing presence reflected dramatic—if gradual—changes in the balance of power between English and Indians and between different groups of Indians, the history of the place continued to assert its influence on the geography of trade. Like Fleet's experience with the Anacostans who acted as middlemen between the Piscataway and Iroquois Massawomecks, English traders to the southwest who tried to bypass traditional middlemen encountered resistance from those reluctant to surrender their roles in the trade. When traders tried to go due west across the fall line boundary, they failed. Powhatan guides knew little of the area and lacked connections with enemy Indians. Furthermore, the complete lack of trails, reflecting years of Siouan-Algonquian hostility, made travel almost impossible.

The most active traders among Tsenacommacah's southwesternmost chiefdoms, and the southwestern Siouans and Iroquoians most involved in earlier trade to the Powhatan chiefdom or to the English colony, reacted to English expeditions in a variety of ways. Their disparate responses reflected each group's understanding of how a direct trade between English colonists and southwestern fur sources, especially Iroquoian-speaking Tuscaroras, would affect their own role as either traders or middlemen. Weyanocks, Appamattucks, Quiyoughchohannocks, and Warraskoyacks, the Powhatan chiefdoms south of James River who had the closest access to the southwestern trade routes and had the most contact with the Iroquoians to the southwest, acted as the traders between the Powhatan chiefdom and these tribes. A Weyanock werowance told the English that he traveled to the Anoags (possibly Tuscaroras) ten days to the southwest, knew the Anoags' language, and had brought back "their Commodityes . . . [and] Presents to Powhatan."[62]

These southwestern Powhatans—middlemen for the Powhatans and for the English during the first half of the century—employed different strategies in response to English explorations and trading ventures after midcentury. Each strategy reinforced the importance of precontact economic exchange patterns for the English. The Appamattucks most frequently provided guides for the English. The Weyanocks, in contrast, tried several times to preserve their position as middlemen and prevent the English from trading directly with the Tuscaroras. Siouan-speaking Occaneechee Indians, located in the piedmont near the present-day Virginia-North Carolina border, also tried to preserve a middleman role. The travel accounts left by English explorers and traders illustrate how Indian interaction patterns shaped English opportunities for travel, English perceptions of Virginia's boundaries, and English Virginia's long-distance contacts with the regions beyond those boundaries. The first of these traders' accounts also illustrates the varied responses of southern Powhatan trading nations to English expeditions.

In late August 1650 the Appamattuck guide Pyancha led merchants Edward Bland and Abraham Wood with four other Englishmen from Fort Henry (the site of present day Petersburg) at the falls of the Appomattox River "intending a South westerne Discovery," in part to trade with the Iroquoian-speaking Tuscaroras.[63] Wood, a member of the House of Burgesses, lived at Fort Henry and managed it for the colony, using it as a base for his fur-trading business. Pyancha led Wood, Bland, and the rest of the English party from town to town along well-traveled paths that connected Indian allies with one another, linked Tsenacommacah/Virginia to its southwest, and made up part of the network of paths that covered the eastern part of the continent.[64]

After leaving Fort Henry, Pyancha and his party came first to an Iroquoian Nottoway town. Initially wary, the Nottoways only appeared after discovering that the party included Pyancha "our Guide whom they knew." Pyancha knew which paths led to Indians with pelts to trade, and his personal connections in the Nottoway town gained the English admittance. Though the Nottoways later proved less than receptive to the idea of direct English-Tuscarora trade, Pyancha's presence allowed the English to communicate and receive at least temporary hospitality.[65] After they left the town to continue their southwestern journey, the Nottoway werowance Chounterounte came to their camp "with a scornefull posture" and "a countenance noting much discontent" trying to convince them to turn back. Chounterounte claimed to have heard reports that Captain John Flood, a fur trader and interpreter living east of Fort Henry, had told the Weyanocks (Flood's own principle Powhatan trading partners) that Governor Sir William Berkeley would not allow English colonists to trade directly with the Tuscaroras. Because the 1646 treaty had designated Flood's house and Fort Henry (managed by Wood) as the only two places south of the James River where Indians could legally come to trade, the two men may well have been rivals.[66] Bland and Wood assured Chounterounte that "the Tuskarood King had envited us to trade, and our Governour had ordered us to go." Chounterounte persisted, insisting "that the way was long, for passage very bad by reason of much raine . . . and many rotten Marrishes and Swampps," but the English party pressed on.[67] Whether or not John Flood wanted to stop Bland and Wood, Chounterounte clearly did, and not from concern for their comfort in the swamps or worry over whether they enjoyed Berkeley's blessings. Rather, Chounterounte, as a Nottoway, led a tribe that had straddled one of the two main paths into the Chesapeake. The growing dependence on European trade of Indians farther and farther west and the increased scale of Anglo-Indian trade promised real gains to those who could gain a portion of its economic and political proceeds.

Dismissing Chounterounte's dissuasions, the party continued along "the Path" to Maharineck, a town of Iroquoian Meherrins on the Meherrin River, where they found the Meherrins waiting to greet them, a house ready for them to sleep in, and food for their horses.[68] Bland believed the Meherrin welcomed his party just "as they used to doe to their great Emperour Apachancano [Opechancanough] when they entertained him," understanding that he and his English companions traveled along routes formerly used by Powhatans.[69] The Virginia party hired a Tuscarora to run ahead and tell his werowance to meet them at a town called Hocomowananck three days later. That afternoon they met the Hocomowananck werowance, who "seemed very joyfull that wee could goe thither" and told them that the Tuscaroras very much wanted to trade but that "the [Powhatan] Wainoakes had spoken much to dishearten them from having any trade with the English." According to the Hocomowananck werowance the Tuscaroras had tried several times to go to Virginia "but were afraid, for the Wainoakes had told them that the English would kill them." The English acknowledged that the Weyanocks had also tried to hinder English-Tuscarora trade by "likewise [speaking] much against the Tuskarood to the English, it being a common thing amongst them to villefie one another, and tell nothing but lies to the English."[70]

When the Virginia party had almost reached Hocomowananck, where there expected finally to meet the Tuscaroras and trade with them, they learned that Powhatan Weyanocks and Iroquoian Nottoways and Meherrins had cooperated to keep Virginians from successfully invading the piedmont path system and ending their roles as middlemen. The runner they had hired to carry their message to the Tuscarora werowance had never done so. Instead, he had spread the rumor among surrounding Indians that the English party was hostile and "come to cut them off." The supposed Hocomowananck werowance was a Meherrin, "and no Werrowance." The English realized that yet another attempt at direct trade had failed, and began to perceive that in fact they had placed themselves in danger. A Nottoway asked Pyancha "why we did not get us gone, for the Inhabitants were . . . angry with us."[71]

On hearing this warning, the Englishmen gave up all hopes of reaching the Tuscaroras and "resolved to return" to Fort Henry "another way," via a path about eight miles above their previous route. Pyancha had learned from his Meherrin "Sweetheart" that "some plots might be acted against us," if they returned the way they had come.[72] That the Appamattuck Pyancha had a Meherrin sweetheart suggests, like his initial welcome from the Nottoways and his detailed knowledge of the area, that he had long been a trader. He described to his party in detail more distant trade routes, explaining to the English that "three dayes journy further to the South-West, there was a far greater Branch so broad [the Roanoke] that a man could hardly see over it." Where the river curved "Northward above the head of James River unto the foot of the great Mountaines," "many people" lived, most importantly the Siouan Occaneechees. The Occaneechees inhabited an island in the Roanoke River at a point near present-day Kerr Reservoir, where the river was "fordable, not above knee deepe." Although Bland did not reach the Occaneechee town in his travels, it attracted his attention because the Occaneechees controlled a point of the Roanoke River easily crossed and therefore important for trade, and because Pyancha had impressed on Bland that the Occaneechees were important traders.[73]

The party's experiences illustrate the importance of Indian guides and trade patterns, as well as the dangers posed by Indian hostilities. Despite the fact that Powhatan Appamattucks such as Pyancha had access to trade into and beyond Meherrin land, the Powhatan Weyanocks and Iroquoian Nottoways and Meherrins profited from their own role in bringing goods from the southwest to the English. They therefore stood to gain from obstructing direct trade and perpetuating mutual wariness between English colonists and southwestern fur-trading Indians, particularly the Iroquoian Tuscaroras. Thus, while preconquest routes continued to define the shape of trade, and while the English used Powhatan trade patterns and tributary Powhatans to access those patterns, once outside the borders of Tsenacommacah and no longer among Indians they had conquered, they faced resistance to their efforts to travel Indians' paths, even from tributary Powhatans. The Weyanocks offered no further recorded opposition to the English after Wood and Bland's journey, but continued hostilities between Weyanocks and Tuscaroras (they went to war in 1667) suggest that the two continued to fight over access to English trade. The English defeat of the Powhatans in 1646 and subsequent attempts to trade to the southwest sent ripples far beyond Tsenacommacah/Virginia, altering historic balances of power.[74]

Even in the complete absence of any Indian hostility, Indian travel patterns shaped Virginia colonists' opportunities for overland travel. William Talbot, in his introduction to German doctor John Lederer's accounts of his 1670 explorations, dedicated them to Anthony Ashley Cooper, proprietor of Carolina, explaining that "the Apalataeen Mountains (though . . . they deny Virginia passage into the West Continent) stoop to your Lordships Dominions, and lay open a Prospect into unlimited Empires." While true Virginia had higher mountains than South Carolina, they were not impassable. Rather, the rivalries and subsequent danger, lack of a good path system, and lack of Powhatan travel experience or trading relationships hindered Virginians' travel directly west. Lederer's experiences indicate that for the English, Indian paths indicated the possible routes through the mountains and forests, and that attempts to explore without regard to Indian guidance or geographies would fail.[75] When, at a Monacan town in the piedmont, Lederer asked the way to the mountains, "an ancient Man described with a staffe two paths on the ground . . . but my English Companions slighting the Indians direction, shaped their course by the Compass due West, and therefore it fell out with us, as it dows with those Land-Crabs, that crawling backwards in a direct line, avoid not the Trees that stand in their way, but climbing over their very tops, come down again on the other side, and so after a days labour gain not above two foot of ground. Thus we obstinately pursuing a due West course, rode over steep and craggy Cliffs, which beat our Horses quite off the hoof. In these Mountains we wandred from the Twenty fifth of May to the Third of June, finding very little sustenance for Man or Horse; for these places are destitute both of Grain and Herbage." Away from Indian habitation and off of Indian paths, Lederer and his companions got lost, made little progress, and found little food.[76] Most of Lederer's company of twenty Englishmen on horseback and five Indian guides, tired and hungry and afraid of the Mahocks (Mohawks?), gave up and returned east.[77]

Lederer and the rest of the company parted ways. Jackzetavon, a Susquehannock, remained with Lederer as his guide. They changed course from west to south and after four days of difficult travel "without seeing any Town or Indian" they arrived at Saponi on the Roanoke River in Carolina.[78] From there they got back onto the southwestern trail network and continued southwest, following paths "by the Indians['] instructions," which resulted in "easie journeys."[79] They sometimes sought to avoid seemingly circuitous routes that paths occasionally took by attempting more direct routes, but these invariably proved more arduous than the Indian paths, which meandered expressly to avoid the marshes and rocky scrambling that hindered Lederer and Jackzetavon when they attempted short cuts.

After traveling south-southwest almost two weeks from Saponi, they finally reached a passage through the mountains, at a Cherokee town called Sara.[80] Indians at Sara or at nearby Usheree had Spanish coins, and told Lederer that two and a half days' journey to the Southwest would take him to "a powerful Nation of Bearded men." Not wanting to risk an encounter with the Spanish, Lederer returned home.[81] Here European rivalries stopped him, though Indian trade routes could have taken him farther.

At the end of his accounts, Lederer appended advice for future travelers. He informed potential explorers of two passages through the Appalachians. The first was at Sara, the town of Iroquoian-speaking Cherokees. The other he knew only from Indians' accounts. It lay to the north, "at a place called Zynodoa [Shenandoah]." This referred to the Great Indian Warpath, which ran up the Shenandoah Valley, with Chesapeake access where the Shenandoah River joined the Potomac near present-day Harper's Ferry.[82] Lederer's experiences and his explicit advice emphasized the importance of Indian knowledge and trade routes. Talbot's dedication to Lord Ashley suggests yet another challenge for English traders, one caused by the further imposition of European geography onto the southeast. Virginia traders had lost access to northern Chesapeake trade routes a half-century before with the founding of Maryland. Now Carolina's founding challenged their access to southwestern routes. English colonial charters sometimes set colonies' northern and southern borders by choosing points on the coast and extending borders due west until land ended. Using that practice to draw the Virginia-Carolina border placed valuable trade partners like the Tuscaroras and important routes like the passage through the

Appalachian Mountains at Sara within Carolina's boundaries, thereby granting an advantage to Carolina traders. Virginia traders argued that their precedence in the trade, based on long-established Indian paths that led from the
Chesapeake coastal plain to Sara and beyond, established their right to continue trading. Carolina did not agree, and traders from the two colonies fought
over access to deerskin traders. In this case the fact that precontact trade routes
crossed new colonial borders created intercolonial conflict, discussed in more
detail below and in Chapter 7.

In 1673 Abraham Wood, who had traveled with Pyancha and Edward
Bland in 1650, sponsored another trip to the southwest, though this time he
himself stayed home.[83] His experiences provide yet another example of Indians—in this case the Occaneechees—working to preserve a role in trade. More
importantly, however, its timing helps us to understand a crucial context for
Bacon's Rebellion (only three years later) and to understand that the rebellion
represented in part an English effort to end southwestern Indians' insistence on
preserving their role in connecting Virginia to more distant sources of deerskins, furs, and slaves. In April, Wood sent James Needham, Gabriel Arthur,
and eight Appamattucks to discover land (and hopefully sea) to the west.[84] On
their first attempt, "by misfortune and unwillingness of ye Indians before the
mountaines, that any should discover beyond them," the would-be explorers
were forced back.[85] In May they set out again, meeting some Tomahitans (possibly Overhill Cherokees from the Little Tennessee River) who were "journey-
ing [northeast] from ye mountains to ye Occhonechees" and who agreed to
guide the party. The Occaneechees had developed their island town into an
important entrepôt for trade between the English Virginians and fur- and deer-
skin-trading Indians of the southwestern Appalachians, perhaps based on a
similar precontact role. Virginian Robert Beverley noted that Indians' "general
Language here us'd, is said to be that of the Occaneeches." The widespread use
of the Occaneechee language as a trade language indicates the importance of
their town as an entrepôt before the involvement of the English in the southwestern trade.[86] The possession of such an important trading site not only provided them with significant material advantages, but necessarily determined
their role among their neighboring Indians and therefore their place within the
political geography of the region, a place they were loath to surrender.

The Tomahitans led Needham, Arthur, and one Appamattuck (the others
feared proceeding beyond Occaneechee) nine days southwest from Occaneechee to the eastern base of the mountains and west over the mountains (perhaps via the Sara passage Lederer had identified) for fifteen days to their own
town on the other side of the mountains, where they "very kindly entertained"
the English. Gabriel Arthur remained in the Tomahitan town to learn their lan-

guage while Needham and the Appamattuck guide retraced their steps to Wood's house, accompanied by twelve Tomahitan men and women, including one man who had once been a prisoner of Spanish colonists on the Gulf Coast, down river from the Tomahitans. The Tomahitans who accompanied Needham to Wood's house described the Spanish settlements and the routes that led there. Wood subsequently presented everything he had learned to the Virginia Assembly, hoping for assistance in conducting more explorations.[87] He did not receive the aid, but news that a network of paths connected Virginia with the Spanish colonies must have impressed, and perhaps worried, Assembly members, who theretofore normally drew a distinction between European threats from the sea to the east and Indian threats from the paths to the west.

The Occaneechees, wanting to prevent any more English travel beyond their trading town, killed Needham on his trip back to the Tomahitan town and ordered the Tomahitans to kill Arthur.[88] The Tomahitans, who sought direct trade with the English as the English did with them, disregarded the Occaneechee request to kill Arthur and instead helped him return to Virginia. The Occaneechees knew from observing Powhatans' experiences with the English that once colonists had established themselves, they endangered the prior inhabitants. Therefore they strove to gain European goods while preserving their territory and control over path networks from English incursion, keeping it as Indian, not European, geography.

English fur traders' frustration at Occaneechee efforts to preserve their entrepôt fueled some Virginians' participation in Bacon's Rebellion. The two other precipitating factors—endemic frontier violence and the Susquehannock War—were likewise tied to Indian long-distance travel routes. Virginia's defeat of the Powhatans in 1646 and subsequent expansion to Tsenacommacah's borders increased English contact with non-Powhatan Indians, both through direct trade with former Powhatan trading partners and by increased exposure to Iroquois raids. English records claim that Iroquois attacks intensified at this time, something many historians have attributed to an actual increase in Iroquois travel. Indeed, the Iroquois may well have increased raids on the Chesapeake after midcentury to replenish population and supplies following warfare in Iroquoia, directly affecting the English colonists now settling in westernmost former Tsenacommacah, and perhaps also pushing the Monacans east (and closer to English Virginians) to avoid the Iroquois.[89] But it also seems likely that English reports of increased marauding reflected heightened English awareness of seasonal raids that had been occurring long before their arrival. By taking over Tsenacommacah they made themselves, rather than the Powhatans, a more frequent target, and thus more familiar with the regular impact of the Iroquois presence.

English exposure to Iroquois raids raised English fears of Indian attacks, providing a context of heightened anxiety in which Anglo-Susquehannock warfare near the Potomac River fall line precipitated Bacon's Rebellion. During the Anglo-Susquehannock war in late 1675, Susquehannocks responded to an English attack by targeting westernmost English settlers in Virginia and Maryland. English colonists conflated their fear of Susquehannock attacks with their anger that local Indians' claims to land prevented their own acquisition of land, creating support for Nathaniel Bacon's suggested forays against all Chesapeake Indians. His followers, largely English servants or freedmen frustrated by their inability to acquire land, readily complied. Colonists, knowing that the Iroquois traveled long distances to appear in the western Chesapeake, but only possessing a very incomplete understanding of the path systems by which they arrived, felt exposed to an unknown number of possible Indian attackers from afar. The Virginia Assembly shared some of the fears of western colonists. It worried that Virginia's Indian enemies had hired other Indian nations from two hundred or three hundred miles away to join them in an attack on the colony, and that they had all gathered fifty miles up the James River from the westernmost English settlements. Such anxieties reflected English Virginians' knowledge that Tsenacommacah's precontact connections to its outside world were now Virginia's connections to Indians throughout eastern North America.[90]

Bacon and his followers began by targeting "foreign" Indians (the Susquehannocks and Occaneechees), but then requested a license to wage war "against all Indians in general." When Governor Sir William Berkeley opposed Bacon's indiscriminate onslaught, Bacon refused to halt it. When Berkeley declared Bacon and his followers in rebellion, they turned on him and his supporters as well. After a summer of civil war, the rebellion ended with Bacon's death in the fall of 1676. While land acquisition was clearly the motive of many of Bacon's followers, his own involvement (and that of a few of his supporters) was much more complicated. Bacon himself was a trader as well as a planter, and held six Indian slaves on his plantation. He gained the support of other colonial fur traders who found themselves thwarted by Powhatan and non-Powhatan middlemen in their attempts to trade directly with the Tuscaroras and Cherokees. Access to scarce labor and direct trade for furs and slaves, in addition to land acquisition, motivated some of the rebels.[91] Bacon complained that Berkeley was too conciliatory toward those Indians who traded with his own political supporters. The interests of most Virginia colonists would be better served by war, which was a means to acquire land, rather than peace, which was a means to maintain trade. But the recent conflict between traders like Needham and Arthur and the Occaneechees suggests that at least some traders believed they too stood to benefit from Bacon's war against Indians. A desire to eliminate middlemen explains Bacon's otherwise puzzling attack on the Occaneechees who lived well beyond land that Bacon's poorer followers desired for settlement. William Byrd, who had inherited his uncle Thomas Stegge's land at the falls of the James and his active Indian trade, supported the rebellion in its initial stages.[92] The difficulty of land acquisition that motivated so many of Bacon's followers does not explain Byrd's support (or Bacon's own motivation), but annihilation of Powhatans and nearby Siouans like the Occaneechees would have allowed them direct trade with the Tuscaroras. Bacon and Byrd both had fur-trading licences from Berkeley until March 1676, when the Virginia Assembly revoked such licenses and gave responsibility for regulating fur trade to individual counties.[93] Bacon's rampage against Occaneechee Indians and tributary Powhatans may have reflected not merely the kind of out-of-control racist anger that historians have identified but rather a calculated plan to do away with those Indians clinging to their role in the trade.[94]

At the end of the rebellion, the 1677 Treaty of Middle Plantation revised the 1646 settlement between Virginia and the Powhatans. The Pamunkey weroansqua (female werowance) Cockacoeske and three other Powhatans signed the treaty. The treaty was expanded in 1680 to accommodate the request of non-Powhatans to join. Signers of the new version of the treaty included leaders of Iroquoian-speaking Meherrins and Nottoways and Siouan-speaking Monacans and Saponis.[95] These Indians recognized that in Bacon's Rebellion the English had reached beyond the bounds of Tsenacommacah and would no longer confine themselves to appropriating former Powhatan land.[96] Meherrins and Nottoways, among those who had successfully thwarted Bland, Wood, and Pyancha's trip to the Tuscaroras in 1650, now made themselves subservient. The Occaneechees did not sign the peace articles, but tried to retain their entrepôt in the Roanoke River until sometime after 1690, when they moved farther from Virginia, settling and establishing a new trading town down the trading path on the Eno River near what is now Hillsborough, North Carolina.[97] Thus the rebellion altered Indian political and economic geography well beyond Virginia, not only changing the Meherrins and Occaneechees' relationships with Virginia, but also necessarily (in a world of which the English were now inexorably a part) changing their relationship with Indians to their west and south.[98]

Bacon's Rebellion was thus very much about Virginia's place in a much larger world. The colony's Atlantic connections fed the migration of young men expecting land. The colony's North American connections created the situation in which Indian and English traders struggled for control over paths beyond Virginia's dominion and in which westernmost English settlers feared Indians traveling to the Chesapeake on seasonal hunting and raiding ventures. Virginia

Governor Berkeley understood (though imprecisely) that Indians' mobility endangered colonists more than local Indians could, and indeed feared a continental alliance of Indians to attack all English colonies in North America.[99]

Bacon's Rebellion thus marked a new stage in English appropriation—this time of Tsenacommacah's external trade routes. After Bacon's Rebellion, many English traders traveled beyond the falls of the James to the southwest along former Powhatan trading routes, having in fact taken over the position of Powhatan traders.[100] Bacon's rebellion hastened and confirmed a process already occurring gradually. In 1686 William Byrd complained that the number of competing traders had "overstocked" the trade with "one [trader] indeavoring to eat out another."[101] He urged his English suppliers to get his goods to him early to give him an edge over his rivals in the region.[102] By the end of the century there were fifty or sixty traders per year following this pre-contact trading route southwest from Virginia.[103]

Although Bacon's Rebellion increased the number of Englishmen trading, it eliminated neither English reliance on guides nor Indian resistance to English direct trade, though it reduced both substantially.[104] For Englishmen to go beyond Powhatan territories remained dangerous, particularly beyond Occaneechee, still on the Roanoke River until the 1690s. In 1684 Byrd reported a party of five traders in his employ "all killed by the Indians in their returne from the westward, about 30 miles beyond Ochanechee," after having "made a very advantagious journy" up to that point.[105] Whoever killed Byrd's traders refused to accept an English interpretation of Indian defeat during Bacon's Rebellion that extended Virginia's functional boundaries beyond Tsenacommacah's former limits. In addition to Occaneechees, members of the Iroquois five nations still posed a problem in their coming down the Great Indian Warpath to conduct raids on the piedmont-coastal plain boundary of Virginia. In fact, the Virginians' and Marylanders' defeat of the Susquehannocks in the 1675 Anglo-Susquehannock war resulted in the adoption of some Susquehannocks into the Iroquois Five Nations. Those Susquehannocks strengthened the Iroquois just as the weaker Indian presence in western Virginia and Maryland made English colonists more vulnerable to Iroquois attacks. Furthermore, the Susquehannocks encouraged the Iroquois to target English settlers in the Chesapeake, in revenge for the Susquehannocks earlier losses.[106] On Easter Monday 1684, Byrd "spoke with 50 Seneca Indians [the westernmost Iroquois] about 12 miles above my house, they have promised to behave themselves hereafter very peaceable towards the English."[107]

The old boundary between the coastal plain and the piedmont and continued Powhatan unwillingness to go beyond the fall line directly to the untrailed west survived into the late seventeenth century, despite dramatic changes in the relationship between Powhatans and English colonists. In 1688 Byrd wrote that twice he had tried to get some crystal from the Virginia mountains but was both times "disappointed by the fearfulness of the Indians." The Indians whom Byrd employed—presumably Powhatans—felt unsafe in the piedmont and mountains where he wanted to send them, "above forty miles beyond the Christian inhabitants" where they risked meeting Siouans and possibly Iroquois.[108] Weakened by successive Anglo-Powhatan wars during the seventeenth century, they could venture into the piedmont with even less security than they enjoyed in that region before 1607, and refused to endanger themselves for the sake of English trade or exploration. Such reticence on the part of his Powhatan guides reinforced for Byrd a sense of Tsenacommacah's former western border as a boundary. In 1690 he wrote that he lived "att the end of the world," even while his own activities were expanding the colonial world beyond his plantation.[109]

Indian precontact interaction patterns shaped the way colonial Virginians perceived their colony's boundaries after they supplanted the Powhatans as political masters of Tsenacommacah/Virginia, and determined how they moved beyond the Chesapeake coastal plain to trade and explore. Features of physical geography such as the fall line, mountain passes, and swamps clearly influenced the outlines of precontact social and political geographies, but by the time the English arrived, cultural relationships resulted less from topography than from social and political geographies. The topography and the precontact patterns of Indian trade, alliances, and rivalries had embossed an indelible pattern on the land and its masters old and new, seen in the persistence of Indian names for geographic features and in Indian paths as European roads and highways. As the English incorporated these patterns into the governance and commerce of Virginia itself, those precontact path networks affected Virginia's interactions with Indians in regions of North America that were or became other European colonies. As Chapters 7 and 8 will argue, relations between Anglo-Virginians and the Iroquois or between Anglo-Virginians and the Tuscaroras affected late-seventeenth-century intercolonial relations by inciting Virginia-Carolina competition for trade (in the case of the Tuscaroras) or encouraging (admittedly grudging) Virginia-New York diplomatic cooperation (in the case of the Iroquois).[110]

Although for much of the seventeenth century English Virginians were well aware of Indian interaction patterns and trade routes, they had little personal experience with them. Their own long-distance communications remained largely coastal. Despite their knowledge of overland routes to Canada, they interacted with colonists in New England or New Netherland or even Maryland much the same way in which they interacted with those in Barbados or St. Christopher: by using the ships involved in intercolonial trade as means of travel and communication. Because English Virginians had such trouble extending their movements outside of Powhatan lands and knew so little of what lay beyond, they continued for much of the century to interact with other colonies as though Virginia were an island of appropriated Powhatan lands surrounded by a sea of Indian territory.[111] The differences between European and Indian mapping practices strengthened the perception of two interaction patterns during the seventeenth century: coastal-English and overland-Indian. Much of the intercolonial interaction described in this work took place in this context. The English communicated with one another, whether on islands or on the mainland, using coastal shipping, at the same time that they realized that Indians had their own overland networks covering the mainland.

The following chapters explore Virginia's integration into the maritime Atlantic world. But the reader should bear in mind (as seventeenth-century Virginians did) that maritime connections grew while English traders and colonists in Virginia gradually appropriated Powhatan Tsenacommacah and indigenous trade routes. The two processes were intertwined: English weapons and cloth and Caribbean rum traveled inland to Indians, as Indian deerskins, furs, and slaves followed maritime routes out of the Chesapeake to Europe and the Caribbean. While by the end of the seventeenth century the English had gained the upper hand within the Chesapeake, Indians retained control over much of the North American path system beyond European settlement—including the vital Great Indian Warpath north-south artery.

Thus, while Europeans engaged in tying their various colonies to one another and to Europe (and at the end of the century to Africa) via coastal and transatlantic shipping, an alternate network of travel routes controlled by Indians tied the mainland colonies together overland. At the end of the century, those two separate networks would come one step closer as English colonies on the mainland cooperated with one another to try to control travel via overland routes. Their efforts failed to limit Indian movements as they hoped, but succeeded in integrating overland and maritime connections fully enough that Virginia colonists began to understand their connections to other mainland colonies as twofold and significantly different from their connections to other parts of their Atlantic world.

Chapter 2

Shaping the Networks of Maritime Trade

If Indian trade routes determined the overland connections between Virginia and other parts of North America, Atlantic maritime trade patterns provided the routes along which Virginians formed social and cultural connections with other inhabitants of the Atlantic world. Almost every European or African who moved to or was born in Virginia participated directly in the maritime Atlantic world. That world consisted of overlapping transatlantic and intercolonial connections and grew increasingly complex over the course of the seventeenth century as the number of locales immersed in Atlantic connections grew. Transatlantic ties defined Euro-Virginians' place in the Atlantic world early in the century, when there were few other colonies to offer opportunities for intercolonial trade. As the Netherlands and England established mainland and Caribbean colonies in the 1620s and succeeding decades, Virginia's Atlantic world became intercolonial as well as transatlantic. Both the intercolonial and transatlantic aspects of Virginia's Atlantic world were international, with the Dutch especially important through the middle of the century. England's conquest of Jamaica from the Spanish in 1655 and New Netherland/New York from the Dutch in 1664 and the addition of the Restoration colonies of Carolina (1663) and Pennsylvania (1681), made Virginia's intercolonial world more strongly English by the end of the century.

We know a great deal about Virginia's transatlantic trade.[1] When English Virginians learned in the 1610s to grow tobacco that was marketable in Europe, English and Dutch ships immediately began competing to carry that tobacco. In exchange for Virginians' tobacco, English and Dutch merchants brought European goods and, more importantly, a continual supply of indentured servants, mostly young, English, and male, to build a labor force subject to high mortality rates and low fertility rates. The Chesapeake's tobacco trade grew in volume over the course of the seventeenth century, from around fifty thousand pounds in 1620 to over thirty million pounds by 1700.[2] Tobacco dominated Virginia's transatlantic trade, though beaver and deerskins acquired in trade with Indians were also destined for European markets. As tobacco prices went through several cycles of boom and bust, Virginia's economy reflected those cycles. Until the end of the century, tobacco collection was inefficient, with vessels collecting their cargoes piecemeal, and uncertain even of finding full ladings when they arrived in the colony. In order to better their chances in a difficult trade, London merchants successfully lobbied Parliament for help in competing against the Dutch traders. Those London merchants provided much of the impetus for three Anglo-Dutch wars, in 1652–54, 1665–67, and 1672–74. English victory in those wars indeed reduced Dutch traders' dominance in the north Atlantic, but London merchants quickly found new competition (more important in the eighteenth century) from Scottish and French tobacco traders. However, the weakening of the Dutch had another significant impact on Virginia at the end of the century, in allowing English traders to gain a growing portion of the transatlantic slave trade, some of which they began to carry to the Chesapeake. That added a new element to Virginia's transatlantic connections. For most of the century, slaves entered the colony via intercolonial trade.

We know much less about Virginia's intercolonial trade.[3] What follows represents an attempt to outline that trade and place it in its Atlantic context. Intercolonial trade provided Virginians with important diversification from the 1630s on. It established intercolonial maritime connections that facilitated intercolonial migration and emulation. Attention to intercolonial trade is necessary if we are to understand distinctions between different regions of Virginia in the seventeenth century. By outlining the patterns of intercolonial trade that linked Virginia to Barbados, Massachusetts, New Netherland, and Carolina, this chapter provides a map for understanding the social, cultural, and political connections that followed such trade routes.

Intercolonial and transatlantic trade often intertwined. A 1639 voyage illustrates the often complicated (and sometimes tenuous) nature of Virginia's Atlantic trade, which commonly involved multiple English and Dutch colonies as much as England and Europe. That summer, Barnaby Brian sailed from Virginia's Eastern Shore to New England to trade tobacco on behalf of some Eastern Shore colonists. Rather than returning with the tobacco's earnings (in goods or bills of exchange) to the Virginia growers and shipowners, Brian lingered for months in New England and Manhattan, spending all the proceeds carousing, though his seamen testified that he could have returned in ten days with bills of exchange. (Collecting a return cargo would have taken longer.) While in New England, Brian spent his time in a Boston ordinary and sometimes at the Noddles Island house of Massachusetts merchant Samuel Maverick. Having taken liquor and fish in exchange for the tobacco, Brian drank away the liquor with his fellow revelers at Noddles Island and gave away the fish in Manhattan. With little reason to return to his Virginia creditors and considerable incentive to avoid them, Brian decided to go to the Caribbean instead, and recruited men in Boston for a voyage that he apparently never made. When he ultimately returned to Virginia without the tobacco or anything to show for it, his clients took him to court.[4] Brian's own foibles brought his clients to grief. In the process, however, his story demonstrates the highly social nature of the maritime world and illustrates the complicated, flexible trade practices required for mariners to make multiple voyages to several colonies before returning to their home port.

Trade patterns evolved in response to the desire to find markets for goods

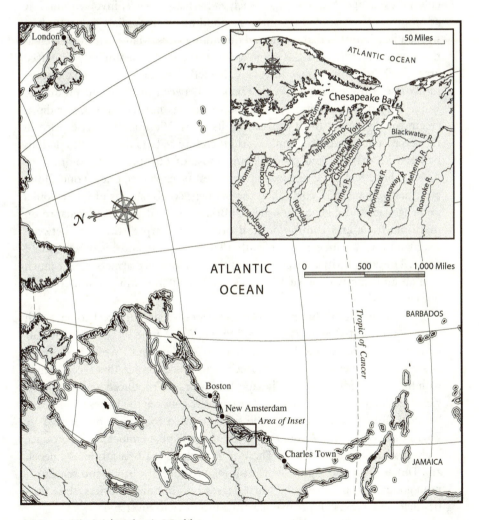

Map 6. Virginia's Atlantic World

in nascent colonial economies already undergoing significant regional special-
ization. The intercolonial networks that subsequently grew around economic
exchange also provided the shape of intercolonial social and informational
links. Because maritime trade so pervaded the Chesapeake, the mariners whose
labor moved the trade interacted constantly with the people producing and
consuming the goods traded, ensuring that social connections would follow
the patterns established by trade and would similarly pervade the Chesapeake.
An exploration of Virginia's maritime trade patterns provides a necessary pre-
lude to understanding its patterns of transatlantic and intercolonial social and
cultural exchange. Many voyages, such as Barnaby Brian's, involved multiple
adventurers from several colonies, responding to immediate opportunities
with ad hoc journeys that connected disparate places. Many mariners, such as
the men he recruited in Boston to go to the Caribbean, similarly displayed
great flexibility from voyage to voyage. Nonetheless, each commercial opportunity that arose reflected specific relations between markets and producers.
While requiring flexibility, the Atlantic world was not haphazard, nor did it
create equally strong links between all its parts. Virginians' precise place in
the seventeenth-century Atlantic world therefore reflects the specific relations
between its markets and products and those of Europe, other colonies, or
Africa. Those economic relationships can best be explained one by one. However, that process risks concealing the frequent combinations of intercolonial
exchanges in multiple voyages such as Brian's. Indeed, colonists' reliance on
maritime trade and communication precluded sharp distinctions between
mainland and Caribbean colonies that later colonists and historians would
make. The complexity of exchange and the mobility of mariners meant much
overlap and intertwining of Virginia's various Atlantic links into a complex
but patterned web.

In the regions of Virginia most dependent on tobacco, direct contact with
mariners connected settlers largely to Europe. These areas—the three peninsulas between the James and Potomac Rivers (like Maryland's Western Shore)—
possessed the overwhelmingly tobacco-driven economies that we associate
with the seventeenth-century Chesapeake. Their soils produced higher tobacco
yields and higher-quality tobacco. The counties between the James and Rappahannock Rivers could produce the sweet-scented tobacco most desired by
English markets and the counties north of the Rappahannock could produce
high-quality Orinoco tobacco. These regions therefore best attracted English
and Dutch ships coming to the Chesapeake to collect tobacco and sell European goods. Except during the worst depressions in tobacco prices, the counties that were most competitive saw little incentive to diversify.[5]

In contrast, Virginia's Eastern Shore and the counties south of the James

River grew poor-quality Orinoco tobacco. Much of the soil in Lower Norfolk, Accomack, and Northampton counties was unsuitable for any tobacco production.[6] Those who did grow less-competitive tobacco found themselves at much greater risk during periods of low tobacco prices or when shipping was scarce.[7] Colonists responded by raising cattle and hogs for export as livestock or meat, producing naval stores such as pitch, tar, and pipe staves, and growing or acquiring from Indians surplus corn. These goods sold to other colonial rather than to European consumers. As a result, the Virginians who produced and traded these goods became enmeshed in intercolonial trade networks that afforded them multiple contacts to other colonies as well as to Europe, linking them most closely to Massachusetts, New Netherland (and after 1664 New York), and Barbados.[8] Though intercolonial traders existed in every seventeenth-century Virginia county, such trade was especially important (and important earlier) for colonists on the Eastern Shore and south of the James. Thus, though not rigid, regional patterns in Chesapeake intercolonial trade were pronounced. Barbadian trade was most important to the Southside counties of Lower Norfolk, Princess Anne, Nansemond, and Isle of Wight, although Caribbean trade grew in importance for all Virginians toward the end of the century. The Eastern Shore counties of Accomack and Northampton maintained much of Virginia's trade with New Netherland, and both the Eastern Shore and Southside regions of the Chesapeake were disproportionately involved in New England trade.[9]

Observers of the Chesapeake recognized early on the potential for intercolonial trade.[10] In 1618 the merchants Captain Andrews and Jacob Braems proposed a voyage in the *Silver Falcon* to "fish upon the coast of Canada, and exchange the fish when salted for commodities in Virginia."[11] Moreover, because Virginia had passed its starving time before England established its other American colonies it could provide colonists elsewhere with food until they had established the means to grow their own. The downturn in tobacco prices at the end of the 1620s encouraged some Virginians to diversify into food production, allowing trade between Virginia and New England to begin early. In 1632 Governor John Harvey wrote that Virginia's "Planters are carried with a great forwardness to seeke trade abroade, to which purpose we have now 7 or 8 pinnaces and Barques bound to New-England and the Northward."[12] And in 1634, Harvey announced that Virginians had successfully decreased excessive tobacco planting and increased the growth of corn. That corn, plus an abundance of cattle and swine, had permitted Virginia to feed twelve hundred newcomers and to export ten thousand bushels of corn that year for the relief of New England. Virginia, he claimed, "is now become the granary of all His Maj[es]ty's northern colonies."[13]

Because some of the corn surplus that English Virginians traded to other colonies came from the Chesapeake's Indians, rather than from colonists, Indian and coastal trade overlapped, perhaps as early as 1624.[14] Henry Fleet and William Claiborne, who traded with Indians in the Potomac and northern Chesapeake for beaver skins, were also among the earliest intercolonial traders. They purchased corn from Indians along the Potomac and on the Eastern Shore and carried it to New England. Eastern Shore colonists and Indians traded some corn to the western shore, but found its most important markets in other colonies: New Netherland, Maryland, the English Caribbean, and especially New England.[15]

Henry Fleet's travel accounts provide one of the earliest and most detailed descriptions of Virginia-New England corn trade. In the 1630s Fleet traded corn from Potomac River Indians to New England. While Fleet and his companions most concerned themselves with the beaver trade during their 1631 and 1632 Potomac River trading expeditions, a complementary trade in corn provided a more secure backup when they found no beaver skins. On his first recorded voyage, in 1631, Fleet left England in July and sailed to Piscataway in New England. While there, he promised the settlers that he would return with corn from Virginia.

When Fleet arrived in the Potomac in October 1631, he described himself as "engaged to [deliver] a quantity of Indian corn in New England." After collecting his corn in the Potomac, Fleet, despite being delayed in Jamestown until January 1632, arrived at Piscataway the following month with seven hundred bushels of corn. After delivering it, Fleet continued to Massachusetts Bay, where he obtained English goods for more Indian trade. Massachusetts settlers sent a twenty-ton pinnace with Fleet on his return to Virginia, in order for him to freight it with more corn for them.[16] By May he, his mariners, and those from New England returned to the Potomac, where they failed to get the beaver but loaded the pinnace with corn and left for New England on June 1. While conducting his trade, Fleet took care to preserve good relations with Virginia officials so that he could continue trading in the Potomac, where he "conceived all my hopes and future fortunes depended upon the trade and traffic that was to be had out of this river."[17]

Coastal and overland trade overlapped because individuals such as Fleet used coastal and overland networks to complement one another. His interactions with northern Indians who arrived in the Potomac River with European trading goods they had acquired from English or French colonists in New England or Canada shows that intercolonial trade involved traversing political, cultural, and imperial boundaries as it traversed geographic space for Indians as well as for Europeans.[18] Indians' multiple trade contacts, available because of their precontact travel routes, accessed the Atlantic coast and navigable rivers in several places, thus providing them with bargaining power that came with their ability to compare the quality and price of different Europeans' goods.

As cattle and swine populations thrived in Virginia, colonists began to export livestock and meat to other colonies as well, and these products made up an increasingly significant proportion of their inventories. In 1654 for example, the estate of Norfolk County commissioner Cornelius Lloyd had an appraised value of 40,361 pounds of tobacco, more than half of which (25,540 pounds) consisted of eighty-seven cattle. Other midcentury estates in Norfolk County and on the Eastern Shore show a similar concentration of cattle, valuable because of colonial markets for livestock and beef. Eastern Shore planter and intercolonial merchant Edmund Scarborough leased a plantation with 109 cattle and "a parcel of hogs" to William Brenton of Boston, thus highlighting the link between cattle and intercolonial connections. In 1645 another Norfolk estate (that of Cesar Puggett) contained forty-two cattle which were worth 17,500 pounds of tobacco out of an estate valued at 24,215 pounds. The county had 546 cows over three years old in 1647 when its population contained only 360 tithables. The Eastern Shore provides similar examples. Between 1665 and 1669 (when the county had no more than 177 households) 236 people recorded cattle marks. Many of those people who recorded their livestock marks possessed multiple cattle.[19]

The significance of cattle in the Eastern Shore landscape emerges clearly from the description of overland paths leading "from one kowpen to the other."[20] The importance of intercolonial trade goods in the Eastern Shore economy similarly surfaces in the occasional use of meat rather than tobacco as currency.[21] Apparently, this trade grew so quickly that it temporarily outpaced the cattle population's ability to reproduce itself, because in 1640 the Assembly ruled that Virginians could export only one out of every seven cattle to New England or other "neighboring" colonies.[22] Virginians exported enough corn and other grain during the seventeenth century to warrant similar prohibitions on exports when Virginia needed them to sustain its own subsistence needs. After a 1667 storm, the Assembly prohibited the export of grain, pulse (beans and peas), meal, or bread until late October 1668.[23] Almost ten years later, in preparation for war, the Assembly made a similar order.[24]

Commercial relations between New England and Virginia's Eastern Shore continued throughout the seventeenth century with little change in pattern. In the spring of 1641 George Lamberton, a merchant of Quinnipiac (New Haven), acknowledged receiving eighteen cattle from Nathaniel Littleton, a merchant and planter on the Eastern Shore.[25] That summer, the Accomack court recorded testimonies from Edmund Scarborough, Nathaniel Littleton, and Captain William Stone that they had witnessed bargaining for one hundred barrels of corn bound for New England.[26] In the 1650s and 1660s New Englanders exchanged salt, wine, liquor, beer, and fish for Chesapeake tobacco, corn, beef, cattle, pork, and beaver.[27] By 1664 an observer could claim that New England sent three hundred vessels to trade to Barbados and Virginia, as well as Spanish Madeira, and French Acadia.[28] Through the end of the seventeenth century, Virginia vessels made up a significant proportion of New England's entire intercolonial trade. In 1687–88, for example, thirteen recorded ships entered Boston from Virginia, thirty-three from Barbados, thirty from the Leeward Islands, fourteen from Jamaica, twelve from Pennsylvania, seven from New York, and five each from Carolina and Maryland.[29] The most important development came as New England traders carried more of Virginians' Caribbean trade, thereby linking many Virginians' New England and Caribbean connections, just as it linked Barbadians' Chesapeake and New England contacts and New England merchants' Caribbean and Virginia trade.[30]

By midcentury, then, several prominent Eastern Shore and Lower Norfolk planters recognized better opportunities in producing provisions than in tobacco. Imperfect records make it difficult to assess precisely the importance of tobacco versus other goods and transatlantic versus intercolonial trade to these counties, but existing data suggests relatively equal significance in these regions. For example, historian James R. Perry identified eighty-three likely nonresident merchants, mariners, and captains known to have traded to the Eastern Shore between 1641 and 1655. (That includes only those whose business required that they make use of the county courts.) Of those whose place of origin could be clearly identified, the number from New Amsterdam and New England equaled that from England: eighteen were from England, fifteen from New England, ten from Holland, three from New Amsterdam, and seven from other parts of Virginia or Maryland.[31] Moreover, poor soil conditions coupled with farmers' vulnerability to protective legislation (designed to raise tobacco prices during periods of depression by prohibiting the export of poor quality weed) make it difficult to imagine continued reliance on uncompetitive tobacco in volatile markets.[32] Caribbean populations expanded continually during the seventeenth century, and therefore except during periods of warfare that interfered with shipping, markets for foodstuffs expanded as well (though competition from other food-producing mainland colonies increased).[33] Intercolonial markets thus provided economic opportunities for Chesapeake planters who could not afford prime tobacco land or whose intent was to produce goods for intercolonial, rather than transatlantic, trade. In 1656 promoter John Hammond wrote that from Virginians' "industry" and their "great plenty of

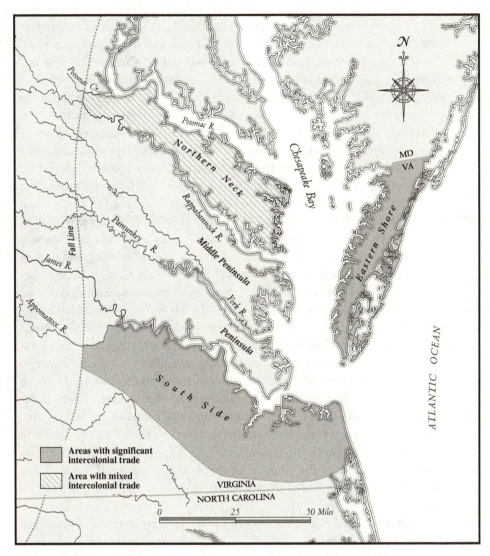

Map 7. Virginia Trade Regions

Corn not only New England hath been stocked and relived, but all other parts of the Indies inhabited by Englishmen." He claimed that the "great plenty of Cattel and Hogs (now innumerable)" allowed colonists to sell "beife, pork, bacon, and butter &c. Either to shipping or to send to the Barbadoes and other Islands; and he is a very poor man that hath not sometimes provision to put off."[34]

Dutch prominence in seventeenth-century Atlantic shipping, Dutch markets for tobacco, and Dutch sources for dry goods and slaves made Dutch and New Netherland traders crucial to seventeenth-century Chesapeake planters.[35] Dutch presence in the New World consisted of both trading activity and colonization, which were closely intertwined. The Dutch trading presence in the Atlantic far exceeded its colonial presence, but its colonies, especially New Netherland and the Caribbean island of Curaçao, served as important entrepôts through which Dutch and English colonial merchants channeled trade between English and French colonies and Rotterdam and Amsterdam.[36] Peter Stuyvesant governed both Curaçao and New Netherland from 1647 to 1664 and encouraged strong ties between the two colonies, a connection that allowed New Netherland to acquire slaves, thereby increasing its attractiveness to Chesapeake traders seeking goods they could easily resell in a labor-hungry Chesapeake market.[37] They traveled to Curaçao to procure slaves and to New Amsterdam because it afforded cloth and other goods not easily available elsewhere and also because traders there could sometimes avoid English duties on Chesapeake tobacco bound for Europe.[38] Dutch and New Netherland merchants were especially valuable to Eastern Shore and Lower Norfolk (Southside) tobacco producers because while English markets demanded the sweet-scented grown between the James and Rappahannock and the high-quality Orinoco grown north of the Rappahannock, Dutch traders provided growers of poor-quality Orinoco access to Amsterdam markets. There, various European and Chesapeake tobaccos were blended and shipped to continental markets where consumers did not object to stronger flavors.[39] Thus, the poor soil that made many residents of the Eastern Shore and Lower Norfolk region eschew tobacco altogether in favor of specifically intercolonial products also made those who continued to produce tobacco more likely to market it via intercolonial traders.

Dutch traders' importance to Chesapeake planters increased dramatically during the 1640s when the English Civil War seriously disrupted English transatlantic shipping. While Dutch merchant David Peterson De Vries reported only 4 Dutch ships (out of 34 total) loading tobacco in Virginia in 1643, in 1648 the number of Dutch ships had risen to 12 (of 31 reported.)[40] The Amsterdam and Rotterdam Notarial Archives report only four ships bound from the Netherlands to Virginia between 1637 and 1642 but as many as 33 between 1643 and 1649.[41] During the 1640s Virginians actively sought Dutch commerce as well. The director of the Dutch West India Company reported in 1646 that Virginians traveled to Curaçao seeking trade with the Dutch there.[42] The Virginia Assembly explicitly protected Dutch trade in 1643, reflecting its expectation that diverse markets and shippers would prove crucial during the political upheaval then beginning in England.[43]

During the second half of the seventeenth century, the English Navigation Acts and the Anglo-Dutch wars complicated Virginia's interactions with the Netherlands and with New Amsterdam, but did not stop it.[44] The importance of Dutch commerce for Chesapeake planters led them to defend it as part of their right to "free trade" when Parliament began to regulate imperial commerce. In the 1640s, when London merchants began lobbying for regulations limiting Anglo-Dutch trade, Virginians grew concerned, and in 1647 the Virginia Assembly declared Dutch trade necessary for the colony's survival.[45] When Parliament passed a 1650 law (precursor to the 1651 Navigation Act) prohibiting trade between foreigners and English colonies, Virginia Governor William Berkeley protested the exclusion of the Dutch in particular, on the grounds that the Dutch had "rescued" Virginia during the English Civil War. The Virginia Assembly responded to the same law by reasserting its belief in Virginians' right to free trade. Their experiences of reduced English shipping during the war had taught them the danger of dependence on only English traders.[46] Virginians' opposition to the 1651 Navigation Act encouraged the colony to continue resisting the Interregnum government, precipitating England's use of a military fleet to force the colony's submission in 1652. The act, which required trade from English colonies to travel directly to England on ships owned and manned by Englishmen, contributed as well to the first Anglo-Dutch War of 1652–54. During the war the capture of several Dutch ships in Virginia showed that hostilities hindered but did not eliminate Dutch-Virginia trade: else no ships would have been there to be captured. Once the war ended, higher volumes of Dutch commerce resumed.[47]

During the three Anglo-Dutch wars illegal Anglo-Dutch trade in the Chesapeake became dangerous, but English colonists in Virginia and Dutch merchants alike tried to continue the trade despite its hazards. Dutch ships in the Chesapeake attacked competing English ships during the second and third of the three wars, but they did not target tobacco-producing colonists.[48] English colonists dependent on Dutch merchants resisted English officials' efforts to prevent its colonists from trading with the enemy. During the first Anglo-Dutch War, New Netherland Governor Peter Stuyvesant, by order of Dutch West India Company, tried to negotiate a commercial alliance with Virginia so that the two colonies could continue to trade despite war between their home countries. In the spring of 1653 he sent envoys to Virginia to negotiate an alliance; a few months later he sent minister Samuel Drisius to propose "a provisional continuation of the commerce and intercourse between the two places" if Virginia Governor Richard Bennett had not received instructions to the contrary. Drisius, a Puritan minister living in New Netherland, not only negotiated, but also preached while on this trip to Virginia, illustrating the intertwining of religious and commercial and political connections linking the Chesapeake, New England, and New Netherland as an American archipelago of northwestern European Protestantism and commerce.[49]

The two colonies did not sign the "Articles of amitie and commerce" until 1660, after William Berkeley had resumed Virginia's governorship. Chesapeake colonists' amity toward Dutch traders recognized the access Dutch merchants and ships provided to African labor sources. In the 1660 agreement, Virginia charged higher tobacco export duties for Dutch shippers than English, *unless* the Dutch had brought slaves into the colony.[50] The act proved short-lived, however, because Parliament's 1660 Navigation Act followed shortly thereafter, requiring that all ship masters and three-quarters of crew members sailing into England's colonies be English, and that the Chesapeake's tobacco go directly to England. The 1663 Navigation Act stipulated that all European goods going into the colonies be from England. Traders found ways to skirt these Restoration Navigation Acts as they had the Interregnum Navigation Acts, and merchants of Dutch descent who had settled in the Chesapeake colonies remained there and maintained their positions in Dutch-English trade networks.[51] After the English conquered New Netherland in 1664 many Dutch merchants remained as New Yorkers and continued to trade as before, able to do so legally because English authorities allowed "free denizen" status to Manhattan burghers.[52] Some volume of illegal trade (by definition difficult to quantify) continued as well. Ships whose Chesapeake voyages were recorded only because they encountered authorities enforcing the Navigation Acts show that even ships trading between the Chesapeake and another English port often had non-English crews and captains.[53] In 1674, for example, ship masters Isaac Foxcroft of the ship *Carolus Secundus*, John Harlow of the *Charitas*, and Jeroln Jerolnson of the *Liefde* received special permission from Charles II to sail to Virginia with their "own outlandish [foreign] seamen" and to trade as freely as natural born subjects of England. Foxcroft and Harlow, described as strangers, apparently Anglicized their names, a common practice among Dutch merchants trading among the English.[54] Foxcroft made further show of his commitment to the English by naming the *Carolus Secundus* after the English king.

Virginians' Dutch and New England trades commonly intertwined, so that Virginia's intercolonial trade provided Chesapeake colonists not just with connections to multiple discreet places but also with the keen awareness that such disparate locations were also connected to one another, creating a complex Atlantic world crisscrossed with overlapping ties. Because of its location,

New Amsterdam served as a common stopping point between New England and Virginia. Eastern Shore merchant Stephen Charleton and ship captain John Stone, owners of the pinnace *Virgine*, used it to trade corn from Virginia to New England, stopping in New Netherland to get water en route.[55] While continuing to trade in New England in the early 1640s, Charleton simultaneously did business with the Dutch, shipping tobacco on the *Water Duck* of Rotterdam for pipes of wine, Holland sheets, and other articles.[56] Charleton had a storehouse on one of his plantations, probably to collect his own and his neighbors' tobacco and to store Dutch goods for later trade on the Eastern Shore.[57] As New England and New Netherland established their own transatlantic trade routes, the Eastern Shore colonists most involved in sending food to the north also traded some of their tobacco to those colonies, usually in exchange for fish, liquor, Dutch cloth, or slaves. The New England and New Netherland merchants who purchased this tobacco reexported most of it to Europe.[58]

Not only did many colonists in Virginia maintain contact with the Dutch in the Netherlands or in New Netherland, but more significantly, those with Dutch connections proved disproportionately instrumental in forging and maintaining Virginia's intercolonial trade with other *English* colonies. The largest Dutch presence was on the Eastern Shore and in Lower Norfolk, where trade with other colonies mattered most; almost all the intercolonial traders in these regions had some Dutch connection or experience recorded in personal, legal, or commercial documents. Two of the wealthiest Eastern Shore merchants, Stephen Charleton and Edmund Scarborough, traded extensively to both New Netherland and New England.[59] Residents of Lower Norfolk acted as attorneys for Rotterdam merchants, took voyages to "the Duch Plantacon," or willed substantial bequests (£400, for example) to siblings in Amsterdam.[60] Maintaining a relationship with family in Amsterdam or Rotterdam could have as much value for a Virginia merchant as family in London. County courts recorded the frequent presence of Dutch merchants and sailors without reference to any need for translators or difficulty in communication, showing that language rarely impeded commerce.

After the English conquered New Netherland in 1664, trade between the two regions continued, often involving the same Dutch merchants who had acquired free denizen status in New York and therefore could continue to trade legally. In 1669 Barnaby Brian's drinking companion merchant Samuel Maverick came to New York. Maverick, who had traded between Virginia and New England for three decades and had lived in both regions, hoped in the 1660s to establish a trade in fish from New York to the Chesapeake. He wrote in 1669 that the English in New York had had good success with cod fishing and that "most of the vessels that go to Virginia take good quantities."[61] His moves epitomize the synergy between migration and intercolonial trade. The networks and knowledge he had acquired living in the Chesapeake subsequently facilitated his trade between the two regions. After spending about a year in Virginia during the mid-1630s, he returned to Boston in October 1636 with two pinnaces, fourteen heifers, and eighty goats.[62] His decision to take livestock with him in his move exploited the New England market for food, animated by the influx of Puritans during the Great Migration to New England between 1630 and 1642.[63] When he moved from New England to New York he used his experiences with that New England-Virginia trade to seize a new intercolonial trade opportunity opened in the newly English New York. Evolving commercial possibilities of intercolonial trade often encouraged such migration, a subject Chapter 4 will explore in detail.

After the English settlement of Maryland in 1634, some trade passed between the two eastern shores, with the Pocomoke River as its marketing center.[64] Virginians and Marylanders used both coastal and overland routes to trade with one another. As with other newly established colonies, much of this began with Virginians sending livestock and other provisions to Maryland, a commerce more controversial than other intercolonial trade, because Marylanders competed with Virginia colonists for English tobacco markets.[65] Some Virginians, moreover, viewed Baltimore's colonists as usurpers of Virginia land and Indian trading rights. In 1634 Virginia Governor John Harvey wrote that many Virginians so opposed Maryland "that they cry . . . that they would rather knock their cattle on the heads than send them to Maryland."[66] Maryland livestock soon flourished, however, and Maryland became a cattle exporter along with Virginia.[67]

Although trade between Virginia and the Caribbean began before 1650, it flourished during the second half of the century.[68] As Barbadians began to produce sugar in the 1640s, they left little land for cattle or other livestock, and began to import most provisions. Sugar production also created a market for draft animals to turn sugar mills. Most such imports initially came from Virginia.[69] The trade in livestock and meat remained central to the economies of the Eastern Shore and Southside regions of Virginia into the eighteenth century, despite competition from New England, New York, and Pennsylvania. As the century progressed, some merchants from other Virginia counties began Caribbean trade as well, though tobacco remained overwhelmingly dominant between the James and Potomac Rivers.[70] Barbadians also imported other provisions, lumber and wood products, and naval stores from Virginia.[71] The two colonies traded enough that even in Virginia sugar sometimes replaced tobacco as currency in large transactions on the Eastern Shore and in Lower

Norfolk.[72] Their county records contain numerous references to Caribbean voyages.[73] In one particular instance, Charles Scarborough (Edmund Scarborough's son) and other Eastern Shore planters engaged James Armitage to sell bacon for them in Barbados. Armitage sold all of it except Scarborough's. Denouncing Scarborough's bacon as so poor that Scarborough should pay freight for it, he used it to provision the ship's crew, leaving for posterity a comment on the diet of seventeenth-century mariners. The Accomack court subsequently ordered Armitage to pay Scarborough for the bacon in goods of the same kind as bacon sold for in Barbados, suggesting either that Armitage made Caribbean voyages often enough or that Barbadian goods were common enough on the Eastern Shore to make such a sentence reasonable.[74]

Virginia accounted for a significant proportion of Barbados's intercolonial trade.[75] Ten of twenty-seven colonial-bound vessels making duty payments in Barbados in 1679 sailed for Virginia, nine to New England, four to Carolina, two to New York, one to Bermuda, and one to Newfoundland.[76] On February 10, 1673, Barbadian Governor William Lord Willoughby wrote that a conflagration in St. Michael's Town had consumed thirty or forty houses and many of their provisions from New England, Virginia, and Bermuda, as well as a great magazine of pipe staves and hoops, many of them likely from Virginia also.[77] At the end of the century shipping records began regularly to include both entries and clearances, illustrating the overlapping of various intercolonial trade routes. For example, in 1699 fifty-two ships entered Barbados from Massachusetts but only seventeen left Barbados for Massachusetts. Only fourteen ships entered Barbados from Virginia while twenty-four left Barbados for Virginia. These imbalances between incoming and outgoing voyages suggest that multicolony voyages were commonplace.[78] Later, in the first decade of the eighteenth century, the Virginia Council wrote to the Board of Trade that "what [intercolonial] trade they had was with Barbados," and that they sent corn, pork, pitch, tar, lumber, and tobacco in exchange for rum, sugar, molasses, cocoa, and ginger. The councilors also stated that Virginians sent cider and European goods to South Carolina and Bermuda in exchange for sugar, Madeira wine, salt, cocoa, and rice. They explained that American-owned vessels carried all intercolonial trade except some of the trade with Barbados.[79]

Virginians' trade with New England and the Caribbean, like that with New England and New Netherland, frequently intertwined. New England ships combined their voyages to Virginia and the Caribbean, just as Virginia ships combined their voyages to New England and New Netherland. Some of the ships in the Caribbean reported as New England-owned carried Chesapeake goods as well as New England products. New England vessels carrying

Chesapeake-Caribbean trade became more common as the century passed. On August 26, 1672, for example, a Boston court heard descriptions of a voyage by Henry Lawton, quarter owner of the ketch *Recovery*, and John Bonner, the ketch's master. Sailing from Boston to Virginia, they loaded goods for Barbados. Lawton stayed in the Chesapeake and consigned to Bonner a parcel of tobacco, pork, peas, and tar to sell in Barbados. From there Bonner returned to Virginia, whence they sailed to Ireland and England before returning from England to Boston.[80] As New England ships gradually carried more of other colonies' trade goods such combinations of intercolonial trade grew more common.[81] The growth of New England's merchant fleet thus augmented the networks that linked Virginia to other English colonies on the mainland and in the Caribbean, as well as with Europe.

During the last three decades of the seventeenth century, Virginia's intercolonial trade expanded to include Carolina. This trade too consisted of provisions (primarily livestock) sent from Virginia to the new colony, with the nearby Virginia counties south of the James River by far the most involved.[82] Early Carolina officials frequently noted the arrival of Virginia cattle and hogs, which burgeoned in the Lowcountry as they did in the Tidewater.[83] On March 2, 1671, Carolina Governor Joseph West wrote to Proprietor Anthony Ashley Cooper that the stock from Virginia, hogs especially, "thrives very well."[84] In some cases this trade involved multiple colonies from the outset and depended on the already established Virginia-Barbados trade to procure provisions for Carolina. On May 1, 1671, for example, the Lords Proprietors of Carolina gave Captain Mathias Halstead instructions to get timber in Carolina and trade it for rum and sugar in Barbados, where he was also to take on passengers for Carolina. After taking those migrants to Ashley River, he was to go on with the rum and sugar to Virginia to trade for cattle for Carolina. Possible contingency plans (in case of disease or saturated markets) involved brazilwood from the Bahamas and salt from Tortuga.[85] As livestock populations in Carolina grew, the new colony depended less on Virginia to feed itself and instead began to compete with the Chesapeake to supply Barbados with food and lumber. Indeed, it may well have been in viewing the Virginia-Barbados trade (and its concentration in Virginia's southernmost regions) that the Barbadian contingent of Carolina planters saw initial opportunity in the Carolina project. Carolina could provide an outlet for Barbadian emigrants, but could also (as its earliest colonists complained) serve Barbados.[86]

The mariners who carried Virginia's intercolonial and transatlantic trade possessed an Atlantic worldview that informed the outlook of its less mobile colonists in a variety of ways. Because they lived their lives throughout the American colonies and beyond, merchants and mariners often formed personal and economic relationships in several places, most commonly illustrated by the frequency with which mariners and merchants served as attorneys for those who had debts to collect in other colonies. In 1656, for example, the Charlestown, Massachusetts, merchant Nicholas Davison appointed his "Loveing freind" merchant William Kendall of Accomack County, Virginia, his attorney to collect debts from Edmund Scarborough or anyone else in Virginia.[87]

Another 1656 case illustrates the intertwined personal and economic relationships that characterized intercolonial trade. Salem, Massachusetts, merchant John Thorndike made "his faithfull & beloved freind Capt Francis Pott in Virginnia" his attorney to receive debts or gifts due to him from Stephen Charleton's estate. Charleton, an Eastern Shore merchant and ship owner, had traded to New England, the Netherlands, and New Netherland. Thorndike ordered the proceeds from Charleton's Chesapeake estate paid to his accounts with Virginia merchant William Kendall. This round robin of debt, trust, and friendship developed among these trading partners on Virginia's Eastern Shore and in Massachusetts.[88]

When Europeans or colonists appointed attorneys to collect multiple debts, they sometimes appointed only one to deal with business in multiple locations, a practice that relied on and facilitated intercolonial interactions. In June 1671, for example, the Bristol merchant John Nethway, living on the Portuguese island of Fayal in the Azores, appointed his "loving friend" Captain James Neale of Maryland his attorney to collect debts in Virginia or Maryland "or any of their parts." Boston courts recorded the letter the following December, suggesting that Marylander Neale had traveled to New England to collect debts due there to Nethway.[89]

While New England shipping grew more important for Virginia and all colonies, and English ships facilitated intercolonial interactions by traveling to two or more colonies in one voyage, Chesapeake ships carried much of Virginia's intercolonial trade.[90] Those Virginians involved in intercolonial trade owned their own ships much more often than even the most wealthy Virginia tobacco traders to England. Intercolonial trading vessels, because smaller and less specialized, required much less investment than transatlantic ships. Some of the wealthiest intercolonial traders in Virginia owned several vessels, and merchants sometimes sold these boats to their trading partners in other colonies.[91]

Shipowning by Virginia merchants and captains encouraged mariners and shipwrights to make the Chesapeake their primary residence.[92] Brothers John and James Bowdoin, Boston mariners, traded with Eastern Shore colonists and found the area appealing enough a base for their maritime activities

to purchase land in Northampton County, Virginia. In 1707 James sold his
share of the land to John and returned to Massachusetts while John stayed in
Virginia. Their decision to live in two different colonies allowed them to continue their intercolonial trade without the risks involved in trusting nonfamily
members. John, while making Virginia his primary residence, commanded the
brigantine *Northampton* and made James his attorney to collect debts for him
in Boston.[93]

Seamen who settled in Virginia shared their familiarity with Atlantic networks and their broad experiences in multiple Atlantic locales with their Chesapeake neighbors while working and socializing together when not at sea. The
pervasive maritime culture in seventeenth-century Virginia made merchant-
planters and even mariner-planters common. Time and time again, local
courts had to postpone cases involving free colonists at all economic levels
because one of the participants was "out of the countrey" on business. The
headright system, allowing fifty acres per person to people who could transport themselves or others to the colony, enabled elite mariners and common
seamen alike to acquire land at minimal cost.[94] The opportunity for seamen to
obtain fifty acres (often combined with mistreatment from their shipmasters)
encouraged them to desert in the Chesapeake and provoked searches for their
return.[95] If they continued to sail, they could avoid middlemen by carrying
their own products directly to markets. The 1649 author of "A Perfect Description of Virginia" claimed that "Most of the masters of ship and chief Mariners
have also there Plantations, and houses, and servants, &c. in Virginia."[96] A
half-century later, in 1697, Governor Sir Edmund Andros reported to the
Board of Trade that Virginia had few or no seamen because they became
planters when they arrived, though in fact court records frequently cited men
claiming dual roles as mariners and planters. Mariner John Wallop owned land
in Accomack, including seventeen hundred acres "near the seaboard side." In
1662 and 1663, Robert Pitt, commander of the ship *Mary* of London, patented
four thousand acres in northern Accomack County where he and his sons were
transatlantic and intercolonial merchants, and an additional four thousand
acres in the Southside County of Isle of Wight between 1637 and 1664.[97] These
mariners, like most migrants to Virginia, brought recent English experience
with them, but also brought broader knowledge of the Atlantic, encompassing
other colonies and perhaps Africa and other parts of Europe.

As the presence of planter-mariners makes clear, intercolonial merchants'
direct involvement in their trade integrated their maritime and local Chesapeake worlds.[98] Edmund Scarborough, one of the Eastern Shore's most active
and successful intercolonial traders, owned his own ships and traveled regularly to the other colonies with which he traded (New Netherland, New

England, the Caribbean, and Maryland) and accumulated over thirty thousand acres on the Eastern Shore.[99] Scarborough, like other successful intercolonial traders, brought his experiences in other colonies to bear in Virginia's political world. His primary trading partner, Boston merchant Edward Gibbons, was a selectman for Boston, deputy to the Massachusetts General Court, and commander in chief of Plymouth troops fighting in Narragansetts in 1645.[100] When Scarborough made trading voyages to Massachusetts, he thus learned not only of its markets, but of Gibbons's experiences as an official in the New England colony, which he surely used in his capacities as sheriff of Northampton, burgess, speaker of the Assembly, and surveyor general of Virginia.[101] His close friendship with a commander of troops fighting Indians may have contributed to his notoriously violent behavior toward Eastern Shore Pocomokes, with whom Virginia was officially at peace, in 1651.[102] Stephen Charleton, another Eastern Shore coastal trader, had county and colony political positions that allowed his intercolonial experiences to inform an arena beyond his plantations and personal circle. A member of the county's first vestry in 1635 and a court commissioner after February 1640, he served as a burgess in 1645 and 1652, and patented a total of 3,950 acres on the Eastern Shore by the time he died in 1654.[103]

Seamen's travels sometimes made them the vehicles for Atlantic commerce beyond the transport of their ships' cargoes. Such services put sailors in contact with merchants in each of the locales they visited. For example, in August 1640, Virginian Henry Peddenden gave a small fowling piece to William Quick to carry to New England for repair. Peddenden's request required Quick to expand his network in New England and may have extended the intercolonial contacts beyond the shipyards and taverns in Boston.[104] Individuals with a few items to sell sometimes asked mariners to dispose of them. In 1641 the estate of deceased Eastern Shore mariner Daniel Beddle included, in addition to seafaring equipment, twelve pounds of skins in the hands of Massachusetts merchant Edward Gibbons, three hogsheads of tobacco in New Netherland, wages due in New England, and two hundred pounds of tobacco due from Thomas Cooke of Jamestown.[105] Beddle, like other intercolonial mariners, had become economically (and therefore personally) involved in several of the colonies to which he traded others' goods.

Although New England developed as an American center for shipbuilding and repair during the seventeenth century, and though Virginia shipowners sometimes had ship work done in New England, one could also have ship repairs done in Virginia.[106] Indeed, some contemporaries exaggerated the lack of shipbuilding and shipowning in Virginia, possibly because it lacked a visible focal point such as Boston or Salem. Clearly less ship work took place in the

Chesapeake, but shipping mattered as much to the Chesapeake economy as to New England's. Outsiders' complaints about their difficulties in finding shipwrights may have contributed to seventeenth-century Virginia's reputation as a place without shipbuilding, and may have stemmed from the fact that like everything else in the Chesapeake, shipbuilding was dispersed, so Virginians could more easily engage a carpenter or a shipwright than could outsiders. Strangers' difficulties getting work done may have resulted from an inability to find craftsmen.[107] Certainly, Virginia ship repairing would not have matched the convenience for traders of New England's, where trading and shipwork concentrated in Boston and other port towns. But Virginians saw shipping as too important to the Chesapeake to rely solely on England or New England shipwrights to supply it. Shortly after the colony's establishment, one observer noted that colonists "built boate of all sorte, vizt Barges Pinaces Frigatts Hoyes shallops and the like."[108] In 1632 Governor John Harvey told the Virginia Commissioners that the colony had made some headway in the establishment of shipbuilding, reflecting conscious attempts to that end.[109] In addition, the expanding volume and scope of Virginia's trade created a market for vessels to carry it, a market that drew Virginians as well as outsiders into shipbuilding and repair. In 1641 Phillip Taylor provided William Stephens with tools and materials to work on his ships. Taylor owed Stephens for a house and for four days' work on the *Phillipp and Jane*, four days' work on his shallop, four days' work on the *Phillipp*, and for work setting up bedsteads, trimming two boats, making a pair of oars, and whetting two saws.[110] Taylor also hired the carpenter William Berry to build a boat for him.[111] Dutch merchant David Peterson DeVries described a creek near Newport News "where they build boats" and in 1645 described being entertained in the home of a carpenter who lived there.[112] Virginia's production of provisions and naval stores, in addition to providing coastal trade goods, proved useful for mariners and carpenters, who depended on such products to complete their work in Virginia.[113]

A 1648 observer wrote that Virginians "have . . . pinnaces, barks, great and small boats many hundreds, for most of their plantations stand upon the rivers' sides or up little creeks . . . so that for transportation and fishing they use many boats."[114] While most of these boats were small vessels used for local travel and transport, their widespread dispersal among English Virginians suggests colonists' familiarity with day-to-day waterborne travel that, together with their likely experience traversing longer distances across the Atlantic and between colonies, gave them personal experience that allowed them to comprehend more easily the ways in which Atlantic maritime ties connected them to residents in other Atlantic world locales. Virginians continued to build, repair, and provision ships through the end of the century, bringing a maritime Atlantic world closer to Virginia by multiplying opportunities for interaction between mariners and settlers.[115]

This maritime culture encompassed ever-growing regions and numbers of people as the seventeenth century witnessed expanding volumes and varieties of trade.[116] In Virginia, a growing colonial population continued to settle along navigable waterways. Trade provided the driving force for the sustaining networks that grew apace, for few Virginia colonists lived without connection to external markets. Early Atlantic trade was thus a matter of commodities and linkage to markets, but it also involved people—mariners and merchants, farmers and fur traders, captains and commoners—the whole polyglot array that gave human meaning to the Atlantic world shaped by the seventeenth-century routes created for the purpose of exchanging goods.

Chapter 3
Mariners and Colonists

In 1688 the Reverend John Clayton wrote of Virginia that "the great number of Rivers and the thinness of the Inhabitants distract and disperse a Trade." Because the Chesapeake's expansive network of navigable waterways provided colonists direct access to shipping, "all Ships in general gather . . . their Loading up and down an hundred Miles distant; and the best of Trade . . . is only a sort of Scotch Pedling; for they must carry all sort of Truck that trade thither, having one Commodity to pass off another." Clayton, like many of his contemporaries and historians since, blamed the lack of towns in the Chesapeake on the number of rivers and their estuaries that allowed colonists to spread out (along their banks) and settle in dispersed patterns without isolating themselves. Chesapeake settlers found direct shipping access convenient, and because, in Clayton's words, "every one being more sollicitous for a private Interest and Conveniency, than for a publick, they will either be for making Forty Towns at once, that is, two in every County, or none at all," an attitude that rendered port towns unnecessary.[1] Though many praised towns as efficient and safe in theory, colonists resisted giving up their own direct access, which would have necessitated taking their goods to other shipping points.[2]

One of the most important aspects of Virginia's maritime trade was that it pervaded society, in part because almost everyone produced goods for transatlantic or intercolonial trade, and in part because of the dispersed nature of shipping that Clayton described. The 1649 author of "A Perfect Description of Virginia" estimated that there were about fifteen thousand English colonists in Virginia, and that the over thirty ships that visited per year employed seven hundred to one thousand mariners.[3] Even allowing for the hyperbole common to promotional literature, the ratio of mariners to settlers was high enough to make mariners a real presence in the colony, especially because settlement patterns and trade methods brought settlers into frequent contact with mariners. Ships' practice of sailing into the navigable rivers and estuaries to numerous trading points maximized the opportunities for colonists and mariners to interact, and so the Chesapeake's geography encouraged contact between seamen and settlers. Ships and their crews stayed in Virginia for months to collect cargo or to wait for favorable weather or for other ships to form a fleet (during war). Ship captains commonly stayed with wealthy Virginia merchants and officials; seamen stayed on the ship or with colonists. Taverns and the ships themselves became centers of social interaction and information exchange between mariners and settlers. In the Chesapeake, geography created a set of trade practices in which mariners shared their broad Atlantic experiences directly with many colonists. Thus, colonists' involvement in the Atlantic world went far beyond their production of trade goods destined for various Atlantic markets or their consumption of goods produced by its distant residents. Rather, Chesapeake settlement patterns and trade methods brought the maritime aspects of the Atlantic world directly to Virginia colonists, servants, and slaves. Their own reliance on waterborne transport, discussed in Chapter 2, their lengthy and intense interaction with mariners, and the immigrant nature of seventeenth-century Virginia discussed in Chapter 4, all ensured their full immersion in Atlantic culture and likely adoption of Atlantic, rather than insular Virginian, worldviews.

Most seventeenth-century Atlantic trade required the cultivation of personal relationships, but in Virginia those personal relationships, like the trade itself, disseminated widely into the colony.[4] Lading a ship in Virginia was frequently time consuming and often engaged mariners and colonists with one another to complete the task. For example, although shallops collected tobacco from particular neighborhoods to facilitate the transfer to ships, often this collection did not occur until the ships had arrived with their mariners who then participated in the process.[5] Ships trading in intercolonial goods such as livestock, meat, grain, and naval stores, found even less cargo collection and storage prior to their arrival than those trading in tobacco. Intercolonial trading vessels commonly picked up livestock directly from its grower, who slaughtered and processed meat on the spot, with crew members watching or helping. The colony's leaders tried several times to concentrate trade (to aid the formation of fleets as a safety measure during periods of warfare and to facilitate the collection of taxes) but never succeeded during the seventeenth century.[6] Throughout the seventeenth century, intercolonial trade and the mariner-settler interactions described in this chapter changed very little. It was not until after 1700, with the extension of European settlement beyond the fall line and development first of Norfolk and later of other port towns and cities, that trade began to concentrate and significant proportions of the population lived out of reach of direct contact with the maritime world.[7]

Chesapeake geography and settlement patterns, then, linked the majority of colonists directly to a wider world throughout the seventeenth century. In an economy in which almost everyone produced goods for export, and in which no towns provided regional cultural centers, interactions with mariners provided settlers with contacts to markets, news, and distant social contacts. Participation in shipping may in fact have carried social as well as economic privileges in such a society. Planters often also acted as merchants, commonly traveling with their cargoes, sometimes on their own ships as captains, masters, or mariners. These multifaceted merchants and mariners sat on county and colonial courts and held various offices, providing them with arenas in which their continued ties to England and their broad Atlantic experiences could inform political developments in Virginia.[8]

Mariners and merchants tied seventeenth-century Virginians to other American colonists, to Europeans, and to Africans. Not only did the labor of elite merchants and common seamen build trade links tying Europe, Africa, and the Americas together economically, but the same mariners likewise created the human links connecting people around the Atlantic basin to one another socially, culturally, and politically. The links that mariners provided between settlers and a larger world were possible, in large part, because the arrival of ships provided social opportunities for Virginians and mariners alike. The European and African residents of Virginia and Maryland were especially likely to interact directly with mariners because of the Chesapeake's dispersed and time-consuming trade. Those mariners spent time working and socializing with Virginians, allowing wealthy and poor planters, merchants, officials, servants, and slaves to communicate with their counterparts in other colonies and across the Atlantic, and thereby to understand their own relationship to the other residents of the Atlantic world.[9]

Mariners provided, as did Indians, a useful source of knowledge about the wider world for settlers. Indeed, settlers often relied on these two sources to understand their geographical position and to connect themselves to other regions. In 1684 Thomas Hinckley wrote from New Plymouth, New England, to William Blathwayt (auditor general of the colonies), sending a map "whereby you may see that the mouth of Narraganset Bay or River (as it is indifferently called by coasters) lies between Seaconett and Point Judith. . . . Its commonly said by coast[al traders], that there are in Virginia far greater bays than this of Narroganset, which are called rivers." He enclosed testimonies that Indians described no other rivers.[10]

Fortunately for historians, David Peterson De Vries, a Dutch ship captain, trader, and would-be colonist, left accounts of his Atlantic peregrinations that allow us to discern patterns of commercial and social interactions in place in the 1630s and 1640s. Mariners and traders played crucial roles establishing and maintaining these networks. De Vries, as one of them, had a firsthand view of the process whereby colonists and mariners interacted to create Atlantic networks. In addition, his indefatigable curiosity, multilingual abilities, worldwide travel experience, and status as an educated member of the Dutch elite uniquely qualified him as an observer, analyst, and reporter of the evolving Atlantic world. His interactions with various Virginians allow us to see how he (and countless others who did not record their travels) engaged in myriad human interactions that gave the Atlantic world social and cultural as well as economic meaning. In seeking to build economic networks in Virginia's dispersed maritime economy that required direct and sustained involvement of mariners and settlers with one another, they immersed Virginians in the Atlantic world.

De Vries left accounts of his voyages that both explain some of the developing patterns of intercolonial trade and detail the social interactions by which mariners linked colonists to one another throughout the Americas. De Vries and his seven crew members met other ships all over the Americas. He described their business, telling his readers about shipping patterns in the process. He also described the interlacing of colonists' and mariners' social worlds. In almost every colony he visited, De Vries met the English or Dutch governor and often stayed with him. In 1632 on the first of his three voyages, De Vries traveled first to Nevis where he met Governor Thomas Littleton. Littleton asked him to convey some Portuguese captives and, en route to St. Christopher, transfer them to Captain John Stone's English ship. De Vries stayed in Nevis a month, much of it with Littleton.[11] At St. Christopher, where he "came to the great roadstead" dotted with English ships, he met the English governor Captain Sir Thomas Warner. He transferred the Portuguese prisoners to Stone's ship and sailed with him to St. Martin, where Stone steered for Puerto Rico, while De Vries went north to the mainland.[12]

In January 1633 in the Delaware Bay, De Vries and his crew found local Indians left by warfare with little to trade. Consequently, De Vries sailed to Virginia to get corn from the English colonists there.[13] At Kecoughtan (Point Comfort) a James River pilot boarded to guide them to Jamestown. An English merchant joined them for passage upriver (possibly also seizing the opportunity to make contact with a Dutch merchant). As they proceeded, they met planters eager for their company. At Blunt Point near Newport News "one of the most distinguished citizens," Councilor Samuel Mathews, persuaded De Vries and his men (as well as the pilot and the English merchant) to stay overnight at his house, where he treated them with hospitality. At Littleton "a great merchant," Mr. George Menefie, "kept us to dinner and treated us very well." While there a message arrived from Governor Sir John Harvey, who had heard of their arrival and wanted to meet them. At Jamestown, they found Harvey waiting on the beach, with halberdiers and musketeers to welcome them. As De Vries stepped on shore, Harvey bid him welcome, and asked from where he came. De Vries told the governor he had come from the South Bay of New Netherland (Delaware Bay), which prompted Harvey to escort De Vries to his house, where he welcomed him with a glass of Venetian sack, and presented a map, showing that what the Dutch called South Bay the English called "My Lord Delaware's Bay," and announced that the English considered it their own, not part of New Netherland. De Vries answered that no Englishmen had been there for ten years, while the Dutch had long maintained Fort Nassau there. Harvey expressed surprise to "have such neighbours, and have never heard of them," but his comment that the Dutch were in no danger from Virginia but should watch out for New England coming too close to them suggests that he not only knew about New Netherland but that he saw advantage in cultivating a relationship with the Dutch colony even if at the expense of Virginia's relationship with New England. Assuring De Vries of his opinion that "there was land enough" and they should be good neighbors, Harvey invited De Vries to stay for dinner and spend the night at his house.[14]

The following day John Stone arrived after delivering the Portuguese prisoners to Puerto Rico where he had received good treatment from the Spanish Governor. Harvey extended the same hospitality to Stone as to De Vries, inviting both captains to dinner. At dinner De Vries told Harvey that he could speak French and Italian, as well as English and Dutch, and had traveled to Italy, Africa, and the East Indies. Another English guest, who had visited the East Indies, expressed disbelief, and quizzed De Vries about people and places there. When De Vries answered, Harvey remarked that "mountains could not, but men who go and see the world can, meet each other," thus connecting the people of the world across great distances.[15]

After a week in Virginia, De Vries left for New Netherland with six goats and a ram on board as Harvey's gift for the Dutch governor, who had no goats. His gift created another tie linking his part of the colonial world to another. On his trip down the James River, De Vries again stayed with Captain Samuel Mathews at Blunt Point. Mathews kept a dairy and sold butter, cheese, and beef to ships leaving the Chesapeake.[16] De Vries bought some of the hogs, which his crew slaughtered and salted for provisions. De Vries after two days left, took in water at Newport News and bought more provisions at Point Comfort, where he waited for good wind.[17]

On March 29 De Vries arrived in Delaware Bay at Swanendael, where he sold salt he had bought in the Caribbean.[18] From there he went on to New Netherland for two months, spending much of his time with Director-General Wouter Van Twiller. On June 15 De Vries and his crew weighed anchor for the

Netherlands, and on the way out to sea warned an Englishman sailing toward them of a sandbar. The Englishman turned out to be Captain John Stone, his ship laden with corn and young cattle from Virginia bound for New England, stopping at New Amsterdam for water. Trusting their friendship to help him, Stone asked De Vries to furnish him a man to pilot him in. De Vries asked his crew whether any of them would willingly transfer to Stone's ship. Illustrating an interdependence among mariners that crossed national lines, a volunteer shifted to Stone's ship, while De Vries headed for Europe.[19] International ship's crews commonly included Dutch, English, Portuguese and sometimes French, Spanish, or African seamen.[20]

All this to-ing and fro-ing in the Atlantic basin showed De Vries obviously comfortable in English and Dutch plantations alike, but he drew distinctions between them. On his first voyage, De Vries expressed wonder at the English practice of risking their servants as stakes in bets, observing that he "had never seen such work in Turk or Barbarian, and that it was not becoming Christians."[21] English mariners familiar with the Dutch had some similar difficulties understanding the Dutch. During the spring months De Vries spent in New Netherland, a New Englander arrived to trade and invited Governor Wouter Van Twiller on board. De Vries accompanied Van Twiller, along with several officers of New Netherland. The Dutch officers "became intoxicated, and got into such high words, that the Englishman could not understand . . . such unruliness among the officers of the Company, and that a governor should have no more control over them; he was not accustomed to it among his countrymen."[22] Although easy communication and interdependence prevailed between the Dutch and the English—particularly among mariners— they both clearly perceived differences between them. Thus, while the maritime Atlantic world was international, its international character did not erase ethnic, cultural, or national boundaries. Rather, it facilitated contact across those boundaries.

On De Vries's second voyage to the Americas, which began in July 1634, he planted an unsuccessful colony in Guiana, meeting French and English settlers who offered him their hospitality.[23] The following spring, after leaving Guiana, he and his crew met a fishing boat and a wooden sloop at the Caimites, on the west end of Hispaniola, both laden with English fleeing the Island of Tortuga after the Spanish attacked their fort. At their request De Vries took on board the twenty-five people from the sloop and twenty-five from the overburdened fishing boat and took them to Virginia.[24] There he got provisions to sail to New Netherland. It was out of season to obtain tobacco, so he left all of his cargo in Virginia with directions to trade when the tobacco crop ripened, indicating that he would return in September after the unhealthy

Chesapeake summer had ended.[25] Once again he spent the summer in New Netherland with Governor Van Twiller. On September 1 he set out for Virginia to collect reimbursement for rescuing the English from the Tortugas and for the trade goods he had left there in May. While he was saying goodbye to Van Twiller, the West India Company's bark arrived, carrying fourteen or fifteen Englishmen who had captured Fort Nassau (empty of Dutch at the time). De Vries delayed his departure for six days to take the English to Virginia, where they expected assistance. The English "took their leave of Wouter Van Twiller . . . and came, bag and baggage, on board my vessel" for Virginia.[26] Not only De Vries, but the rest of the Dutch in New Netherland, including Van Twiller, also assisted the captured English, even while expelling them from the territory in question.[27] Thus, despite national competition in establishing colonies, in these cases at least, mariners cooperated to ensure survival and protect potential trade contacts even while vying for control of contested land. Such cooperation suggests a willingness on the part of Van Twiller and De Vries to recognize the international character of their colonial setting and work to ensure future peaceful (and potentially profitable) interactions between them, and an unwillingness to back down where competing land claims were concerned.

In late September 1638, De Vries left the Netherlands on a third voyage "in order to plant a colony upon Staten Island" for himself and his kinsman Frederick De Vries.[28] After wintering in New Netherland, De Vries went to New Haven on June 8, 1639, where he "Remained at night at this English fort, where we were well treated by the governor." The following day he visited the Dutch outpost, where Gysbert Van Dyke commanded fourteen or fifteen soldiers and where the English, despite the Dutch presence and claim to the land, had built a town with a fine church and a hundred houses. Van Dyke asked De Vries to protest the English use of Dutch land "which we had bought of the indians." At dinner with the English governor, De Vries declared it wrong for the English to take the West India Company's land. The governor answered that the lands had lain idle, a sinful waste of such productive acreage. The English at this settlement impressed De Vries by living "soberly, drink[ing] only three times at a meal, and whoever drinks himself drunk, they tie to a post and whip him, as they do thieves in Holland." The New Haven Puritans asserted "that they are Israelites, and that we at our colony are Egyptians, and that the English in the Virginias are also Egyptians."[29] Again, despite their obvious differences, there prevailed easy correspondence through which the English and Dutch involved gained a picture of the breadth of the colonial American world. In the eyes of some New Englanders, in fact, English Virginians and Dutch New Netherlanders more resembled one another (as "Egyptians") than either did the New Haven colonists ("Israelites"). Both De Vries and the New Haven colonists looked across national boundaries to gauge themselves against "outsiders" in cultural terms, yet they did so without apparent hostility or violence, willing perhaps to recognize that the functioning of the Atlantic world depended on commercial cooperation despite national, ethnic, cultural, and religious differences, while also creating proximities that made such differences more familiar.

De Vries spent almost five years in New Netherland trying to establish his settlement at Staten Island. By 1642, he "was daily with Commander [Willem] Keift [by then New Netherland director-general], generally dining with him when I went to the fort." As commander, Keift "built a fine inn, . . . stone, . . . to acommodate the English who daily passed with their vessels from New England to Virginia." Keift had "suffered great annoyance," providing hospitality for all these English, "who might now lodge in the tavern." Keift may have exaggerated by describing the English arrivals as "daily," but his statement indicates significant volume and intercolonial traders' and travelers' expectations of receiving a hospitable welcome. De Vries thought the inn good for travelers, but worried how it might affect the reputation of New Netherland, so crucial to trade, given Puritan comments comparing rowdy Dutch New Netherlanders to "Egyptians." De Vries told Keift that New Netherland also needed a church to replace the mean barn in which the Dutch worshipped, a scandal to English eyes considering that the English (presumably meaning New Englanders) always built a fine church after their dwellings. He recommended that the Dutch also build attractive churches, particularly "as the West India Company was deemed to be the principal means of upholding the Reformed Religion against the tyranny of Spain."[30] De Vries identified the Dutch West India Company as the primary challenge to Spanish Catholicism and "tyranny" in the Atlantic world, a role that the Puritans claimed for themselves. Their shared Calvinism and their competition for the right to claim primary status as anti-Catholics suggests another element to his conversation with the New Haven colonists and his decision to report it. His concern that New Netherland possess a good church to enhance its reputation among New Englanders may have been part of a larger concern over Atlantic world commerce in which reputation played a crucial part, as was Kieft's more practical decision to promote trade by providing lodging for travelers.

By late summer 1643, Indians had destroyed De Vries's Staten Island plantation and he determined to leave New Netherland. While De Vries awaited passage, a ship arrived from Rotterdam. The master, Jacob Blenck, had one hundred pipes of Madeira wine to sell in Virginia. He had sailed up the coast from the Caribbean but had missed the mouth of the Chesapeake and gone all the way to New England, where he could not sell the wine "because the English there live soberly." He could not sell it in New Netherland because of the West India Company's tax. In New Amsterdam, however, he had met an English merchant, perhaps a Virginian, who bought the wine and arranged for Blenck to deliver it to Virginia. Learning that De Vries wanted to go to Virginia, Blenck enlisted him as pilot; they left for the Chesapeake in early October.[31]

On their way to Virginia, they sailed up the Delaware Bay to three Swedish forts. They found the governor, Captain Johan Printz, at the third fort, where he welcomed them with a silver mug of beer for Blenck and a large glass of Rhenish wine for De Vries. Blenck traded wines and sweetmeats for furs. After five days awaiting a favorable wind, better weather came on October 20 and they sailed for Virginia.[32] Arriving at Point Comfort the following day, Blenck "inquired for his factor," who "immediately came aboard" and told Blenck to take his wines upriver to Jamestown. There, De Vries and Blenck met Governor Sir William Berkeley and renewed the acquaintance of Virginians he had met on his previous voyages. When De Vries told Berkeley that he had come to Virginia seeking passage to London and thence to the Netherlands, the governor responded that he would have to winter in Virginia. When the tobacco ships left in the spring, Berkeley would arrange passage for De Vries on a good ship. Meanwhile, De Vries could stay with him over the winter and "have as good as he himself, for I was a man who had seen the world, and had sailed as a commander over all of it; that he had heard many speak of me before I came into the country now; that I had treated their nation well, and on that account he should use me well, and would have my society during the winter, as he was fond of, and in need of society." De Vries had promised to help Blenck, a newcomer to Virginia, lade his ship, but he visited Berkeley several times over the course of the winter.[33]

De Vries and Blenck spent the winter going "daily from one plantation to the other, until the ships were ready, and had their cargoes of tobacco."[34] In his accounts of his travels, De Vries had warned that because Chesapeake tobacco trade lacked any geographic centralization, Dutch merchants should establish a permanent presence there.[35] As Blenck and De Vries traded, De Vries "examined their plantations," discovering that some colonists who had exhausted their soil with tobacco had shifted to crops of wheat or flax. De Vries told his readers that New Netherlanders should emulate the Virginians and do the same.[36] De Vries's advice shows that those interested in colonial projects looked for models and examples to solve problems common to several European colonies. The extensive travel of mariners such as De Vries, and their communications with colonial settlers and officials facilitated such transfers of information.

In April 1644, having passed most of his winter "in going up and down the river" collecting tobacco, De Vries thanked Berkeley for his friendship and sailed on a ship bound for London, which left Jamestown on April 13. As he had on previous trips, he once again stayed the night with his "good friend" Captain Samuel Mathews at Blunt Point.[37] An incident that transpired on his way back from Mathew's house to his ship showed that the Atlantic network of personal acquaintance De Vries described and helped build included commoners as well as governors, merchants, and captains. He encountered a resident ship carpenter who welcomed him "in his house, as I had, some years ago, on board of my ship, well treated him, and he hoped to treat me well now." The carpenter killed a turkey and some chickens for dinner and took De Vries back to his ship in the morning. De Vries did not mention Samuel Mathews's forty slaves, who operated his cattle, dairy, shoemaking, rope-making, and linen-weaving businesses, but they, too, living at a hub of maritime activity, spoke and worked with mariners from dozens of Dutch and English ships each year.[38]

De Vries's experiences, though not rare, have unique value because he wrote accounts of them. They allow us to see the extent and pattern of mariners' interactions with other mariners and with settlers, as well as the ways in which mariners facilitated the formation of economic and social webs—well established two decades after the first permanent English colony—that created an Atlantic world despite polyglot nationalities, small populations, and great distances between settlements. De Vries's welcomes from the governors of Nevis, St. Christopher, Virginia, New Netherland, New Haven, New Sweden, and the English and French in Guiana, together with his descriptions of John Stone's similar welcomes in St. Christopher, Puerto Rico, Virginia, New Netherland, and New England, give a sense of the world in which ship captains moved, the extent of their interactions, and their importance in the spreading information and shrinking the colonial world for those who lived in it. His account of his winter spent helping Blenck collect cargo in Virginia highlights the unusual nature of Chesapeake trade that increased the numbers of people interacting and the lengths of time they did so, thereby expanding and intensifying the integration of mariners' and settlers' worlds—making Virginia Atlantic. Though his high status makes De Vries atypical, his account reveals that other ship captains played similar roles and suggests parallel interactions among ships' crews and colonists, people less likely to record their encounters systematically. As the seventeenth century unfolded, no accounts similar to De Vries's appeared; however, a vast weight of detailed evidence, much of it in court records, survives to document the extension, expansion, and ramification of the mariner-settler interactions revealed by his accounts.

In April 1643 in Virginia, New England mariner Phillip White, Virginia innholder Anthony Hodgkins, and Rhode Island seaman George Roome bound themselves to Virginia merchant Thomas Bushrod (who a few years later provided Barnaby Brian with the liquor he drank in Noddles Island) to deliver twelve hundred pounds of pork to Manhattan tailor Richard Clecke and one thousand pounds of pork to Manhattan merchant and intercolonial migrant Isaac Allerton by the end of the year.[39] That a New Englander (likely from Massachusetts), a Virginian, and a Rhode Islander made themselves partners to transport pork from Virginia to New Netherland provides a striking illustration of the degree to which intercolonial trade had fostered the development of economic webs linking Virginia to other colonies. These webs testify to the colonists' realization that they lived and prospered in a set of communities linked directly to one another by expanding commerce and, with the passage of time, the legal addenda of such commerce.

Sailors, ship captains, and merchants played an important role in spreading personal and political information about the colonies and about Europe in colonial Virginia. The long stays required for ship repairs and cargo collection provided social opportunities for Virginians and mariners alike and facilitated the formation of commercial and personal relationships. During the 1670s, English merchants estimated that their traders in Virginia might need as long as 210 days to load a ship with three hundred hogsheads of tobacco.[40] When, in April 1667, the *Dove* loaded in Virginia, Master Robert Pitt employed two sloops to bring the freight of tobacco on board. One carried forty-two hogsheads, the other twenty-seven, and the sloops remained continually employed on the *Dove*'s business for four months. The ship also had repairs done and remained in Virginia for at least seven months.[41]

During the months required for lading and repairing ships, sailors and captains mingled with colonists, sharing gossip and news about events in England or in other colonies. In a Chesapeake region pressed for labor throughout the seventeenth century, sailors became laborers enmeshed in the local economy while waiting for their ships to sail. Though most of their work related to their trade and involved preparing colonists' cargoes for shipment, it nevertheless established social ties to the region by taking them to people's houses to labor for extended periods. Because Virginia's geography discouraged the development of port towns to collect and store cargos and where mariners would congregate, colonists spread over a wide area of the Chesapeake had direct contact with mariners during these long stays. While in colonies such as Massachusetts and New Netherland the port towns of Boston, Salem, and New Amsterdam became the foci of the most dynamic interaction between residents and the mariners who connected them to the wider world, in Virginia and Maryland those interactions were, like trade and settlement, dispersed along the navigable waterways. Virginians' use of ship arrivals and departures to mark dates (for example, a two-year-old memory that a particular heifer wandered away "the same daye that Garretts Pinnace came from New England") indicates the importance of shipping to their lives.[42] Colonists' certainty that shipping held the same meaning for court members who heard their depositions further shows the significance of shipping and the degree to which it permeated the consciousness of Chesapeake settlers.

Colonists' direct contact with mariners during their long stays collecting cargoes took many forms. In the spring of 1655, Mrs. Godfrey told the Lower Norfolk Court that surgeon John Rise owed her husband for several days' meals for himself and "divers seamen" and for washing, storage of his goods, and lodging.[43] In 1699 Philadelphia merchant (and former Jamaican) Isaac Norris gave one of his ship captains explicit instructions that if he could not return from his Caribbean voyage to Philadelphia before winter weather, he was to head for the Chesapeake or Bermuda to sell his cargo and "unship the crew" for the winter.[44] Presumably, they would be on their own to find lodging among Chesapeake colonists until the following spring when the ship would sail again. When seamen stayed with people such as Mrs. Godfrey, they socialized not just with the Godfreys, but with their neighbors and with other colonists and sailors in ordinaries and other private homes. Seventeenth-century Virginia ordinaries were private houses whose owners obtained license to sell alcohol, further personalizing mariner-settler interactions by placing them firmly in the world of colonists, rather than removing them to buildings apart from the daily life of colonists and designated as spaces existing between colonial settlements and the wider maritime world. Sailors sometimes preferred layovers in Virginia to continuing their journeys. In the winter of 1631–32, Henry Fleet had difficulty convincing his sailors to travel from Virginia to New England, "all of them resolving not to stir until the spring."[45] Winter in Virginia would be more comfortable than winter at sea or in New England, but the mariners' resistance also suggests that they found their lodging and social situation in Virginia tolerable enough that they wanted to stay the winter there.

In New England, mariners more often had the option of staying in inns and taking part in well-established port town communities.[46] These options kept their interactions with colonists restricted to the area surrounding the port. In Virginia this option rarely existed, but sailors did congregate in ordinaries in Virginia when they could.[47] There, they met and interacted with Virginians, discussing political events in Europe and other colonies, and engaging in social conversation that extended far beyond the business of their trade and sometimes allowed close friendships to grow. Those mariners connected Virginia colonists not only to other places in the Atlantic world, but also to maritime culture in which commitments to egalitarianism among common seamen tended to weaken (but not erase) national and ethnic boundaries between crewmembers.[48] There is little evidence for interracial mariner-settler interactions in Virginia, but it would be surprising, for example, if crew members had not socialized with merchant Samuel Mathews's slaves when their ships anchored at Mathews's plantation to take in water and the shipping supplies and provisions that the slaves produced there.[49]

In 1642 several Virginians and mariners socialized at Anthony Hodgkins's Eastern Shore house, licensed as an ordinary. Their conversations suggest that the kinds of ties forged in such interactions went beyond casual acquaintanceships. As one of the few ordinaries on the Eastern Shore, Hodgkins's house provided a congregating point for colonists and mariners alike. We know it facilitated Hodgkins's own intercolonial contacts because he was the Virginia innkeeper who sent pork to Massachusetts with the New England mariner Philip White and Rhode Island seaman George Roome. In November 1642, the men at Hodgkins's inn included a Mr. Chaundler, his servant Robert Warder, an unnamed ship's gunner (identified only as belonging to Watlington's ship), and Virginian Andrew Jacobs. With all present, the ship's gunner reminded Chaundler that during an earlier conversation Chaundler had promised to free his servant Warder for £6. The gunner now had the money to buy Warder's freedom, but since their agreement Chaundler had sold three years of Warder's time to another man and now could not keep his promise.[50] The gunner of Watlington's ship probably was not resident in the county, or the court clerk would have identified him by name, but he played a key part in this case. Not only was he at the ordinary with Virginians when the events transpired, but he had previously made the agreement and, more importantly, knew Warder well enough to put up the money for his freedom.

In part this practice of socialization among residents and mariners grew out of the fact that the trade itself required multiple contacts involving several individuals. Particularly in intercolonial trade involving mixed cargoes, ships did much of their business piecemeal on both sides, with settlers buying in small quantities and individual mariners, as well as masters and merchants, doing much of the selling (in terms of the numbers of transactions made, if not the volume sold). This practice required many Virginians to come on board or mariners to leave the ship.[51] A dispute over price illustrates the number of Virginians who could frequent a ship at any given time because of the ubiquity of personal trade. In late summer 1643, Thomas Savage's servant and a Dutch ship's carpenter bargained for some linen on board the Dutch ship. Savage's servant, unsure whether he had negotiated a good price, asked Virginian William Johnson, on board and observing the exchange, to call Savage. Johnson, busy (perhaps bartering for himself), sent Goodman Berry, who told the servant the prices were good. To the carpenter's later chagrin, the servant bought the cloth at what turned out to be a good price indeed. Eastern Shore merchant Edmund Scarborough and the boat's cook and boatswain also witnessed the bargaining.[52] Such shipboard negotiation was a public affair, with boats' crew and colonists always present. Enough of it took place in small quantities to involve colonists, servants, and slaves with the boats and their crew members.

Sometimes the socializing opportunities presented by a ship's arrival rivaled the occasion for trade. In 1679 Labadist proselytizer Jaspar Dankaerts reported that when ships arrived in Virginia or Maryland "with goods, and especially with liquors, such as wine and brandy, they attract everybody." Then the masters and planters, whose carousing Dankaerts witnessed, "indulge so abominably together, that they keep nothing . . . yea, do not go away as long as there is any left."[53] Chesapeake residents who could not afford European wines and brandies nonetheless welcomed the arrival of ships, and may have celebrated in similar fashion when intercolonial ships arrived with cargos including less expensive American rum.

The complexity of loading a ship, the multiple uses of a ship's journey, and in some cases, the ships' plural ownership, all ensured involvement of colonists with ships and their crews, an involvement often documented by ensuing court testimonies. Court cases provide evidence of two ways in which the movements of mariners connected England's (and the Netherlands') American colonies during the seventeenth century. First, their use of local courts to address issues involving multiple colonies and England legitimized those courts as legal custodians of the Atlantic world, not just their own limited jurisdictions. Second, the appearance of mariners as witnesses to other cases and the existence of cases involving shipboard events reflects the involvement of mariners in Chesapeake society, illustrating how ship captains and common seamen alike became an integral part of Virginians' world when their ships were in port, adding a decidedly worldly element to individual Chesapeake locales. In the 1650s, Major Thomas Lambert of Lower Norfolk County shared ownership of the ship *Seahorse* with Mathew Fassett, the ship's master. Fassett, as master, stayed constantly with the ship, and habitually made decisions about it without consulting his co-owner Lambert. Collecting lading involved both Fassett and Lambert with colonists. In the early winter of 1653–54, Fassett purchased cattle and hogs in Virginia for sale to Barbados the following spring.

He bought the livestock from several different owners. He and Lambert traveled to each of the plantations, some of them several times, to view animals and visit with colonists in their houses. For example, in mid-November, Fassett went to the house of John Martin and bought twenty hogs. About a month later, Lambert and Fassett went to Martin's house together and asked him to get the hogs ready in three or four days when Fassett and some of his seamen would come to "see to the killing of the hogs."[54] Fassett bought livestock for the voyage from other planters as well, and each sale presumably required similar multiple interactions.[55]

Just before Christmas, Lambert and Fassett fell out over Fassett's purchases. Descriptions of their argument further reveal the social interactions of these mariners while they wintered in Virginia, gradually lading their vessel. Gentleman Edward Lloyd, a visitor at the house of Robert Ewins on December 23 "in a roome together with Maior Thomas Lambert," saw Fassett come in and tell Lambert that he had paid too much for biscuit.[56] This disagreement apparently led Lambert to question Fassett's meat purchases as well. Lambert had recently told Lemuel Mason (from whom Fassett had bought some of his cattle) that Fassett had no power to buy anything without his consent.[57]

The Lower Norfolk justices who heard the case decided in Fassett's favor and awarded the very high damage payment of five thousand pounds of tobacco, perhaps swayed by the potential damage that Lambert had done to Fassett's reputation. Reputation was crucial to traders, who had to rely on their good name among settlers in all their trade locations and among other mariners in order to enter into agreements or receive credit. The jury decided that Lambert had vilified Fassett's by calling him "Rascall, Knave, & foole, in the open Cort, & Speakinge in a disparraginge way thee sd words (you are [not] fitt to be a Marchant, I hope none is soo madd now as to trust you)." The court decided that Lambert had "grossely abused & scandalized" Fassett, threatening Fassett's reputation "to ye great impoachmt of his good name & creditt, not onely in this Country, but it may be farr more in forraine ptes where ye sd Fassett may come to ye losse of his voyages, or his utter undoeinge."[58] The court understood that in a maritime world, information spread quickly and easily "to far foreign parts," not only from this region of Virginia to Barbados, but to other colonies where Fassett traded as well. Fassett, like many intercolonial traders, was involved in more than two colonies. In October 1652 while in New Amsterdam, he bought the twenty-six ton bark the *Hopewell* from merchant Thomas Willett.[59] When New Englander Willett had moved from Plymouth to New Amsterdam in 1644, William Bradford sent a letter of recommendation to New Netherland Director-General Pieter Stuyvesant, referring to Willett as his special friend, who desired to continue trade with the Dutch. Willett also was a partner of Eastern Shore merchant Edmund Scarborough, and put up security for Scarborough in New Amsterdam when Scarborough exported forty-one slaves in 1656.[60]

Testimony in this case also shows how ships' trading movements facilitated travel by colonists. Fassett agreed to transport Francis Anketill and his goods up the Chesapeake to Patuxent, Maryland, for one thousand pounds of tobacco. Fassett may have had to go to Maryland to collect part of the ship's lading there, or perhaps the ship could make such voyages while waiting to accumulate goods in Virginia. In either case, Anketill depended on the trading ship to move himself and his goods, and the use of his ship for this purpose extended Fassett's contacts in the Chesapeake. By late in the century, intercolonial travel was common enough that wealthier colonists could plan to move from one colony to another seasonally, in patterns that sometimes overlapped with trade concerns but that were sometimes unrelated. In the spring of 1687 Virginian Mr. Parker planned to leave the Chesapeake in May for health reasons, spend the summer in Pennsylvania and New England, return to Virginia in October, and then go to Barbados for the winter.[61]

Other evidence for sailors' interactions with colonists often comes from court cases in which sailors from anchored ships served as witnesses to events on land or cases that centered on encounters that took place on ships at anchor in Virginia. Many of these had nothing to do with the commerce that officially brought the ship into the colony, instead reflecting that while in Virginia, ships became gathering places, providing interaction among colonists, between colonists and sailors, and between colonists and passengers traveling with the ship through Virginia and on to further destinations. While in the bay and its estuaries, ships became like ordinaries, temporary and mobile nodes of communication. All these situations served to make colonists constantly conscious of their links to other parts of the world and other colonies in the Americas.

The regularity with which settlers boarded ships provided Virginians in 1635 with the opportunity to send Governor John Harvey back to England when his conciliatory position toward the new colony of Maryland displeased them. Apparently willingly and unsuspectingly, Harvey accepted an invitation onto a ship only to find himself "suddenly carried away."[62] If colonists' visits to ships had not occurred so regularly, Harvey may not have found himself trapped so easily. This kind of easy access to ships was long-standing. On April 19, 1626, concerned about rumors that foreign enemies were headed to Virginia, London officials instructed Virginia Governor George Yardley to prohibit colonists from boarding arriving ships until they received a warrant to do so.[63] The prohibition was necessary only because colonists commonly did board ships, foreign as well as English.

In 1661 the York County Court recorded a shipboard interaction that illustrates the role of ships as gathering places and communication centers. Virginians Thomas Bushrod (the merchant, now a Quaker, who in the 1640s had entrusted Barnaby Brian with liquor and traded pork to Manhattan for Eastern Shore innholder Anthony Hodgkins, New England mariner Philip White, and Rhode Island seaman George Roome) and Justinian Aylmer (an Anglican minister) got into an argument over religion and church attendance aboard a ship riding in the York River. Bushrod verbally abused Aylmer; Aylmer sued him. The court records explain that Aylmer had gone on board to buy a servant, but do not mention why Bushrod, county court justice Captain Augustine Warner, and several other witnesses were on the vessel because the justices would have needed no explanation of the gathering of numerous colonists, including at least one member of their own court, on the ship.[64]

Tens of Virginians, from seamen to gentlemen, were aboard Richard Ingle's ship the *Reformation* in Accomack county to witness "a great dispute" between Ingle and the brothers Francis and Argoll Yardley (sons of former Governor Sir George Yardley) in the summer of 1643. The argument started when "young" Francis, supporting Charles I, and Ingle, supporting Parliament, began to discuss the English Civil War. Their discussion turned into an argument and the argument deteriorated into name-calling. As tensions rose, Ingle rushed into the cabin of the ship where a group of Virginians was talking, grabbed a poleax and a sword, and stormed back on deck. Argoll Yardley, a justice of the peace, accused Ingle of intending to use the weapons against Francis, and arrested Ingle "in his Majesties name." Ingle, retorting that if Yardley had arrested him in the name of the King and Parliament, he would have yielded, instead drew his sword and ran it at Argoll Yardley's chest, "as if hee would have peirced his body but touched him not," whereupon Yardley prudently fled to shore.[65] Then Ingle, "in a dominereing way florished his sworde and Comaunded all the Virginians saying gett you all out of my shipp." But before they could all disembark, he weighed anchor and sailed to Maryland with eighteen or twenty men "that did belong unto Accomack" still on board.[66] The day after they arrived in Maryland, in the words of one Virginian, many "Planters and others in Maryland" came aboard the ship, along with the Virginians and the crew, and Ingle (in the presence of the Virginians) bragged to the Marylanders of his actions in Accomack.[67] In this case the use of ships as congregation points led to Ingle's hauling away twenty Virginia planters (which included only those unable to get off the ship before it weighed anchor) up the Chesapeake, where they encountered the "planters and others" of Maryland. Moreover, the argument between Ingle and Yardley reveals a contest over authority—between its master and the local justice—aboard the mobile ship.

This case appears in the records because of the politically explosive argument, occurring in the midst of the English Civil War, over the relative authority of Charles I and Parliament and because of Ingle's dramatic response, but it illustrates the numbers of "planters and others" from Virginia and Maryland found on board many ships, conversing about commercial transactions and about events in England and other colonies, though usually with less contentious results. Because important news spread most easily between places most closely linked by trade, commercial routes linking Virginia economically to England, and Eastern Shore and Southside counties to Barbados, New Netherland, and New England, also facilitated the development of social ties and paths of information exchange along the same routes.

Similar interactions involving Virginia merchants and mariners took place when they traveled to other colonies. On June 3, 1632, the Massachusetts Bay Court of Assistants fined Mr. James Parker and Mr. Samuel Dudley forty shillings each for drunkenness committed aboard a Virginia ship.[68] Sometimes opportunities for their merchants to socialize in other colonies caused local and colonial courts concern. On October 21, 1657, the New Haven Colony Court fined William East £50 for drunkenness and warned him to stay sober or risk whipping. East's peripatetic drunkenness led to problems not only at home, but also when he traveled to other colonies. Witness Richard Baldwin said that he had heard from the Dutch, by way of a trustworthy man, that East's "cariage ther was exceeding gross, that Vergenia men and sea-men would scoff at him and reproach religion for his sake, saying, This is one of yor church members, but some answered, No, but he is not, for he is cast out [at home] for such courses."[69]

Passengers for one destination often accompanied a ship to other places while it traded and collected lading.[70] The need for passengers to travel the ships' routes on the way to their destinations facilitated the formation of social ties throughout the century. In the fall of 1622, the English ship *Discovery*, which had been exploring the coast between Virginia and Cape Cod, came into Plymouth Colony to trade.[71] John Pory, who had been secretary of Virginia, was on board the ship as a passenger to England. While the ship was in Plymouth to trade, he visited with colonists there. After his departure, he wrote to Governor William Bradford and to Mr. William Brewster, praising their libraries and their learning, and telling them how much he had appreciated their hospitality in having him stay with them while the ship was in port. He thanked them for loaning him religious books while he was there and told them how much he had enjoyed their learned conversation about the books and religion.[72] Pory's need to follow the ship's coastal trade route to get from Virginia to England resulted in the creation of new and long-distance friendships and religious ties.

Colonists sometimes learned through mariners information about events in Europe, from political developments such as those surrounding the English Civil War to personal news such as the death of a family member, from other colonies via intercolonial shipping, because communication was faster that way than from England directly.[73] Indeed, this was likely more often the case for Virginia colonists than for most others. Virginia's location (along with Jamaica and the Hudson Bay) in what Ian K. Steele has called "farthest America" in terms of traveling time from London may have served to increase the significance residents gave to the intercolonial ships that might provide the quickest source of news from other colonies and from Europe.[74] In 1632, for example, Henry Fleet's crew carried letters from Virginians "to their friends in London, and elsewhere in England" as he sailed from the Chesapeake to New England. From New England, the Virginians' letters "were safely conveyed" to London, indicating the significance of intercolonial trade in facilitating transatlantic as well as intercolonial interactions.[75] On January 1, 1662, a New Englander wrote that a mariner, Mr. Wats, who had previously lived in Plymouth, had recently come from Virginia with rumors of "a general discontent among the seamen against the King" in England. Wats had this from a ship captain Higginson, who had recently come from London to Virginia, and also by speaking "with many other seamen, as well Bristol men as Londoners, who were formerly for the K: but are now discontent[ed] with him, & wish for another Cromwell."[76] While providing information about events in England seamen naturally colored their reporting of those events with their own political and economic opinions, likely to be radical.[77] Usually, they provided the first and sometimes only source of information about events elsewhere, information doubtless distorted through retelling but nevertheless eagerly seized upon by colonists so far from their mother countries.[78] A French visitor noted the connection between shipping and access to news when he reported in 1687 that "Virginia loads regularly a hundred & fifty [ships] each year, & through this means can send to & receive news from the whole universe."[79]

Local courts' jurisdiction over the affairs of intercolonial merchants and mariners highlighted the position of such individuals as people who lived and worked in an Atlantic world as much as in any one locale. The use of colony and county courts by mobile merchants and mariners validated those courts as Atlantic (not just local) authorities and expanded the world view of county court members, as well as that of anyone else present at court during an intercolonial case. Sending letters of attorney was the most obvious legal activity requiring intercolonial recognition.

The most common reason for letters of attorney and other intercolonial use of courts was for collection of debts incurred through trade. In September 1655 Thomas Young acted as attorney for Boston merchant William Brenton and convinced the Northampton, Virginia, court that Eastern Shore merchant Edmund Scarborough owed Brenton twenty-four thousand pounds of tobacco. The court ordered Scarborough to ship the tobacco to Boston at the first opportunity of wind and weather in his ship the *Mary*.[80] The same year, Scarborough petitioned the Northampton county court to collect debts owed him by his Massachusetts trading partner Edward Gibbons. Basing its decision partly on the testimony of mariners who had witnessed distant transactions, the court ruled that a judgment against Gibbons's estate would stand.[81] The New Englander had to abide by the decision of a Virginia local court, in part because, as a trader, he owned dispersed property available for seizure by courts outside that of his primary residence.

Other routine transactions involving intercolonial merchants and mariners also sometimes required non-Virginians to use Virginia local courts. For example, New Englanders used Virginia courts to make New England real estate transactions and vice versa. Intercolonial movement of trading ships meant that witnesses could travel and testify to the sales. In 1680 Boston mariner John Clarke and Boston merchant Jarvis Ballard were both in Virginia when Clark sold his two-and-a-half-story house on Boston's Back Street to Ballard for £395 8s. Two of the Virginia witnesses, Eastern Shore merchant William Kendall and Daniell Neech, later traveled to Massachusetts and testified that the sale had occurred.[82] In December 1643, when William Smythson and Eastern Shore mariner Nicholas Waddelowe were in New England, Smythson sold land he owned on the Eastern Shore to Waddelowe. The two of them had enough intercolonial experience to choose between opportunities provided by multiple colonial locations and enough mobility to require the involvement of courts in two locations. Robert Gibson, who had witnessed the transaction in New England, indicated his similar mobility when he testified to the sale in the Northampton county court a year later.[83] The Northampton court recognized the legality of the land sale that took place in another part of the English American world. The intercolonial nature of their world made these kinds of transactions among mariners likely and also allowed information to spread to the local officials who needed to approve them.[84]

Court members were often also traders themselves and realized the ability of people and information to travel and the importance of information spread by word of mouth. In 1655 in the New Haven Colony Court, Isaac Allerton,

Ensign Bryan, and a Mr. Augar sued James Roggers of Milford because "by reason of bad biskit and flower they have had from James Roggers at Milford, they have suffered much damage." As a result, flour from Milford lay "under reproach at Virgenia and Berbadoes," so that while men from elsewhere found "a ready markit for their goods, that from [Milford] lyes by and will not sell."[85] The quality of Roggers's flour had affected not only his own reputation but that of his fellow townsmen as well.

Virginia courts heard cases involving Dutch seamen, and New Netherland courts heard cases involving English seamen, suggesting that the legitimizing effects of courts contributed to the creation of an Atlantic world that was of necessity international, not fractured into national bailiwicks. The economic creation of an Atlantic world required legal courts that could deal with the complexities, unpredictability, and dispersed nature of transatlantic and intercolonial business. Before the establishment of colonial vice-admiralty courts at the end of the seventeenth century, traders' needs for legal action throughout their voyages required the involvement of local colonial and county courts (which sometimes, but not always, indicated when they were following admiralty rather than common law) in the maritime Atlantic world. English admiralty law had developed in response to the specific needs of traders. Beginning in the fourteenth century, it followed continental European maritime law, which grew out of Roman civil law with adaptations developed by continental European merchants. English admiralty law, then, was separate from English civil law. It provided for quick trials that wouldn't interfere with voyages, and a procedure that would be recognized by foreign as well as English mariners.[86] In the early 1620s, Dutch crewmembers of the *Everett*, after having "lost" their original ship and pinnace in the Caribbean, appealed to the Virginia General Court for release from any obligation to stay with their master. Several of the crew members had deserted the ship and hired themselves out on arrival in the James River. They complained that their master refused to provide sufficient food and that the ship was unsound ("eaten with worms," lacking rigging, and having only one anchor). Alwin Danyell, one of those who "tooke away his chest without the M[aste]rs [knowledge] or consent," said he would "rather loose his wages, then go with the M[aste]r."[87] These Dutch seamen helped push the Virginia court into international maritime law, because while the outcome is unknown, the court applied itself to the case. New Amsterdam courts reciprocated, and in fact were particularly likely to act on seamen's behalf if the ships in question were foreign. In 1655 the seamen of Eastern Shore merchant Edmund Scarborough's *Mary of Galeanock* abandoned the ship in Manhattan and complained to the court that Scarborough had hired them for ten or eleven months but so far they had served fourteen and were yet to be paid. Scarborough told the court that he had hired them for sixteen to twenty months. The New Amsterdam court ordered the seamen to complete the voyage and ordered Scarborough to pay them half their wages on the spot and half at the voyages completion. Despite the order, some of the crew succeeded in deserting to the Dutch colony.[88] New Amsterdam officials in 1658 arrested the English master of a ship on its way from Virginia to New England because two of his crew members complained he owed them back pay. The court refused to allow him to continue to New England until he put up security, even though he asserted that the seamen were deserters and that he was on official business for Virginia Governor Samuel Mathews.[89]

Just as international trade depended on the development of widely accepted international maritime law, intercolonial and transatlantic trade depended on its participants' acceptance of individual local courts' decisions throughout the Atlantic world. One case, a midcentury disagreement between London merchants and a Salem, Massachusetts, shipowner and master, involved a Boston ship and events in the Caribbean, the Chesapeake, New England, and England that came to a head in Lower Norfolk County, Virginia. Traders' reliance on local colonial courts and traders' respect for and obedience to those courts reinforced the ties linking the far-flung English and Dutch colonial world. In September 1654 in London, the English merchants William Selby and Joseph Huffey rented the ketch *Hopewell* of Boston for an American voyage. Salem, Massachusetts, merchant William Chichester (who carried on regular trade with Virginia), part owner and master of the *Hopewell*, commanded the voyage. He agreed to take Huffey and Selby and their goods on his Boston ship from England to Ireland, from there to Virginia or Maryland, and then back to England or Holland. They followed the most common route from the British Isles to the American mainland colonies, stopping in the Caribbean to refurbish supplies and perhaps to trade. While in Antigua, shipmaster Chichester borrowed from merchants Huffey and Selby to pay for provisions and ship repairs. The Antigua court recorded Chichester's promise to repay Huffey and Selby in Virginia tobacco within thirty days of arriving in the Chesapeake.[90] Selby decided to stay in Antigua and in the Antigua court appointed his partner Joseph Huffey his attorney to trade in the Chesapeake, receive the debt due from Chichester, and send the ketch on to England or Holland.[91]

Three months later the ship lay in Virginia, where Huffey sued Chichester in the Lower Norfolk county court for repayment of the ship repair costs Chichester had borrowed in Antigua. Huffey presented the Antigua bills as evidence to the Lower Norfolk court, depending on and fostering the expectation that both courts worked as part of a larger legal apparatus that shared evidence as well as the common purpose of facilitating trade.[92] In a second case, shipmaster Chichester sued merchant Huffey for past due rent from a voyage (from Boston to Barbados to Virginia to Holland or England to Boston) the previous year.[93]

The Lower Norfolk court called several of the *Hopewell's* crew members to testify. Described only by occupation—mate, carpenter, boatswain, and three seamen—rather than by place of origin, presumably many of these Boston-based ship's crew members hailed from New England. They described events in Antigua and in England, making it clear that ordinary seamen, in addition to ship captains and masters, were privy to many of the events and communications that masters and captains encountered at each stop. The mariners dealt with courts in Dartmouth (England), Antigua, and Lower Norfolk. Their experiences and testimony in courts throughout the English Atlantic world and their cooperation with the Lower Norfolk court suggests that they accepted this local Virginia court (made up of men deeply involved in either intercolonial or transatlantic trade) as part of their world and competent to deal with complex intercolonial and transatlantic issues.[94]

Although the outcome of the case remains unknown, the significance of the case lies in its unexceptional nature. None of the men involved was a Virginian, but all needed their problem solved there and saw Virginia courts as legitimate adjudicators. When courts ruled in cases such as this one, as they routinely did, they heightened the perception that Virginia was part of an Atlantic and intercolonial world that recognized the legitimacy of colonial jurisdiction over trade. Such cases also tied mariners more closely to multiple colonies, and connected court members and any other colonists present to mariners (who stayed in Virginia for the duration of the case) and to their intercolonial maritime world.[95] This respect for the decisions of local colonial courts, necessary before the establishment of vice-admiralty courts in the colonies, followed the maritime practice that in England had encouraged the use of continental (Roman) civil law rather than common law to expedite international trade cases by allowing for the development of consistent trade law applicable throughout Europe and its colonies.

Mariners understood that individual colonial courts enjoyed respect throughout the colonial world and they used those courts to maintain their reputations intact; they knew that damaging rumors could spread along trade routes as easily as goods, people, and other kinds of information. One night in 1664 Timothy Blades and a Mr. Morgan argued on board a sloop in the Potomac River. The argument turned violent, and during the struggle both fell overboard. Others aboard the ship had trouble seeing the men in the dark water and feared both would drown, but Timothy Blades sported a white cap that enabled them to spot him and pull him out safely. Authorities accused Blades of murder, but Governor William Berkeley, noting that Morgan had started the argument, instructed the Westmoreland County Court to acquit Blades. The court obliged the governor, and Blades, to protect himself against the damage long-distance gossip could do him, took a copy of the acquittal to Boston and had it copied into the record book there the following year.[96] Blades's concern that news of the accusation in the Chesapeake would harm his reputation in New England reflects his knowledge that such information readily traveled from the Potomac River to Massachusetts Bay and that in a world of such personalized commerce, one's reputation was crucial.

At times the mobility of mariners and their ability to use courts through-out the English world caused problems for local justices who had to sort out conflicting documents. When he died in 1647 or 1648, New Haven resident Nathaniel Draper bequeathed seaman Philip Galpin £9 in back wages, by a will recorded in New Haven. Mr. Leach, one of the will's overseers, authorized the executor to pay Galpin. The executor refused because some Virginians had told him that Draper had made another will in Virginia that left the wages to a Mr. Sellicke.[97] Because of the frequency of intercolonial travel, the overseer Leach could confirm the existence of the second will by the following year. He reported to the New Haven court that he had found the Virginia will and, following it, he had paid the due wages to Sellicke instead of to Galpin.[98] Once more, the intercolonial ties created by mariners' travels required and enabled court justices to consider events and evidence far beyond their own jurisdictions, and to recognize their own courts as components of a linked Atlantic world.

Even in cases where mariners themselves did not use the courts, their mobility sometimes raised legal issues that colonists could resolve only by using intercolonial networks. In 1661 in New Haven Colony, Mary Andrews requested a divorce from her husband, mariner William Andrews, Jr., on the grounds that he had absented himself from Mary and from New Haven for eight or nine years and had married another woman. Evidence in the case came from all over the Atlantic world. Witness Thomas Kimberly, Sr., told the court that his son had written him from Virginia that he had heard in Bristol that Andrews was married in Ireland and his other wife was alive in New England. Richard Miles, Jr., told the court that, "being in Barbados in Sep-temb" 1660, he had seen William Andrews, who belonged to a small vessel called the *Charles*. The master of the *Charles* told Miles that Andrews was married to a Cornish woman living in Ireland. The court accordingly granted Mary Andrews a divorce.[99] Not only did William Andrews's position as a mariner provide him with the mobility needed to create such a predicament, but the similar mobility of other mariners and merchants all but ensured that information about his actions would eventually reach New Haven and his first wife.[100] The seventeenth-century Atlantic rim was truly "a world on the move."[101] People and information circulated. Migrants usually, but not always, crossed the Atlantic, moving from east to west. Those who moved by choice did so largely because they thought that they stood to make money or at least gain their independence by participating in an economy created to send goods from west to east to Europe. As the English colonies matured, many of their residents discovered that opportunities, sometimes better opportunities, lay in various exchanges between colonies. As transatlantic, international, and inter-colonial trade routes evolved, they carried more people, not just west but north and south and east too, and along with them, circulated news and cultural practice and ideas that knit the very different parts of that world together.

Intercolonial maritime trade, following particular regional patterns, linked Virginians to colonies in the Caribbean and on the mainland. Because of their dispersed settlement patterns, Virginians lived in a world in which shipping and sailors were familiar to every European colonist and servant and every African slave. The willingness of Atlantic mariners to respond to dispersed markets with dispersed trading (and the fact that seventeenth-century Chesapeake products did not require warehousing) allowed the Chesapeake to continue without urban centers through the century. The intercolonial experiences of mariners like De Vries and his crew members, and all the motley panoply that preceded and followed them thus broadened the world of all Virginians, offering Chesapeake society a substitute for some elements of the urban culture that geography denied them, most notably allowing Chesapeake residents to hear news of distant Atlantic world locales directly from mariners who had witnessed events (or learned of them from word-of-mouth channels without officials' filters). The travel of all those merchants and mariners involved in trade thus allowed Virginians and other Atlantic world residents opportunities for physical mobility and provided them with information and contacts that placed them firmly in a maritime transatlantic and intercolonial world.

Virginia's dispersed settlement shaped the particular nature of its inhabitants' interactions with the mariners whose movements spun the Atlantic world web. Trade fostered increasingly close economic and personal ties between merchants and those with positions of local political influence, permitting the formation of an increasingly well connected Atlantic network of traders and local colonial officials who shared an interest in ensuring that Atlantic networks perform well their original function of moving goods. One way they did this was through the evolving colonial court systems that adapted to a tradition of international coordination in the interest of commerce through their performance of admiralty law. Although court justices might share the interests of shipmasters rather than seamen, common seamen, with some success, used the courts to protect their own interests as well. From the perspective of local courts, in Virginia and other colonies, guaranteeing seamen's wages was an important part of maintaining a functioning Atlantic world.

Virginia's legal and social and political ties to the Atlantic world were not unique, and suggest that we cannot understand colonial English America in relation to the Atlantic world without paying close attention to the ties that connected individual places like Virginia to the rest of that world. Virginia's Atlantic trade and the social networks it facilitated acquired meaning well beyond trade and merchant family networks. As the following chapters show, it also shaped migration paths for Africans and for Europeans of all socioeconomic levels, influenced the religious map of Virginia, and even prompted officials' attempts to harden colonial boundaries.

Chapter 4

Intercolonial Migration

In 1654 Thomas Baldreage of Barbados wrote a letter to his cousin (also named Thomas Baldreage) in Virginia. The Barbadian asked his Chesapeake relative for help in acquiring "any plantacon of 4 or 5 hundred Acres" in Virginia. Additionally, he requested "a true L[ett]re of what condicon ye country stands . . . for here are many good people that are minded to come for Virginia."[1] During the half-century following Baldreage's request, thousands of people indeed moved from Barbados to Virginia, part of a much larger pattern of remigration throughout the Atlantic world. This included not only the "good people" to whom Thomas Baldreage referred (Europeans with sufficient means to enable them to be "minded" to go), but also many with less choice, ranging from free laborers through indentured servants to black and Indian slaves.[2] Their movements followed routes established by trade, but added human ties to those economic ones, making the Atlantic world a place understood by its inhabitants to be extensive and varied and sometimes frighteningly far-flung, but connected. Some migrants, particularly merchants and occasionally ministers and colonial officials, moved for the very purpose of forming a new link in Atlantic networks.

The numbers of colonists migrating to Virginia from other colonies never approached those coming directly from England. Virginians in the seventeenth century owed their basic social, cultural, and legal inheritance to England. Connections to England persisted through the colonial period. Continual migration in the seventeenth century, remigration to England, and transatlantic travel reinforced Virginia's English origins.[3] Measuring the relative numbers of intercolonial and transatlantic immigrants with any precision is impossible because, while estimates exist for transatlantic migration, evidence for intercolonial movement is almost entirely anecdotal.[4] The one year—1679—for which we have a count of migrants to Virginia from another colony (Barbados), the island recorded sixty-two emigrants to Virginia. The same year, Virginia saw an increase of under five hundred taxables and 748 headright grants, numbers that include enslaved Africans as well as the European migrants recorded in the Barbados emigrant lists.[5] There are many problems in comparing these numbers.[6] But they suggest that intercolonial migrants from Barbados (and other colonies that never recorded their emigrants) constituted a meaningful proportion of new immigrants. Moreover, intercolonial immigrants were reportedly more likely to survive their first few years in Virginia, having experienced exposure to American diseases in their previous locale. This is not to say that intercolonial migration challenged the significance of transatlantic migration. After all, the vast majority of intercolonial migrants had made the transatlantic voyage as well as a subsequent intercolonial one and thus brought European perspectives that reinforced those of the majority of Virginia colonists who arrived directly from England. However, intercolonial migrants, regardless of the proportion of the population they constituted, brought with them knowledge of another part of the Atlantic world in addition to their probable English place of birth. They made unique contributions to Virginia's economic, legal, diplomatic, and social development. Migrants' previous experiences, whether in England, Africa, or other colonies, affected their responses to new locales and facilitated the transfer of ideas and social models. Intercolonial migrants' knowledge proved especially important to aspects of colonial life that lacked clear English precedent. To understand seventeenth-century colonies fully, then, we need to develop an awareness of their intercolonial as well as their transatlantic context. Intercolonial ties linking England's colonies strengthened Virginians' realization that they participated in a growing English Atlantic empire, within which they shared interests and competed with Barbados and Massachusetts. But the colonial Atlantic context was also international. Spanish colonies provided precedents when England could not, and Virginians' world included New Netherlanders and Dutch traders.

Intercolonial migrations began early and continued throughout the century.[7] They represented one expression of great early modern English population mobility. In response to very high unemployment and economic dislocation, English people moved from the countryside to towns, and from all parts of England to London, boosting the population of that city from 200,000 to 490,000 over the course of the century. Migration across the Atlantic often represented migrants' second or third long-distance moves. Once in America they continued to move, from one county to another within particular colonies, between colonies, or back to Europe.[8]

For the same reasons that Virginia could provide provisions to other colonies, it attracted those whose ventures had failed or proved more difficult than participants wished. As an already established colony with available food sources, Virginia offered less serious risks to potential settlers than did new colonial projects. Once established, Virginia provided food and refuge for mainland and Caribbean colonizers whose plans faltered or failed. The Tortuga colonists and the English invaders of Delaware Bay, whom De Vries took to Virginia during the 1630s, provide two such examples. In the 1620s, Lord Baltimore, after finding Newfoundland too cold, went from there to Virginia, where he looked to establish a plantation south of the James River before eventually receiving a patent for Maryland.[9]

Several observable intercolonial migration patterns involved Virginia. English colonists of all socioeconomic levels and African slaves moved from Barbados to Virginia in large numbers during the second half of the seventeenth century, part of an even larger emigration from Barbados to other American colonies in the Caribbean and on the North American mainland. This connection proved particularly important for Virginia, because the influx of slaveholders and slaves affected the nature of slavery as it expanded in Virginia. English Puritans, some from New England, settled on the Eastern Shores of Virginia and Maryland beginning in the 1640s. Some Virginia Puritans from the Eastern Shore and counties south of the James River moved to Maryland at midcentury. Both of these migrations shaped the religious map of the Chesapeake. Dutch and Huguenot colonists from New Netherland and from Europe moved to the Chesapeake, sometimes bringing servants and African slaves. As English colonists pushed farther inland over the course of the century, some Virginia Indians moved south to land that became parts of North and South Carolina.[10]

These migrations all followed routes well established by trade. That migrants followed trade patterns reflected more than shipping routes. Planters and traders who moved to places actively trading with their former colony had a head start procuring credit and trading partners, and intercolonial traders sometimes encouraged colonists to travel with them.[11] As a result, the distribution of intercolonial migrants in Virginia varied from region to region, a function of intercolonial trade connections. Thus, residents of the Eastern Shore and Southside counties, fully enmeshed in intercolonial trade, maintained close social and familial ties with colonists elsewhere. At least 9 percent of seventeenth-century Eastern Shore landowners had kin in other colonies, a number representing only those connections preserved in surviving records. At least 12 percent of adult resident landowners represented nonresidents in local court cases, another indication of ties.[12] Barbadians moved in greatest numbers to Lower Norfolk and other counties south of the James River; Dutch, Huguenot, and English colonists from the Netherlands and New Netherland settled in Lower Norfolk and on the Eastern Shore, where their presence influenced the regions' social development, which differed from the rest of Virginia's; and New Englanders moved disproportionately to the Eastern

Shore. Although it is possible to identify such patterns to intercolonial trade, because transatlantic and intercolonial trade networks overlapped and intertwined, the intersections of intercolonial migration and trade were often equally complex.

The routes established by the intercolonial exchange of goods provided all colonists with opportunities to move between colonies, both temporarily and as permanent migrants. Trade routes also limited intercolonial travel. People could much more easily go where the ships customarily went to trade. Ships did not travel between colonies just to transport passengers, except in the case of servants or slaves or initial settlement projects. Consequently, migration patterns mirrored those of trade and created social networks along the same routes. Because the early modern business world lacked limited liability, and because slow communications hindered the spread of market information, trusting one's partners was crucial. Establishing trade networks of family members, friends, or sometimes coreligionists facilitated the trust needed for long-distance trade.[13] Merchants trading with nonfamily members therefore sought to strengthen their relationships with one another by encouraging their children to marry or by acknowledging strong relationships with godparentage. These social networks strengthened over time and provided the trust and close relations needed to create even more trade.[14] Thus, once established, economic and social links reinforced one another.

Access to intercolonial trade facilitated migrants' integration into new locales. In July 1642 Londoner William Webb wrote letters of introduction for Mr. Thomas Cobbs, who was moving to the Chesapeake. Webb asked readers to assist Cobbs in stocking his plantation. To make it clear that Cobbs's presence would benefit the region, Webb assured readers that Cobbs would arrive "well provided with such [things] as are usefull in those parts," that he would have the support of wealthy friends and kinfolk in England, and that he owned a plantation in Barbados and stock with his uncle Captain Pellham in St. Christopher. If he liked the country and found good friends among the settlers there, he intended to employ all those resources in establishing his new Chesapeake plantation.[15] In his letters, Webb declared that Cobbs would prove valuable not only for his material resources, but also as a source of information about "the troubles which here hang over" London, and how the Londoners "stand in great Feare of Tumults and Cumbustiones" of the Civil War.

The Accomack County, Virginia, court recorded the letters the following winter, so Cobbs likely stopped there. The network of names and connections laid out in Webb's letters shows how among elites personal connections translated into economic contacts that facilitated intercolonial migration and made individual moves economically viable. Information about Cobbs's English and

Caribbean friends and relatives, his plantation in Barbados, and his uncle in St. Christopher assured his new neighbors that he would have goods to establish himself and a market for his (and possibly his new neighbors') produce. Also, these connections increased his chances of succeeding, so that his neighbors could more safely lend him what he needed—and possibly gain access to valuable new intercolonial contacts by doing so.

The movement of people from Barbados to Virginia that Thomas Baldreage described in the opening vignette of this chapter, like the migration of Barbadians to all other English colonies, resulted largely from land shortages on the island.[16] After the island's establishment as an English colony in 1627, the economy roughly resembled that of the Chesapeake, with mixed free, indentured, and enslaved labor producing tobacco, food for the island's population, and cotton. In the 1640s some English planters (with the help of Dutch merchants and planters from Brazil and probably Brazilian slaves) began producing sugar, much more profitable than the island's mediocre tobacco. Very quickly those Barbadian planters with enough capital switched to sugar production and bought out many smaller landowners. Employment and land-owning opportunities for freed indentured servants declined, and many left for other colonies. Planters in search of greater opportunities or cooler climates left as well, sometimes taking servants and slaves with them.[17] In 1652 Colonel Thomas Modyford wrote that Barbados "cannot last in an height of trade three years longer" and he hoped that "this great people" could find maintenance and employment somewhere.[18] A decade later, Barbadian Governor Francis Lord Willoughby echoed Modyford, writing that, "As Barbadoes decays fast, the people must be placed somewhere."[19] In 1675 Barbados Governor Jonathan Atkins wrote that "People frequently go to the other plantations in America, some for change, others with persuasion of mending their fortunes." He expected many would find the Anglo-Indian wars then under way in the Chesapeake and New England too great a deterrent and return to Barbados. However, he recognized that freed servants found Virginia, New York, and Jamaica, "where they can hope for land," far preferable to Barbados, "where there is none."[20] Some Caribbean colonists fled international rivalries playing out in the Caribbean. In June 1666 after the French overtook St. Christopher, "they transport[ed some of the English] to New England, to Virginia, and about 1,500 hither (to Nevis)."[21] The following year Sir Peter Colleton wrote that some Caribbean planters feared the growing French presence in the Caribbean and moved to the North American mainland because they believed it safer.[22]

The migration involved slaveholders, nonslaveholding whites (including freed servants), indentured servants and slaves traveling with their masters, and slaves brought by merchants and traders. In December 1647 in England, bricklayer and plasterer William Eale signed a four-year indenture as the servant of Mr. John Lownes, a Barbadian merchant trading with Lower Norfolk.[23] Eale arrived in Barbados on March 3, 1648, and served there until he moved with Lownes from Barbados to Lower Norfolk sometime before the end of 1651. Lownes brought six people into the colony: his wife, Eale, George Gosden, Mary a Negro, Henery Lambert, and maidservant Mary Gouldsmith.[24] In Lower Norfolk, a focus of livestock and meat production, Lownes used his Barbadian connection to carry on a trade with the island and befriended other Virginians in the county who traded to the Caribbean.[25]

The bricklayer William Eale served Lownes in Virginia for one week beyond March 3, 1652, the date that should have ended his four-year indenture. Lownes, in an attempt to avoid releasing Eale, took him to Maryland. In December 1652 Eale petitioned the Maryland Governor and Council for his freedom. He produced the original written indenture and further claimed that while still in Barbados, Lownes had promised to give Eale three months time in return for "Comminge wth him from the Barbadoes to Virginia."[26] The ongoing migration from Barbados to Virginia replicated Lownes's and Eale's travel many times over. As the wealthy like Lownes moved, they took laborers such as Eale, maidservant Mary Gouldsmith, and "Mary a Negro" with them. Servants, slaves, and free migrants brought with them their experiences in the island, for many the first place of contact with English America. Wealthier migrants maintained strong connections to the island long after settling in the Chesapeake. They stayed in contact with family members and friends by visiting, exchanging property, and intermarrying. They maintained commercial relationships with Barbadian merchants and returned to the island to do business and to visit. Most of the indentured and enslaved left no records of their own, but their tracks appear in the family, legal, and commercial records of the elite. They not only assured elite acquisition of quantities of land through headrights, but also assured the means to profit from it.

Some Caribbean colonists may have moved to Virginia in order to grow higher quality tobacco and avoid competing with sugar planters for increasingly expensive land. In the spring of 1664, the Nevis Council and Assembly wrote of hardship for "Many of the meaner sort . . . , wholly employed in the manufacture of tobacco." Unable to compete with better Chesapeake tobacco, they could not sell their tobacco to English traders, were prohibited from selling to the Dutch, "and not being able to produce sugar, they are forced daily to desert the island."[27] Emigrants from the Caribbean who had spent years growing tobacco perhaps moved to the Chesapeake in the hopes of continuing to produce it. They contributed to Virginia's northern expansion into regions with good tobacco land in the Northern Neck.

However, most Barbadian immigrants settled disproportionately in the counties south of the James River that produced naval stores, live cattle and hogs, and beef and pork for export. Economic contacts sometimes provided Barbadians with personal connections in Virginia that eased their move from the island to the mainland. Once in Virginia, some former Barbadians used their knowledge of the island and their contacts with merchants or planters there to produce exports specifically for the Caribbean. Like many later Barbadian settlers to Carolina, those to southern Virginia knew of particular trade opportunities between the mainland and the Caribbean and could, in the Chesapeake, find economic opportunity for themselves by producing a commodity of value to Barbadians.

Just as Chesapeake-Caribbean trade intertwined with other transatlantic and intercolonial trade, many Barbadian families who moved to Virginia maintained their contacts with the Caribbean and cultivated ties with other colonies and Europe. The far-flung activities of Virginians in Lower Norfolk reveal the permeability of colonial boundaries in the seventeenth century and show how little those boundaries actually separated the Caribbean and mainland colonies. Some prominent Barbadians in Virginia—for example, the Emperor family—interacted with almost all elite families of Lower Norfolk and Princess Anne, the Virginia counties in which they resided. The Emperors, merchants in Barbados and Virginia, lived in the eastern half of Lower Norfolk County in Virginia, which, after the division of Lower Norfolk in 1691, became Princess Anne County.[28] Francis Emperor came to Lower Norfolk County, Virginia around 1650 and settled on the Eastern Branch of the Elizabeth River in Puritan Lynnhaven parish. Despite his youth (about twenty-two at his arrival), he quickly established himself as a prominent member of the community, holding many of the highest local government positions during the 1650s, including county court justice, surveyor, high sheriff, and collector.[29] Throughout the decade he received individual land grants totaling at least 750 acres and shared a 1,000-acre grant with two other men.[30]

"Captain" Francis Emperor was a merchant and possibly a ship captain. He had three siblings in Barbados. His brother John Emperor, a merchant, also "Captain," lived in Bridgetown, Barbados. His two sisters, Elizabeth Emperor Horbin and Sarah Emperor Oistin Leigh, both married members of elite planter families in Barbados.[31] Francis Emperor used his own ship, the *Francis and Mary*, to trade with his brother John.[32] With a merchant brother in Bridgetown, Francis may have settled in Lower Norfolk specifically to establish this trade. Although colonists throughout Virginia desired Barbadian rum, sugar, and slaves, those in Lower Norfolk and its neighboring counties produced the meat, livestock, casks and staves, and naval stores that Barbadians needed from the Chesapeake. As a result, Barbadians found good reason to trade with (and therefore to migrate to) this region of the Chesapeake.

After moving to Virginia, Francis traveled to Barbados to trade and to visit his brother and sisters.[33] He traded with, traveled to, and corresponded with other colonies. In November 1655 he wrote to Barbadian Captain Thomas Willoughby for help obtaining a Puritan minister for Lynnhaven parish.[34] The following July found Emperor in Boston, perhaps attempting to recruit a minister. While there, he translated Dutch documents from New Amsterdam for the Massachusetts Court. Back in Virginia that November, Emperor wrote to Puritan minister Mr. Moore in New England, planning for Moore's upcoming voyage to Virginia, suggesting Moore may have agreed to serve the Puritans in Lower Norfolk County. Emperor made multiple voyages to New Netherland.[35] He conducted widespread trade in Virginia; when he died in 1661 his estate inventory included active accounts with twenty other Virginians, many in Lower Norfolk, but some in other counties and in Jamestown.[36] His own ties to Barbados, New Netherland, and Massachusetts thus provided Virginians beyond Lower Norfolk with Barbadian goods and secondhand contacts to the Caribbean and to other mainland colonies. Traders such as Emperor and Willoughby were best able to actively recruit ministers to their clergy-poor colony, just as their travels helped them acquire workers in a labor-poor colony. Traders—those with the strongest links in the Atlantic world—may have exercised disproportionate influence in determining the kinds of ministers (and laborers) who came to their parts of Virginia.

Francis and his wife Mary Tully Emperor had four surviving children, Francis Tully Emperor, Tully Emperor, William Emperor, and Elizabeth Emperor Phillips. Francis Tully Emperor, born about 1655, maintained and strengthened his family's connections to Barbados. In 1679, at Christ Church Parish, Barbados, he married his cousin Sarah Oistin of Barbados, daughter of his father's sister Sarah Emperor Oistin Leigh, by then a widow owning 172 acres and fifty-two slaves.[37] This marriage perpetuated the close connection between Francis Tully's and Sarah's families in Barbados and Virginia and the economic benefits of keeping roots in the two colonies. Francis Tully, a merchant like his father, acquired extensive estates in Christ Church Parish, Barbados, through his marriage to Sarah Oistin and enlarged his inherited estate in Princess Anne County. He served as justice of Princess Anne from 1691 to 1693. The county clerk referred to him as a gentleman, indicating his wealth and high social status.

Francis Tully Emperor traveled often enough between Virginia and Barbados during the 1680s and 1690s to father at least six children, all of them born in Barbados, while making numerous documented appearances in Princess Anne County.[38] He spent enough time in Barbados to make friends beyond his extended family; as executors of his will he named "three trusted and well beloved friends," all "Gent of ye Island of ye barbados."[39] When in September 1691 Emperor bought a 650-acre plantation from a departing Princess Anne neighbor, the clerk described Emperor as "late of Barbadoes, now resident in the eastern branch of Eliz. river," suggesting that despite his Virginia birth, some of Francis Tully's stays in Barbados lasted long enough for others to regard him as a resident of the island.[40]

Sarah Oistin Emperor, Francis Tully's wife, also traveled between the two colonies, though perhaps not as frequently. Although in Barbados for the birth of all their children, she seems to have been in Virginia at the writing of her aunt Elizabeth Emperor Horbin's will in December 1693.[41] In a 1697 deed, Francis Tully Emperor postponed completion of a deed of sale because his "wife Sarah Emperor is now gone to the Island of Barbados and [therefore] cannot at present . . . relinquish her right of dower to the said land."[42] The language Emperor used, that Sarah "is now gone to the Island of Barbados," shows that she had resided in Virginia for a time. However, she wrote her will in Barbados on March 20, 1702, and died there on October 25, 1709. She left her estate to her daughter Elizabeth Emperor and to the children of her sister and brother-in-law Miles and Elizabeth Oistin James, all in Barbados.[43] Apparently her personal ties to Barbados remained stronger than those to Virginia.

Other family members helped the Emperors bridge the distance between the Caribbean and the Chesapeake. Elizabeth Emperor Horbin, the sister of the elder Francis Emperor and aunt of Francis Tully Emperor and Sarah Oistin Emperor, moved to Virginia after her husband died. In her 1693 will she called herself "late of [the] Island of Barbados, now in Princess Ann County, Virginia." Five Barbadians managed her estate, which remained in Barbados. She made her niece Sarah Oistin Emperor her executrix and gave her £100 and a slave woman named Jeane. She made additional bequests to family in Barbados and Virginia totaling £135, and made two of her Barbadian estate managers overseers of the will written in Virginia.[44] Though she had spent most of her life in Barbados, where her widowed sister Sarah remained, Elizabeth Emperor Horbin felt her ties to Virginia strong enough to move to the mainland and away from her living siblings in the island. Her bequests to her siblings' grandchildren in both colonies reinforced the ties binding the Virginia-Barbados family for subsequent generations. As with John Lownes and his servant William Eale (who moved from Barbados to Lower Norfolk within a year of Francis Emperor and appeared in court when Emperor was a justice), the

Emperors' movements too dictated the intercolonial migration of other individuals. One of their Chesapeake slaves, Oistin Judah, most certainly came from Oistin plantations in Barbados and likely the Emperors' other Chesapeake slaves also came from Barbados to Lower Norfolk, where they met or were reacquainted with other former Barbadians.[45]

Members of the Emperor family also moved from Barbados to South Carolina. Francis Tully Emperor had a Barbadian niece Elizabeth and a nephew John in Charleston in the 1690s, grandchildren of Francis Emperor senior's Barbadian brother John. The younger John was a captain and merchant, like his grandfather, father, and uncles.[46] Intercolonial networks involving merchant families involved multiple colonies because economic networks expanded to encompass newly colonized regions and changing local economies.

In a pattern familiar to students of migration, Francis Emperor's success encouraged others to follow, and Barbadian immigrants in Virginia formed or renewed friendships with one another. Barbadian merchant Thomas Walke and his family came from Barbados to Lynnhaven Parish in 1662. His story illustrates the relationships former Barbadians maintained with one another in Virginia and also shows how they helped other Virginians trade with Barbados merchants. The Walkes were friends and neighbors of the Emperors in Princess Anne and perhaps linked with the Emperors by marriage ties in Barbados.[47] Throughout the late seventeenth century, Emperors and Walkes lived in close proximity and witnessed one another's deeds and wills. Because of the two families' closeness in both colonies, Walke and Emperor slaves who moved to Virginia may too have been able to sustain relationships after moving. Walke received headright patents for almost 500 acres of land in Virginia, but also used his Barbadian contacts to buy land, as others had before him. In January 1691 he purchased 360 acres in Lynnhaven Parish from ship captain William Hillyard for six thousand pounds of pork. Hillyard, who traded regularly between Barbados and Princess Anne, had purchased the land from a Barbadian who had purchased it from a Barbadian.[48]

Born in Barbados, Thomas Walke left behind his sisters and brothers (including merchants Robert and Jonathan).[49] Thomas traded to Barbados, and the three brothers remained in contact with one another, as did their children. In Virginia, he produced commodities for the Barbadian market and shipped them in his own vessels.[50] Walke, like Emperor, continued to travel to Barbados after moving to Virginia.[51] He too achieved positions of influence: colonel of the militia, military governor of Norfolk County, vestryman of Lynnhaven Parish, and attorney for Bermuda governor John Wilkinson.[52] During the 1680s he encouraged William Byrd I to initiate a trade relationship with

his brother Jonathan.[53] Walke's ties to Byrd (one of Virginia's most elite planters and traders living at the falls of the James River in Henrico County) suggest
Walke's stature as a merchant whose connections enabled him to link Virginians well beyond Lower Norfolk County to Barbados. Virginians such as Byrd,
who produced goods primarily for European markets, increasingly sought
Barbadian exports. Many Virginians interested in Barbadian trade sought African slaves from the island. Barbados also likely provided Byrd with a market
for Indian slaves he acquired in exchange for Barbadian rum. Like Francis
Emperor's, Thomas Walke's business extended beyond the two colonies of
Barbados and Virginia.

Thomas Walke and his Barbadian brother Robert Walke, like the Emperors and other Barbadians and Virginians, left wills documenting the closeness
of the family across colonial boundaries.[54] His Barbadian brother Robert
Walke's 1699 will (proved in 1704) left luxury goods, money totaling over
£1,400, land, and slaves to family in Barbados and Virginia, including £100 and
one Negro boy each to his Virginia nephews Anthony Walke and Thomas
Walke when they reached the age of twenty-one. He left the majority of his
estate, including a plantation in St. Thomas Parish, to his Barbadian nephew
John Walke in Barbados. Next in line for the estate came his Virginia nephews,
Anthony and Thomas, followed by another Barbadian nephew, John Downes.
Robert Walke's will demonstrates not only the closeness of the intercolonial
tie but also that extensive travel and relocation made the gift of a Barbadian
plantation to a Virginian (in preference to one of his Barbadian nephews) reasonable.[55]

This pattern of family, trade, and travel recurs in the records of other
Barbadians in the Norfolk region and played a crucial role in the area's development. In the 1690s and the early eighteenth century, the three Princess
Anne-Norfolk residents who initiated the establishment of the town of Norfolk, Virginia's first commercial town (exporting products in great demand in
the Caribbean), all had Barbadian connections.[56] The lives of people like the
Emperors and Walkes show the highly permeable nature of the late-seventeenth-century English colonial world. With frequent travel between colonies,
some social and economic communities easily bridged geographical distance
and political boundaries. The Emperors played a role in shaping religious ties
linking Virginia and northern colonies, and Virginians beyond Lower Norfolk
found their access to Barbados valuable. Barbadians' connections to colonists
such as Byrd expanded their influence. The extensive interaction between Barbados and Virginia reflects the degree to which the perception of various
English colonies as completely distinct places should yield to the contempo-

rary inhabitants' view of seventeenth-century English colonies as parts of a larger Atlantic world.

Migration and social links between Virginia and New Netherland similarly followed the patterns established by merchants' economic networks. As a result, the most intricate social networks between the two colonies centered, like the economic links, on Virginia's Eastern Shore. The Eastern Shore court records contain multiple denizations for settlers explicitly described as Dutch or with obviously Dutch names. (A denizen was a foreigner who received citizenship but could not hold public office or inherit real property.)[57] As was the case with Barbadian migrations, some servants and slaves moved with their masters from New Netherland to the Chesapeake. Those involuntary migrants, like their masters, brought broadly American experiences with them to their new colony and based their actions in the Chesapeake in part on their prior experiences in other colonies.

The Varlett-Herman-Hack-Boot extended family offers the most clearly documented example of New Netherland-Eastern Shore family ties. Huguenot merchants Casper Varlett and Judith Tentenier moved from the Netherlands to the Dutch fort Good Hope (site of Hartford, Connecticut) in the 1630s and from there to Fresh Water on Manhattan. Varlett and Tentenier's only son, Nicholas, married Anna Stuyvesant Bayard, the sister of New Netherland Governor Peter Stuyvesant and widow of Samuel Bayard. Nicholas Varlett, also a merchant, traded to Curaçao and imported tobacco to New Amsterdam from Virginia. An officer for the Dutch West India Company, he held several public offices in New Netherland. In 1660 and 1661 he went to the Chesapeake to help negotiate the commerce treaty between Virginia and New Netherland.[58]

Two of Casper Varlett and Judith Tentenier's five daughters moved to the Chesapeake.[59] Anna and her husband, German-born surgeon George (Joris) Hack, moved to Virginia by 1651 and acquired over three thousand acres in Virginia and Maryland.[60] Anna Varlett traveled to New Amsterdam several times between 1651 and 1661, apparently by herself, in order to take care of their business there and to visit her family. Because George Hack was repeatedly referred to as a surgeon, and not a merchant, and because Anna did all of the recorded commercial traveling to New Amsterdam and came from a merchant family, their impulse to trade probably came more from her than from her husband. In a New Netherland lawsuit she claimed a shipment of tobacco sent to her from Virginia by her husband as her private property.[61] Her activities in New Netherland and the Chesapeake exhibit the commercial activity common to women in Dutch merchant families and demonstrate her capacity to participate in legal activity to promote or defend her economic interests.[62]

George Hack and Anna Varlett traded African slaves and Dutch goods such as Holland cloth for their own and their neighbors' tobacco, which they sent to New Netherland, in their own vessels, for reexport.[63] George and Anna's continued trade contacts with New Netherland helped them facilitate further migrations from New Netherland to Virginia and Maryland. Much of their land came from headrights acquired for migrants who reflected New Netherland's ethnic diversity and included people of English, Dutch, Huguenot, German, Bohemian, and African descent.[64]

One of those headrights, Bohemian Augustine Herman, was Anna Varlett's trading partner. He had moved from Prague to New Amsterdam in 1643 and by the early 1650s was regarded as New Amsterdam's "greatest merchant." He traded to the Dutch and English Caribbean, the Chesapeake, Southern Europe, and the Netherlands.[65] In December 1650 or 1651, he married Anna Varlett's sister Jannetje in the Dutch Reformed Church of New Amsterdam. He traded extensively in Virginia and was well known on the Eastern Shore, where colonists saw him as "of [New] Amsterdam in the New Netherlands Merchant," rather than as Bohemian.[66] In the mid-1650s Herman and Jannetje Varlett followed Anna Varlett and George Hack to the Eastern Shore. The two families maintained a commercial partnership and patented land near one another in both Maryland and Virginia.[67] They traded tobacco in their ships to New Netherland for Dutch cloth and for slaves, serving as merchants to other colonists on the Eastern Shore.[68] Even Edmund Scarborough, who owned more land than anyone else on the Eastern Shore and who traded to New Netherland in his own vessels, also relied on the Varlett-Hack-Herman family to carry some of his trade.[69] Herman and Varlett did not hesitate to use Virginia and New Netherland courts to pursue their debtors. Court members' favorable decisions and their respect for Herman indicate his importance to their respective economies. In 1657 Herman complained to the Northampton County Court that gentleman Captain John Stringer (a New Netherland-Virginia trader resident in Accomack) owed him seven thousand pounds of tobacco for a bark he had purchased from Herman the pervious summer. However, Herman could not stay long enough to pursue a lawsuit, his affairs "not permittinge his longe staye in the Countrye." So the clerk registered the protest and promised Herman that Stringer would see it.[70] Herman's position as merchant required incessant travel, which all colonists, including court members, understood.

On the Eastern Shore, networks of personal communications necessary to conduct trade in the Chesapeake (without ports) involved the whole society in maritime trade communities that were Dutch or New Netherland centered as much as they were English. New Netherland merchants in the Chesapeake, such as Herman, connected English colonists to New Netherland and Dutch markets. In late April 1657 Augustine Herman arranged to transport the tobacco of several Northampton County colonists to New Netherland, whence it could reach continental markets tolerant of the Eastern Shore's strongly fla-vored Orinoco.[71] John Custis, born in the Netherlands of English descent and naturalized in Virginia, first consolidated the tobacco at his house and then delivered it to Herman.[72] The mariners who loaded the tobacco onto Custis's sloop worked at individual plantations located in "assorted places," meeting the owners of each plantation and probably also their servants and slaves as they worked.[73] Those crew members, some based in New Netherland and some in Virginia, planned to travel to Manhattan with the tobacco. Dutch-connected traders and settlers thus became a significant presence on the East-ern Shore, a presence that many English colonists appreciated because of access to markets for their tobacco and other goods.

After George Hack and Jannetje Varlett both died in 1665, Augustine Her-man (who had acquired over four thousand acres in Maryland by that point) and Anna Varlett remained business partners and kept their Virginia land-holdings.[74] In 1665 in Northampton County, Virginia, Anna Varlett engaged James Fookes to build her a sloop that could carry thirty-five hogsheads of tobacco, indicating her intent to carry on with business. Varlett was to supply the sails and rigging, for which she depended on other mariners of her acquaintance: in September 1666 she bought a sail from the ship *Daniell of Dublin* and the following winter she bought some rigging for his sloop and bolt ropes for the sails from Mr. Martindale's ship.[75]

After a brief marriage to New Netherland merchant Nicholas Boot, who died about a year after marrying Varlett, she continued to manage her business and build trade contacts with fellow New Netherlanders and Dutch colonists in Virginia and Maryland.[76] Around 1670, she sold half of a sloop to her long-time attorney Cornelius Vanhoofe.[77] When he did not pay in due time, she sued him. Unsatisfied with the judgment of the county court, she requested an appeal to the Virginia General Court, which intervened in her favor.[78] Despite her preference for a Dutch attorney (a preference that this experience may have weakened), Varlett's willingness to appeal to the General Court reflects her comfort with the workings of Virginia's colonial government. Not only did she trade independently, she used the English colonial courts to protect her interests just as male merchants commonly did, and just as she had done in New Netherland. Her success in the appeal to the Virginia General Court indi-cates the ability of Dutch merchants to act effectively in the public sphere in various colonies.[79]

The lives of merchants Anna Varlett Hack Boot and Augustine Herman illustrate the ease with which Dutch-connected merchants operated in Virginia and Maryland, both before and after emigrating from New Netherland. Their financial success in Chesapeake-New Netherland trade and their ability to use Virginia's county and colonial courts to their advantage embody their rise to prominence in the colony. Their Caribbean contacts (through Herman's own trade and Anna's brother Nicholas) may have helped them access sources for slaves that they traded to the Chesapeake and that undoubtedly increased their attractiveness to Chesapeake planters impatient for labor sources.[80]

Anna Varlett's career supports the claim that Dutch women in early modern Europe more commonly engaged in long-distance trade than did other European women, and that in New Netherland as in old, women acted as merchants and as their husband's business partners.[81] Margaret Hardenbroeck, the wife of David Peterson De Vries, was an independent merchant in New Amsterdam during their marriage, her widowhood, and her second marriage. After De Vries's 1661 death, Hardenbroeck invested in two ships which she used for transatlantic trade for thirty years, often sailing with her ships. Her second husband, Frederick Philipse, was also a Manhattan merchant who traded slaves from Africa to New Netherland and to the Chesapeake.[82] Anna Varlett's continuing activity as a merchant, even after moving to Maryland and Virginia, suggests that Dutch women's participation in such trade extended across the Atlantic not only to New Netherland but also to parts of English America.[83]

In 1650 Lower Norfolk County merchants William and Susan Moseley, "late of Rotterdam in holland" (and friends of the Dutch-speaking Barbadian immigrant Francis Emperor), sold emerald, diamond, gold, ruby, and sapphire jewelry worth 612 guilders to Francis Yardley (married to Amsterdam-born Ann Custis) for nine head neat cattle, two draft oxen, two steers, and five cows. Before the sale of the jewelry, Susan Moseley wrote to Francis Yardley, agreeing to the terms of the sale and explaining that the decision to sell was because of *her* "greate wante of Cattle." She assured Yardley that she herself had gone from Rotterdam to The Hague to confirm the value of the jewelry with goldsmiths there.[84] The Moseleys sold the jewelry soon after they arrived in Lower Norfolk, when cattle were much more important than jewelry to their economic establishment and ability to develop a niche in an intercolonial trade network. Susan Moseley's decision to sell her jewelry for cattle shortly after arriving in the Chesapeake from Rotterdam, provides further evidence that Dutch trading practices survived among women and men of Dutch heritage, even after they moved to English colonies and found themselves surrounded by English settlers with quite different expectations of women's commercial roles. The lack of any objection or comment in English Chesapeake records suggests acceptance, or at least tolerance by the English colonists for whom Dutch trade was so important economically.

At least one Dutch-connected woman in the Chesapeake continued to follow Dutch rather than English naming practices, using her name Barbarah DeBarette rather than her husband's (Garrett Vanswaringen). More notably, the Maryland court recorded her name following Dutch practices, even when naturalizing her in 1669.[85] Some Dutch immigrants to Virginia used Virginia courts to write wills conforming to Dutch inheritance practices, whereby husbands left their entire estates, and the management of those estates, to their wives first, then to be divided between sons and daughters.[86] English inheritance more often provided for the eldest son to inherit the estate, with the widow receiving the use of a "widow's third" of the estate as maintenance for the remainder of her life. Virginia courts commonly did not protect even widows' right to the use of that third until the end of the century.[87]

Ann Taft (or Toft), a spinster living in the Pungoteage region of the Eastern Shore (where Anna Varlett had her plantation), did business and made personal and economic contacts from New England to Jamaica, providing further evidence that in this region with significant Dutch presence gender conventions differed from those elsewhere in English colonial America. In 1666, Taft appointed Connecticut Governor John Winthrop, Jr., her attorney to recover her half of the goods in the ketch *Virginia Merchant* (belonging to Dutch merchant Simon Overzee, who had moved from Lower Norfolk to the Eastern Shore and had hosted Augustine Herman as ambassador from New Netherland to Maryland in 1659–60).[88]

Three years later, in 1669, Ann Taft was still shipping goods in the *Virginia Merchant* (by then known also as the *Providence*), this time trading between the Eastern Shore and Nevis. When difficulties arose, the Northampton County Court sent Barbadian immigrant (and Carolina promoter) Colonel John Vassall as envoy to Nevis to gather information. When they instructed him to seek the help of the Nevis Lieutenant Governor Colonel James Russell, Ann Taft, apparently an acquaintance of Russell's, assured the Northampton Court that it could trust Russell to see to a thorough examination of the concerns of the *Providence*.[89]

Ann Taft also owned a four-thousand-acre plantation in Jamaica's St. Elizabeth's parish. In 1672 she conveyed the land "along with all negroes, &c." to the executors of Eastern Shore intercolonial merchant Edmund Scarborough (who had brought forty-one Africans from Manhattan to the Eastern Shore in 1656), apparently to repay debts she owed his estate.[90] Taft did business that involved her in at least three other colonies and required that she make personal contacts throughout the Atlantic world. Her residence in a county with Dutch settlers, her repeated use of a vessel owned by Dutch immigrant Simon Overzee, and her trade with Scarborough and others familiar with New Netherland may have eased her entry into a commercial world not commonly the domain of English colonial women.[91]

Dutch merchants and settlers provided important economic contacts for many English colonists in the seventeenth-century Chesapeake. Financial concerns weakened ethnic prejudices and significantly reduced any Chesapeake commitment to English metropolitan mercantile visions. Such easy incorporation of Dutch merchant activity and settlement in the Chesapeake did not occur without Dutch cooperation.[92] The apparently conscious effort some Dutch merchants made to fit in—by Anglicizing their names, Anglicizing their boats' names, speaking English, and seeking out fellow Calvinists among English Puritans—contributed to their easy acceptance in Virginia and Maryland that may have provided leeway for Dutch women to maintain independent economic activity. The Dutch themselves pragmatically exhibited a lack of attachment to a separate ethnic identity, a pattern that formed part of a commercial strategy aided by shared religious identity among English Puritans and Dutch Calvinists.[93] Many of the "Dutch" merchants who exhibited the greatest flexibility in the Chesapeake were, in fact, not Dutch but were Huguenots (Varletts), English Calvinists (Moseleys), or other protestant merchants (Herman) who had taken advantage of Dutch tolerance and commerce to flee religious persecution elsewhere and establish Atlantic trade networks based in New Netherland. Seventeenth-century Virginians' frequent dependence on these Dutch-connected merchants and seamen for sufficient access to European goods and markets and African slaves, particularly during the English Civil War, affected English colonists' perspectives on international rivalries and on national and individual goals of colonization in ways that facilitated significant Dutch involvement in local Chesapeake society.

Migrations between New England and Virginia also followed trade routes and therefore also concentrated on Lower Norfolk and especially the Eastern Shore. These connections differed from those discussed above in that migrants traveled in both directions and that those from New England to Virginia seem to have spread more evenly throughout Virginia.[94] Because some of these contacts had a religious component, and because so many Virginia Puritans migrated to Maryland, Virginia-New England-Maryland intercolonial migrations intertwined. A similar result nevertheless ensued: the creation of economic and familial networks that also helped to shape the social and, in this case, religious, worlds of colonists in the Chesapeake.

Though not New Englanders, some Virginia settlers had experienced colonial life in New England because they came from England to Virginia by way of New England. Many references to ships with passengers for both places exist.[95] The stay usually lasted several weeks to a few months, but in some cases people lingered longer, clearly learning about at least one way to live in an English American colony. In at least one case in the 1620s, a ship with passengers for both New England and Virginia came to New England first, where it "fitted her self to goe for Virginia." Some New Englanders joined the passengers for Virginia, "some out of discontent and dislike of ye countrie."[96] To these migrants, the English colonial world offered multiple possibilities. In 1625 Captain Thomas Wollaston came to New England with three or four partners, each of whom brought servants, provisions, and tools to begin a plantation. They began to plant in Plymouth, but the results seemed unlikely to achieve the profits they expected. To make some money, Wollaston took many of the servants to Virginia, where he sold their time. Wollaston wrote back from Virginia to one of his partners in Plymouth, telling him to bring more servants to Virginia to sell.[97] The tobacco boom then underway in Virginia assured a good market for servants, and while it also likely provided those servants with a reasonable chance for financial independence if they survived their indentures, the experience of being shipped from one colony to another in response to labor markets provided a rude and early introduction to the Atlantic world's demand for mobile labor and disregard for the laborers themselves.

Some New England colonists migrated to Virginia to escape censure and restrictions. Others suffered expulsion for misbehavior or an inability to support themselves.[98] In 1672 Rebeccah Turel petitioned the Massachusetts Bay Court of Assistants for passage to Virginia (where she hoped to find her husband), so she could obey the court's expulsion order. She was too poor to transport herself and her child, unwilling to lie in prison, but unable to go unless sold as a servant, which probably would make her condition worse. The court ordered the treasurer to supply her passage to Virginia because she was "utterly unable to pay any thing herself," and to do it immediately "so the Country may be freed from further charge."[99]

Like Turel and her husband, other migrants moved to reunite with or escape from their families. In 1643 Virginian Francis Martin owed Eastern Shore merchant and trader Stephen Charleton three hundred pounds of Virginia tobacco for transporting Martin's wife to him from New England.[100] Conversely, Mary Chichester's husband William (the Salem-based master of the *Hopewell* and defendant and plaintiff in Lower Norfolk lawsuits) abandoned her in Salem and moved to Virginia.[101] Massachusetts officials' success at controlling the character and religious behavior of their colonists prevented some Virginians from moving to that colony. Boston officials noted that Virginia tailor John Tompson, trying to move to Massachusetts, was the son of Roman Catholics, and that James Worth, who wanted admission, was "a laborer cast away upon the cost of Virginia having a wife and child and nothing to maintain them," information not likely to result in either man's welcome.[102]

Some of the most striking connections involved groups of families on the Eastern Shore and New England. Again, these close ties resulted from intercolonial trade that facilitated communications and migrations. William Stone migrated to Virginia before 1628 and settled on the Eastern Shore by 1629, where he acquired 5,250 acres and became justice of the peace and sheriff for Accomack County.[103] In addition to tobacco, Stone raised cattle and grain for trade to New England. His brother Captain John Stone (the English trader whom David Peterson De Vries met so frequently) carried grain and cattle for him from Virginia to Boston during the early 1630s.[104] When he lived in St. Christopher, he and Accomack planter Stephen Charleton co-owned the *Virgine*.[105] He served as attorney for Captain William Epps, a former Accomack County resident and partner of John Stone's, who had moved to the island of St. Christopher in the Caribbean. In July 1633 Stone visited his "loving friend" Epps on the island. Epps kept land in Virginia and conducted trade that included Barbados, St. Christopher, Virginia, and New England.[106]

William Stone, a Puritan, became a member of Accomack's Puritan-leaning vestry in 1635 (joining other New England traders such as Stephen Charleton).[107] Stone's wife Verlinda was the sister of William Cotton, a Puritan minister in Accomack. Stone's sister married William Cotton, making the two families in-laws twice over.[108] Stone moved to Maryland in 1648, when Lord Baltimore invited him to become governor of the province. Hundreds of Puritans followed him, establishing paths along which migration would continue.

Many more Puritans came to the same region, making moves that undoubtedly were facilitated by contacts with traveling merchants. Nathaniel Eaton, first president of Harvard, fled to the Eastern Shore rather than face an investigation over charges that he had botched the college's finances and abused students. Brother of Congregational minister Samuel Eaton and of New Haven merchant and Governor Theophilus Eaton, Nathaniel likely knew William Stone before moving.[109] He married Stone's sister after William Cotton died.

Francis Doughty, also a Puritan and friend of William Stone's, had numerous intercolonial experiences before and after living on the Eastern Shore. He first went to Massachusetts in 1636, moved to Plymouth but was forced out in 1638 for supporting the halfway covenant, and by 1641 had moved to Rhode Island. He convinced the Dutch to grant thirteen thousand acres on

Long Island to him and other New Englanders. In 1643 attacks by Mohicans and Matinecocks forced them to Manhattan, where Doughty remained for a time, supported by English parishioners and by the Dutch Reformed Church. By 1655 he had moved to Virginia's Eastern Shore where he stayed for four years, preaching to Puritans there. By the fall of 1659 he had moved to Patuxent, Maryland, perhaps following Stone. After two years in Patuxent, Doughty returned to Virginia, this time to Rappahannock County. In 1669 when his nonconformity once again forced him to move, he went to the Caribbean, while maintaining his previous contacts and expanding his network.[110] He also married Stone's popular sister after both William Cotton and Nathaniel Eaton had died.[111]

Daniel Gookin, Jr., migrated from Virginia to Massachusetts by way of Maryland. He, like Stone, was an intercolonial merchant and moved along routes that he had traveled many times as a trader between the Chesapeake and New England. In 1620 his father Daniel Gookin, Sr., transported cattle into Virginia from Ireland. He established a plantation (Marie's Mount) at Newport News and brought more cattle and hogs for breeding, thus setting up a plantation well stocked in goods for intercolonial trade. By 1631 his sons Daniel Gookin, Jr., and John Gookin had followed him to Virginia. John patented land in Nansemond County and became a justice of the peace in Lower Norfolk and a burgess for Upper Norfolk (Nansemond) in 1639.[112] After a return to London and marriage there, Daniel Gookin, Jr., and his wife Mary Dolling Gookin settled in Nansemond in the early 1640s and, with other Nansemond Puritans, tried to recruit a New England minister to their parish. Daniel Gookin, Jr., was a burgess for Nansemond in 1642 and the county's militia captain that year. In addition to his land in Nansemond, Gookin acquired fourteen hundred acres along the Rappahannock for transporting twenty-eight people.[113]

As Nansemond militia captain, Daniel Gookin, Jr., negotiated with Nansemond Indians in southern Virginia, experiences he doubtless drew on when he became Indian commissioner for Boston.[114] When Daniel and Mary Gookin moved to Boston in 1644, the First Church of Boston admitted Daniel only six days after they arrived and made him a freeman three days later, uncommonly fast. His trade between the colonies afterward and his quick admission to the church and community suggest that Gookin's earlier trade to New England had made him well known in the colony. Five months later, on October 12, 1644, the church accepted his wife Mary as well.[115]

After his move, Gookin continued to hold his land in Virginia and to trade and travel between Massachusetts and the Chesapeake, using goods from his Chesapeake plantations in this trade. In 1647, according to John Winthrop,

Gookin arrived from Virginia in a ship "bought by him [of] the governour there." If Winthrop was correct, the ship purchase illustrates Gookin's interaction with Governor William Berkeley and Berkeley's direct participation in maritime trade.[116]

Gookin's intercolonial trade, like that of other merchants and captains, provided other colonists with the means of migrating.[117] Gookin's migration from the Chesapeake to New England also facilitated the creation of a different kind of connection between the two regions when he helped two Virginians attend Harvard during the 1650s. He paid fees for Virginian Nathaniel Utie, who attended the college from 1651 to 1655. Utie was the stepson of Richard Bennett, a Puritan who had been Gookin's neighbor in Nansemond, had joined Gookin in the 1642 attempt to bring a minister from New England to Nansemond, and had become governor of Virginia during the Interregnum.[118] In the summer of 1655, during Nathaniel Utie's residence at Harvard, "Mr Bennete fellow Commoner," Richard Bennett's son and Utie's stepbrother Richard, Jr., entered the college at the head of his class (a position measuring his superior wealth and status, not academic performance). Fellow commoners such as Bennett paid double, received the honorary title *Mr.*, and did not have to uncover their heads to upperclassmen.[119] The first payment Bennett made to the college included "for vtye £2 9s 9d," indicating that Bennett arrived from Virginia with payment for Utie's expenses. Bennett rented a study, expensive and unusual for a first-year student; in the middle of his first year he upgraded to the most expensive Senior Fellow's study, recently vacated by another intercolonial scholar, Samuel Megapolensis, son of New Amsterdam minister Johannes Megapolensis. Though Bennett apparently left school before completing his first year, his presence there made a lasting impression on the college. In 1659 three years after he left, the room he had rented was still designated Mr. Bennett's study.[120] Utie completed his course work at Harvard and returned to the Chesapeake where both he and his stepbrother acquired large landholdings in Maryland on the Sassafras River near Augustine Herman, Jannetje Varlett, George Hack, and Anna Varlett.[121] Their experience at Harvard broadened their connections as it has for generations of undergraduates for three and a half centuries since, introducing them not only to students from Massachusetts but to Calvinist elites from multiple colonies.[122]

Migrations between Virginia and New England resulted from more complicated motives than many of those from Barbados or New Netherland to Virginia. Religious affiliations as well as trade figured actively in their decisions. Nonetheless, this migration pattern, like those discussed earlier, also followed shipping and trade routes. Puritans who migrated and maintained connections between the Chesapeake and New England often made their initial contacts through trade. The concentration of Puritans (and Calvinists from New Netherland) on Virginia's Southside and Eastern Shore, the regions most active in intercolonial trade, reflected the continued importance of trade routes in shaping migration patterns, whatever their underlying motivations.

Other intercolonial migrations resulted from more orchestrated efforts. The founders of Jamaica and Carolina looked to other colonies for settlers. Virginians figured more prominently in the plans of Carolina than of Jamaica. In 1663 the Lords Proprietors of Carolina requested that the governors of Barbados, the Caribbee Islands, Virginia, New England, and Bermuda not hinder free and unengaged persons from moving to Carolina.[123] Barbados made significant contributions to Carolina's settlement, but other colonies, including Virginia, played major roles as well. Carolina depended on Virginia migrants for settlers, on Virginia's proximity as a haven for retreat and a source of supplies, and on Virginia interpreters' and traders' knowledge of Carolina Indians and their languages, for a less risky start than previous colonies had had, and for quickly establishing overland trade in deerskins and slaves.

Founded at a time of decreasing economic opportunity for many Virginians and Barbadians, Carolina offered a potentially attractive destination for migrants from both colonies. In 1665 Carolina surveyor and interpreter (and former Virginia interpreter) Thomas Woodward noted that to attract Virginians, Carolina had to provide better opportunities for landowning. He wrote from Albemarle County in Carolina to Proprietor Sir John Colleton in London that most people resented the small land grants in Carolina and that "the very rumor of them discourages many who had intentions to remove hence from Virginia." He continued, noting that if the Carolina Proprietors hoped to lure Virginians, they should learn from Lord Baltimore's experiences in Maryland "that men will remove from Virginia" only if offered easier conditions for acquiring acreage "it being only land that they come for."[124]

By the early 1670s, Carolina promoters had developed strategies to attract Virginians and other English American colonists. Carolinians planned to disperse copies of their laws and concessions in New England and Virginia. Sir John Yeamans, a Barbadian sugar planter who led migrations to Carolina and served as governor from 1672 to 1674, wrote to Proprietor Anthony Ashley Cooper that a seven-year custom-free period for Carolina tobacco would "draw the Virginians" and that he had sent word to Virginia that from Carolina they could carry their goods where they wanted.[125] Three Virginians, one perhaps an earlier Barbadian migrant to the Chesapeake, wrote to the Lords Proprietors that they intended to move from Virginia to Carolina and proposed a special boat designed to carry cattle and passengers. The three men told the Lords Proprietors that many "inclined to remove from Virginia to

Carolina." Others wrote to England confirming that many hoped to remove from Virginia but lacked transportation.[126] Carolinian W. Owen wrote to Anthony Ashley Cooper asking that tobacco from Carolina to England remain custom free for some time because "This the Virginians hearken after."[127]

Carolinians not only looked for intercolonial settlers and supplies but also looked to other colonies for instructive examples. They soon discovered that their reputation in other colonies could affect the success of their project. In October 1667 Barbadian John Vassall (whom the Northampton Court later sent as envoy to Nevis to help settle Ann Taft's affairs) wrote from Nansemond County, Virginia, to Sir John Colleton explaining difficulties he had had while in charge of their Charles River plantation in Carolina.[128] Vassall wrote that he did not understand why the project failed until he came to Virginia. There he learned that "all that came from [Charles River to Virginia] made it their business to exclaim against the [Carolina] country," claiming it as "unfit for a Christian habitation." That news, of course, discouraged Virginians from moving to Charles River or trading there, which in turn made the "rude rabble of inhabitants" of Charles River "daily ready to mutiny" against Vassall for trying to keep them there without sufficient supplies. After they discovered how to travel from Carolina overland to southern Virginia, "neither arguments nor authority" could keep them there, and Vassall had to send for ships to carry away those who remained. According to Vassall, their troubles started because the Lords Proprietors' "hard terms" discouraged potential supporters from Barbados as well as from Virginia. Once again confirming that the fates of earlier colonial projects were at the fore of colonial planners' thoughts, he worried that Carolina would fare no better than Roanoke unless something were done "to encourage their stay, for they [have] great cause of complaints."[129]

The regions of Virginia south of the James engaged most actively in the settlement and supplying of South Carolina because of their proximity and access, because they already had a livestock-based economy that addressed a Carolina need, and perhaps because numerous Virginians in this region had ties to Barbadians who were also involved in the Carolina project. If Carolina settlers intended to supply Barbados, many Virginians already had goods, economic ties, and experience useful for the Carolina project. In 1673 Edmund Lister of Northumberland County (in the Northern Neck area, which also had fairly significant Barbadian and New England trade) bought one hundred acres on the Ashley River on Oyster Point. He "Transport[ed] Severall Negros, out of . . . Virginia, into Carolina and did there Settle them upon a Plantacon, together wth Some Cattle." In 1676 his widow sold the land to another wealthy Virginian and slaveowner.[130]

While not so consciously intercolonial projects, other Restoration colonies such as Pennsylvania grew from intercolonial as well as transatlantic migration. Some Atlantic world residents, after time in Virginia, moved on to other colonies or even back to Europe. Their mobility reflects seventeenth-century Virginians' view of an Atlantic "world on the move" that offered varied opportunities. Just as those who left took something of their lives in Virginia with them, Virginia's reception of migrants from other colonies and from Europe provided a means by which the political, religious, and cultural developments in other parts of that Atlantic world informed Virginians' perceptions of their world. Migrations to and from Virginia created overlapping and intertwining connections, suggesting that an Atlantic web is in fact an accurate metaphor for describing the relations linking distant locales via the maritime world. English fur traders at the rivers' falls represented the Atlantic world's overlap with yet another web; that of overland Indian trails that became more and more fully integrated with maritime trade as the century wore on and as human slaves as well as animal pelts moved along both kinds of trade routes. Despite the regional nature of Virginia's links to the wider world, the impact of each of those links—to England, to Barbados, to Iroquoia—spread throughout the Chesapeake. Contacts to England always defined Virginia, but the influence of others contributed to Virginia's political, social, and diplomatic development, intensifying at particular moments when events made intercolonial maritime or overland connections especially relevant.

Chapter 5
English Atlantic Networks and Religion in Virginia

Puritan, Quaker, and Dutch Reformed merchants predominated intercolonial American trade during the seventeenth century. The transatlantic and intercolonial trade and migration routes that shaped Virginia's economy and its settlement patterns also influenced the colony's religious map. The Church of England was strongest in the Peninsula and Middle Peninsula counties that grew the best tobacco and therefore maintained the closest connections to England. Puritans and Quakers, who made up a significant proportion of Virginia's population in several counties during the middle decades of the seventeenth century, concentrated south of the James River and on the Eastern Shore, the areas most involved in intercolonial trade, and constituted a disproportionate percentage of Virginia's intercolonial merchants. Seventeenth-century Puritans and Quakers constituted Atlantic communities that included England and the Netherlands and multiple colonies. These nonconformists in Virginia depended on intercolonial networks of family and trade. Intercolonial religious and economic networks thus overlapped and reinforced one another.

The Virginia Company established an Anglican parish system that lasted through the end of the colonial period. That parish system divided the colony geographically into parishes that, like English parishes, encompassed all English residents. The parishes were intended to collect tithes, oversee poor relief, enforce church attendance, and provide discipline for some ethical transgressions. Because Anglican clergy required theological training and ordination by a bishop, and because neither was available in the colonies, Virginia's Anglican church necessarily depended on transatlantic ties. The Anglican clergy who traveled to Virginia not surprisingly chose (or were chosen by) wealthier parishes in counties with the best access to England and the highest quality tobacco (important not only because it created better transatlantic contacts but also because clergy salaries were paid in tobacco). Their English educations, their relationships with former classmates and other clergy in England, and their subordination to English episcopal hierarchy all served to reinforce for Virginia parishioners their membership in a religious world centered in England.[1]

However, the number of Anglican clergy in Virginia was always insufficient to supply the population, and for most of the century most English residents had no access to regular Anglican worship. Between the 1640s and 1670, as the colonial population of Virginia increased from about eight thousand to about thirty thousand and spread throughout the coastal plain, there were seldom more than five to ten ministers resident in the colony at any one time.[2] Even by the end of the century, the average parish encompassed about 270 square miles, and many of those parishes often went without clergy many Sundays.[3] Those parishes that were active in seventeenth-century Virginia did not conform to a particular vision for the Church of England but, rather, represented a wide range of theological and liturgical preference that only became controversial at midcentury. When Virginia was planned and established at the beginning of the century, the church of Elizabeth and James I encompassed a spectrum of practice from Puritan to very high church. During the late 1620s and 1630s, Charles I and his archbishop William Laud worked to enforce a more narrow definition of the Church of England and ultimately created sharp distinctions that forced many Puritans within the church to choose between a more elaborate worship form (and the theology that such liturgy represented) and separation from the church. The Great Migration to New England in the 1630s stemmed from pressure on Puritans to conform to Laud's vision of Anglicanism.[4] Into the 1640s, transatlantic and intercolonial interactions alike supported both Puritans and non-Puritans within Virginia's Anglican church. However, the Eastern Shore and Southside counties with closer ties to New England already began to encourage the emergence of the regional religious pattern in which nonconformist tendencies followed immersion in intercolonial trade. By the mid-1640s, Virginia was no longer able to persist in earlier more locally flexible parish system. The English Civil War that began in 1642 spread religious conflict throughout the English Atlantic, and royalist Governor Sir William Berkeley, who arrived in Virginia that year, came with a perspective on the church derived from Laud's England in the 1630s and a conviction (as the Civil War began) that Puritans represented a serious threat to the English world, and he intended to enforce his Laudian view of the Church of England in Virginia. Thus, by the 1640s the English Atlantic imposed on Virginia a clear distinction dividing Puritans from Anglicans.[5] Thereafter, the links joining strong intercolonial connections and nonconformity, on the one hand, and relatively stronger transatlantic connections and Anglicanism, on the other, grew more pronounced.[6] As Quakers emerged in the 1650s, they too depended on transatlantic and intercolonial communication, but even those Quaker evangelists who came to the colonies from England relied on intercolonial networks once they had crossed the Atlantic, so in Virginia they arrived via other colonies along intercolonial shipping (or overland) trade routes.

Commercial and familial intercolonial webs such as those maintained by the Emperors, the Gookins, and the Varletts, helped foster the development of dissenting religious communities in seventeenth-century Virginia and strengthen Virginia's dissenting communities that already existed. The development of long-distance ties between American nonconformists occurred through written correspondence, intercolonial migration, and the intercolonial travel of ministers. Puritans and Quakers, like Anglicans, perceived themselves as members of Atlantic communities, which they actively and consciously fostered. Their intercolonial movements, like almost all colonial migrations, followed patterns established by coastal trade routes.

In addition to larger migrations, ministers sometimes moved between colonies especially to serve religious needs or to build connections between dispersed congregations. In the case of Quakers, building such ties involved a well-established practice, in which traveling ministers (Public Friends) left their homes in England or one of its colonies to travel for months or years at a time, visiting Quaker meetings to proselytize, serve religious needs, or build connections between dispersed Friends. Unlike many other migrations, Quaker ministers' travels followed Indian overland paths in addition to shipping routes. The migrations of Puritans and Puritan ministers between colonies and the intercolonial and overseas traveling by Quaker men and women ministers indicate the permeability of colonial boundaries and served to break down those boundaries further. Quaker traveling ministers not only preached but also visited, sometimes settled, and invariably brought news of family, friends, and events elsewhere.

The porosity of intercolonial boundaries, especially pronounced for those merchant families involved in coastal trade, allowed intercolonial travel and migration for religious reasons, strengthening nonconformist communities within Virginia. Many of the most important intercolonial traders in Virginia were nonconformists who lived in the parts of Virginia (the Eastern Shore and the Southside of the James) most heavily dependent on intercolonial trade. By the middle of the seventeenth century, Puritans and Quakers constituted a significant presence in Lower Norfolk, Nansemond, Isle of Wight, Accomack, and Northampton Counties, all counties with substantial trade to other American colonies. Religious and commercial links reinforced one another, and commerce was a part (perhaps both as means and as end) of the nonconformists' attempts to build intercolonial communities.[7]

Puritan, Quaker, and Dutch Reformed conversions and intermarriages created families that included a variety of nonconformists and involved multiple Atlantic world markets and locales. A few connected individuals clearly illustrate this aspect of intercolonial networks. Isaac Allerton, his son (also Isaac Allerton), and their associates exemplify the ways that several intercolonial trade, migration, and communication routes overlapped to form a complex intercolonial web and a broadly colonial world with Puritan and Dutch connections central to its maintenance.[8] Isaac Allerton, Sr., born in London between 1583 and 1585, moved to Leiden in 1609. He, his wife Mary, and three of their children traveled on the *Mayflower* to Plymouth as part of the Puritan migration there in 1620. Allerton, a merchant and the wealthiest of the migrants to New England, owned several trading vessels and played an instrumental role establishing intercolonial coastal trade and the New England fishing industry. He disagreed with the New England religious leadership on issues of tolerance and moved to New Amsterdam around 1636. For the next ten years he lived mostly in New Amsterdam, where he was involved in intercolonial trade and tobacco reexport and owned a warehouse. While living in New Amsterdam, he traveled to Virginia, the Caribbean, and New England. He helped Massachusetts ministers get to Virginia when they wrecked on Long Island.[9] He did business with Govert Loockermans of New Amsterdam who traded with the Chesapeake and later moved to Maryland where he became naturalized.[10] In 1643 Allerton became one of eight assistants to New Netherland Governor Willem Kieft, obviously having earned a place of high status in the Dutch colony. In 1646 he moved to New Haven, where he lived the rest of his life, continuing to travel and trade to New Amsterdam, Massachusetts, and Virginia.[11] He died in early 1659.

His son Isaac Allerton, Jr., followed his father's footsteps as an intercolonial trader. Born in Plymouth in 1630 to his father and second wife Fear Brewster, he graduated from Harvard in 1650, just before the arrival of Virginian Nathaniel Utie, stepson of future governor Richard Bennett.[12] Allerton, Jr., accompanied his father on trading voyages between Plymouth, New Haven, New Amsterdam, and Virginia, and gradually became a partner with his father in intercolonial trade. By the 1650s he managed much of his father's business.[13] When his father died, Isaac, Jr., away from New Haven at the time, returned to settle the estate, which included debts in Barbados, Delaware Bay, Virginia, and New Netherland.[14]

Isaac, Jr., purchased his father's New Haven house from creditors for his mother to live in.[15] In the 1650s, Isaac, Jr., and his wife Elizabeth lived in New Haven and had three children there. By 1655, however, he had purchased land in Virginia, at Wicomico in Northumberland County. He moved to Virginia after his first wife died (around 1660) and became close friends with Thomas Willoughby of Elizabeth City. Willoughby was the only son of Barbadian trader and immigrant Captain Thomas Willoughby of Elizabeth River in Lower Norfolk County, who had delivered Lower Norfolk's 1654 request (written by Francis Emperor) to find a minister in New England. Allerton married Elizabeth Willoughby, daughter of his friend, granddaughter of the immigrant, and widow of Dutch Eastern Shore merchant Simon Overzee (who had traded Ann Toft's goods in his ship and entertained Augustine Herman on a 1659–60 official voyage to Maryland for New Netherland). Isaac and Elizabeth Allerton named their son Willoughby Allerton.[16] Isaac Allerton became justice of Northumberland County in 1663, and a member of the "Committee of the Association of Northumberland, Westmoreland, and Stafford Counties" in 1667. In September 1675 he and Barbadian-connected immigrant Colonel John Washington led the Virginia forces that pursued Doeg Indians across the Potomac river (after the Doegs killed Barbadian immigrant Thomas Matthew's servant) and thereby helped precipitate the Virginia-Susquehannock War and Bacon's Rebellion. The Northern Neck (and southern bank of Rappahannock River) was another Chesapeake region that attracted intercolonial immigrants, and those immigrants seem to have disproportionately participated in precipitous events of the mid-1670s there.[17] Such involvement apparently did not hurt Allerton's political career. By February 1677 he was a member of the House of Burgesses.[18] Throughout his life, he maintained the nonconformist beliefs of his parents (and probably his wife).[19] Isaac's and his second wife Elizabeth's son Willoughby furthered and strengthened family involvement with other nonconformist traders by marrying Hannah Keene, widow of intercolonial trader John Bushrod, whose father was a Quaker merchant.[20]

The strong link between nonconformist religion and intercolonial trade emerges clearly in the lives of seventeenth-century Virginians: moreover, the Puritans in Virginia played a greater role than many historians have supposed, requiring that we rethink not only the Chesapeake's religious history but its economic and geographic history as well. The regions most deeply enmeshed in intercolonial trade—the Eastern Shore, the Southside Counties, and to a lesser degree the Northern Neck-Rappahannock area—also had the largest Puritan and Quaker populations. The connections that residents of those regions maintained in other colonies placed them firmly in an intercolonial world. Their trade contacts facilitated a development of religious communities transcending colonial boundaries. As well, their long-distance interaction webs put these individuals at the forefront of the economic, social, and political negotiations and transfers that provided the context for the development of Chesapeake slavery and that grew into the larger intercolonial networks of officials who worked to regularize colonial administration and fight the emergent creole identities that became so forceful in eighteenth-century Virginia.

While Anglican officials in Virginia supported the exchange networks intercolonial traders created, they opposed the strengthening of nonconformist intercolonial communities that accompanied the growth in trade. They realized that freedom of movement between colonies bolstered the position of religious minorities within Virginia. In response, Anglican officials attempted to prevent nonconformists from using intercolonial trade networks to build intercolonial religious communities. Though never able to keep Puritans and Quakers out of Virginia, by trying to enforce Virginia's political borders as effective cultural (though not economic) boundaries, officials did succeed in adding a perceived cultural meaning to Virginia's political borders. In doing so, they helped define Virginia as an Anglican colony.

Puritans formed an important part of Virginia's population from the outset of its colonization. English Puritans had gone to the Netherlands, mostly to areas near Middleburg and Amsterdam, during the late sixteenth and early seventeenth centuries to escape persecution in England. Some of the largest Puritan settlements in Virginia came from these English congregations in Holland. As well, the Virginia Company included several Puritans with broadly American plans and aspirations involving two or more colonies. For example, the Puritan Robert Rich (second earl of Warwick) was a prominent member of the Virginia Company, sat on the Virginia Council, and was involved as well in the New England, Somers Island, and Providence Island Companies and in the colonization of Guiana, Newfoundland, and Barbados. His cousin Nathaniel Rich, also a Puritan, was a member of the Virginia Company as well, in addition to the Somers and Providence Island Companies.[21] The Virginia Company planned that Puritan minister Patrick Copland would be rector of the college they hoped to establish at Henrico in Virginia.[22]

Puritans settled and converted in the largest numbers on the Southside of the James River and on the Eastern Shore. These areas contained Virginia's clearly Puritan congregations, as well as the largest number of Anglican parishes with Puritan leanings.[23] As in England, many nominally Anglican parishes in early seventeenth-century Virginia had nonconformist tendencies. In the 1620s and 1630s several hundred Puritans settled in Nansemond and Isle of Wight Counties, many of them adjacent to one another. Puritans Christopher Lawne, Nathaniel Bosse, and Edward Bennett patented adjoining landholdings in Isle of Wight County, Bosse and Bennett receiving their patents within three days of one another in 1621.[24] Bennett, formerly an elder of Johnson's ancient church in Amsterdam, established the largest Puritan settlement south of the James. More than three hundred settlers came to Bennett's plantation by early

1622, fifty-three of them killed in the March 22 Indian attack. Bennett survived and continued to recruit settlers, bringing as many as six hundred Puritans to Virginia from the Netherlands and England. He used his own ships to transport colonists and to trade. His nephew Richard Bennett became leader of those Puritans, and later friend of Daniel Gookin, governor of Virginia, and father and stepfather to Harvard students Richard Bennett, Jr., and Nathaniel Utie.[25]

As the Civil War began and Berkeley arrived in Virginia as governor, theological differences among Virginians grew much more visible and became political. Virginia's Puritans, beginning to feel threatened, looked to New England as a source of guidance and clergy. In May 1642 seventy-one Virginians from Nansemond, including Richard Bennett and Daniel Gookin, sent a letter (hand delivered by Philip Bennett) to the "Pastors and Elders of Christ Church in New-England and the Rest of the Faithfull" explaining "their sad condition for the want of salvation" and requesting that ministers be sent to them from New England.[26] The writers described themselves as "the Inhabitants of the County of the upper Norfolke [Nansemond] in Virginia," rather than as a particular group from the county. As the tithables in Nansemond County in 1637 numbered about five hundred, the seventy-one men who signed the letter constituted a substantial minority of the county's population.[27] They wrote so "that the word of God might be planted amongst us by Faithfull Pastors and Teachers."[28] Their actions and words indicate that Puritans in Virginia and Massachusetts considered themselves part of a spiritual community that transcended space and linked people with one another across both political boundaries and physical distances. When Philip Bennett delivered the letter, he explained the needs of the Virginia Puritans to the elders, who according to Edward Johnson of Massachusetts, hoped "to take all opportunities for inlarging the kingdome of Christ."[29] Because English reformed thought held that both understanding the Bible and achieving salvation depended on "the work and preaching of upright clergymen," the lack of ministers in Virginia (particularly of ministers that Virginia Puritans could consider "upright") potentially prevented salvation for the colonists there and thus intensified the need to recruit clergy.[30]

Shortly after the Nansemond parishioners requested ministers, Norfolk County Puritan William Durand wrote to John Davenport, pastor of Christ Church in New Haven, sharing his fear that the unworthy Anglican priests in Virginia would doom Virginia Puritans: "If we continue under these wreched and blind Idoll shepards the very bane of this land we are like to perish."[31] Durand painted a picture for Davenport of the ways in which Puritans in Virginia belonged to the same community as Davenport and other New England Puritans, connected by spiritual links reaching across geographical boundaries.

Though the two men had never met, Durand trusted that Davenport would concern himself in a matter as important as "the Enlargement of christs kingdome and the good of many poore soules in Virginia." Durand wrote that he (and others in Virginia) had benefitted from hearing Davenport preach in London, which to Durand indicated that they were already spiritually linked to one another. Those of the Virginia faithful who had not heard Davenport in London were nonetheless joined with him in their mutual love of Christ, which "doth even bind the hearts of all christians," and further connected with one another through prayer. Durand believed that the growth of Puritanism in Virginia answered prayers he knew Davenport had offered "for the conversion of such as abide in the shadowes of death, and chaynes of darkenesse."[32] Durand's belief that spiritual links overcame physical space enabled him to initiate a more tangible connection with the New Haven minister. In other words, Puritans' belief in their spiritual unity encouraged them to form relationships that would involve migration and strengthen trade connections.

In response to the request of Lower Norfolk Puritans, the elders of Christ Church in Boston decided to dispatch William Tompson from Braintree and John Knowles from Watertown.[33] Massachusetts Governor John Winthrop later wrote that the court and the congregations sending ministers to Virginia welcomed the chance to contribute to the growth of Virginia Puritanism. According to Winthrop, they considered the men sent "as seed sown, which would bring us in a plentiful harvest, and we accounted it no small honor that God had put upon his poor churches here, that other parts of the world should seek to us for help in this kind."[34] Puritans in colonies other than Virginia also looked to New England for religious leadership. Winthrop noted that at about the same time as the Virginia request, two trading vessels brought letters from Barbados and other Caribbean islands asking for New England ministers.[35]

Tompson and Knowles sailed for Virginia in October 1642, along with a third minister, Thomas James of New Haven, but were shipwrecked near Manhattan.[36] The Dutch director-general apparently did little to help them, but Isaac Allerton, Sr., a Puritan merchant and Massachusetts-New Netherland-New Haven migrant whose son Isaac Allerton, Jr., moved to Virginia, took care of them in New Amsterdam and got them a pinnace and enough supplies to continue to Virginia. They arrived in mid-December, eleven weeks after leaving New England.[37]

In Virginia, according to Winthrop, the three ministers were well received in several places. The Virginia Assembly initially approved of their arrival. Governor William Berkeley, however, did not welcome them, despite their letter of introduction from Winthrop. In March 1643 the Virginia Assembly ordered the ministers out of the colony. In June John Knowles returned to

Massachusetts from Virginia, bringing letters from his congregation and from other Virginians to the Christ Church elders. The letters, read in Boston at an open lecture, indicated that, despite the Assembly's order, the Puritans' ministry had succeeded in "inflaming" the hearts of some Virginians, who organized services in private houses once the parish churches were off limits.[38] A year later, the Powhatans' 1644 uprising against Virginia colonists demanded the attention of Virginia officials and prevented them from fully implementing their directive to suppress Puritanism in Virginia. In Massachusetts, Winthrop wrote in his journal that God had obviously sent the attack to express displeasure at the Virginia Assembly's persecution of Puritans.[39] Edward Johnson, in his *Wonder-working Providence of Sion's Saviour in New England* (1653), similarly saw in the Powhatans' attack "the hand of God against this people, after the rejection of these Ministers of Christ." Johnson also pointed out that the attack stopped just short of the Puritan settlements in Lower Norfolk and Nansemond. When it neared "that place where Christ had placed his little flock, it was discovered and prevented from further proceeding." To Johnson, this development proved that "the Lord pittied the little number of his people among this crooked generation."[40] Winthrop claimed that the Indian attack forced Virginia Anglicans to acknowledge that God had punished them for expelling the New England ministers.[41] New Englanders clearly regarded their beleaguered fellow Puritans in Virginia as part of their religious community, mandating communication between the colonies to ensure that members of "the kingdome of Christ" could look out for one another.

After the Assembly's order and the 1644 Anglo-Powhatan war, several Virginia Puritans left the Chesapeake for New England. In the mid-seventeenth century, persecutions by the Virginia government sparked further communication that encouraged Puritan leaders in other colonies to continue attention and concern for Virginia Puritans.[42] Berkeley's attempts to suppress Puritans and define Virginia as an Anglican colony within its political boundaries did succeed in encouraging emigration and decreased the visibility of Puritans who remained. However, Anglican hostility strengthened Virginia Puritans' ties to New England, binding them more fully into the intercolonial Puritan network on which these Chesapeake nonconformists depended.

Most Puritans who left Virginia in response to official persecution went to Maryland or New England. In the early 1640s, Richard Bennett, Daniel Gookin, and William Durand considered establishing a Puritan settlement on the Rappahannock, farther from the reach of Virginia officials. They decided on Maryland instead, but the settlement in Rappahannock of intercolonial traders and migrants such as Puritan Isaac Allerton, Jr., suggest the region remained attractive for some Puritans.[43] Gookin himself moved to Boston, where he and his wife quickly joined the Roxbury congregation.

During the English Civil War, Lord Baltimore, Catholic proprietor of Maryland, needed to ensure continued religious toleration for Maryland Catholics and so actively courted Puritans. He welcomed Virginia Puritans and also in 1643 sent an agent to New England to recruit New England Puritans who might prefer a warmer climate. Baltimore continued such attempts to ensure toleration for Catholics in his colony during the Interregnum. In a move designed to position himself favorably vis-à-vis Puritan England, he appointed William Stone, a Puritan from Virginia's Eastern Shore and brother of deceased ship captain (De Vries's acquaintance) John Stone, as governor. In choosing his new governor, Baltimore perceived an intercolonial talent pool, rather than one encompassing only Maryland and England. Baltimore stipulated that when Stone came to Maryland as the new governor (in 1648), he bring five hundred colonists. In 1649 about three hundred nonconformists migrated from Virginia (mostly from southeastern Virginia) to the Severn River in Maryland, though by 1649 English laws guaranteed Puritans religious freedom in Virginia as well.[44]

Despite these migrations, the Southside Puritan community persisted. Its members maintained connections to New England, strengthened by migrations and shared projects early in the decade. Thomas Harrison, Puritan minister to Elizabeth River Parish in Lower Norfolk county in the 1640s, also saw New England as a source of guidance and corresponded with John Winthrop, though he himself did not possess prior ties to New England or English Puritan networks but rather had come to Virginia as Berkeley's Anglican chaplain.[45] In April 1645 the Elizabeth River church wardens brought charges against him for not reading the Book of Common Prayer, not catechizing on Sunday afternoons, and not administering baptism correctly. He and his followers considered migrating to New England and were "in a posture of removing" by 1646, but when they consulted Winthrop about the move, he suggested they stay in Virginia.[46] In November 1646 Harrison wrote that Winthrop's arguments carried "weight and worth and force enough in them to have stakd us down againe."[47] So his congregation of Virginia Puritans stayed in the Southside counties and Harrison soon reported to Winthrop that his church was growing.[48] The Massachusetts elders clearly enjoyed respect as leaders of Puritanism in America not only from their own parishioners but from those in Virginia as well, who looked to them for decisions about their own church. That they could carry on such a correspondence depended on intercolonial traders such as Edward Gibbons (Eastern Shore merchant

Edmund Scarborough's trading partner), who carried at least one letter from Harrison to Winthrop.[49]

During the English Civil War, New England leaders saw the distinct possibility that Puritanism might increasingly define the English Atlantic world, including Virginia. Harrison, however, knew that such a development did not seem imminent to those on the ground in Virginia. He told the Massachusetts elders that he needed to consider other options. One possibility involved William Sayle's plans to settle Eleutheria in the Bahamas. Sayle had drawn up a covenant for all potential participants providing for liberty of conscience, "wherein . . . the civil magistrate should not have any cognizance of any matter which concerned religion, but every man might enjoy his own opinion or religion, without control or question." When Sayle, in Virginia seeking provisions for his project, discovered that the Virginia government had oppressed Puritans and threatened them with expulsion, he tried to persuade them to move to Eleutheria. Interested, but, according to Winthrop, "very orthodox and zealous for the truth," they would not decide before receiving advice from New England, which Harrison asked for when in New England. Winthrop and other New England religious leaders sent aid to Eleutheria but returned letters to Virginia dissuading Harrison and his congregants from joining under the terms of Sayle's commission.[50] Sayle's project ultimately failed and the Committee for Trade and Plantations sent instructions to Jamaica to rescue any English left on Eleutheria. The involvement of Puritans from at least three other colonies and the expectation that Puritans in various colonies would migrate between colonies in order to further Puritanism in the Americas nevertheless illustrates the sense among Puritans that their religious ties transcended political boundaries. Their understanding of these ties as spiritual forged their "kingdome in Christ" unbound by physical or political geography. Two years later, however, because Harrison had disobeyed Berkeley's orders to conform to Anglicanism, the Lower Norfolk county officials in May 1648 followed the governor's and assembly's orders and commanded the inhabitants of Elizabeth River to stop their illegal meetings. Justices of the Peace Cornelius Lloyd and Edward Lloyd and several other county residents refused to obey, and instead helped William Durand, in trouble for lay preaching, avoid arrest. In response, Berkeley banished Durand and Harrison.[51] Durand later helped move former neighbors and parishioners to the Severn River in Maryland.[52]

Other New England Puritans besides John Winthrop followed these events in Virginia. Humphrey Atherton wrote to John Winthrop, Jr., in August 1648 that "the Church in verginy is in sum truble there minster is cam to boston: I thinke hee is bannished."[53] Two days latter Adam Winthrop wrote also to (his brother) John, Jr., at Pequot that "Mr Harrison the paster of the church at verjenya being banished from thence is arrived heer to consult about some place to settle him selfe and his church some thinke that youer plantation [Connecticut] will be the fittst place for him, but I suppose you have heard more amply before this."[54] Puritans in both Virginia and New England considered themselves enough a part of an intercolonial Puritan world that such a group migration from one colony to the other neither antagonized nor surprised them.

In New England, Harrison reported that his church in Virginia had grown to 118 people "and many more looking towards it."[55] He asked the Massachusetts magistrates and elders "whether their church ought not to remove" because of Anglican prosecution, and, if so, where they should go. The New Englanders answered "that seeing God had carried on his work so graciously hitherto, etc., and that there was so great hope of a far more plentiful harvest at hand, (many of the council being well inclined, etc., and one thousand of the people by conjecture,) they should not be hasty to remove, as long as they could stay upon any tolerable terms." Harrison, however, moved on. Following his expulsion, he stayed in Boston long enough to marry Governor Winthrop's niece, Dorothy Simonds.[56] He returned to Virginia briefly during the winter of 1649 before going to England and then serving as Cromwell's chaplain in Ireland. The Nansemond vestry and parishioners petitioned the Council of State in England to have him reinstated, but to no avail.[57] Continued strong ties to New England (or possibly an attraction to intense spiritual experience that encouraged their support of both Puritanism and Quakerism) may have contributed to Lower Norfolk's being the only region of Virginia to experience significant witchcraft accusations during the seventeenth century. However, the county officials' greater immersion in an Atlantic world in which rationalism was overtaking belief in the supernatural may in part explain why Lower Norfolk officials reacted so differently than New Englanders. Instead of investigating such claims, the Lower Norfolk court imposed a fine of one thousand pounds of tobacco on persons who, by their "divers dangerous & scandalous speeches," had accused "severall women in this Countie" of being witches, thereby ruining "theire reputacons."[58]

After the Puritan leaders' expulsion, Lower Norfolk lacked a minister, though Puritans did enjoy reduced persecution after 1649 English law guaranteed them religious freedom and the 1652 "reduction" of the colony by an English fleet defeated Anglican royalist holdouts and installed Puritan governor Richard Bennett. In 1655 the Lower Norfolk county court, including Francis Emperor, asked Barbadian ship captain (and later father-in-law of Isaac Allerton, Jr.) Thomas Willoughby to try to "p[r]ovide a Minister of Gods word for us" as he traveled to England, presumably to trade. The following year they asked minister John Moore, part of the New England settlement on New Netherland's Long Island. Both attempts apparently failed.[59]

Even during the Interregnum, some hoped to find a more supportive community in New England and migrations to New England for religious reasons continued. In July 1657 Mrs. Rebecca Burrows told the Roxbury church that she had moved there from Virginia in order to "enjoy God in his Ordin. in N. E."[60] However, many Virginia Puritans who had remained in the colony throughout the repression of the 1640s found the 1650s a much better decade. Some nonconformist intercolonial traders, such as Francis Emperor and Isaac Allerton, Jr., appeared for the first time in the Chesapeake during the 1650s. Many Puritans gained political offices in Virginia during the Interregnum. After Richard Bennett helped organize the 1649 migration to Maryland, he stayed for several months in the new settlement on the Severn, but kept his property in Virginia, returned there to live, and became governor of Virginia. Edward Major and Colonel Thomas Dewes, both Speakers of the Assembly under the Commonwealth, were Puritans from Nansemond. John Hill, who had signed the 1642 petition to New England for ministers, stayed in Isle of Wight and in the 1660s, as sheriff, prosecuted Quakers. Edward Lloyd went to Maryland, but his brother Cornelius stayed in Virginia and was a burgess for Lower Norfolk County in the 1652–53 session.[61] The decade of Puritan government provided opportunities for nonconformists to establish and strengthen intertwined economic and religious networks, which remained strong enough to persist after the 1660 Restoration. Some, like Allerton, continued to hold office and retain prominent political as well as economic positions beyond 1660.

Before 1676 nonconformists on the Eastern Shore encountered less oppression than did those elsewhere in Virginia.[62] Nevertheless, a number migrated up the peninsula to Maryland. Visible by 1637, the movement peaked in 1649, the year after William Stone moved to become governor.[63] Stone's move from the Virginia Eastern Shore to Maryland and his recruitment of Southside Virginia Puritans to join him reflected and reinforced ties joining Eastern Shore and Southside Virginia Puritans. At least three ministers served both Southside and Eastern Shore churches.[64] Their presence surely helped attract New England Puritans such as Nathaniel Eaton and Francis Doughty, discussed in Chapter 4. The presence of Dutch Reformed Calvinists on the Eastern Shore and English Puritans who had lived in the Netherlands, and ties between New England Puritans on Long Island and in New Netherland and the Dutch Reformed Church complicated the Puritan leanings of Eastern Shore Virginians. In 1653 when New Netherland Governor Peter Stuyvesant sent Dutch Reformed Dominie Samuel Drisius from New Amsterdam to the Eastern Shore to try to encourage the resumption of intercolonial trade after the 1652 Anglo-Dutch War, Drisius preached at Hungar's parish in Northampton County, where New England Puritan Francis Doughty served as minister.

A prominence in intercolonial trade of individuals who had both Puritan and Dutch ties may have originated in the communities of English Puritan exiles in the Netherlands and been further strengthened by their common Calvinism. Moreover, the strong positions of New England and New Netherland in intercolonial trade may have given Puritan and Dutch Virginians an advantage in intercolonial trade. The connections between religious and economic ties surface in Stuyvesant's sending a Calvinist minister (whom he could reasonably hope would be well received by Puritan Governor Bennett) to address his concerns about trade relations between the colonies.[65] Ultimately, it was Anglican Governor Berkeley rather than Puritan Governor Bennett who approved the proposed trade agreement, illustrating that while religious and economic networks overlapped for many, some Anglicans such as Berkeley hoped to promote intercolonial economic networks while severing them from their frequent connections to religious networks.

Puritans used intercolonial shipping patterns to communicate with one another and build religious networks spanning the English and Dutch Atlantic world. Intercolonial traders from other colonies who spent time in Virginia (such as John Stone, David Peterson De Vries, Edward Gibbons, Isaac Allerton, Jr., and Augustine Herman), were likely to be Puritans or members of the Dutch Reformed Church. In Virginia, Puritans lived in the regions best connected to New England and New Netherland commercially. The migration of intercolonial merchants such as Edward Gibbons, Isaac Allerton, Jr., and Augustine Herman further increased the Calvinist presence in those Chesapeake regions most immersed in intercolonial trade. Local Puritan leaders in Virginia, such as Cornelius and Edward Lloyd, William Stone, Daniel Gookin, Thomas Willoughby, Francis Emperor, and Isaac Allerton, Jr., numbered among the most prominent intercolonial traders.

After the 1650s, webs of Quaker interaction patterns overlapped with those of Puritans in Virginia. Although Quaker reliance on overland trade routes made them less dependent than Puritans on intercolonial shipping, their success in converting Virginia Puritans, their involvement in Atlantic trade, and their focus on creating an intercolonial American community ensured that their presence too would be strongest in the Southside and Eastern Shore intercolonial trading regions.

Quakers very consciously attempted to build a transatlantic and intercolonial religious community. In Virginia, Quakers best succeeded in areas with strong nonconformist traditions because the strength of trade with other colonies provided transportation that put residents in contact with coreligionists elsewhere. In addition, the regions that produced more intercolonial goods and less tobacco had inferior connections to England, less economic success, and therefore appealed less to Anglican ministers, whose scarcity gave them some choice about where they went in the Chesapeake. Quaker belief that every person possessed an inner light (a divine spark whose presence precluded the need for sacraments or ordained clergy to mediate between laity and God) also held special appeal to regions plagued throughout the seventeenth century by a lack of clergy, necessary for full worship in Anglican and Puritan religion.[66]

The first traveling ministers brought Quakerism to Virginia in the 1650s. Conversions happened both when these Public Friends held meetings, and on a more local level, through the activities of family and friends. Between 1652 and 1702 almost 150 Quaker ministers visited America from England. Many of these included Virginia in their travels.[67] They made converts and established Quaker meetings in several counties. Most came from England by way of Barbados and Jamaica, and some had spent time in New England before traveling to the Chesapeake. The first Public Friend whose voyage to Virginia is recorded, Elizabeth Harris of London, arrived in Virginia in 1656 and stayed for about a year. When she returned to England she wrote letters and sent books to those she had converted (or who were Quakers before her arrival).[68] The next Public Friends to go to Virginia, Josias Coale and Thomas Thurston, came in late 1657 and stayed until the following summer.[69] Their activity prompted an order from the General Court to leave Virginia by the first ship available. Virginia officials at first imprisoned Coale and Thurston without pen and ink until a ship arrived but during the winter released them and allowed them to go to Maryland.[70] During the same year, William Robinson, Christopher Holder, and Robert Hodgen arrived. They went first to the Eastern Shore, where they held meetings in private houses. They spent over a year in Virginia, traveling throughout the colony. Robinson spent at least six months in jail there. After their work in Virginia, Robinson continued to New England, where his ministering got him hanged.[71]

In 1661 at least five ministers included Virginia in their trips: Josias Coale (on his second trip), George Wilson, George Rose, Elizabeth Hooten, and Joan Brocksoppe. The end of 1662 found Joseph Nichelson, John Liddal, Jane Millard, and John Perrot in the colony. In 1663 ministers Mary Tompkins, Alice Ambrose, and Wenlock Christison all went to Virginia. John Burnyeat made two trips, in 1665 and 1671. In the latter year, Daniel Gould from Rhode Island also came; William Edmundson came in 1672 and 1676.[72] In 1672, Quaker founder George Fox visited Virginia with Robert Widders, Joseph Lancaster, and George Patteson. In 1677 William Gallway of Scotland died preaching in Nansemond. In 1678 John Bowater visited most of the settled meetings. Thomas Story, Thomas Chalkley, and William Ellis also visited Virginia.[73]

Quakers elicited a stronger reaction from Anglican authorities in Virginia than did Puritans, in part because their belief in a universal inner light posed potential challenges to the social order. Moreover, officials perceived Quaker intercolonial networks, when combined with Quaker pacifism, as a unique threat to the colony that went beyond cultural concerns to impinge on military considerations. Quakers consequently faced imprisonment, fines, whipping, or expulsion. A 1660 act ordered a £100 fine on shipmasters transporting Quakers into the colony, reflecting the Assembly's recognition of shipping's importance to the Atlantic Quaker community that nourished its Virginia members.[74] That officials correctly gauged the importance of shipping can be seen in a 1663 incident in which later the Lower Norfolk County sheriff broke up a meeting "aboard the Shipp Blessinge rideing at anchor in the southern branch of Elizabeth River."[75] George Fox described a 1673 meeting on the Eastern Shore of Maryland at which "there was 4 new England men masters of shipps and marchants: the truth spreads blesed bee the lord."[76] Both incidents illustrate the role of intercolonial shipping in the spread of nonconformity. Because New England officials persecuted Quakers so vigilantly, the New England ship masters and merchants present at the Maryland meeting may have depended wholly on their intercolonial travels to express their Quaker sympathies. William Chichester, the Salem, Massachusetts, master of the *Hopewell*, who deserted his wife in Salem and relocated to Lower Norfolk (the county whose court had heard his 1654 lawsuits with Joseph Huffey and William Selby), later appeared as a Quaker and householder.[77]

Virginia officials quickly noted the intercolonial aspect of Quaker communities. The preamble to a 1663 anti-Quaker statute stated that the Quakers, by assembling in great numbers in different parts of the colony under the pretense of religious worship, spread terror among the people and endangered the public peace; moreover, they kept up a constant and secret correspondence with each other, separated themselves from the rest of the king's subjects, and avoided regular congregations. The Assembly further noted the importance of coastal trade in advancing the development of the intercolonial Quaker networks that strengthened Quaker communities within Virginia. The law instructed shipmasters who brought Quakers to Virginia to keep them on the ship while in the colony, prevent them from communicating with colonists, and carry them out of the colony when the ship left.[78] Virginia officials punished Quaker outsiders much more harshly than those resident in Virginia.

Virginians who converted apparently never suffered worse punishment than a fine, but those who came into the colony from England or other colonies faced harsher penalties such as whipping and imprisonment.[79]

The fact that travel to more tolerant Maryland legitimately took ships through Virginia's portion of the Chesapeake Bay provided cover for Quakers illegally traveling into Virginia, the shipmasters who brought them, and the colonists who hosted them. Ambrose Dixon, a prominent citizen of North-ampton County, having already given bond that he would not entertain the Quaker minister William Robinson, continued to violate the statute forbid-ding the importation of Quakers. Under pretense of transporting them up the Chesapeake Bay to Patuxent, he landed them at Nassawaddox on the Virginia Eastern Shore, where there was a Quaker meeting house, and where Living Denwood (one of Augustine Herman's business associates) welcomed them.[80]

Despite the oppression, some Quakers managed to obtain or maintain important positions in their counties or in the colony. For example, the Quak-ers John Porter, Sr., and his son John Porter, Jr., were both Lower Norfolk justices of the peace in 1665. John Porter, Jr., was sheriff in 1660 and a burgess in 1663. He married the daughter of another justice and burgess, Colonel John Sidney. William Robinson was a justice of the peace in 1660. Mary Emperor, a Quaker, married Puritan Barbadian immigrant Francis Emperor, a justice and sheriff of Lower Norfolk and Princess Anne Counties and a surveyor of Vir-ginia. All of these relatively prominent Quakers lived along or near the Eliza-beth River, an area with strong Puritan traditions.[81]

By the 1670s, Quakers permeated all parts of Virginia. Most numerous on the Eastern Shore and south of the James, they also lived on the Rappahannock and Potomac Rivers and in York County, and included many justices and some burgesses.[82] In 1672 William Edmundson converted the Puritans Richard Bennett and Thomas Dewes, who had been governor and speaker of the Assembly, respectively, during the Interregnum.

The pattern of travel for Quaker missionaries resembled that of other travelers from England to Virginia, following trade routes that commonly dic-tated a first stop in Barbados. Friends considered Barbados the center of American Quakerism before the 1682 establishment of Pennsylvania. In 1661 one Quaker called Barbados "the nursury of the Truth." English Quakers who wrote circular epistles to multiple colonies often named Barbadian Quakers first in their lists of intended audiences.[83] Because ministers so often came to Virginia directly from Barbados and before traveling elsewhere, Virginians usually heard most about Quakers in Barbados (after England) and about Bar-bados in general from these traveling public friends. Because of the prevalent trade patterns, Quakers coming to the Chesapeake from Barbados were more likely to find passage to the Lower Norfolk area than to any other part of Virginia.

From Virginia the ministers went either overland or by sea to other colonies. Ministers traveled overland and by canoe more frequently than other travelers because they wanted to stop at all meetings and potential meetings to try to convert colonists and Indians along the way, and perhaps because Virginia officials' efforts to prevent shipmasters from bringing Quakers into Virginia hindered their maritime access to the colony. Their overland travels therefore depended on precontact Indian trade routes and on guidance from Indians who knew them. Whether maritime or overland, religious travel ultimately relied on networks whose primary purpose was trade.

Apparently these ministers did not plan ahead, instead trusting divine "leadings" and "drawings" to tell them where to go.[84] The continuing missionary tradition fostered a sense of an intercolonial and transatlantic community of Quakers.[85] They relayed more than religious news. In 1697 a friend asked traveling minister William Ellis to look for a family member of his in West Jersey "and take account from them of their welfare, both as to the things of this life and to the Truth."[86] Ministers fostered community by discussing Quakers' experiences in England and other colonies as well as by establishing meetings on the English pattern in the different places they went. George Fox was particularly concerned with establishing a common organization.[87] In August 1671 Fox and several other Quaker ministers left England for its colonies. In October they arrived in Barbados, where Fox met with Deputy Governor Christopher Codrington. The Quaker ministers held several meetings with white and black Barbadians.[88] From there they dispersed, with some remaining in Barbados while others went to Jamaica and from there to various mainland colonies. During the next two years described in Fox's journal, the ministers who had parted ways in Barbados crossed paths several times in their respective travels throughout the English colonies. Fox himself went from Jamaica to Maryland, from Maryland to Rhode Island and through New England, back overland to Maryland, and first arrived in Virginia in 1672.

When Public Friends dispersed in their travels, they planned to reunite at appointed places. They clearly conceived their sphere of operation to include all the English world, and they knew well of the existing commercial, familial, and social networks that allowed them to include all colonies in their travels.[89] George Fox, coming to Maryland from Virginia, reported arriving at John Mayor's house "where wee mett with some from New England which before wee had left behind there, & glad wee were to see each other after our longe travells." Those arriving from New England informed Fox that Quakers had left New England for Jamaica, Ireland, Barbados, the Leeward Islands, New

Jersey, and "the New Countries" to visit Friends.[90] Though Public Friends claimed to follow divine leanings as they felt them, they clearly made some prior arrangements and relied on the intercolonial movement of letters and word of mouth information to know the whereabouts of sympathizers and Quaker settlements. Maryland, perhaps both because of its central location and its policy of tolerance, was a common rendezvous point for Quaker traveling ministers in America. Fox describes going in Maryland to Quaker William Stephens' house, which he described as a place "where frinds mete that hade bee[ne] abrode."[91]

The Quaker traveling ministers stayed with whoever would have them. Their reputation and news of their imminent arrival often preceded them. In Nansemond County, Virginia, when Fox and other Quaker ministers arrived, "there came an old man a Justice to a friend, and saide that Geo ffox was a very famous man." In his journal Fox repeatedly reported his fame and the desire of Quakers and non-Quakers to meet him or to attend meetings. He reported that non-Quakers beyond Somertowne in North Carolina ("their was no friends in those parts") "had heard of mee, & had beene at ye house where wee lay, & had a great desire to heare & see us but miss'd us: The truth sounds abroade everyway."[92] Fox expressed confidence in intercolonial information networks. Several times after describing meeting Quakers in his travels, especially where missionaries had not traveled, he ended his story with the words "the truth spreadeth," noting that information and interest had preceded the arrival of the ministers themselves.[93] Both Friends and "people of the world" welcomed the arrival of Quaker ministers, who had meetings whenever they could, stayed with colonists in settled areas, and, while traveling overland, camped or stayed with Indians. They tried to convert everyone with whom they came into contact.[94]

The Quaker meetings that visiting ministers attended were popular in Virginia. Thomas Jordan wrote to George Fox from Virginia in 1687 that many colonists went to meetings when visiting Friends appeared there "but few will com & sett & waight wth us then they are gon." If more visitors came to Virginia, wrote Jordan, Quakerism there would benefit, clearly suggesting that intercolonial and transatlantic travel strengthened Quaker communities in Virginia.[95]

Quaker ministers' journals enable us to explore how Quakers created an intercolonial community and describe in more detail than many other sources the logistics of overland and coastal travel. They also allow us to consider the overlapping of Indian and colonial geographies on the mainland. Ministers stayed for weeks at a time in each colony and for days at each location. Their practice of traveling overland as well as by sea partly stemmed from their interest in converting Indians, but it also allowed them to avoid officials and reach areas Europeans had sparsely settled, that lacked clergy, and perhaps felt most open to Quaker teachings.

Fox's journal contains several references to passing through "Indians Countryes," often hiring Indian guides to take them part way or canoes to cross rivers.[96] As they traveled, they slept sometimes "in the woods by a fire and sometimes in the Indian Cabbins" until they "came at last & lay at one Indian Kings house and hee & his queen received mee lovingly and his attendants allsoe and laid me a mat to lie upon." At the next Indian town, the chief, who could speak some English, greeted Fox "very lovingly." Fox "spake to him much and his people" and procured from him a second guide who took them from New Castle to Middle Towne in New Jersey.[97] When they returned from New England they again traveled overland on a "longe Journey through the woods toward Mary Land, & soe hired Indians, for it was upon me to passe thorrow ye woods" on the other side of the Delaware Bay. They again passed through many Indian towns and over rivers and bogs, several times hiring Indian guides.[98] Precontact Indian travel routes, then, allowed Quaker ministers (like European traders) to travel overland across colonial boundaries, bypassing the more usual method of travel for colonists. Such association with Indians aided their travels, but could not have endeared them to Anglican officials who already regarded Quakers as subversive, secretive, and dangerous.

Indians served as guides, not just between colonies, but in them. They commonly came to Quaker meetings, sometimes as expressly invited guests, sometimes on their own initiative. Quaker teachings or other aspects of Quaker meetings appealed to some Indians. Their frequent appearance without active Quaker recruiting and their seemingly easy attendance at meetings imply frequent interaction between colonists and Indians. Sometimes interpreters at the meetings were Indians, sometimes colonists.[99] In Maryland, Fox referred to an "Established and setled" meeting at a Friend's house on the Eastern Shore. The "Judge of that Couenty," his wife, three other justices, the high sheriff and his wife, the "Indian Emperour & an Indian King & there speaker" all attended, "& all was very loving." Shortly after that meeting, Fox and his party went by water about ten miles to the Indian town where the tayac lived. Fox had sent him a message ahead of time so that he could ask the "Kings & there Counsell [to come] togeather" for a Quaker meeting. Two justices and some other English Quakers accompanied Fox as interpreters and attendees.[100]

Such meetings indicate Quaker belief in potential for a religious community that not only transcended political borders between English colonies using shipping routes, as Puritans did, but also political/cultural borders between

Indians and Europeans using overland routes discussed in Chapter 1. George Fox's explicit belief that Indians could be Quakers gave Anglican officials further cause for concern. After meeting a werowance "a pretty sober man" in Carolina, Fox argued in the presence of "the Governor & ye people" that "the Light & the spiritt" were present in everyone. As proof, he asked an Indian whether "when he did wronge, was not there somethinge in him, that did . . . reproove him." The Indian confirmed that he did in fact possess such a conscience, which according to Fox, provided proof that Indians possessed inner light just as Europeans did.[101] Many Indians saw great distinctions separating Quakers from other English colonists. Indeed, Jaspar Dankaerts reported in 1679 that "The Indians . . . say [the Quakers] are not Englishmen, always distinguishing them from other Englishmen. . . . The Indians say 'they are not Christians, they are like ourselves.'"[102] Such an identification with Quakers may have resulted both from Quaker theology and from Quaker travel patterns.

The combination of Quakers' challenges to such cultural boundaries and their disregard for political borders was what caused such concern among Anglican officials. Thomas Thurston, a Public Friend who traveled in several colonies, often stayed with Indians from whom he received "the most Courteous Entertainment." When Virginia officials jailed Thurston in 1657, some Susquehannocks with whom he had stayed came to visit him in prison.[103] Susquehannocks lived in Maryland, Delaware, New York, and what became Pennsylvania, so in this instance Quaker travel encouraged Indian intercolonial travel, facilitating cultural and political boundary crossing, not a situation calculated to improve Quaker standing with Virginia officials. Just as the Quaker combined use of overland and coastal travel depended on both Indian and European (and increasingly overlapping) trade routes, Quakers' belief in the possibility of a spiritual community including Europeans and Indians depended on the existence of already overlapping and interacting physical worlds. Sometimes Indians they met spoke English. The journals make it obvious that Indians interacted with English colonists in a variety of ways on a casual or daily basis, particularly in areas less central to the English.

The travels of English Friends in American colonies facilitated the intercolonial travel of American Quakers. While George Fox and other Quaker ministers were in Barbados, John Jay, described by Quaker John Stubbs as "a pretty rich planter in Barbados," decided to accompany the ministers to New England, New Jersey, Long Island, Delaware, Maryland, Virginia, and Carolina. After his travels through the mainland colonies, Jay returned to his wife, plantation, and family in Barbados, taking news about the mainland colonies that would contribute to American Quakers' sense that they belonged to a shared world.[104] Other American Quakers also used English traveling Friends' journeys to facilitate their own intercolonial travel. While in Elizabeth River, Lower Norfolk County, Fox reported that "wee passed about 6 miles by land and water to take in freinds for Maryland" before leaving Virginia.[105]

After returning to England, Fox and others wrote letters encouraging American Quakers to visit other colonies. In a 1684 circular letter, Fox urged Friends to visit Virginia and Carolina.[106] In 1699 James Dickinson encouraged Friends to "visit remote parts that want help; as Virginia, Carolina, New England, Barbados, Jamaica, Antigua, Nevis."[107] Fox suggested that Public Friends in Pennsylvania and New Jersey, where there were more in ministry, "divide [themselves] to other meetings, and two and two to visit friends" in New England, Maryland, Virginia, and Carolina.[108]

Fox's writing also reveals his expectation that Quakers would continue to travel between colonies beyond his explicit recommendations. Quakers sometimes in fact traveled across intercolonial boundaries not to proselytize but simply to attend meetings. In a 1673 letter from the Worcester jail to Quakers in Virginia, Fox wrote that if they went "over again to Carolina," they should ask Captain Nathaniel Batts, "the Old Governor," about a paper Fox had left with him to read to "the Emperor and his Thirty Kings under him of the Tusrowres, who were to come to Treat for Peace with the People of Carolina."[109]

Persecution itself could encourage communication, travel, and migration between American Quakers. Fox reported a meeting at the Clifts in Maryland "and there Came a Justice from potomake in virginia a prety man & had beene under persecution & threatned by the preeste & others hee & his man came 40 milles on fote hee hath a greate love to the truth."[110] John Copeland, a Quaker who had his ears clipped in Massachusetts, later moved to southern Virginia, possibly hoping to escape persecution.[111] George Wilson, persecuted in New England in 1661, went to Virginia but fared worse there and died in jail in Jamestown.[112] Quaker minister William Edmundson reported that, having visited in North Carolina in 1672, he met Henry Phelps. Edmundson wrote that "Henry Phillips and his wife had been convinc'd of the Truth in New-England, and came there to live (1665), who having not seen a Friends for Seven Years before they wept for Joy to see us."[113]

Fox and other ministers clearly tried to foster conformity and a sense of unity among Quakers throughout the English Atlantic world. In Rhode Island during the summer of 1672, Fox reported that he and those accompanying him came from New England to Rhode Island for a general meeting, which they had encouraged and helped organize. Planned to last ten days, "by the Continued comeing of people in sloopes from divers other Collonies & Jurisdictions it Continued longer." Fox planned the 1672 Rhode Island General meeting as the first of many that would supplement annual meetings within each colony.[114] During his visit, Maryland may have held a general meeting as well. For several days after the 1672 Rhode Island General Meeting many of the Quakers stayed and had more large gatherings. At one of them "A Marriage for Example sake," which Quakers and non-Quakers attended, took place at the house of the Quaker and former Deputy Governor William Coddington to serve as "an Example to all the rest of the Jurisdictions, some [people] out of many places was there."[115] Unity in ceremony would foster the Quakers' sense of belonging to an Atlantic community of Friends.

Quakers also sent circular letters to meetings, which read them publicly and sent them on.[116] These epistles and those sent from one American meeting to another had the potential to produce mutual shared assumptions on a variety of subjects. Those who carried the letters formed further contacts between meetings, carrying news and experiences from one place to another. In the summer of 1672, Fox, still in Rhode Island, gave a public lecture recounting his travels in Jamaica, Virginia, and through "the Indian Countrey" to New England. He sent a copy of the narrative to Thomas Rouse in Barbados to be read in meetings there. He intended that it also be read at the London meetings and copies of it distributed throughout Quaker meetings in England.[117] In addition to organizing meetings to conform to a common model, Fox and other ministers hoped to encourage American Quakers to continue communicating with one another and maintain their intercolonial and transatlantic community. He continued in his writings to encourage them to travel and hold a yearly North American meeting. He also wanted them to send minutes and epistles with religious and other advice from meeting to meeting.[118]

With its founding in 1682, Pennsylvania became a new center for Quakerism in America. The large-scale migrations of Quakers to the new colony and the political power of Quakers within that colony made Pennsylvania a de facto, though not official, influence on other Quakers and also made it a primary line of communication between American Quakers and the London meeting. Some Pennsylvanians adopted a sense of responsibility for Quakerism in America.[119] In 1683 William Penn suggested "a general meeting of friends from New England to Carolina." In 1684, representatives from Maryland and Rhode Island held a yearly meeting where they made plans for another yearly meeting and asked meetings in the colonies to "send two or three for each province to our Yearly Meeting here being a center or middle part that so communion and blessed union may be preserved among all."[120] These general meetings were not to include Quakers from Caribbean colonies, perhaps reflecting that the importance of overland travel for Quakers on the mainland and the presence of possible Indian converts created a distinction between island and mainland colonies just beginning among other

English colonists. Their overland travels perhaps led them to an early perception that as Restoration colonies filled in the once vast spaces between England's mainland colonies, they were less "islands" of English settlement, like the Caribbean, but began to form a contiguous whole that did not include the Caribbean.

Tracing the spread of one Quaker heterodoxy and the effort to prevent the spread of another shows the facility with which ideas spread within the Quaker intercolonial network. "Perrot's heresy," which involved a denial of all outward signs of worship (including removing one's hat as a sign of respect to God when another Friend prayed), began in England in 1661. John Perrot carried his doctrine to the Caribbean and thence to Virginia and Maryland. It spread eventually to New York and Rotterdam.[121] In a similar case thirty years later Pennsylvania Friend George Keith attacked the Quaker belief that the inward Christ alone saved, with or without faith in a historic Christ or in biblical scriptures. In 1692 the Philadelphia Yearly Meeting disowned as many as one quarter of the Quakers in Pennsylvania and New Jersey for ascribing to Keith's heresy. Soon afterward, Quakers in Barbados, Virginia, Maryland, New Jersey, Long Island, and Rhode Island censored him, indicating both that the news had spread and that Quakers considered it useful to voice opinions across the distances their community spanned.[122]

Because Quakerism combined an intercolonial community with significant challenges to the social order, with a greater acceptance of Indians as potential spiritual equals, and with pacifism, officials perceived them as posing a unique threat that rested on intercolonial communication and strengthened other kinds of intercolonial dangers, particularly those posed by Indians' traveling. Officials responded with increased attempts to prevent Quaker travel, thereby attempting to make their political borders serve as religious boundaries as well. Though James II's "Declaration for Liberty of Conscience and Indulgence in Religious Matters" assured toleration for nonconformists, and the Glorious Revolution in 1688 assured its continuance, Quakers in Virginia remained subject to suspicion.[123] The strength they derived from their intercolonial community, combined with the challenges they presented to social order, created a threat, especially with regard to fears about Indians crossing political and cultural boundaries. As a result, persecution of Quakers continued and officials increased their attempts to create firm religious boundaries along their political borders.

In 1691 when France and England were at war, Virginia Governor Francis Nicholson and his Council heard that the Quakers of Pennsylvania had declared that if the French and Indians came to their settlements armed with rifles, tomahawks, and torches, Pennsylvania would offer no resistance. On hearing this report, Virginia councilors worried that if French colonists and their Indian allies invaded the Chesapeake they would obtain provisions in Pennsylvania and that the pacifism of Penn's colony would provide them with a safe retreat after raiding Maryland and Virginia. The Virginia Assembly noted that recently many Quaker meetings in Virginia had assembled without informing the local authorities, as the Toleration Act required. The Council worried that if the French and their Indian allies took Pennsylvania, they would learn Virginia's strengths and weaknesses through the frequent communication between Virginia and Pennsylvania Quakers and through the Quaker practice of welcoming Indians into their midst. The French and their allies could thereby discover the best way to attack the Chesapeake.

Nicholson and his Council issued a proclamation warning Virginia Quakers not to "come together" in a general assembly unless they had informed officials of their meetings. Most importantly, Quakers must send a message immediately to the nearest "magistrate" if a Pennsylvania Quaker came with a message from the Pennsylvania government. Magistrates were to summon any traveling Quakers instantly and question them closely, finding out where they came from, why, and their destination. If the replies seemed suspicious, the magistrate was to send the travelers to Jamestown.[124]

Meanwhile the Church of England increased its presence in Virginia. Henry Compton, bishop of London (with authority over the colonial church) for the final decade of Charles II's reign and again under William and Mary, took much greater interest in the colonial church than had his predecessors. In 1677 he initiated an investigation into the quality of Virginia clergy, and in 1680 required that colonial governors ensure that parish clergy possessed certificates issued by Compton himself. He sent clergy to Virginia and for the first time appointed a commissary (bishop's agent) to oversee church governance in the colony.[125] James Blair, commissary during the 1690s, used increased transatlantic flow of clergy and money to strengthen Anglicanism in the colony. He failed in some attempts to assert the Church's authority, as in his effort to reestablish church courts to discipline clergy and laity for their moral failings. Nicholson, as governor of Virginia, supported the effort as part of an overall desire to bring England's colonies into greater conformity with one another and more firmly under England's control, and backed plans to establish the College of William and Mary, which would serve in part as a training ground for Anglican clergy. The decade also saw renewed support for the appointing of an American bishop, and in 1701 the establishing of the Society for the Propagation of the Gospel in Foreign Parts, an Anglican missionary society that devoted much of its attention to England's unchurched colonists in America.[126]

Anglican church officials, in their criticisms of Quakers, detailed the ways in which Quakers created and maintained their intercolonial networks. In November 1702 the Anglican (and former Quaker) George Keith and a committee of six others were charged with investigating the state of the Church of England in America. Their report included twenty-four headings on the ways in which Quakers supported their meetings and schools, including "organization, uniformity of discipline, circulation of literature, . . . active missionary enterprise," and collections of a common fund with which they financed printing and meeting house buildings. Keith also noted that Quakers strengthened their position in the colonies "By keeping there Trade within themselves and maintaining a strict Correspondence and Inteligence over all parts where they are" and "By suffering none of themselves to marry but with those of their own profession."[127] Documenting the scope and efficiency of the Quaker network, the Anglican Reverend John Talbot, in a 1703 letter to the secretary of the Society for the Propagation of the Gospel, expressed his concern that "The Quakers compass sea and land to make proselytes; they send out yearly a parcel of vagabond Fellows that ought to be taken up and put in Bedlam. . . . Their preaching is of cursing and Lyes, poysening the souls of the people with damnable errors and heresies, and not content with this in their own Territories or Pennsylvania, but they travel with mischief over all parts as far as they can goe, over Virginia and Maryland, and again through Jersey and New York as far as New England."[128]

Keith and his fellow committee members recognized clearly the links between intercolonial religious networks, the marriages that formed long-distance family ties, and the colonial shipping that shaped seventeenth-century intercolonial networks and held them together. His comments on Quaker endogamy and trade would have held for Puritans in the seventeenth-century Atlantic world as well. Quaker and Puritan bonds functioned for some like family ties in providing a basis of trust on which to form commercial linkages.[129] Enough Puritans (including merchants) converted to Quakerism to procure similar and overlapping networks. The movements of ministers, the best documented, provide the geographical outlines for more general migration patterns. Ministers' movements both created and reflected the sense among nonconformists that they belonged to communities not bounded by political colonial borders. The fact that these networks mirrored almost exactly the intercolonial trade routes (encompassing most fully those regions of Virginia that traded most extensively with other colonies) substantiates the high degree to which the religious, family, and economic networks intertwined.

The Church of England changed by the end of the century, exhibiting greater toleration that accompanied the growing influence of latitudinarian beliefs in rational religion. Religious dissent increased in England after 1660.[130] The Toleration Act of 1688 assured non-Anglican protestants the right to worship and hold office, so Anglican officials' victories in confirming Virginia's official status as Anglican did not limit Virginians' options as it might have had Berkeley succeeded in suppressing them in the 1640s. In 1699 the House of Burgesses reduced Virginians' church attendance requirement to once every other month, recognizing that Virginia's geography and demography and history limited the colony's ability to impose a more meaningful Anglicanism on unwilling inhabitants.[131] Puritans' and Quakers' persistence to that time had depended on intercolonial ties that allowed them to survive until Virginia allowed greater toleration. Those intercolonial ties did not end with toleration, but continued into the eighteenth century, existing alongside the elaborated transatlantic ties to England that accounted for the growth of the Anglican Church, and ensured that Virginians' religious lives, while lived largely in local parishes and meeting houses, kept them firmly ensconced within the British Atlantic.[132]

Because Anglican officials realized the dependency of nonconformists in Virginia on their links to other American colonies and to England, they attempted to limit the religious travel of Quakers and Puritans across colonial borders. While all colonists recognized the necessity of economic links between colonies, in the case of religious intercolonial networks of nonconformists, authorities contested the fluidity of colonial boundaries. Virginia Anglicans attempted to strengthen and add cultural meaning to intercolonial political boundaries in response to the intercolonial religious networks described in this chapter. The interaction between nonconformists and Anglican officials in Virginia embodied a contest over the fluidity of boundaries and over the cultural definition of Virginia. Easy movement between colonies strengthened Quaker and Puritan communities south of the James River and on the Eastern Shore. As long as other colonies remained only partially Anglican, fluid boundaries allowed some degree of religious diversity in Virginia, despite periods of persecution at the hands of Anglican officials. In response to nonconformists' reliance on porous intercolonial borders, Virginia officials tried to seal those boundaries, at least against Quakers and Puritans. By the end of the seventeenth century, when Virginia officials, impelled by their colonists' frequent intercolonial interactions, succeeded in defining Virginia as an Anglican place theoretically, its history of religious diversity was fully established and facilitated the successes of future nonconformist proselytizers. We must, therefore, reconceive Virginia as a place where intercolonial trade and travel altered colonists' religious choices and allowed them to contest officials' attempts to make Virginia an exclusively Anglican colony.

Chapter 6

Chesapeake Slavery in Atlantic Context

Virginia's Atlantic world context powerfully shaped the nature of slavery as it evolved there. Slavery, like indentured servitude before, marked a significant departure from English labor practices. The widespread use of indentured servitude and slavery in Virginia required that laborers move, voluntarily or involuntarily, from one part of that Atlantic world to another. Masters and legislators throughout the English Atlantic communicated with and emulated one another (and sometimes their Spanish, Portuguese, and Dutch counterparts) as they moved farther and farther from English traditions of servitude. Servants and slaves likewise observed and attempted to affect regional variations and temporal changes in labor systems. As a result, English American slavery developed within a context of intercolonial conversations—spoken and implicit—regarding the parameters of the institution and the choices available to individuals living within it.

Information about enslaved Africans in Spanish and Portuguese America reached England in the sixteenth century and affected future colonists' earliest impressions that the place of Africans in a colonial American context was as slaves whose labor profited European colonists. That the earliest African-Americans in Virginia arrived as slaves (and with Iberian names) reinforced those impressions. Later in the century, migrations from the Caribbean to Virginia and trade between the two regions shaped the cultural expectations of both slaveowners and slaves in the Chesapeake. Connections between the Eastern Shore and New Netherland and New England affected the lives of African-Americans in Accomack and Northampton Counties.

This chapter argues that the Atlantic context that encompassed Chesapeake localities defined the emerging institution of slavery in Virginia. The origins of colonial slavery ensured that that Atlantic context would profoundly influence colonists and slaves as they set parameters for the institution in Virginia. First, because the vast majority of slaves in the seventeenth century were imported into rather than born in Virginia, their very presence in the Chesapeake depended on the Atlantic world. Second, because until the 1670s most of them came not directly from Africa but from other colonies, the ways in which the institution had developed in other places informed the decisions of almost all participants. Because little English precedent for perpetual inherited enslavement of an imported and ethnically distinct population existed, English colonists expected that Iberian American identification of Africans with slavery would apply to their own colonial projects. Once they had brought the institution to their own colonies, English colonists in different locations looked to one another when altering their inherited English legal and social apparatus to define the institution of slavery in their particular colonial contexts.

Consequently, the Atlantic context in which seventeenth-century Virginia existed affected the pace and nature of Virginia's transition to a slave society throughout its disparate locales. In the early seventeenth century many English colonists first encountered Africans as slaves in Spanish and Portuguese colonies.[1] Despite the complexity of English attitudes toward Africans in Africa and in Europe, English people knew that Africans in the Americas were not servants, but slaves who toiled involuntarily for the enrichment of their masters.[2] The earliest Africans in Virginia arrived in just that situation, a stark manifestation of the impact of the existing international context. English adoption of Iberian words such as negro, mulatto, and pickaninny (pequeño niño) illustrate the affect of prior Iberian models on English perceptions of Africans and African-Americans in America.[3] More importantly, most English Virginians first encountered Africans as slaves for sale, available because of the slavery existent in Spanish and Portuguese America by the early seventeenth century; indeed, Virginia's first census identified Africans only by first names, most commonly Iberian first names.[4] Virginia tobacco planters may intentionally have sought Spanish Caribbean slaves with experience cultivating tobacco. In 1618 Bermuda planter and Virginia Company shareholder Robert Rich wrote to his brother Nathaniel that he intended to have a Caribbean slave plant "west endy plants, wherein hee hath good scill," and asked his brother to purchase from Captain Powell (who had been to the Spanish Caribbean to buy slaves for Bermuda planters) another slave named Francisco because of his exceptional "judgment in the curing of tobackoe."[5] The very close relationship between Virginia and Bermuda during that decade, when Virginians also acquired Spanish slaves, and the involvement of the Rich family in both colonies, makes it likely Virginia planters also knew about Spanish Caribbean slaves' tobacco expertise and of Bermuda planters' strategies to profit from such expertise.

Slaves lived in Virginia beginning in the 1610s, but Virginia was not a slave society (one dependent on the institution and defined by it) until the end of the century. Rather, indentured servants, most of them English, traded four to seven years of labor and freedom (at first to the Virginia company and for most of the century to individual masters) for a chance at economic independence if they survived their servitude. The system of indentured servitude as it developed in Virginia marked a significant departure from English servitude, with fewer protections for servants and an increasing regard for them as commodities.[6] The system met a demand for labor throughout England's American colonies, and poor economic conditions in England ensured a willing supply of servants until the 1660s. Colonists in England's other colonies adopted this system Virginia investors and planters had developed, and indentured servants found themselves growing cotton and tobacco in the Caribbean and Maryland by the 1630s and, in smaller numbers, working in New England as well. Colonists thereby created a system of servitude that was uniquely American; one that many contemporaries regarded as inhumane in comparison to English servitude.[7]

While colonial indentured servitude represented a new and distinctly American creation, it nonetheless depended on a tradition of English servitude, as historians have long recognized. Historians now understand that a (largely Iberian) Atlantic context also shaped the early seventeenth-century role of African Americans in Virginia, and are working to understand the impact of transatlantic connections linking colonies to Africa. However, the continued influence of intercolonial relations on Virginia slavery and race relations later in the century has received less attention, despite repeated recognition of two relevant facts: that much of Virginia's seventeenth-century enslaved population came to the Chesapeake from other colonies and that the men most likely to purchase slaves and create laws to define their status and govern them were members of a highly mobile group of English Atlantic elites.[8]

In the 1630s Providence Island off the coast of Nicaragua and Tortuga (Association) off the coast of Hispaniola, both governed by the Puritan Providence Island Company, became the first English colonies whose populations were over half enslaved Africans. The English on both islands feared those slave majorities, partly because of the military danger they posed in the event of Spanish attack, and partly because they might rebel against their English masters, as the slaves on Providence Island in fact did in 1638. Both African and English residents of the Providence Island Company's possessions moved to Virginia. The English on Providence Island, to increase the ratio of English to African residents, considered selling slaves to Virginia and other colonies on several occasions and in 1638 did sell some to Virginia and New England.[9] When the English fled Tortuga after a Spanish attack in 1635, Dutch captain David Peterson DeVries, as we have seen, carried fifty of them to Virginia, where many remained.[10] Those English who remained on or returned to Tortuga abandoned the island for good in 1638 out of fear of their lack of control over the black majority on the island—a demographic situation they themselves had created. In 1641 the Spanish conquered Providence Island. Refugees from those two evacuations likely dispersed to locations throughout the English Atlantic world, including Virginia. They took with them both their conviction that African slave labor made economic sense ("more easily kept, and perpetually servants" according to the Providence Island Company) and their experiences that indicated to them that such laborers were safe only if carefully controlled.[11]

In the 1650s and early 1660s, the Dutch cultivated ties between their colonies of New Netherland and Curaçao, in part to facilitate the importation of slaves into New Amsterdam to labor there, "but . . . moreover [to be] exported to the English and other Neighbors."[12] Some of the Africans who came to Virginia via this route spent time in New Amsterdam before their resale to the Chesapeake. The forty-one Africans from Benin who arrived on the Eastern Shore as Edmund Scarborough's slaves in 1656 had spent seven months in New Amsterdam. At midcentury, Virginia elites with connections to New Netherland were more likely to own African slaves than were colonists without Dutch contacts. Also at midcentury, Barbados became the first English American colony to move from indentured servitude to slave labor when acquisition of African slaves accompanied the colonists' hugely successful turn from tobacco and cotton to sugar production, perhaps with the aid of Dutch merchants and African slaves from Pernambuco, Brazil. Those who could afford to purchase African slaves did so, preferring lifelong laborers to temporary servants.[13] This transition occurred under Governor Philip Bell, who had been governor of Providence Island in the early 1630s.[14] Barbados's transition to sugar and slavery thus occurred in an Atlantic context as well, one in which English planters and governors had already learned that slavery presented dangers as well as economic benefits and therefore should be encouraged but controlled. After sugar production began, Barbados gained a reputation throughout the Atlantic world as the worst English colony for laborers, and planters found it increasingly difficult to procure willing servants.

Having developed a profitable slave system in their own colony, Barbadians, through migration and communication, clearly catalyzed the development of slavery in South Carolina (where Caribbean migrants, mainly Barbadians, made up nearly half the early colonists and office holders) and Jamaica. Those Barbadians who colonized Carolina and Jamaica during the late seventeenth century brought the institution with them.[15] This connection between slavery in Barbados and in South Carolina and Jamaica has implications for the institution's expansion in the Chesapeake. Virginia and Barbados traded extensively with one another throughout the colonial period, Barbados providing Virginia with a principle source of slaves until the final quarter of the seventeenth century.[16] Prior to the 1670s, Virginia merchants and planters with intercolonial connections (to New Netherland or Barbados) thus possessed an advantage over others in acquiring slaves. When transatlantic slave traders bringing Africans directly to the Chesapeake began to arrive in the 1670s, the much larger scale of this trade quickly surpassed intercolonial trade, but enslaved and free immigrants from the Caribbean continued to arrive in the Chesapeake into the eighteenth century, and their experience with the organization and regulation of labor in a slave society provided them with an influence over Chesapeake slavery likely greater than the Europan migrants or slaves from Africa who outnumbered them. Virginia's transition from indentured servitude to African slave labor as the primary unfree labor source occurred largely during the last quarter of the seventeenth century, contemporaneous with the Barbadian-influenced settlement of South Carolina, when as many Barbadians migrated to the Chesapeake as to South Carolina or Jamaica.[17]

Notwithstanding these connections, most historians have assumed that the Virginia slave system developed independently from that of other American colonies. Discussions on the origins of Chesapeake slavery have focused principally on the questions of whether slavery or racism came first, and what specific economic and social factors in Virginia and England accounted for the transition from indentured servitude to slavery as the primary source of unfree labor.[18] Although historians have acknowledged that the prior existence of the slave trade made the increase in Virginia's enslaved population possible, they have paid little attention to the relationship between the previous existence of slavery elsewhere in the Americas and its evolution in the Chesapeake.[19]

Barbados, as the most powerful seventeenth-century English colony, a slave society by 1650, and a continual source thereafter of intercolonial and transatlantic migrants, played a particularly crucial role in the growth of Chesapeake slavery. Seventeenth-century Virginia planters well knew that many Caribbean colonists were growing rich using enslaved African laborers. Strong commercial ties between Virginia and the English West Indies fostered communication between the colonies. Virginia planters' contacts with Caribbean planters and merchants, as well as with the English and foreign traders who supplied West Indian planters, aided Virginia's transition to slavery. Chesapeake planters, like Barbadian planters, preferred permanent to temporary laborers if they could afford them and if they could gain access to traders who could supply them. Before 1675, when almost all slaves came to the Chesapeake via other colonies, intercolonial migrants and traders held a distinct advantage because they possessed access to merchants in Barbados and New Netherland who could provide them with slaves. As early as the 1640s, shipmasters from Barbados sold slaves to planters in Lower Norfolk County, demonstrating that the economic and social links between that region of Virginia and Barbados facilitated Lower Norfolk's early acquisition of slaves.[20]

Most planters (perhaps especially those tobacco planters from the "central" areas of Virginia best connected to England but least connected to other colonies) had great difficulty acquiring enslaved laborers. Those who did, such as William Byrd, relied on Barbadian immigrants in the Southside counties, like Thomas Walke, to help them establish the Caribbean contacts needed to acquire slaves. Because of their English connections, however, Virginia planters between the James and Potomac Rivers had best access to the steady supply of servants who arrived in Virginia during its first fifty years of English colonization. But after the early 1660s the pace of servant immigration stagnated and in the 1680s and 1690s it fell. Because population growth continued rapidly through this period, the ratio of servants to planters declined beginning in the early 1660s. In the decade following the start of that decline, the majority of slaves continued to arrive in Virginia in small numbers on intercolonial trading vessels. Intercolonial traders continued to have the best access to those slaves, and between the early 1660s and the mid-1670s were likely most important as sources of unfree labor. In the late 1670s when ships began to sail directly from Africa to the Chesapeake, wealthier tobacco planters from the Peninsula and Middle Peninsula regained first access to labor, because their greater wealth meant they could afford to purchase larger numbers of slaves and thus made them more attractive to ship captains and the Royal African Company.[21]

Other American colonies and the regions of the Chesapeake best connected to them, were thus central to Virginia's acquisition of slaves before the mid-1670s. For the remainder of the century, when slaves came to the Chesapeake from both Africa and the Caribbean, an Atlantic context continued to shape the development of Chesapeake slavery, which developed partly in ways specific to the Chesapeake demographic and economic context, and partly in ways reflecting a broader Atlantic world in which English American slavery grew and became institutionalized. Many aspects of Virginia's plantation system developed with indentured servants as the principle laborers, most notably the ability to buy and sell laborers (and a resulting regard for workers as property) and the system of gang labor.[22] These developments, and an increased length of service (four- to seven-year contracts rather than one-year contracts) reflect important departures from English servitude and were, like slavery, developments that spread via intercolonial communication and imita-

tion. Barbados and Maryland planters followed Virginia's lead in using indentured servants to populate their colony with laborers and in restricting the
rights of those servants more than was customary or legal in England. Thus,
even those aspects of slavery that built on indentured servitude reflect earlier
intercolonial communication as well as later emulation of Barbadian modifications specific to slavery.

Migrations such as that of the Emperor family facilitated the most important and most direct Barbadian influences on Chesapeake slavery. Individual
migrations from Barbados to Virginia, like those of the Emperor family, were
part of a widespread movement of people during the middle and late seventeenth century. A 1667 writer claimed that between 1648 and 1658, twenty-four
hundred Europeans left Barbados for Virginia and Surinam.[23] The emigration
that began in the 1640s continued into the eighteenth century and involved
tens of thousands of people, free and slave. Between 1660 and 1675 alone seven
to eight thousand Europeans departed for other islands, the mainland, or
England.[24] In 1680 Governor Jonathan Atkins of Barbados compiled a list
including the names and destinations of the 593 Europeans granted tickets to
leave the island in 1679. The governor's list reveals a wide dispersal of Barbadian emigrants, including seventeen large-scale planters who left in 1679, indicating a high degree of mobility among a class made up entirely of
slaveholders.[25] A total of 154 migrants went to other Caribbean Islands; 151
went to Europe, primarily England; 233 went to the English mainland colonies.
Of the last, sixty-two went to Virginia, the second most popular destination
after Boston, which attracted sixty-eight Barbadians. Carolina was the third
most popular destination with thirty-eight. Jamaica attracted thirty-five. In
Carolina, Caribbean immigrants made up half the colonists between 1670 and
1680 and transferred many political and social practices, including those surrounding the institution of slavery.[26]

The Carolina experience raises significant questions concerning Virginia's
history. The influx from Barbados to Virginia came after Barbados had established itself as a slave society but with Virginia still in the midst of the process.
Virginia, as a more fully established colony with a far larger population than
Carolina during the late seventeenth century, felt the affect of Barbadians pro-
portionally less than did Carolina.[27] The numbers of Barbadian immigrants
reported in the 1679 statistics nevertheless sufficed to make a significant
impact. Those who went to Virginia, like those who went to Carolina, included
slaveholders who moved with creole slaves and experience with the successful
use of them, and also had contacts with slave traders. Slaves, their masters, and
others who had experienced life in a Caribbean slave society based their
actions and interactions in Virginia on slavery and race relations in Barbados,

and thus the Caribbean experience helped shape the institution of slavery and ideas about racial distinction as they acquired explicit legal definition and regulation in Virginia. Even those planters who brought small numbers of slaves found themselves, in a period when there were few Africans in Virginia, economically and socially advantaged in the Chesapeake.

Family connections like those the Emperors maintained with Barbados, in some cases accompanied by documented acquisitions of what in seventeenth-century Virginia constituted large numbers of slaves, show the importance of such intercolonial contacts to the procurement of African labor. Although the sixty-two Barbadians who moved to Virginia in 1679 made up a small percentage of the total Virginia population of between thirty-five thousand and forty thousand in that year, the Barbados colonists who brought Africans with them to the Chesapeake in the middle and late seventeenth century constituted a far higher proportion of the slaveholders in the colony. Several held prominent political positions in Virginia (and Maryland) and thus could influence developing legislation governing slavery.[28] Such men also provided valuable word-of-mouth information about slaves and slavery, which gave them the potential to shape the social and economic organization of the institution as it developed in the Chesapeake. Additionally, with estimates of an African population in Virginia of only between one thousand and three thousand in 1674 and still only between six thousand and ten thousand in 1699, the dozens documented as arriving from Barbados after living there as slaves constituted an important component of the total.[29]

The Barbadian slave society in which both slaveowners and slaves were immersed affected them in concrete and personal ways. In 1685 the Barbados Council paid Francis Tully Emperor and four other men between £17 and £24 each "in compensation for . . . negro[es] executed."[30] For those slaves, masters, and neighbors who knew the executed slaves, Barbadian legal and social definitions of slavery were not abstractions. Emperor learned in Barbados what white Barbadians considered appropriate responses to particular black behavior (or white suspicions)—knowledge that he brought back to Virginia with him. The Emperors' slaves who knew of the execution and subsequently moved from the island to the Chesapeake might have either drawn assumptions about limits they could not cross or tried to set different limits in a colony new to them and newer to slavery.[31] This documented incident, as well as countless daily interactions and experiences that went unrecorded, shaped the definition of slavery for Emperor and his slaves and would in part determine their behavior in Virginia.

The experiences the Emperors and their slaves brought with them were important not only because of the examples they set, or the opinions Francis

Tully Emperor may have expressed at the County Court, but also because Emperor had friends and neighbors who held positions in Virginia's colonial legislative bodies, the House of Burgesses and the Council.[32] Similarities between the slave codes in the two colonies suggest that whether brought by Emperor or by others with similar connections, Virginians and Barbadians participated in a continuing Atlantic discussion about slavery and referred to these communications when constructing their own legal definitions of the institution. Furthermore, Francis Tully Emperor provided slaves to others in Princess Anne and Norfolk Counties, and possibly elsewhere in Virginia.[33] Virginians for whom he procured slaves—for whom slaves came from a Barbadian merchant family—may have been more likely to associate slavery with Barbados and therefore look to a Barbadian example. Thus Emperor's role as a slave dealer strengthened any example he set or advice he gave about slavery. The slaves who moved may have had only prior Barbadian experience with which to understand the Chesapeake.

Like the Emperors and their acquaintances, other Barbadians brought or arranged to bring African slaves to the Chesapeake. John Lownes, the Barbadian embroiled in an indenture dispute with his servant bricklayer William Eale, received a headright for "Mary a Negro" and sold a slave to fellow Norfolk County resident (and Dutch immigrant) William Mosely in 1652.[34] Thomas Goodrich, who claimed seven slaves as headrights in 1653, was a close enough friend to Virginia-Barbados ship captain Matthew Wood (also a partner of Lownes) that he administered Wood's estate after his death the same year.[35] Thomas Mathew (whose disagreements with Doeg Indians helped precipitate the Virginia-Susquehannock War of 1675) exemplified Barbadian immigrants who aided the growth of slavery in Virginia. In February 1680 the Northumberland County court, in a notable example of one man's ambition propelling the migration of many, granted Mathew thirty-eight hundred acres of land "for the transportation of seventy-six persons into the colony, including himself and ten negroes from Barbadoes."[36] Mathew lived as merchant and planter in the Northern Neck where he could only have organized his Virginia plantation based in part on his Barbadian experiences. As justice of Northumberland in 1672 and 1676 and a member of the House of Burgesses in 1676, not only did he himself engage in the direct importation of Barbadian slaves into Virginia, but he also occupied a position through which he could influence others in the colony, both by example and persuasion.[37]

Several other immigrants from Barbados gained prominence in Virginia.[38] Henry Applewhite first appeared in Isle of Wight County in 1668.[39] He maintained his connections with Barbados until at least 1679, when he transported two servants from there to Virginia and appeared in the Barbados census still owning 272 acres, nine bought servants, four hired servants, and 216 slaves in St. Thomas parish.[40] Barbados emigrant lists did not record the transport of slaves, but Henry Applewhite, who had so many slaves in Barbados, likely brought slaves as well as servants to Virginia and certainly brought knowledge about slavery that he shared with his fellow Virginians. He served as a justice of Isle of Wight County in 1680; a burgess in the assemblies of 1684, 1685–86, 1688, and 1691–92 (when several pieces of legislation concerning slavery passed); and a captain of the militia, positions of influence in his county and in the colony.[41]

George Moore also came from Barbados to Isle of Wight County. Arriving by 1663, he too maintained Caribbean connections, transporting one servant from Barbados to Virginia in March 1679.[42] Moore served as an Isle of Wight colonial officer in 1685 with Henry Applewhite.[43] The two served together as justices of the peace in 1688, and on a jury from October through December 1694.[44] These ties between two Caribbean immigrants in Virginia illustrate how past contact in Barbados often influenced the choice of sites for mainland settlement and how friendships continued after migration, reinforcing the regionally concentrated trade ties that linked Barbados most fully to the Southside, the Eastern Shore, and the Northern Neck. The Barbadians likely had the strongest influence on slavery in those areas, although their disproportionate access to Barbadian slave traders ensured that their influence would spread throughout the Chesapeake.

Along with Henry Applewhite, Joseph Woory also represented Isle of Wight County in the House of Burgesses in 1684.[45] Woory was the nephew of Sir John Yeamans, a Barbadian sugar planter who led migrations to South Carolina and became its governor from 1672 to 1674.[46] In 1671 Yeamans took several slaves from Barbados to South Carolina, and apparently both he and his brother Sir Robert Yeamans of Bristol were interested in trade with Virginia.[47] The Yeamanses remained important planters and slaveholders in Barbados through the 1679/80 census, so it is likely that they were also there during Woory's 1684 House of Burgesses term, providing him with connections to the island, and if he did indeed communicate with his uncle, a family example of slaves brought from the island to the mainland.[48]

Anglo-Barbadian immigrants to the Chesapeake used the connections and experience they had to continue their exploitation of African labor and provided information regarding the intercolonial slave trade, thereby helping other Virginians gain trade contacts in the Caribbean. Thomas Walke, the 1662 Barbadian immigrant, convinced Virginia planter and trader William Byrd I to initiate a trade relationship with Walke's brother Jonathan, a merchant who was still in Barbados.[49] That trade contacts between the two colonies began early is revealed in Richard Ligon's comment (based on his 1647 to 1650 visit to Barbados) that a successful planter on the island must have factors in Virginia and New England "to provide you of all Commodities those places afford, that are useful to your plantation; or else your charge will be treble."[50]

In addition to influencing Virginia by way of migration, the English Caribbean islands also affected Virginia through their economic strength. Barbados dominated the economy of the English colonial world in the second half of the seventeenth century, and as the largest English colonial market for slaves, controlled prices throughout the trade. English merchants actively entered the African slave trade around midcentury, specifically to meet the demands of Barbadian planters. The illicit independent traders, both English and foreign, and especially the Royal Adventurers and the Royal African Company, concentrated on the larger market of wealthier Caribbean planters, rather than on the Chesapeake.[51] Caribbean planters' demands continued paramount in the minds of English merchants throughout the seventeenth century (and well into the eighteenth), leaving mainland colonists, who produced far less revenue, a secondary concern.[52]

Linked by commercial ties since at least the 1630s, Virginians not only exchanged Chesapeake grain, lumber, livestock, and meat for Barbadian sugar, rum, molasses, and slaves, but also shared information.[53] By the middle of the century, Chesapeake colonists' direct communication with Atlantic mariners connected them with Caribbean planters and merchants involved in the slave trade.[54] The Caribbean's centrality for London merchants and its importance for Virginia intercolonial traders made the region the nexus of the seventeenth-century Chesapeake slave trade. In 1708 Edmund Jennings, acting Governor of Virginia, reported to the Board of Trade that before 1680, according to older colonists, "what negroes were brought to Virginia were imported generally from Barbados for it was very rare to have a Negro ship come to this Country directly from Africa."[55] Maryland Governor John Seymour wrote the same year that "before the year 1698, this province has been supplyd by some small Quantitys of Negro's from Barbados and other her Ma'tys Islands and Plantations, as Jamaica and New England Seaven, eight, nine or ten in a Sloope, and sometymes larger Quantitys."[56]

Ships sailing directly from Africa delivered large numbers of slaves to the wealthy West Indies where they found a ready market throughout the seventeenth century.[57] Virginia's geography and lack of regional focus long prevented centralized market locations, thereby discouraging ships with large numbers of slaves, such as those chartered by the Royal African Company, from sailing into the Chesapeake. As a result, the company had even less success enforcing its monopoly in Virginia than in the islands. Slaves coming directly from Africa became available to Euro-Virginians in large numbers only after the demands of Barbadian planters increased the supply of slaves and thereby lowered prices.[58] The company's competitors thus provided Virginia planters access to slaves they would not otherwise have had. These competitors included traders from countries other than England (primarily the Netherlands and France), English interlopers in the West African-American trade, and those acquiring slaves in East Africa.[59] In 1679 company agents in Barbados, Jamaica, Antigua, and Nevis reported sighting thirty-two smugglers, of which only four were seized. In this same four-year period seventy company ships delivered slaves to the English Caribbean.[60] Although interlopers generally brought smaller cargoes, they represented almost one-third of the ships and carried a significant proportion of the traffic in African slaves. Relatively high prices for slaves on the mainland (and perhaps the willingness of the slaves anxious to escape the horrific regime of sugar production) inspired some intercolonial traders to steal Barbadian slaves (and servants) to sell them elsewhere. In 1661 the Barbados Assembly complained that "divers Servants and Slaves have been carried off this Island to other Plantations and Colonies, to the great damage and prejudice of many Inhabitants thereof," and tried to enact measures to prevent such theft.[61]

Other competitors included the captains and owners of the ships hired by the Royal African Company. To avoid unnecessary capital expense, the company paid one-quarter to two-thirds of ship owners' and captains' wages in slaves on their arrival in the West Indies. Such payments accounted for almost 20 percent of the total number transported by the company.[62] Once chartered captains dropped off their shipments in the West Indies, they operated on their own until they reached England again.[63] They did not have to sell the Africans received as salary in the same place they delivered those they carried for the Royal African Company. The Chesapeake, although it could not guarantee the same large market, commanded slightly higher prices for slaves during the late seventeenth century than did the Caribbean, which made it attractive to traders with small cargoes. Ships returning from the Caribbean to England followed the Gulf Stream north anyway, so a trip to Virginia did not represent a significant detour. The Virginia slave market was especially attractive to captains who could also acquire Caribbean molasses or rum, both sometimes available when sugar was not, and marketable in North America but not in Europe.[64] There, they could sell both the slaves they had received as salary and those they and their crew members had illegally (and the company suspected frequently) carried from Africa on their own accounts or reported as dead.[65]

English merchant George Tuthill recognized the economic opportunities presented by a Barbados to Virginia to England trade route (rather than a direct Barbados to England route) when in 1680, he ordered ship captain John Friskoe to go to Newfoundland and procure a "loading of reffuse fish fitt for the Barbadoes," sell it in Barbados as food for slaves, and there "take in what goods may be propr for Vi[r]g[ini]a." In the Chesapeake, Friskoe was to trade the Barbadian merchandise for a cargo of "halfe of the best sweet scented Tobacco, and the other halfe ordinary tobacco" and return with it to England. The "goods . . . propr for Virga" that Friskoe acquired in Barbados included rum, molasses, lime juice, and four enslaved African men.[66]

Virginia planters also purchased slaves directly from Barbadian merchants.[67] Rappahannock County merchant Nicholas Ware and Barbados merchant John Vassall traded tobacco for four slaves before 1662.[68] John Vassall, nephew of London merchant Samuel Vassall, traded with other Rappahannock County colonists (and later moved to Carolina as a promoter for the Proprietors and from there to Virginia, where he agreed to travel to Nevis to settle Ann Taft's affairs for the Northampton court). Vassall's daughter Anna married Nicholas Ware and moved from Barbados to Virginia. Like the transaction recorded in Rappahannock county, mid-seventeenth-century slave purchases commonly took place in counties that attracted intercolonial immigrants and often involved individuals, like Anna Vassall Ware, who themselves had moved from Barbados to Virginia.[69] Until the last two decades of the century, these migrations and the economic and familial ties they cemented lay at the core of Virginia's slave trade.

Virginians in other Chesapeake regions relied on immigrants in Caribbean-connected counties such as Lower Norfolk to help them establish relations with Barbadian merchants who could supply them with slaves. After William Byrd I established trade relations with Thomas Walke's brother, Barbadian merchant Jonathan Walke, island merchants supplied him with slaves, sugar, rum, and molasses during the 1680s and 1690s.[70] He testified to the importance of the island for Virginia planters' procurement of laborers when, in 1685 he wrote to English trading partners that "If your design by Barbados fails, wee shall bee fairly disappointed for without servants or slaves, no great crop is now to bee purchased."[71] In February 1686 Byrd wrote to Barbadian merchants Sadler & Thomas requesting that they send him "4 Negro's, 2 men 2 women not to exceed 25 years old." In the same letter he requested twelve hundred gallons of rum, three thousand pounds of muscovado sugar, one barrel of white sugar, three tons of molasses, and some lime juice and ginger, all to "bee sent on my particular account."[72] That Byrd had an account with Sadler and Thomas shows an ongoing relationship with them. The large volumes of rum and muscovado sugar testify to his role as a merchant within

Virginia and his ongoing trade with Indians in Virginia.[73] Through his position as merchant, Byrd probably used his connections in Barbados to purchase Africans for other Virginians in addition to himself. In 1689 and 1690 Byrd sent copies of sales accounts to unidentified Barbadian merchants. The accounts listed seventeen other colonists in addition to Byrd who had purchased Caribbean merchandise from the Barbadian merchants through him, among them Henry Applewhite, Barbadian immigrant to Isle of Wight County, Virginia.[74]

Other Virginians operated in a similar capacity. In 1685 Byrd worried about some of his fellow colonists buying too many Africans and Caribbean goods on credit, in the process creating debts that the following year's tobacco might not cover. He pointed to Richard Kennan and Quaker John Pleasants, both of Henrico County, Virginia (and both elected burgesses), who purchased "34 Negro's, with a consederable quantity of dry goods, and 7 or 8 tun of rum & molasses" from Barbadian slave traders William Paggen and Company.[75]

Byrd's letters also indicate a familiar relationship between him and the ship captains who carried those goods and therefore had contact with planters in both regions.[76] If the time Byrd and other planters spent with ship captains from Caribbean slave societies approximated the time Dutch merchant David Peterson De Vries had spent with Chesapeake, Caribbean, and New Netherland colonists earlier in the century, they had plenty of occasion to hear descriptions of sugar plantations and ask questions about the relationships between servants, masters, and slaves in societies that had made transitions Virginia was then undergoing. Such socializing seems likely, as cargo collection times in the Chesapeake did not improve measurably until the early eighteenth century.[77] Communication with the captains who traveled to the Caribbean provided Virginians not only with access to the markets but also with opportunities to discuss the social and economic nature of a successful slave-based economy and society with someone who had witnessed it.[78]

Given their close commercial contacts, Virginians could not help knowing of many Barbadians' growing prosperity and the connections between that prosperity and an increased reliance on African and African-American slaves. Londoners and residents of all other English colonies learned of Barbadian planters' wealth. A visitor from New England claimed in 1645 that Barbadians "have bought this year no lesse than a thousand Negroes; and the more they buie, the better able they are to buye. For in a yeare and a halfe they will earne (with gods blessing) as much as they cost."[79] To this traveler, slaveholding clearly increased profits. Another observer, positing the same linkage, compared Barbados in 1643 and 1666, noted the enormous increase in the numbers of black slaves—from sixty-four hundred to more than fifty thousand—and commented that "the buildings in 1643 were mean, with things only for necessity" but in 1666 "their buildings very fair and beautiful, and their houses like castles."[80] A pamphleteer in 1676 described "many Costly and Stately Houses" in Bridgetown and "the Hospitality, or Number of the splendid Planters, who for Sumptuous Houses, Cloaths and Liberal Entertainment cannot be Exceeded by [the] Mother Kingdom it self."[81] This reputation and the connection between affluence and the rise of African slavery spread along the trade routes throughout the Atlantic world. Those Virginians who had lived in or visited Barbados had seen for themselves the island's prosperity and emerging slave labor system. Travelers from England often stopped in Barbados on the way to Virginia, the favored route before midcentury.[82] They, too, witnessed slavery there before traveling to Virginia.

Virginians also learned about Barbados through written material. In 1657 the Englishman Richard Ligon published *A True & Exact History of the Island of Barbadoes*, an account of his experiences in Barbados between 1647 and 1650. A 1701 inventory of Virginia planter Ralph Wormeley II's library included a copy of Ligon's *Barbadoes*. Other Virginians besides Wormeley likely read his copy. The expense of books to seventeenth-century Virginians meant that those who had them frequently loaned them to neighbors and that individual volumes often got "read to pieces."[83]

Ligon's family much intermarried with the Berkeley family in England, which made Richard Ligon a cousin of Virginia Governor Sir William Berkeley and of Carolina proprietor John Berkeley. Ligon's brother Thomas moved to Virginia where he entered into a business partnership with Governor Berkeley during the late 1650s. Thomas Ligon accumulated at least two thousand acres in Virginia, some of which he purchased from William Byrd in 1657. A justice in Henrico County, he also represented Henrico in the House of Burgesses in 1655 and 1656.[84] Such familial connections to the most elite of Virginians increased the likelihood that Ligon's views of Barbados (via his published work or more personal correspondence) circulated among Virginians with decision-making power.

Richard Ligon also had a less direct personal connection to Virginia. Captain Thomas Willoughby, the mariner whom Francis Emperor had written in 1655 seeking a Puritan minister, lived in Barbados and Lower Norfolk County. In Virginia he served as a member of the Lower Norfolk County Court, in the Virginia House of Burgesses, and on the Council of Virginia. An uncle of the Barbadian planter Thomas Middleton, he acted as agent for Thomas Modyford, the planter with whom author Richard Ligon lived in Barbados.[85]

Through these connections to elites in Barbados, multiple Virginians gained access to the Barbadian world that Ligon described.

Ligon's first description of Barbados pictured a "happy island . . . extreamly beautiful" with a lively trade in its bustling port of Bridgetown. Although Ligon complained about the climate of the island, he depicted a good life for planters, describing lavish feasts with food from all over the world.[86] Ligon clearly admired the planters and praised them for succeeding, through "honest labour and industry," in rising from modest beginnings to opulence. He particularly admired the planters' ability to run their large, complex plantations smoothly.[87] Additionally, for Virginians who had had little experience with African slavery, Ligon's work provided detailed information about Africans as slaves (especially relevant to Virginia planters who had purchased Barbadian slaves), and the planters' ideas about how to organize a plantation system based on African labor. Ligon described the island as being "divided into three sorts of men . . . Masters, Servants, and Slaves."[88] He asserted that African slaves would not revolt, even though a "bloody" people who outnumbered whites on the island by two to one, because they were not allowed to possess weapons, their spirits were too subjugated to permit such boldness, and they spoke too many different languages.[89] He explained that slaves had Sundays free to rest, play, or work for themselves. He spoke of slaves with an overt paternalism, as in his description of them as "those poor ignorant harmless souls the Negroes."[90] Ligon also compares slaves to animals in several instances, likening them to cows, "every one of them know[ing] his better, and giv[ing] him the precedence, as . . . in passing through a gate"; claiming that African babies had eyes "not unlike the eyes of a young kitling"; and stating that "though we breed both Negres, Horses, and Cattle; yet that increase, will not supply the moderate decrease which we find in all those; especially in our Horses and Cattell." In the midst of a discussion of the sports possible on the island, he recommended Liam hounds as useful for hunting runaway slaves, a recommendation he followed shortly with a complaint that it was cruel to race horses "given to us for our moderate use." He apparently found it only amusing that Colonel Drax had his slaves chase ducks in a pond for the entertainment of Drax's guests.[91] The map accompanying his text showed a planter on horseback shooting at a black man wearing only a loincloth and running away from the planter, an image that recalled hunting scenes and that dehumanized enslaved Africans more than was possible for temporary English servants.

Although Ligon claimed that African slaves, representing a long-term investment, enjoyed better conditions than English servants, his descriptions of food, clothing, lodging, and work routines revealed the opposite.[92] Their

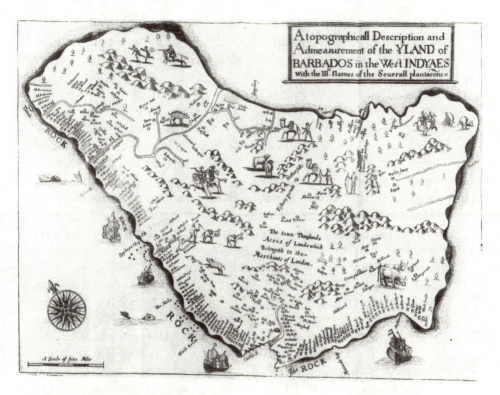

A topographicall Description and Admeasurement of the YLAND of BARBADOS in the West INDYAES with the ſll. ſnames of the Seuerall plantacons

Map 8. Richard Ligon's Map of Barbados. Courtesy University of Pennsylvania Library, Philadelphia.

diet included one bunch of plantains a week, "to this, no bread nor drink, but water." At night they slept on "a board, with nothing under, nor any thing a top of them." In comparison, white servants in Ligon's account received clothes, hammocks, corn gruel, some fish or meat, and orange juice, making them more expensive to feed, clothe, and house.[93]

In many ways, Ligon's comparisons of servants and slaves show that he thought Africans the more desirable workforce, particularly in their ability to stand subjugation better than Englishmen. Although the planters planned defenses against both slaves and servants, according to Ligon the greatest danger came from servants "whose spirits were not able to endure such slavery," particularly when forced to do work "unfit for Christians to do."[94] Ligon's assessment of some kinds of work as "unfit for Christians" but appropriate for African slaves further belied his claim that slaves lived and worked under better conditions than servants. The contradictions within Ligon's account—his claims that African slaves were "a happy people" and "very good servants" coupled with his evidence of inhuman treatment—only served to strengthen his dehumanization of Africans while emphasizing the perceived advantages in Africans as workers.

The arrival of new Virginians, both free and enslaved, from Barbados; the development of social and familial connections between residents of the two colonies; the availability in Virginia of written material describing Barbadian slavery, such as Ligon's *History of Barbadoes*; and business communication between planters, merchants, traders, and ship captains—all these provided colonists in Virginia with connections necessary to purchase African slaves and with information about ways to employ them successfully. Although other factors influenced the development of Chesapeake slavery, particularly local environmental and agricultural characteristics, information from Barbados contributed to the ways Virginians used slavery as a mode of production and organized the society that surrounded the institution.

The members of the House of Burgesses who had come to Virginia from Barbados or who had close ties to Barbadians proved particularly important, not only for the role they played in writing Virginia's legislation concerning slavery but also in the more informal contacts they made through their political positions. The offices they held involved them and reflected their prominence in circles of Virginians most likely to possess slaves.[95]

Recent legal history of slavery and race in Virginia, considered in light of concurrent developments in other colonies, reveals that Virginia legislators' efforts to define slavery and race legally constituted part of a larger conversation within the English Atlantic world.[96] That South Carolina, Jamaica, and Antigua adopted versions of Barbados' slave laws reinforces the conclusion, drawn from less explicit similarities between Barbados' and Virginia's slave laws, that English American legislators did not reinvent the institution anew in each colonial English location. Evidence that legal definitions of race and slavery and regulation of slaves developed as part of an intercolonial exchange raises questions about the explanatory weight historians have given to local events such as Bacon's Rebellion in the evolution of slavery and race in Virginia. Even those elements of slavery that evolved from indentured servant laws reflect intercolonial exchange, because the legal apparatus of indentured servitude developed from English servant law in an Atlantic context, with Virginia creating many innovations that other colonies, including Barbados, adopted.[97] While the evolution of indentured servitude in English colonies provided some basis for legal apparatus surrounding slavery, planters and legislators regarded slavery as a different institution requiring different laws. In an undated Barbados act addressing "the Government of Negroes," the

Assembly explicitly stated that they had to create new laws for slavery because it was a new institution to the English, and because English law lacked statutes dealing with blacks or slavery.[98]

The 1661 Barbados act "for the better ordering and governing of Negroes" created the first slave code in Barbados. The Barbadian legislature reenacted it with slight modifications in 1676, 1682, and 1688; the assembly of Jamaica copied it in 1664; the Carolina Assembly in 1696; and the Antigua Assembly in 1702.[99] While the legal codes of Virginia do not reveal the same extent of direct borrowing from Barbados as those of Carolina, Jamaica, and Antigua, they do contain one near-identity and enough similarities to reveal broad reciprocal influences between Barbados and Virginia. Similarities show that Virginians considered knowledge about Barbadian slavery relevant and those who possessed it derived some authority to influence legal developments surrounding the institution in Virginia.[100]

Laws defining race and regulating slavery reflect a broad discussion taking place throughout the Atlantic world and shaping the thoughts of London officials as well as colonial officials. When Barbados Governor Jonathan Atkins sent Barbados' slave code to England for approval, he feared that English officials would recoil at the harshness of it. Instead, English officials responded by revealing that they accepted Barbados masters' justifications for the laws, believing that blacks were "a brutish sort of People and reckoned as goods and chattels in that Island," and they therefore believed it "of necessity or at least convenient" that repressive laws govern them.[101]

There were three interrelated aspects of law that saw change with the adoption of African slavery in English colonies: defining slaves as property, establishing means for ensuring control over slaves, and developing legal definitions of race that would separate African slaves and their descendants from the rest of the population. As English colonies turned to slavery, their assemblies became concerned with developing precise legal definitions of slaves as property, in particular to govern inheritance and sale. Colonial legislators and slaveowners worked within a framework of English property law that they shared.[102] But their applications of English property law to slaves reflected considerable innovation and intercolonial communication.[103] A comparison of these laws for Barbados and Virginia shows that the many individuals familiar with Barbadian laws influenced the defining of slavery legally in Virginia. A fundamental question concerned whether, in determining the legal status of slaves, they constituted real estate (property like land and buildings), chattel (movable property like livestock, farm equipment and, temporarily, indentured servants), or some combination of the two.[104]

In Barbados, the assembly first addressed this question in 1668, when it defined slaves as real estate, or freehold property (that is, property entitling the owner to freehold status, a position that included voting rights). The assembly noted explicitly that they intended the law to address the problem of estates being too easily divided when someone died without a will. They wanted to avoid lawsuits and ensure "that the Heir and Widow . . . may not have bare land, without Negroes." Therefore, they defined all slaves as "Estates Real, and not chattels, and [they] shall descend unto the Heir and Widow of any person dying intestate, according to the manner and custom of Lands of Inheritance held in Fee-simple."[105] Emphasizing that the law was meant to prevent the separation of slaves from land, the legislators added that it would not apply to slaves owned by merchants, factors, and agents.[106] In 1672 the assembly reaffirmed the definition of slaves as real estate, but amended the law to consider slaves as personal chattel when used as payment for masters' debts.[107]

In 1671, just three years after enactment of the 1668 Barbados code, the Virginia Assembly also explicitly stated that slaves there were not to be considered chattel with regard to inheritance.[108] The next time the Virginia Assembly addressed the issue, in 1705, it copied almost exactly the language the Barbados Assembly had used, stating that "all . . . slaves [were] . . . to be real estate (and not chattels)" that descended "unto the heirs and widows of persons departing this life, according to the manner and custom of land of inheritance, held in fee simple." The only exceptions, slaves held by merchants or their factors before sale, were to be considered personal estate, and slaves of indebted masters, considered "chattels of personal estate for payment of debt," the same as in Barbados.[109] The laws' resemblance shows transmission to Virginia, possibly through Barbadian immigrants, of the island's developing inheritance laws for slavery. The similar language suggests that a copy of Barbados laws (or of this one Barbados law) existed in Virginia.[110]

Colonists in Barbados and Virginia also shared common concerns about the relationship of slaves to land, and legislators in both colonies arrived at a common conclusion that slaves belonged legally within landed estates.[111] Some wealthy colonists in late seventeenth-century (and eighteenth-century) Virginia entailed their slaves, legally binding them to a particular estate (and preventing their heirs from selling them or willing them away from those estates) in order to protect the value of the land by ensuring it would have laborers to work it.[112] Barbadian lawmakers labored early in the eighteenth century to protect estates for heirs during the temporary possession of widows (tenants in dower) or tenants for life. The 1709 "Act to secure the peaceable possession of Negroes and other Slaves, to the Inhabitants of this Island,"[113] stipulated that such tenants not sell or dispose of any "Negro or Negroes, Slave or Slaves" without the lawful consent of the heir, if of age, and also of the executor or administrator. Anyone who disobeyed the law owed the estate "treble the full value of such Negro or Negroes so sent off," showing that the legislature regarded slaves' value to an estate greater than their market value, as this triple fine applied only to slaves, not to other property associated with the estate.[114] Worrying that guardians and executors sometimes undersold (to themselves) slaves on estates under their trust "even to the ruin of the Plantations to which they belong," the assembly prohibited the sale of slaves belonging to estates, including for debt, "when there are other effects, personal Estate of the deceased, liable to the payment of any such debt."[115] Most importantly, "for the better preserving Negroes on Estates in this Island, and keeping them entire together from ruin, by the recovery of Legacies left by Testators, and just debts due from their Estates," the assembly stipulated that even in cases of debt slaves continued to be defined as real estate rather than as moveable chattel.[116] The incidence of entail in Virginia and the passage of legislation in Barbados prohibiting widows or tenants for life from selling an estates' slaves represent similar solutions to the problems slaveowners in both colonies saw following from the dissociation of land and enslaved laborers. If some Barbadian slaves were entailed, that would explain why some migrants with dozens or hundreds of slaves in Barbados, but whose families maintained their Barbadian estates, did not bring larger numbers of those slaves to Virginia.

A basic decision about the hereditary nature of slavery represented departure from English common law. In 1656 the Virginia Assembly recognized that "by [English] Comon Law the Child of a Woman slave begott by a freeman ought to bee free."[117] In 1662 the Virginia Assembly reversed itself and, like Barbados, declared that the status of a child of a slave and a free person would follow the mother.[118]

The legal codes of the two colonies also contain striking similarities in the specifics of maintaining control over slaves. The majority of legislation regulating slaves in both colonies consisted of policing measures. While such regulations were distinct legally from definitions of slaves as property, the two issues were related in the minds of seventeenth-century Englishmen, such as the English official who in the late 1670s, in approving Barbados police laws that Governor Atkins had feared too repressive, noted that such laws were desirable because they believed Africans to be "brutish" *and* because Africans were "reckoned as goods & chattels in that Island."[119] While the Board of Trade was wrong about the specific kind of property in most cases, their larger point was that because Barbados legislators had defined slaves as property that inhumane treatment of them was permissible.

The Barbados Assembly explicitly noted, in the preamble to their 1661 slave code, that they needed legislation specific to the policing of slaves because "in all the body of that Lawe" of England there was "noe track to guide us where to walke nor any rule sett us how to govern such slaves."[120] However, while they found English servant law insufficient, they did use elements of sixteenth-century English laws that had provided for the policing of vagabonds, wanderers without fixed homes. These Tudor laws of social control included requiring individuals not in a master's service to carry passes, branding offenders with the letter of their crime, using a "hue and cry" to capture "masterless men," and sending runaways or vagabonds from district to district for punishment. These were laws that emphasized shared public responsibility of householders for controlling the "masterless," which differed from the more private relationship governing interactions between masters and servants. Virginia masters applied some elements of these public police measures to indentured servants, but tempered them with protections that English law ensured servants. English colonies applied vagabond laws more widely to enslaved Africans, expanding the notion that, like vagabonds and unlike servants, controlling slaves was the responsibility of all propertied men. Similar Virginia and Barbados police laws reflected their common English legal heritage, but they looked to one another, perhaps unconsciously, when reaching the common decision to apply particular elements of laws regulating vagabonds to African slaves.[121]

In Barbados, Sundays worried planters because slaves normally did not work and instead often traveled to other plantations for markets and for visiting, both of which resulted in dangerously large gatherings and opportunities to plan revolts. In 1661 the Barbadian Assembly required that thereafter slaves leaving their masters' plantations on Sundays had to carry tickets stating the expected hour of return. The law also exhorted free white men who found unticketed blacks to give them a "moderate whipping," which, according to a visitor's account, could mean as many as fifty lashes.[122] Virginia's laws dealing with fear of insurrections followed and resembled those of Barbados. In 1680 the Virginia Assembly passed "An act for preventing Negroes Insurrections," which stipulated that because "the frequent meeting of considerable numbers of negroe slaves under the pretence of feasts and burrialls is judged of dangerous consequesce; for prevention whereof for the future," no slave could thereafter carry arms or "goe or depart from his masters ground without a certificate from his master, mistris or overseer, and such permission not to be granted but upon perticular and necessary occasions." Any African man or woman (the law said "negro," not slave, and therefore applied to free blacks) found without a certificate was to be sent to the nearest constable, who was "to give the said negro twenty lashes on his bare back well layd on" and send him or her home.[123]

Both laws specified a system of tickets or passes required for travel, a practice derived from vagabond law, not English or colonial servant law, though Barbados applied the system to Irish indentured servants as well as to slaves.[124] Both colonies also provided specific punishments for slaves and punishments for masters or overseers who allowed others' or unknown slaves to remain at their plantations. The laws made controlling slaves, like vagabonds and unlike servants, the responsibility of the entire society rather than just that of the owner. Virginia's 1680 "Act for preventing Negroes Insurrections" and an overall late-seventeenth-century increase in restrictions on slaves in Virginia occurred several years before Virginia actually experienced any "Negroes Insurrections." Slaves' participation in Nathaniel Bacon's 1676 rebellion may have convinced some Virginia legislators of slaves' willingness (and ability under existing law and practice) to participate in, if not foment, rebellion. That ability and willingness, however, would not have distinguished them from any other disadvantaged Virginians. Rather, Virginia's extensive communications with Barbados brought word of slave revolts and scares of revolts in Barbados in 1675, 1683, 1686, 1692, and 1702, fueling the fears that produced Virginia's regulations. Barbadian contributions to Virginia police laws likely made them more draconian than the Chesapeake situation warranted in 1680, independent of outside connections.[125] Outside connections, however, did exist. In 1678 Jamaican slaves who had known one another in Barbados joined in a conspiracy to revolt against their enslavers.[126] News of this communication may have indicated to Virginia legislators that Barbadian revolts not only exposed the possibilities of revolts elsewhere, but may in fact have encouraged revolts elsewhere.[127] In any case, the Virginia Assembly, presented with a problem much like one earlier faced by the Barbadian legislature, responded with a similar solution.

Both colonies prevented slaves from carrying arms, a regulation that again followed sixteenth-century English vagabond law rather than seventeenth-century servant law. Other similarities independent of either servant or vagabond law included reimbursement to masters for slaves killed as punishment for felony, masters' legal right to kill their slaves, denial of recourse to the courts, a system of tickets to prevent ship captains from "carrying off" colonists' slaves, and increasing attempts to prevent slaves from trading or buying and selling goods, either among themselves, from European colonists, or for their masters.[128]

The third category of colonial law developed in response to the growth of African slavery was that defining race. In both colonies evolving ideas about racial difference rested in part on European mens' perceptions that African women and their bodies differed in fundamental ways from European women and European women's bodies, suggesting that this subject too was one of broad concern in the English Atlantic world.[129] In both places by the end of the seventeenth century, planters regarded enslaved women as laborers for whom "men's" work was appropriate.[130] The Barbados Assembly outlawed interracial sex between white men and black women in 1640.[131] Virginia's assembly imposed stricter fines for interracial fornication in 1662 and outlawed interracial marriage in 1691.[132] Restrictions against interracial sex were new in an Atlantic context. England itself had no such restrictions, and Spanish, Portuguese, and French colonies permitted marriage between Africans and Europeans. English colonists in Barbados and Virginia (and other English American colonies) reached this decision, unusual in an Atlantic context, in communication with one another.

Records for the two colonies also reveal a similar evolution of notions of race in the first appearance of the word white, rather than English or Christian, in 1691 in Virginia laws and the following decade in Barbados.[133] Notions of "blackness" and "whiteness" among the English predated the appearance of the terms in laws. Quaker founder George Fox, who traveled in both colonies in 1672, used the terms frequently in a pamphlet he directed to the Barbados clergy that year.[134] Likely he had grown familiar with the terms in one or both colonies. His use of the words in his pamphlet at the very least indicates that he had used the words among colonists and slaves throughout the Caribbean and North America as he traveled.

Historians of the Chesapeake have argued that Virginia lawmakers' late seventeenth-century attempts to separate European servants from African slaves by legislating racial difference stemmed from elite fears that slaves, servants, and recently freed landless whites could unite (as some had under Bacon in 1676) against the planter class unless racism prevented them. Although Bacon's Rebellion may well have provided local reinforcement to Virginia elites, they participated in a process that legislatures in the Caribbean and mainland undertook at the same time. In 1686 the Jamaica legislature agreed to award freedom to any servant and £20 to any free white who killed a "rebel negro."[135] After the discovery in 1686 of "an intended rising" of slaves and Irish servants "to destroy all masters and mistresses" in Barbados, the Assembly briefly jailed the Irish conspirators, but executed twenty slaves, revealing the growing racial distinctions that officials encouraged at the end of the century.[136] The development of racial distinctions such as black and white (out of earlier notions of ethnic, religious, and geographic difference) did not reflect an inevitable process. Rather, the hardening of racial divisions in the English Atlantic (compared to the rest of the Atlantic world) depended on information spread by intercolonial migrants and by travelers such as George Fox and many more less literate. In 1697 Francis Tully Emperor drew a distinction between two slaves he had in Princess Anne County, Virginia: "one negro man by name Doctor Mallock & one moletto man named Oistain Judah."[137] While Emperor in that case used Spanish distinctions that already had common currency in English Caribbean and mainland colonies, nonetheless his racial identification of Doctor Mallock and the Barbadian Oistain Judah in a Virginia deed represents his similar use of such racial identifications in casual conversation and illustrates the means by which such ideas, not "natural" or based on English heritage, could spread both formally and informally throughout the Atlantic world.

Many of the parallels between Barbados and Virginia laws, in an area largely without English legal precedent and in colonies growing different crops and facing different demographic situations certainly reflect the communication of information concerning the organization of a slave-based plantation system. Barbados' early economic success with slavery prompted Virginians (and others) to look to it for example and encouraged Barbadian migrants to reproduce, to the degree that local conditions allowed, some aspects of the Barbados system after they moved to other colonies.[138] English American legislatures continued into the eighteenth century to borrow slave law from one another.[139]

Seventeenth-century Virginia developed into a colony economically and socially based on slavery within the context of a wider Atlantic colonial world, dominated by Barbados and other Caribbean colonies. In the slave trade as in other aspects of the development of seventeenth-century Virginia, the influence of white Barbadians emerges clearly from the extensive primary and secondary sources available. Of equal interest, but far more difficult to document, the consequences of slaves' experiences in Barbados on their perceptions of themselves and the world they found themselves in, and the shaping influence of slaves who moved from Barbados to the mainland colonies poses a tantalizing puzzle for historians to unravel from the sketchy surviving evidence.

Sufficient documents do exist to establish that the majority of enslaved Virginians came from the Caribbean prior to the mid- to late 1670s; moreover, although the Barbadian share of slave importations declined thereafter, significant numbers continued to arrive from Barbados through the 1720s.[140] From that solid point of departure, however, the analytical path quickly becomes a twisting and dimly lit series of events difficult to discern in themselves, and subject to ambiguous determination. It seems a logical certainty, for example, that those African-Americans who came to Virginia from Barbados would have interpreted their new situation in the Chesapeake in light of their experiences in the Caribbean. To suggest otherwise would fly in the face of our understanding, imperfect as it is, of human behavior. Those who arrived with their masters came already creolized, and had extensive knowledge of the workings of Barbadian plantations. Logic argues, with perhaps less certainty, that slaves with Barbadian experience played a significant role in the configuration of slavery and African-American culture as it developed in Virginia. Historians have had difficulty enough discerning how Africans used their knowledge from lives in Calabar or Kongo in a colonial American context.[141] The relative similarity between Virginia and Barbados, considered in an Atlantic world stretching from Gambia to the Netherlands to Quebec to Brazil, makes evidence of Barbadian influence on Chesapeake slaves all the more difficult to distinguish from African or English influences common to both societies.

Knowing exactly what impact the Barbadian slaves had in their new Virginia home therefore involves, because of the paucity of evidence, a combination of inference and (hopefully) informed speculation.[142] My own interpretation, which follows here, embodies the same uncertainties, drawn as it is from the fascinating though modest body of relevant secondary literature and my own sense of what the evidence implies. Each sentence that follows bears the weight of implied, if not overt "maybes" and "perhaps," but attempts to construct a picture of the world that existed for denizens of seventeenth-century Virginia.

Slaves who spoke English taught newly arrived Africans the language, as well as work routines.[143] To the extent that salient cultural characteristics of creole societies had formed during the first few decades of Caribbean settlement, the uprooted Barbadians carried an awareness of these creole characteristics with them to Virginia. If they thereafter acted as agents of transfer and replication, then, contrary to much scholarly argument, African-American culture in the Chesapeake emerged before the eighteenth century, shaped in part by prior Caribbean experiences.[144] Some historians have argued that Chesapeake settlement patterns presented Virginia slaves with insurmountable challenges to creating distinct African-American culture in the seventeenth-century Chesapeake. Conceding the difficulties posed by dispersed settlement and small numbers of slaves, I would posit that for many Chesapeake slaves prior experiences in a colony with a black majority, a much more concentrated population of slaves, and developing creole African-American culture added another important variable to the equation. Most Barbadian slaves in Virginia did not possess the autonomy some Atlantic creoles enjoyed.[145] Some Chesapeake slaves with Barbadian histories nevertheless maintained elements of an Afro-Barbadian cultural base transferrable to Virginia in a way African culture could not be, thus providing Barbadian slaves with a much greater ability to negotiate within an English colonial society in Virginia than most Chesapeake historians have assumed.[146]

Slaves with prior Barbadian experiences surely tried to define Chesapeake slavery against the Barbadian model they knew. Barbados gained a reputation throughout the late-seventeenth-century English world as a terrible place for servants and slaves. African slaves carried memories of this severity to Virginia.[147] Recognizing the inchoate character of slavery there, newly arrived slaves with prior Caribbean experience could hope to take advantage of the undefined nature of the institution in the Chesapeake and configure it differently there than in Barbados.[148] The appearance in Virginia records of slaves with names such as Barbados, Barbados Mary, and Barbados Dick points to a consciousness of slaves' Barbadian past, but whether slaves or their owners chose names that recalled that past is impossible to say.[149] In 1667 a Maryland slave who had come from Barbados lived on the plantation of Barbadian immigrant and Maryland governor Thomas Notley. John Batten, agent of Barbadian planter William Bushey, identified the man as belonging to Bushey and having been illegally brought to Maryland. When faced with the possibility of being parted from his wife and returned to Barbados, the man convinced Notley and Batten that "If he had not been prevented, he would have hanged himself." Notley bought the man from Bushey for one thousand pounds of tobacco, double his market value according to Batten.[150] The presence of his wife in Maryland was surely enough incentive to resist return to Barbados, but the comparably worse lives of slaves in the Caribbean added to the Chesapeake's attractiveness. He did not, after all, ask his Barbadian master Bushey to buy his wife so they could live together in Barbados. Slaves arrived in Virginia with expectations of continuing to enjoy the few freedoms they had experienced in Barbados, most importantly that of traveling on Sundays, one particularly important to maintaining connections with other African-Americans in Chesapeake colonies with lower concentrations of slave populations. In 1672 a colonist wrote that in Surry Country "Negroes . . . mete together upon Satterdayes and Sundayes . . . to consult of unlawful pjects and combinations." When, in 1680, whites in the Northern Neck discovered a "Negro Plot," they blamed it on "the great freedome and Liberty that has beene by many Masters given to their Negro Slaves for Walking on broad on Saterdays and Sundays and permitting them to meete in great Numbers in makeing and holding of Funeralls for Dead Negroes," echoing the concerns of Barbadian legislators.[151]

How many of those slaves sent to the Chesapeake by Barbadian merchants (rather than those arriving with Barbadian planters) had spent enough time in the Caribbean for the experience to affect their reaction to the Chesapeake remains unknown. By the 1680s, at least some Caribbean planters sold adolescent slaves born on their plantations to mainland planters.[152] However, we know too little about Barbados's reexport trade to determine how long enslaved Africans normally spent on the island before resale and shipment. Some mainland planters thought it often long enough for them to have adjusted to an American disease environment, gaining the advantage of "seasoning" that made them a less risky investment. While slaves designated for reexport often did not labor in Barbados, they doubtless witnessed slavery there, affecting their expectations of and reactions to Virginia. Perhaps as importantly, they encountered other slaves or learned to speak English or a pidgin language. Relationships that developed early, such as shipboard ties, could have had lasting and kin-like significance for slaves separated from family.[153] Time in Barbados awaiting reexport could have functioned similarly for those slaves who went on to the Chesapeake, allowing some sense of shared experience among Virginia slaves despite the dispersed settlement patterns that for most of the century prevented frequent intense contact after arrival.

The Eastern Shore's particularly close ties with New England and New Netherland provided Accomack and Northampton Counties with additional intercolonial influences on slavery and race relations. For many slaves who came to Virginia's Eastern Shore during the mid-seventeenth century, prior experiences with uncommonly open race relations in Dutch New Amsterdam may have "shaped black aspirations and assumptions," enabling some to achieve a surprising degree of freedom and latitude in that part of Virginia. Dutch immigrants or merchants with Dutch connections often owned slaves earlier than was common. The forty-one slaves from Benin purchased in 1656 in New Amsterdam by Eastern Shore merchant Edmund Scarborough represented the largest group of slaves arriving into Virginia up to that time. In January 1650 two Dutchmen, Derrick Arrisson and Cornelius Clinton, presented a bond to the Northampton County Court stating their intention "to bring in a shipp with Negros into Chirryston Creeke" and to give local planters Nicholas Waddelow and Stephen Horsey first chance to buy the cargo (at two thousand pounds of tobacco per slave).[154] In the 1660s four (of seventy-three) family groups in Northampton County owned about two-thirds of all the county's slaves.[155] Of those four families one (Michael) was Dutch, one (Custis) was of English descent but had lived in Rotterdam for a generation before moving to the Eastern Shore, and one (Robins) had strong ties to New Netherlanders and Dutch colonists. Planter John Robins, son of Eastern Shore-New Netherland merchant Obedience Robins, owned a plantation worked completely by slaves.[156] Members of the Hack-Varlett-Boot-Herman family, brought slaves from New Netherland to the Eastern Shore.[157] A visitor

reported that in 1679 all the laborers on Augustine Herman's Maryland plantation were slaves.[158] At least one of their slaves probably achieved his freedom.
On New Year's Eve 1671, the free black man William Harman visited six slaves
of Dutch Eastern Shore resident John Michael.[159] Frederick Philipse, the largest
New Amsterdam slave merchant (and second husband of David Peterson De
Vries's widow Margaret Hardenbroek) was also one of New Netherland's principle Chesapeake traders.[160] Eastern Shore merchant Stephen Charleton, an
associate of Scarborough, left his daughters large quantities of Dutch cloth
"rec[eive]d from the Dutch Plantation," three slaves, and little else when he
died in the late 1650s, indicating the likelihood that a merchant trading to New
Netherland would own slaves in a decade when slaves were rare in Virginia.[161]

Strong connections with New Netherland and New England may have
reinforced any relative openness in master-slave relations on the Eastern
Shore, and slaveowners' experiences in northern colonies shaped their
assumptions about slavery as well, even in cases where the slaves themselves
may have spent little time in New England or New Netherland. Moreover, our
knowledge that English ideas about gender relations affected the development
of race relations in Virginia and other English colonies makes it worth asking
whether the Dutch influences that allowed more open economic worlds for
women and for Africans in New Netherland were related, and whether Dutch
influence on the Eastern Shore delayed the development of the Virginia patriarchy that ultimately emerged in that Dutch-influenced Chesapeake region.[162]

At least two slaves who were probably former Barbadians managed to
achieve freedom on Virginia's Eastern Shore. Their former experiences as
slaves in the Caribbean gave them knowledge that may have enabled them to
recognize and exploit differences between Barbadian and Chesapeake Eastern
Shore slavery. Philip, [Do]Mingo, and Tony arrived in Virginia between 1641
and 1645 as the slaves of Captain William Hawley. They likely acquired their
Iberian names in Brazil, where Dutch slave traders obtained many of the slaves
they took to the English Caribbean in the mid-seventeenth century. If Brazilian slaves (especially Brazilian slaves desirable in Barbados in the early 1640s),
they likely worked in sugar production. Hawley had been deputy governor of
Barbados during the second half of the 1630s under his brother Governor
Henry Hawley. Both left the island in 1640, Henry going to England and William to Virginia. By 1641 William reached the Virginia Eastern shore and in
1648 or 1649 he moved to Maryland, perhaps following his neighbor and creditor Captain William Stone, who became governor of Maryland in 1648. Hawley's slaves stayed in Virginia.[163]

In 1648, while still in Virginia, Hawley hired Philip and Mingo out for
four years to John Foster. Foster complained about the quality of their work,

and asked Hawley for a written promise for their future performance. In 1649 Hawley made an agreement with Philip and Mingo that, if they served Foster, "they shalbe free from their servitude and bee free men, and labour for themselves." In 1650, after Hawley had moved to Maryland, Philip (now with the surname Mongon) and Mingo (Domingo Mathews) brought information to the Northampton court about a suspected Indian plot against English colonists, and the court apparently freed them in exchange for their information. Mathews disappeared from the records thereafter, but Mongon continued to live in Northampton for at least forty years.[164] Philip and Mingo's lives in Barbados before coming to the Eastern Shore may have helped them perceive opportunities for freedom when they appeared there. The resolve and insight they exhibited in resisting overwork and attaining their freedom supports the notion that as Atlantic creoles, these two men who brought the experience of an Iberian colony and another English colony to the Chesapeake were, as a result of such broad experience, better able to negotiate some control over their lives than were recent African (or European) immigrants. Even if neither Philip nor Mingo had ever been to New Netherland, on the Eastern Shore they met many who had, and probably knew of its reputation among servants and slaves as a location worth escaping to. Most seventeenth-century Chesapeake slaves, creoles when they arrived in Virginia or Maryland, did not possess such a degree of agency. Nonetheless, the large percentage of free and enslaved blacks who followed intercolonial trade routes to settle on the Eastern Shore seem to have possessed greater ability to shape their lives and the institution of slavery than did many black immigrants. Their ability to envision movement and change within the Atlantic world allowed them to recognize a possibility to push for race relations more resembling New Netherland's than Barbados'.

Relatively egalitarian relations among the New England ship crews that frequented the Eastern Shore may also have played a role in shaping race relations there.[165] At least one black sailor decided to move from New England to the Eastern Shore. Sebastian Cane lived in Dorchester from 1652 to 1662, during which time he worked on ships trading between Boston and Virginia. In 1654 he testified in the Northampton county court concerning tobacco transported by a ship on which he had worked during a voyage to the same county two years earlier. In 1662 Cane moved to the Eastern Shore and became a permanent resident.[166] Something in his earlier experiences made the Eastern Shore seem a relatively attractive place for a free black to live for Cane to have moved there from New England. A 1670 attempt by black pilot James and a group of white servants to run away from Accomack County to New England indicates that these servants perceived their chances for freedom to be better in New England than on the Eastern Shore, but it nevertheless also illustrates a strong connection between the Eastern Shore and New England, one that may have given Eastern Shore blacks and whites experiences that contributed to an environment for blacks in Accomack and Northampton more open than that in other parts of Virginia.[167] On the Eastern Shore, close contacts with New England and New Netherland added another intercolonial variable important in defining the parameters of seventeenth-century slavery and race relations.

Slavery in other places affected the pace of slavery's development in Virginia, its regional distribution in the colony, and its character during the seventeenth century. Spanish and Portuguese American slavery and the transatlantic slave trade that existed to supply Latin America put the first Africans in English colonies as slaves. English colonists in the Caribbean and mainland colonies gradually developed legislation defining and controlling slaves out of elements they had inherited from various kinds of English law. Unlike Spanish, Portuguese, French, and Dutch colonists, the English were not restricted by any heritage of Roman law and consequently created legal systems that granted themselves a degree of power over their slaves that was unique in the Atlantic world. While they used a shared English legal heritage to do so, the similarities between the slave laws of various English colonies do not represent a logical development of English legal thought but rather a borrowing of ideas and information that resulted in both clear cases of wholesale copying (Barbados to Jamaica) and instances of concurrent and similar evolution (Barbados and Virginia). Given the close contacts linking various English colonies, a completely independent growth of markedly similar legal solutions to questions uniquely colonial would have been impossible.

Colonists in Virginia's poorer counties, rather than those in the wealthiest counties, played a key role in acquiring the colony's first slaves. The Eastern Shore and Norfolk areas, producing worse tobacco and with more diversified economies as a result, were much involved in the earliest adoption of slave labor, even if only by facilitating a contact between a Virginia planter from wealthier tobacco-producing areas and a New Netherland or Barbadian merchant. That less wealthy counties had the strongest intercolonial connections seems to provide the best answer for that otherwise surprising pattern.[168] Samuel Mathews, whom De Vries visited on his way into and out of the Chesapeake, produced goods for intercolonial trade and to supply the shipping industry. The 1648 author of "A Perfect Description of Virginia" explained that Mathews grew hemp and flax and had spinners to make it into rope and thread and weavers to produce linen from the flax, that he had "abundance of kine, a brave dairy, swine great store, and poultry." In addition to selling meat and dairy products, he had a tanning house and eight shoemakers. The work was done by his forty slaves, skilled "to the trades in his house." The same author estimated the number of slaves in Virginia at the time as 300. If his numbers are correct, Mathews owned more than 13 percent of all slaves in the colony, more than any other Virginian except Edmund Scarborough.[169] That two merchants whose activities focused on cattle products (both plantations produced shoes as well as meat and livestock), supplying ships, engaging in intercolonial trade rather than tobacco planting, and cultivating strong Dutch connections should together own more than a fourth of all slaves in Virginia at midcentury indicates the importance of such connections (and the minimal role of tobacco) in Virginia's early slave economy.[170] The geography of slavery in Virginia underwent a significant change as transatlantic ships brought Africans to the colony beginning in the mid-1670s. Tobacco planters on the Western Shore bought most of those slaves, and the colony began to develop a demography more familiar to historians of the eighteenth century, in which wealthier planters and larger numbers of slaves populated that region, and more modest planters and fewer slaves lived elsewhere, in the areas that are my focus.[171]

Factors other than intercolonial connections, particularly changes in relative availability and price of indentured servants and slaves, proved crucial to the development of Chesapeake slavery. That Virginia's connections to slave societies in other parts of the Atlantic World informed the development of Virginia as a slave society is, however, apparent. Although many definitive characteristics of Virginia's plantation labor system developed early in the colonial period, with indentured servants as the principal laborers, significant social, cultural, and legal modifications accompanied the transition to slavery. Examining the degree to which these modifications stemmed from intercolonial interactions provides insights into the nature of Chesapeake slavery and a vivid illustration of the ways in which the intercolonial webs of trade and association outlined in Chapters 2 and 4 influenced specific aspects of Virginia's legal and social developments.

Chapter 7
Crossing Borders

Some Atlantic world residents traveled expressly to cross political borders. The fur trade required crossing unstable but nonetheless significant political borders dividing colonists from Indians. Indians traveled into regions controlled by Europeans, and European traders increasingly traveled farther and farther into Indian lands. Maritime Atlantic networks and overland trade routes also provided travel opportunities for individuals who moved across the ocean or between colonies explicitly to put distance between themselves and their history or to take advantage of the intercolonial borders dividing the Atlantic world into separate legal jurisdictions. Criminals attempting to escape capture, debtors fleeing their creditors, servants and slaves trying to free themselves all aimed to leave behind the courthouses that held their contracts and the people who knew their histories. Those who fled England for its colonies as their political or religious affiliations endangered their freedom or their lives are familiar. Unscrupulous traders who trusted time, distance, and labor needs to protect them "barbadosed" unsuspecting Londoners to the colonies for involuntary servitude. Colonists wanting to leave behind debts or crimes or servitude and escape notice of officials often attempted shorter journeys within the Americas rather than more difficult voyages across the Atlantic. Such illicit border crossers were critical to the development of an Atlantic Virginia. They, like merchants and mariners and legal migrants, connected Virginia to other American colonies, albeit in ways that colonial administrators did not expect or desire.

For the first fifty years of Virginia's existence, the most immediate boundaries for most of these individuals were those dividing colonists and Indians. Colonial officials expended great effort to exert some control over this boundary, especially early in the century when Indians clearly possessed greater power over the region than did the English. The boundary proved inherently unstable for both sides, however, when increasing European population put greater pressure on Indians, periods of starvation or desperation over the conditions of servitude and slavery led free and unfree colonists to seek refuge with Indians, and both Indians and Europeans sought trade with one another, whether or not their political leaders condoned it. As the number of colonies increased and as maritime networks grew, opportunities for intercolonial flights multiplied, and for most Europeans aiming to flee a colony, other European settlements provided much more attractive destinations than did Indian settlements.

The proliferation of mainland colonies not only altered opportunities for unsanctioned border crossers, but also changed Virginia officials' responses to such migrants. Together, the mobility of border crossers and officials' attempts to control their movements changed Virginia's relationship to the North American mainland. Events as far away as Iroquois-Huron warfare, inspired by Dutch and French presence in New Netherland and New France, increased Iroquois searches for adoptees from as far south as Virginia. The founding of both Maryland and Carolina challenged Virginians' trade with Indians. When criminals or runaways fled capture, the presence of adjacent colonies changed both the nature of escape opportunities and the means of pursuit. Colonial officials worked to control intercolonial travel just as they did travel across Indian-European borders. In doing so, officials expanded their own use of the very networks they were trying to ban others from traveling.

By the end of the seventeenth century, English American colonial officials created some of the most fully articulated and consciously developed intercolonial interaction networks, their communication made possible by maritime trade routes and social webs. In part, official communication operated just like any other: through a combination of individual migrations, word-of-mouth, and written news moving between colonies. These allowed many colonial officials to look to other colonies' experiences for models applicable to their own situations. In addition, over the course of the century, as the web of colonial trade, migration, and communication evolved, officials, especially at the level of colonial (rather than county) government, consciously fostered stronger networks of their own in order to cooperate in addressing common problems, particularly the desire to control who should have legitimate access to the growing Atlantic and overland travel networks.

The attempts of Anglicans in Virginia to keep Quakers and Puritans from forming intercolonial communities illustrates one such attempt. Others revolved primarily around the efforts of runaway servants, slaves, debtors, and criminals to escape to other colonies; the failure of overland traders to respect the limits imposed on their travel and trade by newly established adjacent colonies of Maryland and Carolina. Both unsanctioned border crossers and the officials who increasingly worked across colonial borders to control them enhanced Virginia's position in the Atlantic web. Illicit border crossers by definition established networks that transcended colonial boundaries. Unsurprisingly, they left few records except when officials were able to stop them. Because officials' efforts to stop such unsanctioned travelers required intercolonial cooperation, officials necessarily enhanced intercolonial communication and strengthened intercolonial networks. They created official Atlantic networks of communication whose purpose was to ensure that officials and masters and creditors maintained legal, social, and economic control over their colonies. Because Virginia was Atlantic, criminals, Quakers, servants, slaves, and debtors could move into and out of the colony using maritime and overland trade routes. Thus, even to exert legal, social, and economic control *within* Virginia's political borders, its officials and elites had to enhance their Atlantic outlook as well. Virginia's officials had limited success in controlling the travel of any of these groups, but their attempts helped to define both the theoretical and functional meanings of Virginia's colonial borders.

Most intercolonial interaction among officials operated informally. Colonial officials often served in more than one colony over the course of their careers, at times serving two colonies at once. Their multicolony experiences allowed them to apply cumulative knowledge compiled in previous successes and failures. Colonial officials in Virginia—often aided by economic ties or membership in common social circles and family networks—communicated with officials in other colonies about common issues. Because officials themselves enjoyed mobility and participated in intercolonial networks, they sometimes saw their problems as shared and their interests as linked. County court members, burgesses, councilors, and governors migrated between colonies and maintained intercolonial commercial contacts for many of the same reasons that other colonists did. Some officials moved to take advantage of economic opportunities or to form trade partnerships; some fled political opposition or religious intolerance. Their experiences or connections elsewhere enabled them to bring a more broadly Atlantic view to Virginia. Like Virginians' other Atlantic connections, its officials' intercolonial ties reflected the changing international character of the Atlantic world. At midcentury, Virginia officials communicated with their Dutch and English counterparts to collect debts or pursue runaways. However, as the English conquered New Netherland and established its Restoration colonies, Virginia's official communications increasingly became English. Thus, the local incentives for officials' intercolonial communications corresponded by late century with England's attempts to increase intercolonial communication as a means of facilitating imperial coordination of its American possessions.

Officials who served in multiple colonies and intercolonial migrants who became officials in Virginia embodied the most direct means to transfer their multicolonial experiences. Slavery provides one example of how Virginia lawmakers' earlier colonial knowledge shaped a Virginia institution common to the Atlantic world. Many of the intercolonial migrants discussed in earlier chapters, including Francis Emperor, Henry Applewhite, Joseph Woory, and Isaac Allerton, Jr., held office in Virginia. Daniel Gookin, Joseph West, and Daniel Parke took their experiences as officials in Virginia respectively to Massachusetts, Carolina, and the Leeward Islands. Some migrants from other colonies had held official positions before moving and, while they did not gain office in Virginia, nevertheless obtained positions of influence. Captain William Hawley, Barbados deputy governor to his brother Henry Hawley, served as governor in Henry's place in 1638, just before moving to Virginia with his slaves [Do]Mingo, Philip, and Tony.[1]

A number of officials who had not lived in two colonies had intercolonial experiences through trade. For example, of the seventeen Virginia councilors in June 1650, at least nine traded to, had family in, or had lived in other American colonies and therefore understood colonial interests broadly.[2] Virginia Governor Sir William Berkeley maintained a correspondence with New York Governor Richard Nicolls during the 1660s. Their letters show a personal tie between the two men that fostered economic exchanges and the sharing of news. In a 1665 letter to his "deare Deare Neighbour" Nicolls, Berkeley sent news of a rumor about war with France and asked what tobacco would yield in New York that October. If higher than the market in Virginia, Berkeley proposed to send Nicolls at least two hundred hogsheads.[3] As with other colonists, economic and social webs overlapped. In this case, their correspondence built official webs between colonies as well.

Their participation in intercolonial economic and social networks provided colonial governors with the means to communicate and to add networks based on shared experiences as officials. On at least three occasions, Virginia governors visited other colonies, in part to discuss colonial governance. In the summer of 1680, Virginia Governor Thomas, Lord Culpeper, went to Boston.[4] In 1684 and 1687 Virginia Governor Francis Lord Effingham and his daughter Philadelphia went to New York so that Effingham could negotiate with the Iroquois (with the help of New York Governor Thomas Dongan), the second time detouring to visit William Penn in Philadelphia. Revealing the overlap of official and social networks, Effingham pursued not only treaty making but also the more cosmopolitan social circles New York could offer him and his daughter.[5] The experience broadened his view and affected his governance on issues other than Indian negotiations. In 1685 he described to William Blathwayt his opposition to a separate Northern Neck proprietorship, explaining that the practice would in time create a distinct and inconvenient government.

This prediction derived "from the Experience I have had of this nature at New York, where the Duke hath granted such lopps from the main stem."[6]

Because news often traveled faster via intercolonial routes than directly from England, colonial officials depended on information from their counterparts to learn of European events as well as American ones. In 1689 New York Governor Francis Nicholson wrote Connecticut Governor Fitz-John Winthrop that "Wee have a flying reporte from Virginia that the Prince of Orange was landed in Tarr Bay. . . . But this news I want to have confirmed."[7] Circular letters from England, addressed to several colonies at one time, increased the likelihood that colonial officials would perceive their positions and relationships to England as similar. Shipping patterns often required that packets to colonial governors be sent by way of other colonies and forwarded to their ultimate destination.[8] This method of communication also strengthened a sense of common experience among colonial officials in America.[9]

Knowing that the governors of Barbados and New England had received the same orders encouraged Virginia governors to perceive their positions as similar to those of governors of other colonies. As early as the 1630s the Crown encouraged comparisons between colonies and emulation of approved behavior. In 1637 Charles I wrote to Virginia Governor Sir John Harvey and his Council, suggesting that their colony was too dependent on tobacco production, which required that they "be supplied by the Indians, nay even the Dutch and other Strangers," "whereas Barbadoes & other the Caribbee Islands have already begun with cotton, wools & other useful Commodities and intermitted for some years the planting of tobacco," which Virginians should do as well.[10] Knowledge of other places sometimes encouraged colonial officials to jockey for position with England vis-à-vis their counterparts throughout the colonial world. On December 18, 1662, the Barbados Council and Assembly ruled that exports from England would thenceforth be duty free "as Virginia, New England, &c."[11] In the summer of 1669, Sir William Berkeley complained that his salary was lower than that of any other Governor in America, though Charles II received more revenue from Virginia "than [from] all the Islands together."[12] At times influence and competition between officials took more subtle forms. When Virginia Governor Effingham visited New York in the summer of 1684 he was impressed by the high standard of living there (compared to Virginia) and wrote to his wife suggesting that she bring good silver from England when she came to Virginia so that they could entertain in a manner similar to New York Governor Dongan.[13] New York similarly impressed Virginia planter and merchant William Byrd when he visited the following year and described it as "a pretty pleasant towne" with "convenient lodgings . . . with other conveniences."[14]

Several times during the century, tobacco-producing colonies tried to cooperate to boost the price of their crops. Officials who had other intercolonial experiences usually became envoys during such negotiations. In 1667 in Jamestown, seven Virginia commissioners, including former Virginia and Maryland Governor Richard Bennett and future Leeward Islands Governor Daniel Parke, agreed with the commissioners from Maryland and Carolina on articles for the cessation of tobacco planting in 1667.[15] Lack of trust and planters' refusal to sacrifice a year's income doomed this effort to failure, but it reflects a sense among officials of common interests best pursued through intercolonial cooperation.

Virginians' attempts to imitate Spanish use of Indian tribute systems provide one of the first examples. Other early examples also involved Indians, not surprisingly, because Euro-Indian relations, a crucial aspect of early American colonial experience, had no English precedent. Powhatan Indians' 1622 and 1644 attacks on Virginia colonists' widely dispersed settlements provided a powerful lesson for English colonists throughout mainland North America. Matthew Cradock, governor of the Massachusetts Bay Company, wrote to the settlers in New England of his concern that they "seeme to feare noe enemies." He warned them to keep "a watchfull eye for yor owne saftye" and not to trust the New England Indians. He cited the 1622 Powhatan uprising as cause for his concern about New Englanders: "Our countrymen [have suffered by] theire too much confidence in Virginea. Let us by theire harmes [learne to beware]."[16] In March 1638 Virginia Governor Sir John Harvey wrote to Secretary of State Francis Windebanke that the Virginia Assembly's lack of enthusiasm for a tobacco regulation act derived from its members' fears of "being reduced to the hard condition of the Bermudas."[17] With communication networks linking Virginians to New England, Bermuda, New York, and the Caribbean, good and bad news spread quickly, leading officials to draw parallels and lessons from others' fortunes and misfortunes.

As Chapter 4 suggests, Carolina, as much a project of other colonies as of England, provides a clear example of this kind of increase in cooperation and learning. Carolina colonizers explicitly noted their belief that in many cases the experiences of colonists and officials in Virginia could provide them with valuable precedents. To avoid problems of competition with Virginia, such as those Maryland had had, Carolina promoters consciously tried to foster a cordial relationship by emphasizing the complementarity of the two colonies. The Carolina Proprietors enlisted the support of Virginia Governor Sir William Berkeley, himself a Proprietor of the new colony. In 1663 the Proprietors commissioned Berkeley to appoint a governor for all of Carolina on the northeast side of the Chowan/Albemarle River and to appoint either the same or another person to be governor of the southwest side of the river.[18] The Proprietors enlisted the help of other governors as well to settle Carolina. They sent letters to the governors of Barbados, "the Caribbee [Leeward] Islands," Virginia, New England, and Bermuda requesting that they not hinder free and unengaged persons from moving to Carolina.[19] On April 17, 1676, Berkeley, clearly identifying his dual authority as both "Capt General and Chief Governor of Virginia and One of the Proprietors of Carolina," acknowledged that for £100 he had sold the island of Roanoke in Albemarle County, Carolina, to New England merchant Joshua Lamb. Along with the island, Lamb received the cattle, hogs, and other livestock on the island and the right to expel anyone currently living there. At the recording of the deed on December 20, the witnesses included John Culpeper, who traveled to Boston the following September and confirmed that he had seen Berkeley sign and seal the deed.[20] Berkeley's family, including his brother Proprietor John Lord Berkeley, had long participated in the Carolina project. The Proprietors undoubtedly hoped that Berkeley's interest in Carolina would mitigate Virginia challenges to the new colony. Indeed, Carolina's ultimately successful cultivation of rice with African labor and expertise may have stemmed from William Berkeley's recognition that such a project had potential in North America and his earlier attempt at producing it in Virginia.[21]

In another attempt to learn from difficulties between Virginia and Maryland, former Virginian Thomas Woodward in 1665 complained from Albemarle County to Sir John Colleton of the inconvenience resulting from the "erect[ion of] divers governments to have passage through one another's territories or inlets, as Maryland, having no inlet for shipping but through the Capes of Virginia." He also thought the Carolina Proprietors would receive the best profits from the new colony if for a time they allowed colonists to "take up . . . land . . . according to the custom of Virginia," by headright. He added that inducing planters to settle in towns would probably prove impossible, perhaps learning from Virginia officials' earlier frustrations, but he nonetheless followed their lead in encouraging congregated settlements for safety.

Woodward, with his Chesapeake experiences, became particularly important for Carolina. In September 1671 Carolina Governor Joseph West wrote to Anthony Ashley Cooper that Woodward's absence from Virginia created a big problem because the Carolinians needed Woodward's services as an Indian interpreter (a skill he had learned as a Virginian).[22] The Proprietors took at least some of Woodward's advice. In 1670 they instructed Governor Samuel Stephens and the Council of Albemarle County to allow the inhabitants to hold their lands on the same terms as the inhabitants of Virginia. Concern that Carolinians learn from Chesapeake mistakes in failing to establish towns was a continuing theme of the Proprietors. In April 1671 Lord Ashley wrote to Colonel William Sayle of the importance of overruling men's rashness and folly and insisting that they live in towns rather than dispersing themselves to "expose the plantation to ruin; the difference whereof is apparent in New England and Virginia." Ashley believed it absolutely necessary to force the settlers to congregate "for their safety and advantage."[23] On the same day, Ashley wrote to Sir John Yeamans that he "Recommends to him as very necessary the planting of people in towns, the chief thing that hath given New England so much advantage over Virginia."[24] On September 18, 1671, Lord Ashley sent instructions to Sir John Yeamans for laying out the port town on the Ashley River, cautioning him to "take care of the lesser townships in the several colonies, and that the houses be placed both orderly and conveniently together, so that their nearness to each other may be a security." Ashley wrote that he concluded "by the experience of both Virginia and Maryland that men will expose themselves to the inconvenience and barbarism of scattered dwellings in unknown countries."[25]

After they had established the colony, Carolina Proprietors continued to study Virginia and make a point of benefiting from prior colonial experiences. In 1670 John Locke learned from Carolina colonists that the years' crop, "if it produce according to Virginia," would yield at least a thousand bushels of Indian corn, besides roots and beans.[26] In 1671 the Proprietors gave instructions to Captain Mathias Halstead for a voyage to take passengers from Barbados to Carolina and engage in complementary trade where he could. Joseph West (who had lived in the parts of Virginia most involved in Barbadian trade and presumably understood the supply side of it) was charged with assembling Carolina's goods bound for Barbados. Halstead should "learn as much as he can of the husbandry and manufactures of the places he goes to, particularly in Virginia of the sorts and ordering of mulberry trees and silkworms, some of the best of which he is to plant in Carolina, and the right way of making silk, tobacco, indigo, cotten, &c."[27] These instructions reflected the fact that Virginians, in a half century of trial and error, had learned valuable information that Carolinians could use to avoid the starving times their northern neighbors had suffered. The establishment of Carolina reveals that by the late seventeenth century new colonies did not result from projects organized solely from London but rather involved people throughout the colonial world. Virginia's thorough integration into the Atlantic world assured its influence on Carolina and other later colonial endeavors, as officials moved from Virginia to new colonies, or as new colonial officials looked to Virginia for examples of successes to emulate and failures to avoid.

As servants, slaves, debtors, and criminals tried to take advantage of opportunities for intercolonial travel to escape, they hoped (often mistakenly) that political borders would prevent the kind of intercolonial cooperation necessary to catch them. Some may have just been looking to put distance behind them, but many indicated their intent to reach the other side of a political border. They knew of intercolonial rivalries, such as Virginia's border disputes with Carolina or its conflicts with Maryland over duty collection on the Potomac River. They likely overheard elites' complaints about New England's relative political independence or Barbados's disproportionate influence in London. While all of these Atlantic locales were connected via overland or maritime trade routes, they remained distinctive and developed reputations that emphasized their differences. Those individuals who fled their debts or crimes hoped that colonies' disparate characteristics or rivalries would preclude coordinated efforts to capture them. Many likely succeeded. Others, however, succeeded in reaching other jurisdictions only to find themselves captured and returned to their place of origin. The Atlantic nature of the colonial world that had allowed them to escape permitted their pursuit.

In response to the mobility of runaways, criminals, and debtors, colonial officials consciously increased their intercolonial (and sometimes, but more rarely, transatlantic) communications. They built on the less formal ties of acquaintance or emulation they had developed with one another to deal with runaway laborers, debtors, or criminals who moved from one colony into another. Court cases involving unsuccessful runaways demonstrate that unapproved intercolonial movement encouraged intercolonial cooperation of courts, sheriffs, and colonists to prevent undesired intercolonial interactions. Their cooperation further broadened the authority of colonial county courts to deal with issues spanning not only their county's but their colony's borders. In their attempts to prevent runaways from crossing intercolonial borders, officials tried to define those political borders to allow selective permeability. In many cases officials found such permeability beneficial. Virginia's economy depended not only on the frequent presence of traders and mariners but on their temporary but intense involvement in the colony. Likewise, Virginia officials welcomed European immigrants from other colonies whether they came as propertied elites or as laborers. But the commerce that defined Virginia's place in the Atlantic world and established travel routes also made intercolonial boundaries porous when officials wanted them impermeable. And so officials tried to make their political borders function as barriers to travel and communication they found objectionable while at the same time encouraging the commercial growth that established border-crossing travel routes in the first place.

Debtors were the most frequent illegal border crossers. Seventeenth-century Atlantic commerce required that its participants undertake temporary debt to acquire goods for trade or consumption before their payment was available. In Virginia, planters bought goods and laborers on credit while awaiting the sale of their tobacco or intercolonial trade goods. Such debt was expected, as was the travel of debtors throughout the Atlantic world, but some debtors traveled in order to avoid payment or prosecution. In a seventeenth-century Atlantic world full of substantial economic risk and a Chesapeake region plagued by widely fluctuating tobacco prices, many colonists who had borrowed found it impossible to repay their debts. Facing the certainty of jail, servitude, or property confiscation if they remained in Virginia, many chose instead to attempt escape and a new start. While debtors at all economic levels avoided payment this way, for wealthy colonists who owned real property in Virginia, sudden departure for Europe or another colony meant only a delay in repayment. Debtors inspired many of the powers of attorney discussed in Chapter 2 as their creditors enlisted the help of traveling acquaintances to recover their money. Debtors were migratory enough that many colonies required that those leaving the colony post security for their debts, a process that became routine for mobile planter/merchants who likely owed local and distant creditors each time they left Virginia with their trading ships.[28] But the law reflected the frequency with which debtors defaulted on their loans. In 1653 New Netherland Director General Peter Stuyvesant enlisted Virginia Governor Richard Bennett's help in recovering debts Edmund Scarborough owed to Manhattan merchant Augustine Herman.[29] The attention of such high-ranking officials apparently did not cause him to change his business practices. In 1670 Virginia received a complaint from New York that Edmund Scarborough had evaded government duties or personal debts. In either case, his activities encouraged the New York official or creditor to enlist the help of the Virginia colonial government.[30]

Intercolonial communication to ensure duty collection was even more common between Virginia and Maryland than between Virginia and other colonies, because the Chesapeake Bay and Potomac River (and their similar markets and trade goods) allowed ships' crews to sell and collect cargoes in both Chesapeake colonies. The dispersed trade of the Chesapeake and the complicity of many local officials allowed many merchants to avoid paying duties altogether. If such evasion occurred in both colonies, Crown officials communicated, sometimes disagreeing, over how much duty the ship's traders owed in each colony.[31] Most colonists, however, fled personal rather than public obligations. In 1650 Barbados planter Nicholas Forster complained that the colony's "Inhabitants . . . daily run from the Island in Boats, being much indebted both to the Merchants, and also to one another."[32] In 1701 Carolina

Governor James Moore wrote to Francis Nicholson that "diverse, idle, extravagant and profuse [debtors had] run away from their creditors to Virginia, the easiness of the journey encourages them to run in debt more than they are able or design to pay," suggesting that colonists regarded the possibility of intercolonial flight as potential means of reducing risk when they accepted credit.[33]

Other American colonists took advantage of their mobility between colonies to seek illegal personal gain, thereby prompting the courts to deal with their intercolonial crimes. Labor markets in Virginia tempted some traders, in the colonies as well as in England, to "spirit away" the unsuspecting or unwilling to be servants. In 1660, as the numbers of voluntary servants to the Chesapeake began to decline, Boston resident Hopestill Coney found himself the victim of Elias Parkman (a partner of Daniel Gookin's in his New England-Virginia voyages in the 1650s), who took him to Virginia and sold him there as a servant. When Coney's kinswoman Sarah Fuller complained to the Massachusetts General Court, it ordered Parkman to give £50 security that he would bring Coney back from Virginia to Boston before the following April or bring a death certificate to prove that he could not comply.[34] In 1645 in the New Haven Colony Court, Richard Catchman accused Thomas Hart of stealing away a woman "negroe servant from Virginia." Catchman, as attorney for Virginian Florence Payne, also tried to collect a debt that Hart owed Payne.[35] Those Hart had wronged in Virginia used Catchman's intercolonial travel to pursue him to New Haven. They could do this in part because English colonial courts cooperated to apprehend debtors or criminals who tried to escape across boundaries. Attorneys commonly traveled between Dutch and English colonies to collect debts. However, Virginia and Maryland sometimes resisted official appeals from New Netherland and New Sweden to return boundary crossers fleeing debt or minor crimes. Such fugitives provided population and labor, and their flight from the Dutch and Swedish colonies destabilized both New Netherland and New Sweden as well as Maryland's contested border with them, desirable outcomes in the eyes of many English officials.[36] If attorneys could not collect intercolonial debts between English colonies, however, the problem usually received more extensive cooperation among colonial officials. Court members understood that in such cases it paid to help those from other colonies and thereby build a shared legal culture that could reciprocate to aid their own colony.

Alhough merchants sometimes tried to take advantage of intercolonial boundaries to sell servants they did not own or whose terms had expired, far more commonly servants tried to flee across borders, in attempts to gain anonymity and freedom.[37] In 1643 servants of Marylander Sir Edmund Plowden crossed the border between Maryland and Virginia, fleeing from St. Mary's City, Maryland, to Northampton County, Virginia. Plowden dealt with courts and officials in both Maryland and Virginia to retrieve the men.[38] The members of the Northampton court, certainly more likely to share Plowden's interests than those of his servants, recognized that helping a Marylander recover a servant across the colonies' common border set an important precedent, helping to define colonial boundaries and build restrictions on intercolonial mobility that would protect their control over their own human property. To set such a precedent required officials to increase their own intercolonial interaction and cooperation while at the same time attempting to decrease the porosity of those same boundaries for servants.

Plowden regularly spent time in both colonies. His mobility gave his servants who traveled with him contacts and a broadened worldview, just as it did him. Knowing people and travel routes and having experienced two colonies encouraged some of them to attempt intercolonial escape again only two years later. Plowden's mobility and status gave him official contacts in both places, and this time he enlisted the help of Governors Berkeley and Calvert, both of whom agreed to address an issue that spanned the two colonies.[39] Unfortunately for the servants, Plowden's movements, which may have allowed them to envision escape, also made their capture more likely, as those with status and freedom moved to strengthen their own networks in order to restrict the use of the same routes for runaway servants.

Though adjacent Maryland proved the most common destination for runaways from Virginia, some went farther, to New York or New England, especially if they served intercolonial merchants who traded to those regions or had other access to those shipping routes. Courts in those regions cooperated as well. In 1682 the Massachusetts court investigated Jacob Sayer, a young man staying in Boston. The court knew he had come most recently from New York but had heard reports that he had run from his master in Virginia. The same year the colony refused admittance to butcher Thomas Phillips because of fears that he too had run from Virginia.[40]

In 1663 John Tarr, John Wells, Richard Davis, Bryan Mackmayon, James Michell, Roger Micave, and William Alchurch, all servants of Edmund Scarborough, stole horses, provisions, clothing, a gun, sails, and a boat; escaped from his Accomack County plantation; and headed toward New Netherland and to New England. Scarborough traded with both places, so the servants may have been to the more northern colonies or known that both had the reputation for being kinder to servants. Their theft of a boat and sails and their confidence that they could sail to New Netherland suggests that some, at least, were experienced boatmen, likely for servants of a man like Scarborough who carried on extensive intercolonial trade in his own ships. Certainly the men had many times met mariners, traders, and migrants from both places. Scarborough sent express notices of their escape to the Delaware Bay, New York, and New England, and hired twelve men and two sloops for eight days each to look for the runaways.[41] Scarborough's attempt to take advantage of both communication and travel networks to find his servants succeeded, and the Accomack court assigned extra time to the captured runaways as punishment. Two of Scarborough's servants, John Tarr and William Alchurch, undeterred (or perhaps made more desperate) by the punishment, tried again to escape. Joined by servants belonging to several other Eastern Shore planters, the group apparently made their plans while working together to build a mill house. Altogether the plot involved at least sixteen servants belonging to three different planters. They planned to steal supplies from stores and houses and go to the Dutch Plantation or New England in the vessel the *Black Bess*.[42] Some of these servants had likely traveled to New Netherland or New England, but surely some had not. Working together on the mill house provided an opportunity for those familiar with New Netherland and New York to describe them to the others and enable them too to envision escape and intercolonial travel and to imagine better chances elsewhere.

The pervasive maritime culture of seventeenth-century Virginia, the widespread sailing knowledge, and the presence of at least small boats at many plantations presented runaways like Scarborough's servants with opportunities to escape by water. Even those servants who attempted escape overland needed to navigate the region's rivers, often wide in the coastal plain. From Virginia, Maryland offered the easiest and most common overland destination for runaways, but also the one where their owners could most easily pursue them. Going farther overland depended on using overland trails and enlisting the help of Indians. In July 1638 William Abraham tried to buy "a booke to learne to speake the Indyan tongue" from his master's son before attempting to run with two other servants to New Netherland, where the servants believed they could "live like gentlemen" and where, "when our Master if hee sees us durst not ow[n] us." Better to run, they thought, than to stay in Virginia and "bee slaves."[43]

Indians could prove as useful to planters pursuing runaways as to the runaway servants. In the 1670s an unnamed Indian returned a runaway Indian servant to Virginia from Maryland and received twenty armlengths of roanoke as reward.[44] But encouraging Indians to return runaway servants entailed problems because it required acknowledging Indians' positions as border crossers, even while many Virginia colonists hoped to limit Indians' ability to travel between colonies. The overlap of colonists' concerns about Indian and servant mobility appear in a later seventeenth-century court case involving servants and slaves of William Byrd I. In 1692 Byrd informed the Virginia Council that strange Indians had killed an English woman belonging to him and had taken away a Negro woman and mulatto boy. Byrd understood that the Indians had taken the woman to "the Governmt of Pensilvania where shee now is" and sold her to a Philadelphian. The Virginia Council determined that this event set a precedent "of very dangerous Consequence to all their Ma[jestie]s' Governments in these parts." If colonists bought African slaves from Indians, it would encourage the Indians "to steale from one Govrnmt and sell to another, that it will be difficult keepeing a Servant, and the Inhabitants of these Governments much damnified in their Estates and discouraged Inhabiting in these parts of their Ma[jestie]s' Dominions." Because solving this problem required the cooperation of every single mainland colony, cooperation ordered by London offered the quickest solution. The Council therefore asked William Blathwayt (auditor general of the colonies) to present their problem for consideration to the Committee for Trade and Plantations, which could issue blanket commands to all the colonies and ask them to have the colonies deal jointly with the problem.[45]

In addition to runaways and debtors, other criminals sometimes moved across boundaries. Virginia officials quickly returned immigrants or travelers from other colonies who committed crimes in Virginia. One Marylander who committed petty larceny on Virginia's Eastern Shore endured a relay system of lashes that took him out of Virginia and back to Maryland. He received ten lashes at the Accomack County prison and ten more in each district of the county through which he passed on his return. When the Accomack officials left him in Maryland, they promised him thirty more lashes if he ever returned to Accomack County.[46] This punishment, emphasizing the criminal's travel as much as his theft, provided a graphic example of Virginia officials' attempts to discourage criminals from following intercolonial travel routes into their colony.

When servant Edward Vickars escaped by boat from his master Henry Tripp in Virginia, Tripp pursued him in a canoe. Vickars "shott at him & thought he had killed him, for he saw him fall downe," and continued his flight, ultimately stopping in New Haven Colony. There, in 1671 he ran afoul of the law for "cursing and swearing and giving threatening speeches to the clerk of the iron works." During the course of his trial, evidence emerged of Vickars's escape from Chesapeake servitude and his possible killing of Tripp. The New Haven Colony Court judged him to be "highly guilty of Common & frequent Curseing & sweareing in a most prophane & blasphemous manner," for which he apologized, explaining that "he had beene brought up in such places & company where it was frequently used, & he hoped he should reforme for the future." He suffered a whipping for that guilt, but the court members worried that he was "a dangerous person in other respects," and ordered him to give £20 security until he and his wife could prove him innocent of "the sd suspition of the guilt of bloud."[47] Intercolonial communication networks made such escapes risky, as word of such crimes could easily follow people from one colony to another. Courts paid attention to this sort of tip and reinforced those routes along which rumors had traveled by using them to confirm the intercolonial information or by ordering the accused to use them to prove themselves innocent.

Between 1668 and 1670 the Accomack County court struggled repeatedly with Henry Smith, a planter who beat his wife Joanna and his servants. Smith's intercolonial travel complicated the case. Smith owned property in both Maryland and Virginia and had lived at Patuxent, Maryland, before moving to the Virginia Eastern Shore. His servants, after years of suffering from physical and mental abuse, including rape, malnutrition, starvation, exposure, and an unremitting atmosphere of fear created by Smith's paranoid distrust, finally worked up their courage to complain to the Accomack County court. As the court uncovered more and more evidence of abuse, its justices became less and less comfortable upholding Smith's property rights over his servants and his wife, finally granting his wife freedom to leave him. It did not free his servants (fearing such an action would set a dangerous precedent and encourage other servants to attempt freedom by complaining of ill treatment) but ordered close supervision by neighbors and suggested that it would believe a servant's future testimony over Smith's. The servants repeatedly expressed their fear that Smith would move with them to Maryland "ag[ains]t theire Wills & theire use his Cruellty in a place where he is not so well knowne & understood." The Accomack court ruled that Smith could not remove his servants from Accomack unless the servants declared their free consent in court. Smith did go to Maryland, but it is not clear whether he took his servants with him.[48] Cases like Henry Smith's may have precipitated later regulations that masters could not move away until having their servants acknowledge in court their willingness to leave the colony with their master.[49]

In the case of more notorious criminals, the Crown sometimes encouraged colonies to cooperate with one another. After Nathaniel Bacon's 1676 rebellion in Virginia, the Massachusetts Council, on orders from Charles II, published the fact that "Nathaniel Bacon the younger" had "made himself the head & leader of a Rebellion in Virginia," not only to the obvious great detriment of Virginia, but also "to the danger of other [colonies] neere adjoyneing thereunto." Following the king's instructions, the Massachusetts Council

made a public announcement by beat of drummer to all "Inhabitants People & Traders" of Massachusetts and anyone traveling from Massachusetts
elsewhere to seize Bacon or any of his accomplices who retreated "within the
limits of this Jurisdiction." The Council forbade anyone from joining with
"the said Rebell" or from providing him with any arms, ammunition, provisions, or help of any kind.[50] In June 1678, when bricklayer William Mason,
dancing master Charles Cleate, and his servant fiddler Ceaser Wheeler (surely
using aliases) went from Virginia to Boston, officials refused to admit them to
the city because of a rumor that the three men had participated in Bacon's
Rebellion.[51] Officials throughout English America recognized the need to capture someone like Bacon, who had challenged the governance of his colony
and therefore potentially threatened the authority of all colonial officials. The
participants in Bacon's Rebellion had not only proven themselves dangerous
individuals, but in such a mobile and communicative world, they also set a
dangerous example that extended far beyond the Chesapeake.

Virginia officials who regarded intercolonial interaction and travel, particularly across the Virginia-Maryland border, as too easy, attempted to quash
the notion among Virginia colonists that the border provided them with freedom from Virginia laws. In 1643 in Accomack County, Thomas Parkes
announced to several people socializing in Mr. (Nathaniel) Littleton's kitchen
his distress with local court members, particularly justice Argoll Yardley, about
a ruling made against him. Parkes announced that, if he could not have justice
"here at this Court," he would appeal to another and that, if he could not have
justice there, he would go to the Susquehannocks "and see what I can doe
there." Inability to receive justice in Accomack, he continued, "will be a Reason that will make mee flye to another province." Parkes threatened to "goe
home to his Majestie and have him [Yardley] put out of his place and I will
make my Lord Baltamoore acquainted with his doings." Though they ultimately dismissed the case for lack of evidence, local magistrates expressed
great concern about the seriousness of Parkes's suggestions, emphasizing the
"treasonous" implications of his claims that he could go to Maryland or even
to the Susquehannocks for recourse from Virginia courts.[52]

Twenty years later the same court put a more decisive stop to similar pre-
sumptions. In the winter of 1665–66 Virginians John Anderson and John Williams employed the Indian Jack to hunt for them. Jack killed five deer for
Anderson and four for Williams, using a gun belonging to Williams. When in
January 1666 the councilor Miles Gray arrested Jack for carrying a gun, Anderson complained that "if he could not have licence in Virginia for an Indian to
carry a gun, he could have a licence from the clerk in Maryland" and regretted
that he had not "had tyme to stay (when last there) tell it could be drawne."[53]

After a year and a half of consulting with Governor Berkeley about the case, the Accomack County court found Anderson guilty of mutiny for claiming that he could avoid Virginia laws by appealing to the governor of Maryland. The court punished Anderson, partly "for the prevention of other mutineers" who might also try to use the border to circumvent Virginia's laws.[54]

Overland traders constituted another major group of colonists who insisted on colonial boundary fluidity and provoked official reaction. When the colonies of Maryland and Carolina were carved out of Virginia, already-developed trade routes between Indians and colonists (and between Indians) increasingly required intercolonial border crossing in addition to the intercultural border crossing inherent to such trade. Before the establishment of the neighboring English colonies, Virginians traded in lands later granted to Baltimore or the Carolina proprietors. After the new colonies were established, many Virginians' existing trading activities, which had previously occurred entirely within Virginia's chartered boundaries, became intercolonial and required renegotiation as they came under new political jurisdiction. When Virginia traders' travels to reach their trading partners and Indian traders' travels to reach Virginia colonists crossed newly established border lines they precipitated much of the difficulty between Virginia and its new colonial neighbors.

The boundary between Maryland and Virginia proved particularly problematic because it did not follow a physical geographical boundary. While the Great Dismal Swamp that separated Virginia and Carolina did form something of a physical barrier, especially in the east closer to the coast, the Potomac River served to facilitate rather than impede movement between Virginia and Maryland. Both Indians and English colonists maintained cultural continuity as well as easy communication and travel across the Potomac, but for both the river formed a dubious political boundary. Unlike Tsenacommacah's boundaries to the east, west, and south, the one to the north did not constitute a physical barrier, illustrated by Powhatan's attempts to expand to the north at the time of English invasion. The northern boundary proved similarly permeable for European colonists, and this fact created serious problems for Virginians and Marylanders after the founding of Baltimore's colony.

Overland fur traders, the most active Virginia colonists in the region north of the Potomac before Maryland's founding, precipitated controversy over competing jurisdiction centered on their activities. Traders Henry Fleet and William Claiborne, both closely tied to the conflicts between Virginia and Maryland, responded very differently when the land and water they had become accustomed to using and the Indians with whom they traded came under a new jurisdiction.[55] When the creation of the new Virginia-Maryland boundary moved his Kent Island trading settlement into Lord Baltimore's colony, the Puritan (and anti-Catholic) William Claiborne manifestly declined to transfer his allegiance from Virginia to Maryland.[56] A new Maryland colonist wrote only a few weeks after arriving in the Chesapeake that William Claiborne came "from *parts of Virginia* where we intend to plant," making it clear that Marylanders thought of the land as under the jurisdiction of Virginia.[57]

As soon as Claiborne and his London partners learned of Baltimore's Maryland patent, they complained that the grant included land within Virginia's boundaries, that it included Virginia colonists' places of traffic, and lay so near their habitations that it would "give general disheartening to planters if they be divided into several governments." In 1633 Kent Islanders repeatedly tried but failed to have Kent Island omitted from Baltimore's patent. Maryland Governor Calvert forbade Claiborne to trade in the Chesapeake without a license from him.[58]

Claiborne, his Indian allies, and other Kent Islanders refused to acknowledge the redrawn borders that placed them under Maryland's jurisdiction and continued to trade as they had before, primarily with Indians who lived in what had become Baltimore's colony. In the spring of 1635 a Maryland commissioner searched the Chesapeake for Virginia traders without Maryland licenses and seized one of Claiborne's pinnaces and the goods of another Virginian who had long traded in the area.[59] When Claiborne tried to recover his property, a battle ensued in which three Virginians died. Virginia Governor John Harvey, following royal orders to help Baltimore's plantation, approved of Calvert's actions against Claiborne, inciting the Virginia Assembly, most of which supported Claiborne, to send their governor back to England.[60] As befitted a royal governor, Harvey pursued royal goals, by definition intercolonial, given the Crown's inherent interests in all English colonies. Claiborne continued to resist Maryland's control over the northern Chesapeake into the 1640s, though he increasingly kept his protests within legal limits.[61] The establishment of new colonies drew lines (or in this case, ascribed new meaning to a precontact Indian political border) that could circumscribe the actions of traders such as Claiborne and his Susquehannock partners. Both wanted to continue trading with one another, but after the establishment of Maryland, their activities suddenly became defined as intercolonial and illegal.

Virginia Indian trader Henry Fleet reacted to the establishment of Maryland very differently than did Claiborne. He too considered himself as trading in or at least from Virginia. He felt less allegiance to Virginia than did Claiborne, and assisted Leonard Calvert in exploring the Potomac and selecting the site for St. Mary's City. Perhaps his position as an intercolonial trader and border crosser (and his conflicts with Virginia over licensing) lessened his loyalty to Virginia.[62] Fleet at first seemed willing to stay put and let the boundaries evolve around him, changing his colonial political allegiance from Virginia to Maryland. In May 1634 he received a grant for two thousand acres on the St. George River in Maryland. In 1638 Fleet and his brothers Edward, John, and Reynold all served as members of the first Maryland Assembly, and in February 1639 another legislature planned to assemble "at the house, where Captain Fleets lately dwelt."[63]

His cooperation with Maryland, however, did not reflect permanent dissatisfaction with Virginia. After the English Civil War began, Fleet returned to Virginia, and in April 1645 the Virginia legislature appointed him "as a fit person acquainted with the language of the Indians, and accustomed to intercourse with them, to trade with the Rappahannocks, or any Indians, not in amity with Opechancanough" (who had led the recent attacks against the colony that began the Third Anglo-Powhatan War). The following year the legislature appointed him to organize an expedition against unnamed Indians and to build a fort in the Rappahannock River valley. In December 1652 Fleet represented Lancaster County in the Virginia Assembly, which authorized him and William Claiborne "to discover and enjoy such benefits and trades, for fourteen years, as they shall find out in places where no English have ever been and discovered, nor have had particular trade, and to take up such lands."[64] In 1654 the Rappahannock county records named Fleet as interpreter to a proposed expedition against Indians.[65] Fleet clearly chose a different response to newly established colonial boundaries than did Claiborne. He temporarily gave up his Virginia allegiance to continue trading with Indians north of the Potomac. Like Claiborne, he had to respond to the fact that his earlier practices of living south of the Potomac and trading with Indians north of the river had become illegal and intercolonial with the founding of Maryland. Rather than fighting the change, as Claiborne did, Fleet responded with flexibility about the specifics of jurisdiction.

Though Carolina did not face a challenge like Claiborne's, once settled, its officials, like those of Maryland, tried to stop Virginia traders from carrying on a trade with Indians in areas now within Carolina's legal bounds. In 1670 the Assembly of Albemarle County passed several acts, ratified by the Lords Proprietors, including one "for the . . . prohibiting strangers trading with the Indians."[66] The trade routes to the southwest described in Chapter 1 became particularly important because they afforded both Virginia and Carolina traders access to western and southern Indians who could provide deerskins and slaves. During the seventeenth century, Virginia traders ignored Carolina's laws and faced little effective challenge from other English traders. In the eighteenth century, however, Carolina passed a comprehensive trade act in 1707 and began confiscating Virginia traders' goods, starting a trade war that lasted through the 1710s. That decade saw considerable tension, rather than cooperation, between the two colonies, caused by the fact that historic trade paths crossed the colonies' uncertain border with one another. The contest over trade, however, did not preclude Virginia's aid to Carolina during the 1715 war against the Tuscaroras.[67]

Overlap in overland and coastal trade created increasingly complicated possibilities for illegal intercolonial trade involving multiple colonists and Indians. Courts' ability to respond to complex problems depended on strong communication networks that followed the same overland and coastal routes permitting the illegal trade. In January 1691 North Carolinian Mr. William Duckingfield traveled to Jamestown to inform the Virginia Council that at the beginning of the month eight or ten Tuscarora chiefs had complained to him that they thought English colonists had killed two Tuscarora chiefs. A visiting Meherrin Indian (who clearly understood the growing overlap of maritime and overland trade) told Duckingfield and the chiefs that Daniel Pugh of Nansemond County, Virginia, had captured the two Tuscaroras and sent them to Barbados as slaves. When the Tuscaroras threatened revenge, Duckingfield warned them that violence would cause the English to declare war against them and that instead they should go directly to the Virginia governor who would investigate the report and do them justice. According to Duckingfield, the Tuscaroras agreed to this suggestion.

In the meantime, however, Duckingfield, anxious to maintain the peace required to continue profitable trade, traveled to Virginia to tell officials there what had happened. He went first to Nansemond County, where credible witnesses informed him that Pugh had in fact sent four Tuscaroras out of Virginia, two in a Captain Prout's ship to Barbados and two in Thomas Tyler's brigantine, the *Swallow* of Barbados, to another of the Caribbean islands. When the Council heard Duckingfield's report in January, it began an investigation and ordered Pugh to appear in court the next month.[68] Pugh did not come to Jamestown in February, but Master Thomas Tyler of the *Swallow* came and testified that he had carried two Indians out of Virginia the previous year for Pugh. He produced a bill of lading signed to Daniel Pugh of Nansemond County for the Indians, and Pugh's instructions for selling them. The Council ordered the Nansemond sheriff to arrest Pugh and bring him to Jamestown.[69] The Assembly members, like Duckingfield, understood the high stakes requiring cooperation between the North Carolina traders and the Virginia Assembly in preventing activity such as Pugh's, which endangered relations between colonists and Indians. Pugh's hopes that by taking Indians from North Carolina he could avoid prosecution in Virginia therefore proved wrong. Once again, growing communication among English and Indians across colonial boundaries and the familiarity of both colonists and Indians (such as Duckingfield's Meherrin informer) with the maritime and overland workings of the Atlantic world made his apprehension likely.

Motion defined the Atlantic world. Over the course of the century, many of its residents used the mobility it provided to improve their own position within it. For some, that involved legal moves to establish trade connections or pursue religious goals. Frequently changing seventeenth-century political borders redefined some legal travel, generally that of Europeans trading between the colonies of different nations or Europeans and Indians trading with one another. Other Atlantic world residents crossed borders illegally in order to use the political boundaries to escape intolerable or unprofitable situations. Those individuals—criminals, debtors, slaves, and servants—hoped that borders would prove fluid enough to cross but meaningful enough to allow escape. Inevitably, those travelers provoked energetic response from officials and elites intent to prove the opposite, that the wealthy (creditors and masters) and the courts that existed in part to protect their interests controlled the borders as well as the trade and communication networks that transcended them. We cannot know whether or not official efforts decreased travels. We are by far more likely to learn of runaways returned, as they appeared in court to receive extended terms, than we are of those who established new lives in other colonies or who died trying. Successful runaways, however, may have predominated, given officials' slim resources, the vast spaces not under colonial control, and the possibility that fugitives would encounter not only members of the ruling class intent on stopping their flight, but also people who might harbor them either out of ignorance or for reasons of shared class, religion, or ethnicity. Colonial officials did not succeed in closing borders, which remained porous to legal and illegal travelers alike into the eighteenth century.

What we can know with certainty is that by endeavoring to establish control over Atlantic world travel, Crown and colonial officials strengthened their own communication networks. Their attempts to restrict the illegal movements of debtors, criminals, laborers, and traders involved negotiations about the meanings of intercolonial boundaries. Officials generally respected political boundaries by avoiding pursuit of criminals across boundaries and instead enlisting the help of officials in other jurisdictions (and thereby creating additional intercolonial links). Officials aided their counterparts in other colonies because they realized cooperation was essential to discourage criminals' escape across boundaries. They also understood that cooperation preserved their own jurisdictions. In other words, their help ensured that other officials could continue to respect their authority within their own boundaries.

The existence of continuously expanding communication networks and effective use of them by colonial officials meant that, far from developing the goals and structures of governance in isolation, colonies drew on a shared, growing body of empirical knowledge. Indeed, they could have done little else. For Virginia's officials, the complex nature of the colony's affairs, encompassing its far-flung business activities and the movement, licit and illicit, of free and unfree peoples, together with the legal ramifications of both, confronted Virginia's government with a series of challenges by no means confined within its political borders. The creation of the neighboring colonies of Maryland and Carolina, whose newly erected boundaries crossed existing routes of trade and travel long used by Indians and whites, created substantial competition between colonies and indeed led to violence, which ultimately heightened the need for multicolony cooperation. Networks of overland and maritime trade routes thus precluded isolation and dictated methods of government that depended on communication among the colonies of the English Atlantic world.

Chapter 8

Virginia, North America, and English Atlantic Empire

By the final quarter of the century, colonial officials gained enough power vis-à-vis Eastern Indians that they could contemplate trying to control the seasonal long-distance Indian travel whose patterns predated European colonization. Such efforts required a different level of intercolonial coordination than those discussed in Chapter 7. Rather than defining types of individuals whose movements should be controlled, these efforts required international diplomacy: negotiations with Indian nations and the European colonies—English, Dutch, Spanish, or French—with which they allied. These efforts dovetailed with England's attempts to coordinate colonial administration in the interest of exerting firmer imperial control over its colonial possessions, thereby imposing an English imperial structure on the English Atlantic. Colonial efforts to control Indian movement thus aided English creation of an Atlantic imperial structure. That structure always remained incomplete in the eyes of London officials. Certainly many elements of Virginians' Atlantic world remained outside it. (England indeed made little attempt to include most intercolonial trade or migration within its imperial vision, requiring instead only that trade in "enumerated goods" destined mostly for transatlantic trade receive imperial oversight: hence the mistaken impression left by the many records that therefore omit mention of intercolonial trade.) But the process by which Virginia experienced England's efforts at creating empire—intertwined as they were with Anglo-Indian relations—changed Virginia's relation to other mainland colonies, while affecting its relation with the Caribbean very little. Thus, at the end of the century Virginia's position within the Atlantic world and its relations with continental and island colonies changed.

Concurrent with the gradual evolution of informal Atlantic ties between colonial officials, after midcentury successive English rulers tried to enforce English control over its colonies and regularize colonial administration. Their attempts included a very different type of intercolonial coordination than that described in the previous chapter, one orchestrated by London and designed to serve London's needs rather than those of the colonies. Parliament tried to prevent Dutch trade with the colonies, passing Navigation Acts to limit colonists' Dutch trade and going to war with the Netherlands from 1652 to 1654. Charles II strengthened the Navigation Acts in 1660, 1662, and 1673, fought two more wars against the Dutch, and established several councils and committees culminating in 1675 in the creation of the Lords of Trade, a standing committee of the Privy Council, to oversee England's Atlantic trade and the administration of its colonies. Both Commonwealth and Restoration efforts aimed at ensuring that colonial trade benefit England's economy and England's navy by employing a large enough English merchant marine to supply sailors during war.[1] Colonists and indeed colonial officials often resisted these attempts to regularize colonial commerce and government. As London encouraged intercolonial coordination or emulation that it deemed desirable (for example, in its numerous instructions to Chesapeake colonists that they imitate New Englanders and build towns), colonists resisted or simply ignored the directives. Mid-seventeenth-century attempts to impose metropolitan authority in the colonies and achieve a degree of conformity among colonies were, in any case, weakly enforced. They created a sense of shared experience among colonists and officials, but often in firm opposition to London policy. Indeed, intercolonial networks sometimes provided colonial officials with information that strengthened their resolve to resist English directives. In 1651, on learning that Parliament had forbidden Virginia, Bermuda, Antigua, and Barbados (the four remaining royalist colonies) any foreign trade as punishment for their refusal to accept the outcome of the English Civil War, Virginia Governor William Berkeley argued to the Virginia Assembly that Virginia should follow Barbados' lead in disobeying the act, because while "the men of Westminster . . . have long threatened the Barbados, yet not a ship goes thither but to beg trade, nor will they do to us, if we dare Honourable resist their Imperious Ordinance."[2] Berkeley's resistance ended badly for him: Cromwell sent a fleet to reduce both Barbados and Virginia to obedience and remove Berkeley (and Barbados Governor Francis, Lord Willoughby) from office, and Parliament passed its 1651 Navigation Act prohibiting all American colonies from trading with foreigners. Nonetheless, Berkeley's use of the Barbadian example in his speech to the Virginia Assembly reveals how information spread along intercolonial networks could encourage colonies to assert greater colonial independence from London. Colonial officials, seeking precedents to guide them through novel predicaments, turned to other English colonies.

In the final quarter of the century, however, official intercolonial interactions took on a different character, as the Crown sent a small but energetic

cast of royal officials to enforce conformity to commercial and political regulations and invested its colonial governors with mandates to cooperate with one
another. London moved colonial officials between Virginia and other colonies
and gave single officials authority over multiple colonies as part of a much
more conscious design to impose intercolonial conformity and improve coordination between colonies.[3] While the Crown and its advisors sought to bring
all of its colonies under tighter regulation and more uniform commercial and
political practice, its plans after 1675 for accomplishing such goals represented
a new English view of the Atlantic world: a world into which the North American mainland and the Caribbean for the first time fit differently. Newly visible
differences between mainland and Caribbean colonies depended on several
changes to the political geography of mainland North America: England's conquest of New Netherland and subsequent alliance with the Iroquois, the establishment of the Restoration colonies, the defeat of coastal Algonquians, and an
increase in English population, all of which permitted for the first time a perception of the east coast of North America, from Maine to Carolina, as
English.

The presence of overlapping and intertwined Indian and European political geographies on the mainland, and their absence in the Caribbean, became
newly important to London as well as to the colonies as the Dutch and coastal
Indians lost significant power, enmity between the English and French grew,
and Iroquois influence increased from Virginia to New England, both in absolute terms and relative to local Indian populations. The settlement of Metacom's War in New England and Bacon's Rebellion in Virginia, only shortly
after England defeated New Netherland and gained Iroquois alliance, produced a dramatic reconfiguration of Euro-Indian diplomatic relations on the
mainland. Colonists' decisive victories over New England and Chesapeake
Algonquians and Virginia's piedmont Siouans removed many former adversaries and competitors as serious military threats, making Virginia colonists
instead more vulnerable to incursions from Iroquoians now allied with
English New York. After 1675, under Charles II and James II (1685–88), and
especially during the period of intense anti-French sentiment shared by most
of his subjects under William III (1689–1702), Virginia's efforts to negotiate
within this North American world of redrawn political relationships converged with Crown efforts to impose uniformity on its colonies. The result for
Virginia was a heightened sense that events in other mainland colonies could
be crucial. That sense increased cooperation between Virginia and other
English mainland colonies to coordinate Indian policy in some cases, and
increased conflict between them over how to conduct such policy in others.

Official political borders represented an ideal geography of elites and officials, who hoped to say who would be constricted by such boundaries and who could travel across them. In the case of individual border crossers, this process occurred piecemeal in response to specific unsanctioned journeys. In the case of Indian nations in time of war, the process was a more formal one warranting English imperial attention. Because all intercolonial boundaries necessarily involved two or more colonies, officials from multiple colonies and England negotiated these "ideal geographies" with one another and then tried to impose them on the real world. However, the practical meanings of real boundaries were worked out on the ground.

The administration of James II continued Charles II's project to increase and centralize control over the colonies. James II's Catholicism and his determination to curb the independence of Puritan New England colonies by placing them, along with New York, under the Dominion of New England created factionalism within colonial governments that produced serious disruptions in several colonies in 1689 when news reached America that the Protestant William and Mary had successfully ousted James II and assumed the English throne. William III continued many of the colonial policies he had inherited from James II, retaining many of the same administrators and officials. He reorganized the Lords of Trade into the more specialized Board of Trade in 1696, expanded the scope of the Navigation Acts, created a vice-admiralty court system for the colonies, and attempted to connect the colonies via a postal system. Under William III, London's attempts to foster colonial coordination took on added significance as he took England to war with France, providing military incentive for continental intercolonial coordination, adding to the economic and political reasons London already possessed for enforcing greater colonial regulation.[4]

By the turn of the century, London created for the first time an administrative structure for the English Atlantic that changed both colonial-metropolitan relations and intercolonial relations on the mainland. The successes of London's efforts rested not only in the determination of the Crown and its officials but also depended on a very different international context and a much altered North American political geography. For Virginia and other mainland colonies, English goals to achieve more regular colonial administration and colonial goals for security intersected in one arena: that involving the by then inseparable issues of Indian policy and Anglo-French warfare. This meant that on the mainland by the end of the century, imperial determination to strengthen colonial regulation reinforced the decades-old growth of commerce-based intercolonial communication networks. During King William's War (1689–97), anti-French and anti-Catholic fears convinced not only Crown and colonial officials, but also many colonists that intercolonial coordination overseen by London had become a military imperative. Those beliefs, even though temporary for some colonists and officials, changed intercolonial relations and helped the Crown establish stronger imperial presence to serve its economic, military, and political ends.

One of the primary means by which the Crown and its advisors asserted royal authority and enforced colonial conformity was by appointing governors with tested commitment to Crown goals and then moving them from colony to colony. Francis Nicholson, for example, served the Crown as governor or lieutenant governor in the Dominion of New England, New York, Maryland, Virginia, and South Carolina; Edmund Andros as governor in New England, New York, and Virginia. Both were career military officers who supported London's desire to bring its colonies under stricter control. Governors of multiple colonies could draw on cumulative experiences to try to regularize colonial governments. Given their relatively brief service in particular colonies, they were unlikely to develop the strong attachment to any one place that had led William Berkeley to promote Virginia's interests over London's. More importantly, they brought an imperial view to the governorship of each colony and hoped to spread that view to colonial assemblies. Such a view, especially during periods of international warfare, encouraged Virginia officials to adopt a broadly American perspective rather than an insular colonial one.

London's late seventeenth-century push to control its colonies also involved the efforts of men such as Edward Randolph who held several offices including customs collector and surveyor general; Colonel Robert Quary, an Admiralty judge in New York and Pennsylvania, surveyor general of customs, and advisor to the councils of New York, New Jersey, Pennsylvania, Maryland, and Virginia; and William Blathwayt, who as secretary to the Lords of Trade and Plantations, surveyor general, and general of royal revenues in the colonies, directed much of the entire effort from London.[5] Such people supplied a driving force instrumental in creating intentional intercolonial networks among governments. Their imperial perspective, their widespread intercolonial and transatlantic connections, and their ability to envision a colonial consolidation that would serve the Crown provided a powerful boost to official intercolonial communication and coordination, though sometimes in the face of stringent opposition from colonial assemblies.

The Crown's commitment to fostering official intercolonial coordination at the end of the century rested on its determination to exercise control over colonial trade and colonial assemblies. Control of assemblies mattered especially when the crown saw continental and island colonies as instrumental in fighting foreign wars (and saw preservation of such colonies and the revenues they provided England as a crucial war goal). Although local colonial leaders often resisted such efforts, the royal governors had some success and local cooperation, especially during King William's War, not because colonial assemblies shared imperial goals to reduce the independence and idiosyncracies of colonial governments, but because local and crown officials shared a desire to maintain firm alliance with the Iroquois and other Indians. For the Crown, this desire stemmed from the need to keep the pivotal Iroquois on the English side of the conflict rather than the French. For Virginia colonists it also included an effort to limit the travel of Indians across Virginia's borders, thereby insisting that Europeans, not Indians, now possessed the power to determine the placement and definition of intercolonial boundaries. That goal required Iroquois cooperation.

The gradual defeat of coastal Algonquians, such as the Powhatans, and some Siouans over the first three quarters of the seventeenth century allowed colonists by 1676 to regard those Eastern Indians as bound to a specific colony (that which had conquered them and their land) and thereby by that colony's borders. References to such Indians by English colonial affiliations as "the Maryland Indians" or "our tributary Indians" rather than as Piscataways or Powhatans helped promote the idea among colonists and officials that Indians' movements were appropriately confined by colonial boundaries. However, such terms could not erase the existence of well-established travel routes, nor could it prevent their continued use. After 1676, Indians' travel began to affect Virginia and Maryland in new ways. Since before Europeans' arrival in North America, Iroquois from New York traveled for trade and warfare to the Chesapeake and to destinations farther south along paths that ran north-south through the Shenandoah Valley.[6] Increasingly during the seventeenth century, Iroquois also traveled to recruit allies for their wars with Canadian Indians or to capture potential adoptees in order to replenish population losses sustained during those wars. Meanwhile, as seventeenth-century Chesapeake colonists conquered or drove out most Indians living east of the fall line, they removed a restraint on colonial expansion.[7] As colonists settled near the fall line, they exposed themselves to attacks from "foreign" Indians, primarily Iroquois. In the late seventeenth century after the establishment of New York, Carolina, and Pennsylvania, English colonies spent much energy negotiating their borders with one another. As part of their efforts to define the meaning of often contested intercolonial borders, colonists and officials tried to limit Indian travel across them. Such control over Indian movements was conceivable to Virginia governments after 1676 because seven decades of intermittent war had weakened and decreased Indian populations. The settlement of Bacon's Rebellion brought many piedmont as well as coastal Indians under tributary status and gave Virginia's government considerable power to regulate the movements of "Virginia" Indians. However, members of the Iroquois Five Nations and the Iroquoian Susquehannocks continued to travel through the Virginia mountains and piedmont. Virginia (and Maryland) officials wanted the Iroquois to respect their political borders as inviolable. This desire, combined with fear of the French, brought some members of the Virginia Assembly to cooperate with Crown programs in North America, even when such programs restricted Virginia's independence.

Because English colonial officials understood colonial borders to limit their own political behavior, individual colonies found it impossible to deal unilaterally with mobile Indians.[8] Rather, they increasingly had to communicate and travel across colonial boundaries themselves, negotiating with one another in attempts to formulate cooperative intercolonial strategies to deal with Indians. Because Indian and European political geographies overlapped and intertwined, and because Virginia colonists were highly aware of overland routes connecting the Chesapeake to other regions of North America, those routes inspired additional fear during periods of European warfare. In times of peace these roadways pointed to the economic promise of expansive Anglo-Indian trade. In times of war, they became fissures along which armed Indians might invade dispersed, largely undefended English settlements. During the first Anglo-Dutch War, Iroquois travels south made some Virginians worry that the Dutch intended to prod the Iroquois to attack English settlements.[9] However, these fears were fleeting: London made little of them, and Dutch maritime attacks proved a greater threat. Enough Virginians benefitted from Dutch trade that many resisted London's efforts to encourage colonial cooperation in any of its seventeenth-century wars against the Dutch.

After England's final conquest of New Netherland in 1674, because the Iroquois Five Nations were now allied with English New York, Virginians could address the problem of Iroquois attacks in Virginia only by working with New York colonial officials. To negotiate with the Iroquois over matters that occurred within their own borders, English Virginians thus had to adopt a broadly intercolonial view. In other words, because Indian movements, following patterns established before the existence of colonial boundaries, crossed those boundaries once Europeans set them, English Virginians at the end of the seventeenth century had to see their own interests as closely interwoven with those of other colonies and therefore had to reconsider their relations to those other colonies. New York, because of the strength of the Iroquois within its borders and its proximity to Canada, became the center of England's North American military strategy. Therefore, because of overlapping Indian and colonial geographies, Virginia and imperial goals intersected in Albany, at the nexus of Iroquois-English alliance.

Until 1675, Susquehannocks formed something of a barrier between the Chesapeake and the Iroquois Five Nations. Susquehannocks, Iroquoian-speaking but not yet allied with the Iroquois Five Nations, lived at the head of the Chesapeake and Delaware Bays and during the seventeenth century fought intense wars with the western four of the Iroquois Five Nations over control of the fur trade.[10] Because after 1652, the Susquehannocks themselves allied with Maryland and Virginia, the western four Iroquois Nations considered themselves at war with the two Chesapeake colonies and their tributary Indians. During 1650s and 1660s, the Iroquois attacked Virginia and Maryland tributary Indians and some of the westernmost colonists, with the Susquehannocks joining the Chesapeake colonists and tributary Indians in resisting Iroquois attacks.[11]

When, after a nine-year period of English rule, the Dutch reconquered New York for a brief time in 1673, Maryland feared the Dutch would encourage the Iroquois to intensify attacks on the Chesapeake and so attempted to make peace with the Five Nations. To prevent the Susquehannock-Iroquois enmity from foiling Maryland's attempts to keep Iroquois war parties away, Maryland invited the Susquehannocks to move from the Delaware Bay and head of the Chesapeake Bay (where the Marylanders knew they provided a target for Iroquois traveling down the Susquehanna River) to an abandoned Piscataway fort at Piscataway Creek just below the Potomac River falls.[12] In response to Maryland's invitation, the Susquehannocks moved in 1674. They relocated near the towns of Maryland allies, Piscataways and Doegs. But Maryland's plans for peace with the Iroquois did not materialize, and the Susquehannocks' move diverted some Iroquois attention from the Delaware Bay to the Chesapeake piedmont and thereby intensified Iroquois attacks on Virginia and Maryland fall line settlements near the Susquehannocks' new residence. The Iroquois, some of whom wanted to force the Susquehannocks to surrender and assimilate into Iroquois tribes, traveled down the Potomac River from the Great Indian Warpath to raid the Susquehannocks and other Indians nearby.[13]

The Susquehannocks' settlement on the Potomac precipitated a series of intercolonial problems that resulted in part from the permeability, for both Indians and colonists, of the Maryland-Virginia border. In July 1675 some Maryland Doegs crossed the Potomac to trade in Stafford County, Virginia, at the western edge of English settlement in Virginia. The Doegs took some hogs belonging to planter (and Barbadian immigrant) Thomas Mathew, saying that he owed them money from prior trading. Mathew or some of his servants chased, caught, and killed or beat some of them. The Doegs retaliated and killed Mathew's English overseer. Two local militia captains and thirty Virginians then went after the Doegs, crossing the Potomac into Maryland and killing Doegs and some of the newly arrived Susquehannocks, allied not only with Maryland but also with Virginia. Maryland authorities protested to Virginia Governor Berkeley that the Virginians had killed innocent Indians and invaded Marylanders' territory "in time of peace."[14] Maryland's protest points directly to the reasons colonial officials required intercolonial coordination of Indian policy: as long as the reality of permeable boundaries meant that Indians would travel from one colony to another, colonies had to assist one another or risk armed invasion from another colony's militia. The Potomac River was a relatively clear intercolonial border, but many were under dispute, and such invasions could set dangerous precedents and provide grounds for conquest during future boundary negotiations.[15]

While the two colonies argued about who was to blame, the Susquehannocks began to raid outlying settlers in Virginia and Maryland, and local officials from both colonies acted in concert to stop the attacks. Indian border crossing between the two English colonies thus moved colonists to cooperate across the Virginia-Maryland border in order to maintain the increasingly more important boundary dividing English colonists and Indians in the Chesapeake. On August 31, 1675, Berkeley commissioned (Barbadian-connected) John Washington and (New England immigrant) Isaac Allerton, Jr., to oversee an investigation into the murders, determine the Indians responsible, and attack them.[16] Washington and Allerton skipped the investigation and instead wrote to Maryland officials asking for help in attacking the Indians. Maryland sent 250 soldiers to help 750 Virginians from the Northern Neck militias pursue Susquehannocks.[17] The English surrounded the Susquehannocks' fort, called their chiefs out to negotiate, and killed five of them under a truce flag. The remaining Susquehannocks held out in their fort for six more weeks and then escaped at night through the English camp, killing ten English soldiers on their way. They then began a series of attacks on English settlers. Some Susquehannocks crossed the Potomac and killed about forty Virginia colonists in January 1676; colonists feared further attacks. Virginia's inability to resolve the issue to the satisfaction of many colonists contributed to Nathaniel Bacon's rebellion.[18]

Once the Susquehannocks had killed about fifty English on the frontier (figuring one chief's life to be worth ten ordinary colonists' lives), they calculated that they had gotten their revenge and offered to make peace with Virginia. With the help of an English interpreter, the Susquehannock chief sent a message to Governor Berkeley asking why, contrary to the treaty between Berkeley and the chief, he had taken "up arms against him his professed friend in behalfe of the Marylanders his professed enemies." He regretted that he and his subjects found the Virginians, once their friends, now "without any cause

. . . becom his foes," and so eager to pursue a groundless quarrel "as to perserv the chase into anothers dominions." His letter shows that the chief recognized English political boundaries, tried to learn what practical meanings they held for English colonists and leaders, and understood that borders possessed different meanings for English than for Indians of the region.

His belief that the English border limited European travel more than Indian travel pointed precisely to the problem that the English in Virginia and Maryland hoped to change by joining forces. The Susquehannock chief hoped that the score was now even. He proposed that, if Berkeley would pay for damages the Susquehannocks had sustained in the war "and no more concerne himselfe in the Marylanders quarell," he would gladly renew and confirm the ancient league of amity. Otherwise, he threatened that he and his allies would "fite it out to the last man." Berkeley did not consent to this proposal, so the Susquehannocks continued to attack frontier settlements, with the salient result that Virginians and Marylanders grew more cooperative because of events originating in Doegs crossing the Potomac River boundary to carry on a trade with Virginia colonists. The fact that the Doegs traveled easily across the border made the issue of their killing an English colonist an intercolonial problem. It resulted in official cooperation and joint coordination of troops. The Maryland-Virginia border certainly mattered to officials in both colonies, but the boundary between Indians and English colonists had begun to matter more. Isaac Allerton, Jr., and John Washington, who had initiated the cooperation between Virginia and Maryland forces, both possessed Atlantic experience, making them perhaps less likely to harbor a strong commitment to Virginia or to its rivalries with Maryland.[19]

The 1675 Susquehannock War, coupled with English knowledge of recent Susquehannock mobility and of Indians' long-distance communication in general, also led Virginia leaders to reconsider their relationship with more distant colonies, forcing them to face what they had long vaguely known, that Indian contacts connected them overland to other colonies and required colonies to recognize and act on common strategic interests. The warfare between the Susquehannocks and the Virginia and Maryland militias coincided with Metacom's War between Wampanoags and Plymouth colonists in New England. English colonists in Virginia knew full well that Indians traveled and formed alliances, sometimes over long distances. That most colonists knew of these contacts without completely understanding the specifics of them led English officials, during this time of two simultaneous wars, to imagine Indian contacts before they had certain knowledge of them. These fears of intercolonial Indian movement and alliance encouraged English colonists to strengthen their linkages with one another.

In February 1676 Virginia Governor William Berkeley penned a detailed description of the events in New England, explaining that "a very understanding and sober Virginia Merchant that came lately hence does assure me" that the news was accurate. Through the coastal sea travel of merchants and traders, Berkeley and other Virginians learned of events that gained salience because of overland Indian travel. By enabling them to compare notes, merchant travel also allowed them to increase their knowledge of Indian overland travel. Berkeley thought the common timing of the Susquehannock War and Metacom's War more than coincidence. He wrote that "The infection of the Indians in New-England has dilated it selfe to the Merilanders and the Northern parts of Virginia, and wee have lost about Forty men Women and Children in Patomacke and Rapahannocke kiled as wee suppose by the sesquashannocks."[20] When the Virginia Assembly met a month later, the New England news had heightened the councilors' and burgesses' fear of local Indians. In an address to Charles II, they explained that they had planned to exact revenge on the Indians, "which we should have not doubted (by Gods assistance) in a short time to effect, had their appeared none other danger but from those Indians within our reach." The assemblymen, however, learned that local Indians were "endeavouring (with offering Vast Summes of their wealth) to hyre other Nations of Indians two or three hundred miles distant from us." A "very considerable bodie" of Indians reportedly had come down the James River, where they waited "hovering over" the colonists, fifty or sixty miles upriver. "[A]ll Indians as well our neer neighbours as those more remote" daily made the councilors and burgesses suspicious that "it is not any private grudge, but a generall Combination, of all from New-England hither." The concurrent timing of Metacom's War and the Susquehannock War bolstered the Assembly's suspicion of a general Indian plot. It feared that the New England Indians' success "is and will be a great incouragement to ours here," which made strong defense in Virginia crucial.[21]

The next month Berkeley reiterated that "the Indians are Generally combind against us in al the northerne parts of America." In describing the losses in New England, he outlined the interrelation of various kinds of intercolonial connections. The losses caused to New England directly by the war were "not halfe the New England mens misery." They had also lost their beaver trade and at least half of their fishing "and have nothing to carry to the Barbadoes with whose commodities they were wont to carry away our Tobacco and other provisions."[22] New England's Indian troubles thus reverberated into the broader English Atlantic as overland Indian military alliances impinged on intercolonial maritime trade. New England merchants depended on fur trade for their own intercolonial commerce. When war damaged New Englanders' ability to procure local trade goods, this hurt Virginians, who depended on New Englanders to bring Barbadian commodities to the Chesapeake to trade for tobacco. Berkeley's letter made it clear that such a disruption in intercolonial and transatlantic trade also hurt Barbadians.

Berkeley's realizations that New England's problems touched Virginia prompted him to encourage London to intervene in New England's troubles. Intercolonial interdependencies—in the realms of trade and diplomacy—required that officials in each colony pay attention to events in other colonies. Because of his concern for Virginia, Berkeley wrote to one of Charles II's secretaries of state about New England. He began by hoping "it will not be impertinent to give you the relation of our Neighbours as wel as of ourselves" but defended that as necessary "because their Troubles were the cause and beginning of ours." He criticized New England, blaming its colonists for their mistreatment of Indians there and asserting that New Englanders coveted more land than they could safely hold "from those they have dispossessed of it." When, according to Berkeley, those Indians asked "if this uncharitable expulsion of them . . . were according to the Charitable doctrines they had learned from their God" the New Englanders had replied that "God had given [the] land to them and they would hold it adding farther that the Indians were to[o] weake and Ignerant to contend with them." The "exasperated" Indians understandably, according to Berkeley, sought revenge. "The nearest to the Inglish communicated their sufferings to those farthest of[f] and told them if they did not Joyne to resist the common Ennimie the next complaynt would be theirs." New England's problems became Virginia's because the New England colonists "so much enraged the Indians that presently their were Leauges made with those that were formerly Ennimies and on a sodune they assault the Inglish." When the New England Indians resolved to attack the English in New England, they "sent Emmissaries as farr as our parts to enduce our Indians to doe the like and it is almost incredible what intelligence distant Indians hold with one the other."[23]

Indians in Virginia, as well as those in New England, almost certainly did know what transpired elsewhere. Perhaps the news of events in one place did influence Indians' actions in others, though the common timing of the Susquehannock War and Metacom's War and colonists' fears of continental Indian alliance offer the only evidence of such coordination. The Indians in each place certainly had sufficient local incentives to attack separately. The English colonists' fears, though perhaps mistaken about details, derived from their knowledge that news indeed traveled via Indians' overland trade routes and connections existed among Indians across long distances and certainly across colonial boundaries. Berkeley's expression of those fears reveals an impressive level of detail in intercolonial news and indicates New England Indian as well as colonial news sources. Ironically, the English knew of these Indian connections because they had profited from them and encouraged them in order to acquire furs. However, even in the midst of attempts by traders to use them, colonists (especially those who were not fur traders) always felt ambivalent about them. The trails had served for war as well as trade since before English settlement, and everyone involved must have known from the outset that the networks were potentially dangerous as well as potentially profitable for Europeans.

Berkeley would not have cared so much about New England wars if he had not believed them to affect Virginia. Though Bacon's Rebellion prevented him from attempting to formulate any strategies with New England, his letters reveal that knowledge of Indian communication networks affected his perceptions of the relationships between geographically separate English colonies. His refined understanding of shared interests prompted his willingness to suggest to London officials policy for colonies other than his own.

In addition to encouraging Virginia officials to see commonalities between their own situation and that of New England, the Susquehannock War also strengthened Virginia's connections with New York. Like Berkeley, New York Governor Edmund Andros also observed the hostilities between the Susquehannocks and the Chesapeake colonists and feared general Indian wars. Andros tried to diffuse the violence by inviting the Susquehannocks into New York for protection "from their Enemys." A Susquehannock migration to New York would achieve the New York-allied Iroquois goal of assimilating (and thereby effectively conquering) the Susquehannocks.[24] Andros recognized that Indian trade and warfare connected colonies to one another so that colonists, through their relations with local Indians, found themselves interacting with more distant Indians resident in other colonies. Andros (likely influenced by the Iroquois) realized that Indian warfare and travel patterns required larger and more complicated alliances between Indians and English colonists than the existing system in which each colony conquered or allied with local Indians. Indian long-distance rivalries, alliances, and trade that had, over the course of the century, become intercolonial, required matching English intercolonial connections.

Andros promised the Susquehannocks that he would make peace for them with Virginia and Maryland and with the Iroquois. The colony of New York and the Iroquois Confederacy would both gain strength from their increasingly central place in the network of relationships between Indians and English colonies in North America. Because the developing network hinged on negotiations with the Iroquois, it provided them with power to force negotiations and to force them to be held at Albany. In the Chesapeake, New York Governor Andros's actions meant that Virginia and Maryland had to focus elsewhere to deal with Iroquois' actions within their own governments. The similarity of their predicament also encouraged the two Chesapeake colonies to work together in dealing with the Iroquois and New York.

As news of Andros's invitation spread among the Susquehannocks, some began to move to New York (though some stayed in the Chesapeake). At a June 1676 meeting, the Susquehannocks in New York formally accepted Andros's offer.[25] Maryland, after some wavering, agreed in the spring of 1677 to participate in peace negotiations with the Susquehannocks and the Iroquois. Virginia, busy with Bacon's Rebellion and its aftermath, sent no delegate of its own; however, in mid-May 1677, the Maryland Council sent Henry Coursey as ambassador to Governor Andros to treat with the Iroquois at Albany, instructing him to negotiate for Virginia as well as for Maryland.[26]

In Albany Coursey addressed the Iroquois, not the Susquehannocks. He stated that Marylanders (and Virginians) would forget the past, "you takeing care (as we shall on our Parts) that your Indians, nor none liveing among you or comeing through your Countrey, doe for the future Injure any of our Persons (Piscataway or other our Indians liveing with us) or goods." The Five Nations and the Delawares (as observers) signed the treaty, which helped to form a broad set of English-Indian alliances known as the Covenant Chain that linked Indians and colonists from Maine to Virginia.[27] But because the Susquehannocks had not signed, they remained, in the eyes of Indians involved, unbound by the treaty and therefore free to attack Virginia and Maryland. Similarly, because the Chesapeake tributary Indians had not signed, the Iroquois regarded them as unprotected, despite the language of the treaty that suggested they were.[28]

In 1678 the Susquehannocks, with help from the Iroquois, began traveling via precontact paths through the Shenandoah Valley and down the Potomac, Rappahannock, and James Rivers, attacking Maryland and Virginia tributary Indians. The Susquehannocks wanted revenge for the Chesapeake Indians' help to the Virginia and Maryland militias during the Susquehannock War. The Iroquois wanted to bring those Indians into their own sphere of influence and thereby further strengthen their own position in North America.[29] Coursey's negotiations clearly did not solve Virginia's or Maryland's problems with the Susquehannocks or the Iroquois. The fact that Virginia and Maryland suffered similarly in this conflict, as a result of their work together in the Susquehannock War, encouraged them to continue to cooperate in their negotiations with New York into the 1680s and 1690s. After the 1681 founding of Pennsylvania, the Susquehanna Valley became a refuge for Indians fleeing violence elsewhere. The Iroquois and Susquehannocks, as they traveled through Pennsylvania to raid Indians to the south, could recruit volunteers from among these refugees.[30] Pennsylvania Governor William Penn also recognized the need for officials in various colonies to communicate with one another about Indians' movements. On June 8, 1684, he wrote from Philadelphia to Virginia Governor Francis, Lord Howard of Effingham, telling him that the Pennsylvania Indians, whom he had "partly gained to the obediance" of his government, told him that "the northern Indians are gone down, whither to the Piscatoway [of Maryland] or Virginia Indians" Penn did not know.[31] He did know that the information might be crucial to saving English colonists' lives and that it was imperative for governors to encourage and build on Indian-English intercolonial communication networks to keep abreast of Indian movements.

In the summer of 1684 Effingham went to New York to renew and strengthen the treaty between the Chesapeake colonies and the Iroquois in hopes of ending the raids. Virginians Ralph Wormeley and Edmund Jennings accompanied him.[32] The trip not only fostered official intercolonial contacts but also formed social and personal ones. Effingham's daughter, Philadelphia, went with him, and she and her father spent much of their time socializing. They stayed the summer with New York Lieutenant Governor Thomas Dongan who offered the hospitality of his house rather than let Effingham take a house in town, providing the two governors with ample opportunity to compare notes about their experiences as colonial governors.[33]

Dongan, though willing to cooperate with Effingham, sought to maintain continued Iroquois action against the Canadian French and their allied Indians. So Effingham, though he complained to the Iroquois about the raids, did not demand reparations or threaten the Iroquois, though they admitted having violated the Covenant Chain.[34] The Iroquois thanked Effingham for his forgiveness but did not promise to stop. Rather, they pressed for their own goals. An Onondaga sachem, speaking on behalf of the Five Nations, told Effingham that they wanted "that the Path may be open for the Indians under your Lordships Protection to come safely and freely to this place, in order to confirm this Peace." This demand would have forced Virginia's allied tribes into the Iroquois tributary system, one of the Iroquois' principal war goals. The wording of the request also suggests Iroquois belief that precontact travel routes remained "open" despite the various claims of colonial dominion over the land through which they passed. If the Iroquois succeeded in having Virginia Indians travel to Iroquoia, however, it would presumably also have achieved Virginia's objective of ending the raids as well. The Mohawks and Senecas, who denied complicity in the raids on Virginia, agreed to Effingham's demand that "we must not come near the Heads of your Rivers, nor near your Plantation, but keep at the foot of the Mountains."[35] In treaty negotiations Effingham tried to confirm that the Iroquois would respect Virginia's functional western border as a boundary also, by limiting their activities to land outside it and thereby changing their seasonal travel patterns to forego raids or any other travel into the Chesapeake coastal plain.

The following spring the Virginia Council planned to send "some of our neighbouring Indians" to confirm the Articles of Peace, as appeared "absolutely necessary." The council wanted to send representatives of the government as well to ensure "the safety and honour of the Country." In June the council, in determining "what person is fit to negotiate in soe great an affair," sent William Byrd I as the agent for Virginia and Edmund Jennings as his assistant, "by reason of his formerly being att New York and Albany, and well acquainted with the Peace his Excellency made with those northern Indians, and ye manner of treating with them." Byrd, as a fur trader, government official, and resident of land near paths providing access to the major north-south Indian artery, dealt with those who traveled through Eastern North America, including League Iroquois, and thus also possessed knowledge useful for such negotiations. They traveled by ship, taking an interpreter and two Indians each from the tributary Appamattock, Nanzatico, Chickahominy, and Pamunkey tribes via European-controlled maritime routes in order to have those Indians participate in an exercise that the assembly hoped would establish a measure of European control over overland routes.[36]

Virginia's appeal to New York for cooperation in preventing Indian overland intercolonial travel (along with the Crown's prompting) encouraged the English to think of their colonies as part of a larger English colonial world in which the strategic interests of separate colonies intertwined in ways that required ongoing diplomatic cooperation. Governors were at the center of these increasing intercolonial connections. Edmund Andros, who had overseen the Covenant Chain alliance at Albany, was during the late 1680s governor of the Dominion of New England, with Francis Nicholson as his deputy governor. The creation of the Covenant Chain had not stopped Iroquois raids on Virginia and therefore the need for further negotiations produced more official intercolonial travel and cooperation. Effingham went to New York to negotiate with the Iroquois again in the summer of 1687, stopping in Philadelphia on his way.[37] In 1689 when Effingham returned to England (but while he still held the office of governor), William Byrd wrote to him asking him to encourage the Crown to intervene in intercolonial affairs on Virginia's behalf. Byrd asked Effingham if he could secure royal instructions to New York to keep "the five Nations from rambling this way."[38] While Byrd may not have sanctioned Crown intervention in intercolonial affairs in general, he did solicit such interference (in the affairs of another colony, not his own) to deal with the necessarily intercolonial issue of Indian travel via precontact long-distance trade routes.

The fear of James II's Catholicism created anxiety among Protestant colonists that James's colonial officials would help surrender England's colonies to Catholic France. English Virginians focused these fears on Indian raids on their western borders. In the spring of 1689 "divers wicked and ill disposed persons of the Counties of Stafford and Rappa[hannock] laying hold of some falce and Extravigant reports of the unsetledness of affaires . . . by a pretended Examination of an Indyan" spread the word that Papists had hired "tenn thousand [Iroquois] Seneca Indyans together with Nine thousand Nanticoaks, [who] were all Landed & Joyning their Forces with an Imediat purpose of distroying all the Protestant Inhabitants of Virg[ini]a and Mary Land." The spreaders of this news also tried to convince their fellow colonists that all the Virginia councilors and most of the county justices "were Papists . . . and that they conspired in the designe of Joyneing with the Indians, to Cutt of the Protestants." The news so frightened colonists that several deserted their houses, and many in Stafford and Rappahannock Counties (both of which had experienced Susquehannock and Iroquois attacks and therefore knew firsthand of overland war paths) formed "parties with force of Armes to Rob, Plunder and pillage many the good & Loyall Subjects the Inhabitants of Virginia and Maryland, and to Stirr up and Carry on a Rebellion in both Colony's."[39] Continued Seneca raids in western Virginia prevented these colonists from putting any trust in the Iroquois' alliance with the English. Virginians' anxieties apparently spread, likely via coastal trade routes, to New York. Shortly after the Virginia Council recorded the rumors in the Northern Neck, the almost identical rumor spread through New York that Governor Francis Nicholson planned to help French Jesuits and their Indian allies "cut off" New York Protestants and present New York to Louis XIV.[40]

During the century's final decade, with James II in exile, an English Atlantic context of extreme anti-Catholic paranoia meant that as England went to war with France in 1689, colonial desires for security and imperial goals of intercolonial coordination converged more fully. William III's officials in America used colonial concerns to promote imperial goals. During King William's War (1689–97), overland Indian networks inspired fear among Virginians that Indians and French colonists from Canada could use Indian trails to reach the Chesapeake. These fears helped Virginia Governors Andros and Nicholson and crown officials such as Robert Quary press Virginia and other colonies into greater cooperation with one another than they otherwise would have sought.[41]

Virginia, obligated to help New York fight against the French, felt even more inclined to offer such support because the Iroquois not only protected New York from the French and Canadian Indians but also (in the eyes of Andros, Nicholson, and Virginia councilors) provided a buffer for Virginia against the French and Canadian Indians. French allies included Abnaki and Canadian Iroquois, but were consistently identified in Virginia sources as "Canada Indians." The stakes in New York's war with the French and Canadian Indians were so high for Virginia because many Virginia colonists and officials knew that if the Iroquois lost and became French subjects or allies, the Iroquois could lead the French straight to Virginia. In Virginia records, fears of French attacks on the Chesapeake almost always centered on the piedmont rather than the coast. Virginians always imagined that Indians would accompany French attackers. In fact, many Virginians perceived the French as a threat only because of the French alliances with Indians and the existence of Indian paths from Iroquoia through Virginia. Nevertheless, the incursions of Indians acting alone (New York-allied Iroquois, not French-allied Indians) had convinced colonists of a dangerous potential for French and Canadian Indian invasion.[42] If French colonists and Canadian Indians could reach Iroquoia-New York and the Iroquois could reach Virginia, the French and their allies could also travel to Virginia. Building on the Covenant Chain, William III made New York the cornerstone of his war strategy in North America. His requirement that other mainland colonies aid New York dovetailed with the Crown's now generation-old effort to regularize colonial governance for economic and political as well as military ends, in part because the same personnel could implement the policies and report levels of colonial obedience to the Crown.

Despite the objections of some Virginia Assembly members who thought the colony's independent defense of its frontier a more effective way of dealing with Indians, royal governors and some councilors continued to push for imperial and intercolonial goals requiring increased intercolonial coordination. In part, they could do so because the persistence of raids frightened colonists who, while perhaps not fully comprehending the complexity of Indians' long-distance relationships, knew that the Indians who attacked the westernmost English settlements came from the north. Some colonists therefore saw their problem in intercolonial terms.

The council paid attention to any news about Indians in other colonies that seemed credible, understanding that in this world which the English correctly understood as covered with a web of Indian paths and alliances, such information could mean life or death for Virginia colonists.[43] This attention to intercolonial news became even more pronounced as governors Francis Nicholson and Edmund Andros, who possessed notable intercolonial experience and connections, served the Crown in Virginia during the final decade of the century. Nicholson, who had held office in New England and New York, was lieutenant governor of Virginia from 1690 to 1692 while Effingham was in England. From 1692 to 1698, Andros, a former governor in New England and New York who had negotiated the Covenant Chain, served as governor of Virginia, during which time Nicholson held the office in Maryland. In 1698 Nicholson returned to Virginia as governor until 1705. During Nicholson's brief absences William Byrd, who had gone to New York for treaty negotiations and had multiple trade contacts throughout English mainland and Caribbean colonies, served as lieutenant governor.[44] Nicholson and Andros worked diligently to govern Virginia with an eye to the good of the English Atlantic empire as a whole, particularly with regard to Indian negotiations. Their contacts and experiences in New York and New England intensified Virginia's interactions with the northern colonies and its negotiations with Indians in the Chesapeake region and throughout English North America.[45] While Andros and Nicholson served in Virginia, the New York government readily approached the Chesapeake colony for help, perhaps counting on the governors' intercolonial outlooks to ensure that Virginia would comply with royal orders to aid New York.

In the spring of 1690 information arrived from New York and Maryland that the French soldiers and Canadian Indians had committed "divers barbarous Murthers" near Albany. The council, fearing "that the French, and Canada Indyans, will make some Attempts on the head of Potomack River, or other Frontiers," ordered rangers and militias to prepare for the possibility of such an attack.[46] In June the council received news from New York that the Five Nations, apparently wanting to strengthen themselves against the Canadian attacks, planned to "Send to Our Neighbour Indyans" to persuade them to leave Virginia, ally with the Iroquois, and return with them to New York. The council, concerned that such a migration would endanger Virginia by removing a buffer protecting them from western attacks, ordered that the colony's interpreters go immediately to "the Several Nations of Neighbouring Indyans" and tell them that if any foreign Indians should come "and require them to goe with them" the local Indians should tell them that they enjoyed the protection of the government of Virginia. The local Indians were to take any foreign Indians to the closest militia officer "who is to acquaint those Forreigne Indyans that the sayd Indians, are under the Protection of this Government, and that they are not to goe."[47]

Nicholson and the council, because of their concern about the rumored French and Indian attack at Albany, agreed that "of absolute Necessity ... this

Government [must] be acquainted, of the truth of what is alleadged, that thereby due care may be taken for the preservation of this Colony" and ordered someone "of good Intelligence and understanding" sent from Virginia to New England and New York to learn more. The council sent Colonel Cuthbert Potter, who returned from his trip in October bringing bad news confirming Virginians' fears of "many depredations and Murthers Comitted by Our Barbarous Enemies the French and Indians." Several letters Nicholson received from New York and New England reinforced those concerns. Additionally, information came from Maryland "that there were diverse strange Indians at the head of Potomack, and that there were some of the Piscattaway Indians killed." Despite the fact that when the nearest militia captains went to investigate they could not find "any Indians or tract of Indians" and that when they went to the Piscataway town in Maryland their tayac "declared he knew of noe strange Indyans, nor had any of his Indians killed," the councilors took precautions to prevent any surprises.[48]

In December 1690 more bad news arrived from the north. Nicholson's New England acquaintances wrote him that the French had beaten New England forces in Canada, a report that the master of a New England vessel in Virginia verified. The council feared that the French and Canadian Indians would attack Virginia, "being encouraged by their success against the New England men."[49] More reports and eyewitnesses arrived, confirming the previous accounts and bringing news as well of Jacob Leisler's Rebellion in New York. The Virginia Council feared that French and their Indian allies would take advantage of the political disruption that Leisler's Rebellion brought, attacking the Iroquois, "one of the Great Bulwarks betweene their Majesties subjects in New Yorke and in these parts, and the French," while New York was in no condition to help its Indian allies. So the Virginians renewed their fears that the Iroquois would "be perswaded or inforced" to ally with the French, "which would prove of very fatall Consequence to the Peace and Security of this their Ma[jestie]s Dominion, and Indeede all these parts of America."[50]

Ongoing fear of "foreign" Indian attacks intensified colonists' concerns about the local political disruptions accompanying the Glorious Revolution and heightened the Virginia Council's attention to internal political situations in other colonies. In 1691 the Council noted "that all the Neighbouring Colonies of New England New Yorke and Maryland are in Confusion and have noe Gov[erno]rs appointed by their Sacred Ma[jestie]s," which prevented Virginia from finding out from them "how affaires stand with them" or "what Methods they Intend to take to Secure their Ma[jestie]s Country against the Enemies, that soe wee might be the better Capable to take Measures to Secure this

Country." To make matters worse, the council learned that Quaker Pennsylvanians were spreading the word "that if the French or Indians come against
them they would goe out and Meet them without Armes, and acquaint them
that they had no quarrell with them, nor would not fight." Such a development, the council feared, would furnish the French and Indians with "provisions and a place of Retreate after Mischeif done."

The presence of Quakers in Virginia and their well-known intercolonial
communications made Pennsylvanians' reported pacifism even more frightening. Quakers continued to meet frequently in Virginia without informing the
government as the law required them to do. At their meetings assembled "not
onely the Inhabitants of this Colony, but those of Maryland Pensilvania and
other places . . . by meanes whereof the French or Indians if possest of Pensilvania have fitt opportunityes of knowing the affaires of this their Ma[jestie]s
Government." The council ordered that if "any Strangers from any other Governmt shall come among" the inhabitants, they should inform the nearest justice of the peace, "who is hereby Ordrd to cause the said person or persons to
appear before him, and to take his or their Examinations under his or their
hands to what place he or they belong, wh[i]ther goeing, when, and of all
things Else which may be for their Ma[jestie]s Service." The justice was to pass
on the information to Nicholson.[51] The potential combination of Quakers'
intercolonial stance of pacifism and Indians' intercolonial networks reinforced
among officials the notion that they needed to impose boundaries on the
movements of specific groups (of colonists, as well as Indians) perceived as
threatening.

Because of the danger other colonies' actions posed for Virginia, the
council sent all the information it had "Concerning the State of New England
New Yorke, Pensilvania, and the Caniday Expedition" to various parties in
London who, the councilors hoped, would convince the king to appoint royal
governors in "Our Neighbouring Plantations." Such a step, the council
claimed, would make things much safer for all English colonists in North
America because "all the Govrnmts may Joyne together to Secure these their
Ma[jestie]s Countryes against their Ma[jestie]s and our Enemyes." The council then added its hope that once having made such appointments, the king
would finally establish a postal system in the American colonies "to goe from
one Government to another that soe wee may have a Continuall and Speedy
Correspondence of anything that may happen for their Ma[jestie]s Service"
more cheaply than by sending messengers. The preceding two decades of
Indian relations had convinced the Virginia Council of the necessity for
cheaper and more reliable methods of regular communication between colonies. In the meantime, the council asked Nicholson to keep writing to "The

Gentlemen of his acquaintance in New England and New Yorke" because, especially given the disruptions in their governments, sources of reliable information were rare.[52] Nicholson's former experiences as governor of New York and his resulting social and political connections were crucial in a world where communication, though frequent, depended on the multiple interactions of individuals, each with his or her own personal or economic ties.

By the early 1690s no question remained among mainland colonial officials of the necessity for intercolonial communication to circumscribe Indian travel and foster Indian respect for European colonial political borders. In April 1692 the Virginia Council noted that the preservation of peace required knowledge of "transactions of Moment in the Neighbouring Governments." Before deciding whether to continue the expensive practice of sending out rangers during the following winter, it wanted to know the state of affairs to the north and asked John Perry, traveling to New York and New England, to make inquiries and to return by October 20.[53] Similarly, when in June 1692 the councilors worried about "Indians goeing in great Numbers from place to place at the heads of the Rivers without passes," they wrote the governments of New York and Pennsylvania to request that they order "their Indians when they Intend to come to Our Neighbouring Indians or goe by Our Frontiers to any Nation to the Southward of us, that they take passes" so that Virginians could identify Indians allied with the English rather than with the French. Virginia Indians, "if above three or four of them designe to travel abroad together," were likewise required to carry passes and inform a local justice when they planned to return so "that if any English or other of the Neighbouring Indians meete their Tract, the Country may not be allarumed thereby, as now is usuall."[54] Though these attempts to get Indians to respect colonial political boundaries failed, they reflected colonists' strengthening commitment to coordination of Indian policies in a world interlaced with a web of Indian byways.[55]

However, despite recognizing that New York could potentially help address the problems of Iroquois raids on Virginia's own borders, Virginians divided over their need to help New York and the Iroquois fight the war against Canadian colonists and Indians. The Iroquois continued to raid Virginia tributary Indians, while at the same time fighting for New York and the English against the French, making relations between Virginia and the Iroquois difficult throughout the 1690s, though they were supposedly allied as subjects of England in a war against France. During the late 1680s and throughout the 1690s, New York governors repeatedly wrote to Virginia governors asking for money or soldiers to help in the war against the French and Canadian Indians. The Virginia Council reacted favorably to New York's requests for help, believing that Virginia's peace depended on Iroquois protection from the French, because if the Iroquois became subject to the French and Canadian Indians, "his Majties Subjects of this Colony must Expect to be perpetually disturbed." In 1688 the councilors declared that they "unanimously think it necessary to send help." The House of Burgesses, however, refused to provide money, so the council asked Governor Effingham to take £500 out of quit rents.[56] The elected House of Burgesses was always more reluctant to send Virginia's money away than was the appointed Governor's Council, and at times refused to help New York, forcing the council to send money from the Crown's quit rents or port duties. The burgesses repeatedly expressed concern over the cost of defending Virginia's frontiers against the Iroquois, which they thought a more necessary defense against a more proven danger than helping New York against the French. They, elected by Virginia's freeholders, more quickly than the Crown-appointed councilors, lost faith in the ability of Iroquois negotiations to stop the raids in Virginia but nevertheless paid careful attention to events in New York. They were suspicious that the purpose of New York's war was to protect a trade that profited New York and the Crown but not Virginia. The council, in arguing with the House of Burgesses, insisted that "this Country has not been so highly independent, as you seem to make it" but that the House and council had agreed that New York had exaggerated to the crown its role in defending Virginia.[57]

The Iroquois also grew understandably suspicious of Virginia's commitment to the war, and sought resources to fight the war in part by continuing their raids in western Virginia. Both the House of Burgesses and the council grew less willing to send monetary aid New York. Their commitment to intercolonial communication as a strategy of Indian diplomacy was well established as necessary due to Iroquois mobility, but in funding the Iroquois to fight the French, Virginia also seemed to be funding the Iroquois to raid Virginia's own frontiers, which the colony then had to spend more money to defend. In July 1692, New York Governor Richard Ingoldsby sent Virginia a letter and copies of the most recent treaties between New York and the Five Nations, in which "the Indians Complaine of the want of Assistance from the Neighbouring Governments according to the Articles of Peace made with them." The Virginia councilors noted the expense of defending their frontiers against their own Iroquois allies whom they had paid to help arm. However, wanting to help defend their fellow English colonists from the French (and probably also still wanting to cooperate with the Iroquois in the hopes that the raids would finally stop), they decided to pay £100 to New York Councilor Stephen Van Courtland, as an emergency-only help fund. The council also asked the government of New York to try to prevent incursions into Virginia by the Five

Nations. If they did not stop, they said, Virginia could afford no further help for New York and the Iroquois.[58]

In the face of the Virginia Assembly's growing opposition to the Crown's Albany-centered intercolonial military policy, Lieutenant Governor Nicholson remained committed to intercolonial cooperation. When he found the assembly unwilling to pay its quota for the support of Albany, he resolved that the royal interest should not suffer even though the assembly members refused to understand their own interests. According to Quary, Nicholson, "who by long experience could judge," knew better than anyone that the support of Albany offered the only security for all the mainland governments against the French and their Indian allies and that keeping the Five Nations required the effectual support of Albany. By neglecting Albany the English would not only "lose so many sure friends but would add so many great and warlike Nations to the number of our enemies." If the Five Nations went to the French, then Quary felt sure the French would become "Masters of all Her Majesty's Provinces on the maine, when they please." Nicholson, finding that "the Assembly would not see their own Interest, or comply with Her Majesty's orders," went immediately to New York and out of his own "great zeale to Her Majesty's service and security of Her Provinces" gave his own bills for £900 to cover Virginia's quota, trusting the queen's "favour and justice, in reembursing him again our of Her Revenue in that Province."[59]

New York's requests for aid, the Crown's insistence on intercolonial cooperation, and Virginia's reluctant agreement (accompanied by more complaints about the Iroquois) continued through the 1690s.[60] Throughout the decade the situation posed a quandary because the Iroquois in New York continued their attacks on Virginia, and Virginians recognized that intercolonial cooperation provided much greater potential to regulate Indian activity than did unilateral action. Though Nicholson's and Andros's presence in office reflected increased intercolonial governing at the highest levels, the councilors declining willingness to help New York suggests resistance to pressure from Andros, Nicholson, and the Crown to act in concert and give up independence of action with regard to their own defense. The Iroquois, who formed the keystone of the Covenant Chain alliances, ultimately foiled royal officials' determination to convince Virginia that full commitment to continental diplomacy was in their best interest.

In addition to seeking better communications with colonies to the north, the Virginia Council encouraged colonies to the south to coordinate a response to Indian travel as well. Because the Iroquois' travels extended at least as far south as Carolina, the council sent the government of North Carolina "an account of the Mithods used here for Rangeing."[61] Virginia councilors believed that their knowledge of Iroquois travel patterns could help North Carolinians in their relations with Indians.

The heightened tensions and increased awareness of long distance Indian travel complicated Virginia's fur trade during the early 1690s. In 1691, Nicholson and the council decided to prohibit free trade between colonists and Indians because "the going forth of persons to trade with the Indians in these times of warr, may prove of very dangerous consequence and be a means of Involving this their Majties Country in great trouble." No one should "Send or go without the Inhabitants to trade o[r] truck" with Indians or to hunt, nor sell any guns or ammunition to any Indians except what the law allowed for neighboring Indians. Soon thereafter, however, the Crown ordered free trade with the Indians.[62] In 1692 the council resolved to use Nicholson's knowledge of New York's Indian policies as a model for Virginia.

Nicholson told the councilors in June that he thought Virginia's deerskin trade both inconvenient and dangerous "as it is now managed." When Virginia traders went to Indian towns to trade, they "use[d] them very basely and highly to the dishonor of the English nation, often times killing some of them, and takeing their goods away." Nicholson considered Virginia traders' practice of traveling to Indian towns "a great incouraging of them to persist in their Wickedness, it not being possible to discover what Indians they were that did it." In Nicholson's opinion, New York managed its Indian trade much more effectively. New Yorkers had followed the Dutch pattern and used their trading centers such as Albany, where the Dutch had built a fort and where Indian traders continued to bring their goods to the English. Nicholson and the council asked the Crown for permission for Virginia to manage its trade as did New York "as near as the Circumstances of the Country will beare." Such management, they believed, would "Secure the Trade, keepe the Indians from doeing Mischief, and regain the Honor of the English."[63] Growing communications between colonies, and in this case the governor's experience in multiple colonies, provided a broad base of experience on which Virginians could draw in dealing with Indians. Pennsylvania Governor William Markham's instructions the following year to Robert Brett, clerk of the market, to follow "the Custom of new yorke" suggests that the impression of New York's superior management of trade circulated throughout mainland colonies.[64]

In January 1698 Virginians learned from the Board of Trade of peace between France and England.[65] Because Indians continued to migrate and because Iroquois war parties continued to travel south in attempts to expand their influence, colonies continued to communicate with one another in order to negotiate with mobile Indians. In the following decades, Virginia and South Carolina fought over access to southwestern Indian trade and cooperated to ensure Indians did not control the southern piedmont. Some of Virginia's remaining seventeenth-century connections with New York, however, took on a decidedly new character. In March 1698 after Francis Nicholson returned to Virginia to replace Andros as governor, he received a letter from New York Governor Richard, Earl of Bellomont, "relating to a new trade with the Indians to the west-ward." At the same meeting, Virginian Colonel Cadwallader Jones (former governor of Providence Island in the Bahamas) also made a proposition for "the discovery of a new trade with the Indians."[66] In June, the Virginia Council ordered that Bellomont's letter and "other papers relateing to the discovery and Settleing a New Trade with the Indian be laid before the Committee appointed to Revise the Laws, and recommend to their Consideracon."[67] Iroquois and other Indians' north-south connections had prompted Virginia and New York to communicate about wartime issues and had allied Virginia (however weakly) to the Iroquois. Iroquois military successes against Great Lakes Indians and the 1698 peace between the English and French had opened trade west from New York. That trade provided opportunities for Virginians as well as for New Yorkers, in ways that would have been impossible before the colonies' need for official cooperation had strengthened their ties with one another. English perception that the French and their Indian allies posed a combined danger to all English mainland colonies caused different mainland colonists and officials to see themselves as more united. With enemies to the north, south, and west, and having already expelled the Dutch and Swedes from what could now be considered "middle" colonies, at least some officials in English North American colonies (particularly those with multiple colonial experience such as Nicholson and Andros) began to perceive themselves as a single entity: an English colonial mainland.

At the start of the eighteenth century, Robert Quary recommended to the Lords of Trade and Plantations that they give directions for the mainland governors to meet once a year. He reported to the Lords of Trade and Plantations with approval that Virginia Governor Francis Nicholson had gone to New York to meet with Governor Edward Hyde, Lord Cornbury, "about some matters relating to Her Majesty's service," adding that "There is a good correspondency between these two Governours, which will be attended with very good effects."[68] Among other advantages, such a meeting would remove "all scruples and objections" to a proposal to unite the mainland governments "under one System, Form and Constitution." Quary complained that many Virginians did not have the Crown's best interests at heart, but rather their own. He lamented that Virginia's assembly members considered themselves entitled to all the rights and privileges of England's Parliament "and begin to search into the Records of that Honourable House for Precedents to govern themselves by." Quary noted that the councilors' dangerous notions appeared in their last address to Queen Anne in which they justified disobeying the order for paying their quota for the support of the war against the French and the Indian allies in New York. Quary concluded "that now or never is the time to maintain and support the Queen's Prerogative; and put a stop to those wrong, pernitious notions, which are improving daily, not only in Virginia, but in all Her Majesty's other Governments. A frown from Her Majesty now, can doe more than perhaps an army hereafter."[69]

The Virginians' worst transgression, their conviction that Virginia had "far greater Importance to Her Majesty, than all the rest of the Provinces on the maine," led them to conclude "that they ought to have greater Privileges than the rest of Her Majesty's Subjects." This conclusion prompted them to begin "a nice Enquiry" into the circumstances of their own and other colonies' governments, which then led the Virginians to "the discovery that New England and the Proprietary Colonies are allowed greater privileges, both in respect of their Constitution of Government and Trade."[70] Learning of New England's privileges made the Virginians "very uneasy, and sowers their Temper" so much that no governor could hope to please them and pursue Anne's instructions at the same time. Quary thought that the most effective way to solve this problem would consist of gathering "all Her Majesty's Governments on the maine, under one Constitution and Government, as near as possible."[71]

While many Virginia elites disagreed strenuously with Quary's argument that the Crown needed to curb Virginia's independence, by the turn of the century events of the preceding decade had convinced even Virginia creoles such as Robert Beverley, William Byrd II, and Benjamin Harrison that much greater regularization of colonial administration was desirable. Granted, they suggested changes that would affect proprietary governments rather than their own, but Byrd, in explaining his reasoning, stressed that in the likelihood of future resumption of war with France, all mainland colonies were dependent on the good defense of each, a situation that existed largely due to the access Indian trails provided to each colony.[72]

English colonists originally based their own perceptions of the borders between their colonies on Indian boundaries they encountered early in the century. By the end of the century, they tried to impose the meanings they had attached to these boundaries onto the Indians and tried to claim as their own—those Indians whose primary residence at the time of contact lay within their functional or official political borders. Although these English attempts to impose on Indians their own boundary meanings often failed, Indians continued to travel and communicate across colonial boundaries throughout the seventeenth century. Colonial officials, most notably Quary, Nicholson, and

Andros, responded by significantly strengthening officials' political and social networks and their ability to communicate with one another. Their attempts to form a unified government only make sense within the context of a world linked by Indian travels that followed precolonial patterns.

Colonial officials' attempts to limit the movements and define the boundaries for Indians had the additional effect of linking overland and coastal interaction patterns to one another. Most Europeans, for much of the century, perceived their intercolonial connections as almost entirely maritime, depending on coastal shipping networks that set the patterns for social and religious networks and intercolonial migrations. As Virginia governors and officials traveled coastal routes to negotiate with Iroquois Indians who had been to Virginia via overland routes, settlers and colonists perceived that the two networks combined to provide overlapping webs of interaction firmly tying mainland colonies together in a way that began to draw distinctions between mainland and Caribbean colonies.

Conclusion

Atlantic Virginia attempts to bring together what are too often three separate literatures. The first includes the multiple historiographies of individual colonies, which often imply or assert that colonial America evolved from parallel projects in European expansion that developed separately, in relation to England but not to one another. The second is the history of Euro-Indian diplomacy and the imperial rivalries over access to Indians' land and trade that complicated that diplomacy. The third, more recent, literature is the Atlantic history that usually focuses on commercial, migratory, and cultural ties linking together, via Atlantic trade routes, various locations in Europe, America, and Africa.

Virginia was conceived as an American project at a time when attempts to define any part of America as English entailed a significant challenge to Spain. It is not surprising, therefore, that English Virginians looked first to Spanish examples (even while attempting to define themselves against the Black Legend) when they launched their colonial project. Those examples continued to be relevant for several decades, especially when they provided information about Indians or African-American slavery. As the numbers of colonies—Spanish, French, Dutch, and English—in North America and the Caribbean steadily increased over the course of the seventeenth century, Virginia's intercolonial context became increasingly complex.

Throughout the seventeenth century, intercolonial maritime and overland trade created networks that connected Virginians to people in colonies throughout mainland North America and the Caribbean. Coastal trade, primarily European, functioned similarly between mainland and island colonies. At midcentury, English colonists made little distinction between mainland and Caribbean colonies. Because areas not settled by Europeans separated them, mainland colonies often functioned more as islands in terms of their relationships with one another than as contiguous colonies along a mainland coast. Contemporaries well aware of North American geography sometimes even called Virginia an island, explicitly comparing it to actual islands.[1] For colonists on the North American mainland early in the seventeenth century, functional political borders had more to do with European-Indian relations than with relations among Europeans.[2] While all seventeenth-century Virginian counties participated in intercolonial trade, economic, social, and religious connections to other colonies were far more important to the Eastern Shore and Southside counties than they were for the geographically central counties in the Peninsula and Middle Peninsula. The story I have told, therefore, contains an important regional component. It suggests that we reexamine our assumption that the eighteenth-century dominance of the Peninsula between the James and York Rivers held for the seventeenth century as strongly as it did later. While good tobacco soil clearly led to strong ties with England and resultant political and economic advantages, the production of intercolonial goods led to strong ties with other English and Dutch colonies and different political and economic advantages, possibly the very significant one of greater access to slaves in a decade (the 1660s) of severe labor shortage. Colony-wide decreases in tobacco production in the late seventeenth century reflect decreases primarily in Southside and Eastern Shore counties, areas that could turn from tobacco because of their solid economic connection to other colonies with markets for other products, building on decades-old relationships.[3] Areas immersed in intercolonial trade not only saw the earliest concentrations of slaves, but also the earliest concentration of brick houses in Virginia, reflecting prosperity and commitment to permanence.[4] Because the seventeenth-century Lower Norfolk and Eastern Shore records are better preserved and (in the case of the Eastern Shore especially) more accessible than those of other counties, historians have used them extensively, sometimes to draw broad conclusions about the entire colony or the entire Chesapeake.[5] Rather, we should take care to acknowledge Virginia's varied regional development. The counties between the James and Rappahannock Rivers (the geographic center of Virginia as it had been of Tsenacommacah) were indeed dominated by tobacco and ties to England, including Anglicanism. They faced the Atlantic as we have long understood Virginia to do: with all eyes on London. The counties south of the James River, on the Eastern Shore, and north of the Rappahannock were connected to other colonies by both maritime and overland routes. They traded to New Netherland, New England, and the Caribbean, contained the Chesapeake's contacts to overland trail systems, and lived in the sections of Virginia that bordered Maryland and Carolina. Historians have been uncertain how to fit evidence of Virginia's intercolonial ties with the traditional view of an English-facing but insular colony. The project becomes much easier if we recognize the regional character of Virginia's economy and its links to the Atlantic world.

From the outset Virginia colonists (particularly deerskin and fur traders and colonial officials) sensed that Indians maintained a web of trails and connections that linked the mainland colonies with one another, potentially for Europeans as well as for Indians. Overland travel for much of the century remained primarily Indian and involved only a few European traders and others (such as Quaker Public Friends and runaway servants and slaves) who chose to travel overland. The frequency of coastal and overland trade allowed and encouraged other communications and movements, making intercolonial boundaries permeable to the movement of people, merchandise, and information, as well as cultural and social models.[6] Routes Indians and colonists developed primarily for trade also served as instruments for shaping networks of migration and of cultural and social exchange.

As Europeans established more and more settlements along the coast between Virginia and New England, mainland colonies no longer functioned as islands separated by Indian lands, and colonists had to define more precisely the political boundaries that separated them from one another. In part, colonial officials' efforts to define their borders grew from their desire to limit certain kinds of intercolonial travel. By conquering Indians and non-English Europeans, and by filling in the land along the East Coast with English colonies, colonial officials increasingly contrived to control intercolonial movements. Their efforts focused largely on overland intercolonial movements, more difficult to regulate than coastal trade.[7] Overland travel generally provided more opportunities for unapproved intercolonial movements. Those who used such routes—primarily the Indians who had created them, colonists who traded with Indians, some runaways, and Quakers—found themselves the objects of official attempts to cooperate (using coastal trade routes and their related social networks) to define who could move between colonies how easily and for what reasons.

Attempts to control undesired intercolonial movements articulated officials' efforts to define Virginia socially, culturally, and religiously. In the process of attempting (with other colonies) to limit the travel of individual Indians within colonial boundaries, they defined Virginia and its boundaries (originally Tsenacommacah's) as English, rather than English and Powhatan. By trying to keep "Virginia's Indians" within its colonial borders and other Indians outside of those borders, English Virginians gave new functional meanings to borders derived from precontact Indians' political boundaries, but now operating quite differently. To this end, Virginia officials asserted that Virginia and its boundaries had now become English, regardless of their original Indian definition. As English borders, they would (if English colonists enforced them) import new meanings for Indians, meanings that the similar lines had not carried when serving as Indian or Indian and English boundaries.

In other words, a Powhatan confederacy that extended to the south shore

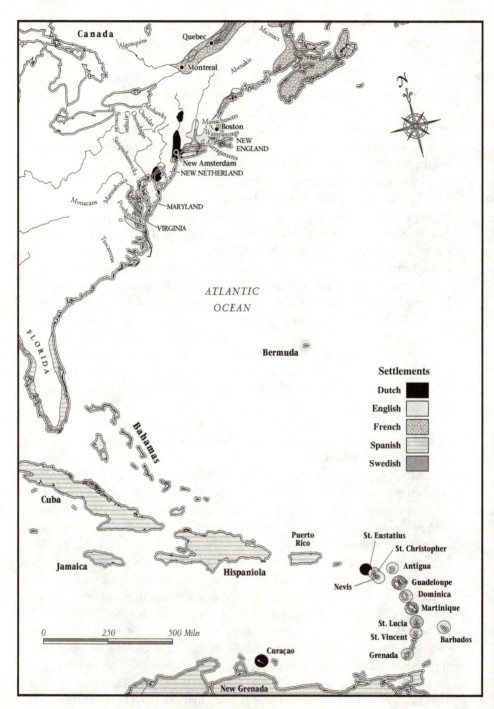

Map 9. Effective European Settlement, 1650

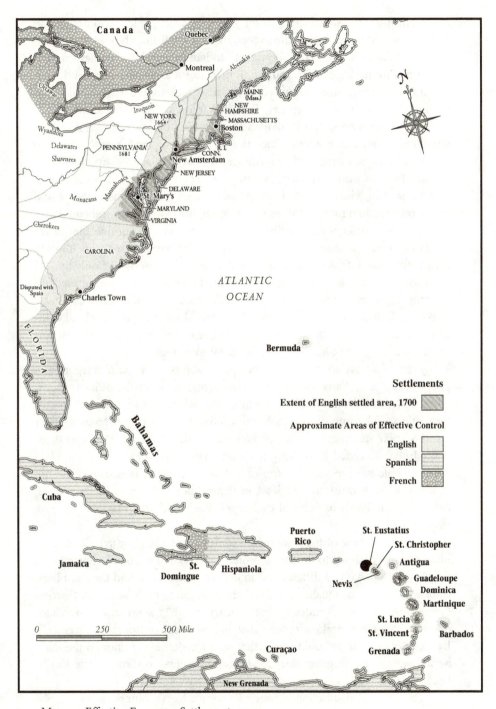

Map 10. Effective European Settlement, 1700

of the Potomac, the south shore of the James, and the fall line had defined an Indian political entity. With the exception of the fall line, however, none of these boundaries had actually "bounded" Indian interaction. Powhatans traveled and communicated with Indians to their north and south and southwest. Iroquois from the north traveled great distances to the Chesapeake and beyond. For much of the century, English Virginians remained powerless to stop such movements, and insofar as they enabled beaver fur, deerskin, and slave trades, did not want to. Once the English conquered New Netherland and New Sweden, established Carolina and Pennsylvania, and surveyed intercolonial borders more precisely, and once many colonies defeated the coastal Algonquians in whose midst they had established their colonies, they could define those Indian movements as violating English boundaries and could better aspire to restrict them. English colonists' attempts to confine the movements of Indians and the overland traders who followed their paths, limiting each to the coastal trade and tax system of a particular colony had only limited success. Ultimately, however, they did constrict overland trade and interaction patterns. Over the course of the seventeenth century, then, as officials sought to restrict Indian movements, they added cultural meaning to mainland colonial political borders. Their attempts to limit religious exchanges between colonies similarly gave political borders cultural meaning.

Even while acting to limit border permeability for certain categories of people, such as Indians and religious dissidents, many of the officials themselves benefitted economically from intercolonial trade and belonged to cultural and social communities that transcended boundaries (often as a direct result of their attempts to limit the mobility of others). Virginia's government never fully succeeded in making its boundaries impermeable, for complete success would have required strategies they never contemplated and could not in any case have mustered. At least in theory, however, they did succeed in delimiting the kinds of cultural exchanges that could take place along these networks.

Over the course of the seventeenth century as the English mainland colonies began to coalesce to deal with problems of Indian overland connections, they began to perceive a differentiation between themselves and the Caribbean colonies. Governors, Quakers, and traders all began to draw such a distinction during the last two decades of the century. In 1685 a Jamaican merchant described his Chesapeake attorney as living on "the continent of Virginia."[8] By 1703 Robert Quarry could advise that their "majesties colonies on the main be united under one government" without reference to those in the Caribbean.[9] In 1650, such a notion would not likely have surfaced.

The growing distinction between England's North American and Caribbean colonies did not in any way diminish trade, communication, and migration between the mainland and the islands. Rather, such correspondence increased in the eighteenth century. Indeed, no cleavage between maritime and overland trade emerged. Individuals whose lives centered on intercolonial (rather than transatlantic) trade often engaged in both. Virginia's role in facilitating the exchange of Indian slaves for Caribbean rum pulled both worlds together. Additionally, different kinds of intercolonial interactions intermeshed in more ways than initially obvious. Not only did individuals often involve themselves in both maritime and overland trade, but the most active intercolonial trade included a disproportionate number of Calvinists (Puritan or Dutch Reformed) or Quakers. The same nonconformist intercolonial traders whose ranks contained many of the Dutch settlers on record in Virginia often incorporated the early slave trade from Barbados into their sphere.

Intercolonial Virginians also appeared as key players during the Anglo-Indian wars of the last half century and the attempts to place limits on Indian overland travel. In this case, their interests combined with those of Virginians looking more to England for direction and assistance. Edmund Scarborough, infamous for his midcentury attacks (inexplicable to many of his contemporaries) on Eastern Shore Indians at peace with Virginia, traded and traveled to New Netherland and New England. His closest trading partner, Bostonian Edward Gibbons, actively engaged in Anglo-Indian warfare there.[10] In the 1670s, many of those Virginians most frantic about the possibility of a continental Indian conspiracy or most active in the frontier wars (William Byrd, Francis Nicholson, Edmund Andros, and in the Northern Neck Isaac Allerton, Jr., and Thomas Mathew) had all lived in or visited other colonies. Some, but not all, engaged in fur trade. Those who most feared an intercolonial Indian-French plot could best imagine it because their long-range American networks broadened their awareness of distant events.[11]

For all of the century the mobility of elites and governors facilitated intercolonial discussion about colonial issues, which meant that officials' decisions were often made in a distinctly Atlantic context. But the results of such intercolonial conversations were often independent of English policy, or indeed sometimes worked against it. That began to change at the end of century because of a series of events including the defeat of coastal Algonquians in North America and English enmity with French rather than Dutch adversaries in Europe. This overlap meant that as James II and William III appointed governors intent on coordinating policy, colonists had less leeway to resist such attempts. It even became possible for creoles to discuss unification of mainland colonies (at least for military purposes) in a way that would have been impossible before. While many Virginia officials opposed such measures, the warfare of the 1690s and the concern that French and Indian fears were one created an American impetus to see North American colonies as part of contiguous place that complemented crown's efforts.

Seventeenth-century Virginians inhabited multiple worlds. My identification of them as Virginians derives from their residence in a colony that began as a settlement within Powhatan Tsenacommacah, took over Tsenacommacah by the 1640s, acquiring an identification wholly separate from the Indian polity that it had replaced. Their residence within the colony of Virginia reveals only one aspect of Virginians' lives. On the largest scale, they resided in an international Atlantic world that encompassed Europe, Africa, and the Americas and possessed meaning for free colonists, European servants, African slaves, and Indians. Atlantic commerce affected every Virginian. Europeans and Africans likely came to Virginia from one or more other Atlantic world places. Indians risked moving along some of the same trade routes as slaves to other colonies. The Atlantic world contained trade connections that allowed migration and other travel, and also contained rivalries that endangered its residents and limited their movements. At the other end of our scale, those residents of Virginia lived and worked in distinct regions that intersected with the Atlantic world differently according to the kind and quality of the commodities they produced or acquired: tobacco for European markets (with the highest quality ensuring strong London contacts); provisions and naval stores for other colonies (early in the century both mainland and Caribbean colonies, by the end of the century most likely Caribbean); deerskins and beaver furs, also for European markets; and Indian slaves for the Caribbean. The relationship between Virginians' region and the Atlantic world had the most basic impact on determining the texture of their everyday life. In the waterside settlements of the seventeenth-century Chesapeake, European and African residents experienced that relationship between their local and Atlantic worlds directly.

It is possible to identify three realms of interaction that operated between the scales of the Atlantic world and Virginia. They were not mutually exclusive and indeed overlapped, but reflect different categories within the Atlantic world that functioned somewhat differently and contained some distinctions recognizable to their inhabitants. Virginians lived in a colonial American world—one consisting of North American and Caribbean colonies. Through the 1660s, Virginians experienced this world, through intercolonial trade and migration and information sharing, as both English and Dutch. They shared challenges, learned from one another, and occupied broadly similar places in relation to the Atlantic world. The North American mainland that included Indian nations and European colonies was distinct from the colonial American world because it included Indians who controlled vast expanses of its land. Colonists, though not Indians, understood this world largely from the perspective of their individual colonies for much of the seventeenth century. However, during the century's final decade the North American world, linked together by Indians' overland connections, created in the minds of English colonists a distinction within the *colonial* world between island and mainland. Finally, Virginians were part of an English Atlantic including England and all of its colonies. That world provided Virginia with its political structure, its laws, its religions, its diplomatic relations to other non-English colonies, and a demographic and cultural context that influenced its settlement patterns and labor organization that in turn determined much about the effect of the colony on Indians and Africans who lived within or near its borders. Each of these constructions—Atlantic world, Virginia, local region, international colonial America, North America, and English Atlantic—functioned in slightly different ways, and each was relevant under different circumstances. They coexisted and intersected. All are necessary for understanding the reality of life in seventeenth-century Virginia that was connected to different parts of its wider world in very different ways.[12]

Many elements of seventeenth-century Virginians' Atlantic world context persisted into the eighteenth century: patterns of intercolonial and transatlantic maritime trade continued, as the volume of trade grew and New England garnered a greater percentage of the intercolonial trade. Trading partners and families continued to maintain social ties along routes of commerce. Information spread along intercolonial and transatlantic routes, and indeed with the establishment of colonial newspapers that reprinted items from other colonies and from Europe, the availability of a variety of Atlantic news may have increased. Indians' use of precontact long-distance trade routes in North America continued, in an Atlantic context of Anglo-French warfare, to encourage intercolonial communications.

However, much about Virginia's relation to the Atlantic world changed in the decades surrounding 1700, making the turn of the century a logical place to stop this study. Overland connections changed in character as European population increased in the mainland colonies. Maritime connections increased, but directly touched a smaller proportion of Virginians. Collection times improved, so that ships turned around more quickly and seamen spent less time among Virginia settlers. While Virginia's population continued to live dispersed throughout the countryside rather than concentrated in urban areas, the establishment of Norfolk at the turn of the century marked the beginning of a change in trade patterns that removed many Virginians from direct access to mariners.[13] By 1700 as well many settlers lived in the interior of Virginia's peninsulas, without their own access to navigable waterways.[14] In the eighteenth century European settlement extended beyond the falls, and tobacco warehousing further reduced the interactions between settlers and mariners. The Chesapeake Bay and its estuaries continued to define Virginia, but for more and more Virginians, this definition no longer personalized their connection to other colonies. Although newspapers provided continued access to Atlantic world news, it was mediated by literate editors and sometimes censored, and was disproportionately available to the literate, creating a very different relationship between Virginians and Atlantic world news than was the case during the seventeenth century, when news came from conversations with seamen and ship captains who provided quite a different sort of filter on information.

Changes in the makeup of Virginia's population also changed the impact that the Atlantic world had on the colony. During the 1690s for the first time the majority of Virginia's English population was Virginia born. This creole majority allowed a consolidation among the elite, for whom a Virginia identity began to outweigh an English or English Atlantic identity, and a stabilization of Virginia politics. Eighteenth-century Virginia slaves were likely born in Africa or Virginia, and most had not spent time in other colonies.[15] Eighteenth-century slaves' African origins created for Virginia new and very different Atlantic world ties. While intercolonial information about slavery, especially about slave uprisings, drew the attention of slaveowners and slaves alike, intercolonial information about the organization of slave labor and definition of race was much less important after 1705, when Virginia wrote its comprehensive slave code.

In the seventeenth century, its place within the Atlantic world so shaped the Chesapeake that many of Virginia's most important developments can only be fully understood in an intercolonial context. Early Virginia's Spanish American context informed its relationships with Powhatans and with Africans who arrived in the colony. Interaction with Barbados, New Netherland, and New England shaped the economic, cultural, and political development of the Chesapeake by facilitating exchanges of goods, people, and information. The pervasiveness of intercolonial contacts argues the need to rethink our picture of life in the Chesapeake to include this reality. Indeed, in the much overlooked intercolonial world of the seventeenth century lies the key to a more nuanced understanding of the Chesapeake than the better-known details of Virginia's eighteenth-century Atlantic world can provide. Perhaps similar attention to Atlantic world contexts might suggest new questions or new answers to old questions about the local specifics of other places within that Atlantic world as well.

Notes

Introduction

1. Alison Games, *Migration and the Origins of the English Atlantic World* (Cambridge, Mass., 1999); Cynthia Jean Van Zandt, "Negotiating Settlement: Colonialism, Cultural Exchange, and Conflict in Early Colonial Atlantic North America, 1580–1660" (Ph.D. diss., University of Connecticut, 1998); Bernard Bailyn, *The New England Merchants in the Seventeenth Century* (Cambridge, Mass., 1955); Richard Pares, *Yankees and Creoles: The Trade between North America and the West Indies before the Revolution* (Cambridge, Mass., 1956); Frederick B. Tolles, *Meeting House and Counting House: The Quaker Merchants of Colonial Philadelphia, 1682–1783* (Chapel Hill, N.C., 1948); Tolles, *Quakers and the Atlantic Culture* (New York, 1960); Ian K. Steele, *The English Atlantic, 1675–1740: An Exploration of Communication and Community* (New York and Oxford, 1986).

2. Exceptions include Bailyn, *The New England Merchants*; Stephen Saunders Webb, *1676: The End of American Independence* (New York, 1984); and Francis Jennings, *The Ambiguous Iroquois Empire: The Covenant Chain Confederation of Indian Tribes with English Colonies* (New York, 1984). Even Ian K. Steele, in describing the multiple interactions that linked the English Atlantic together, concluded that "Initially, it is advisable to study the various routes of the English Atlantic as separate entities with different traffic patterns, levels, seasons, and passage times. As the seventeenth century drew to a close, these routes were still largely independent of each other, like bent spokes of some giant rimless wheel." *The English Atlantic,* 17. John J. McCusker and Russell R. Menard employ similar imagery in their suggestion that "no such thing as a 'colonial economy' developed until nearly the end of the era, after the coastwise trade had performed its work of integration, and then only involving British North America. Rather, there were sets of 'colonial economies' linked more closely with London than with each other or, alternatively, one grand 'Atlantic economy.'" *The Economy of British America, 1607–1789* (Chapel Hill, N.C., 1991), 86–87.

3. Historians of the eighteenth century more often emphasize the intercolonial nature of the eighteenth-century world and the implications of its interaction networks in shaping eighteenth-century lives. See, for example, Julius Scott, "The Common Wind: Currents of Afro-American Communication in the Era of the Haitian Revolution" (Ph.D. diss., Duke University, 1986); Timothy D. Hall, *Contested Boundaries: Itinerancy and the Reshaping of the Colonial American Religious World* (Durham, N.C., 1994); and J. F. Bosher, "Huguenot Merchants and the Protestant International in the Seventeenth Century," *William and Mary Quarterly (WMQ),* 3rd ser., 52 (1995): 77–102. Their work has created among some historians a notion that "the Atlantic world" was a development new to the eighteenth century, reinforcing the notion that during the seventeenth century most colonies were more inward-looking or solely England-facing.

4. James Horn, *Adapting to a New World: English Society in the Seventeenth-Century Chesapeake* (Chapel Hill, N.C., 1994) and David Cressy, *Coming Over: Migration and Communication between England and New England in the Seventeenth Century* (New York and Cambridge, Eng., 1987).

5. Philip Alexander Bruce and Charles Andrews wrote about the links connecting seventeenth-century English mainland and Caribbean colonies, but their insights about intercolonial connections have done little to inform more the historiography of recent decades. Bruce, *Economic History of Virginia in the Seventeenth Century* (New York, 1896); Andrews, *The Colonial Period of American History* (New Haven, Conn., 1934–38). A notable exception, however, is James R. Perry, *The Formation of a Society on Virginia's Eastern Shore, 1615–1655* (Chapel Hill, N.C., 1990). See especially chap. 6 for exploration of "Contacts off the Eastern Shore."

6. The contrast between Peter H. Wood's attention to Barbadian influences on Carolina slavery and Edmund S. Morgan's account of slavery's beginnings in Virginia (as owing much to Chesapeake and English conditions but little to a broader American context) first made me ask whether intercolonial influences might have shaped Virginia's history, as they did South Carolina's. Wood, *Black Majority: Negroes in Colonial South Carolina from 1670 through the Stono Rebellion* (New York, 1974), 3–34; Morgan, *American Slavery, American Freedom: The Ordeal of Colonial Virginia* (New York, 1975). Ian K. Steele proposes several approaches to the study of colonies' relation to the Atlantic world—some, but not all of which I consider here—in "Empire of Migrants and Consumers: Some Current Atlantic Approaches to the History of Colonial Virginia," *Virginia Magazine of History and Biography (VMHB)* 99 (1991): 489–512.

7. These conclusions about the regional patterns of Virginia's intercolonial connections derive from searches in colonywide sources for ties to other colonies. Such searches repeatedly pointed to the Eastern Shore and Lower Norfolk, slightly less often to other Southside counties and the Northern Neck, and much less often to the Peninsula and Middle Peninsula. I therefore pursued my search in Lower Norfolk and Eastern Shore records, which did indeed yield even more evidence of strong ties to other American colonies. A thorough read of the York County court records confirmed my impression that the richest tobacco areas indeed maintained many fewer intercolonial contacts. I did not test it further by reading other county records. The Research Division at Colonial Williamsburg generously made its York County typescripts available to me.

8. Darrett B. Rutman and Anita H. Rutman, *A Place in Time: Middlesex County, Virginia, 1650–1750* (New York, 1984), 29; quoting Darrett B. Rutman, "The Social Web: A Prospectus for the Study of the Early American Community," in William L. O'Neill, ed., *Insights and Parallels: Problems and Issues of American Social History* (Minneapolis, Minn., 1973), 57–123.

Chapter 1

1. See Karen Ordahl Kupperman's discussion of Ralph Lane's descriptions of the area in his "Discourse on the First Colony," in Kupperman, *Roanoke: The Abandoned Colony* (Totowa, N.J., 1984), 164–65, 78. The Virginia Company would have learned

from Lane's account of his 1585–86 exploration north from Roanoke that the Chesapeake was ruled by a strong king with a courageous army that would resist strangers, especially any who wanted pearls. Lane's account is printed in Richard Hakluyt's *Principall Navigations, Voyages, and Discoveries of the English Nation* (1589) (Cambridge, Eng., 1965) (and so would have been available to English readers by 1589) and in David Beers Quinn, ed., *The Roanoke Voyages 1584–1590* (London, 1955), 1:255–94.

Stephen R. Potter suggests that English "unwittingly settled in the midst of one of the most politically complex Indian groups along the Atlantic coast." Potter, *Commoners, Tribute, and Chiefs: The Development of Algonquian Culture in the Potomac Valley* (Charlottesville, Va., 1993), 1. But if Kupperman is correct that the English knew about the Chesapeake from Ralph Lane's accounts, the English Virginians' choice of the James River fit with an intention of finding an indigenous population with sufficient political and economic organization to provide opportunities for trade or tribute.

2. This is a story of persistent geographies and English appropriation, not of Indian agency. It provides an example of the process identified by cultural geographer Wilbur Zelinsky, by which the first settlers who establish "a viable, self-perpetuating society" in a place shape its long-term social and cultural geography more than the settlers who follow and often outnumber them. Zelinsky, *The Cultural Geography of the United States* (Englewood Cliffs, N.J., 1973), 13–14. See also T. H. Breen, "Creative Adaptations: Peoples and Cultures," in Jack P. Greene and J. R. Pole, eds., *Colonial British America: Essays in the New History of the Early Modern Era* (Baltimore, 1984), 195–232.

3. Historians have long understood that while the indigenous empires in Mesoamerica and Peru shaped the outlines of Spanish settlement, the absence of such well-developed indigenous economic and political structures forced Europeans in North America to develop their colonies independent of Indian frameworks. James Lockhart and Stuart B. Schwartz, *Early Latin America: A History of Colonial Spanish America and Brazil* (New York, 1983), 59–121; Ross Hassig, *Trade, Tribute, and Transportation: The Sixteenth-Century Political Economy of the Valley of Mexico* (Norman, Okla., 1985), 160–87.

4. William Strachey, *The Historie of Travell into Virginia Britania* (1612), ed. Louis B. Wright and Virginia Freund (London, 1953), 45.

5. Frederic W. Gleach suggests that the word Tsenacommacah meant "densely inhabited land." Gleach, *Powhatan's World and Colonial Virginia: A Conflict of Cultures* (Lincoln, Nebr., 1997), 25. See also Helen C. Rountree, *The Powhatan Indians of Virginia: Their Traditional Culture* (Norman, Okla., 1989), 7. There has been considerable debate among historians and anthropologists over the political nature of Tsenacommacah, the exact number of Algonquian communities under Powhatan's control, and the strength of his control over lesser chiefdoms in Tsenacommacah. See Helen C. Rountree, "Introduction," in Rountree, ed., *Powhatan Foreign Relations: 1500–1722* (Charlottesville, Va., 1993), 1–3; John Frederick Fausz, "The Powhatan Uprising of 1622: A Historical Study of Ethnocentrism and Cultural Conflict" (Ph.D. diss., William and Mary, 1977), 68–73; Christian F. Feest, "Virginia Algonquians," in *Handbook of North American Indians* 15 (*Northeast*), ed. Bruce G. Trigger (Washington, D.C., 1978), 253–70.

6. He inherited the towns of Powhatan, Appamattuck, and Arrohateck on the upper James River and its tributary Appomattox, and the Pamunkey, Mattaponi, and

Youghtanund on the Pamunkey and Mattoponi Rivers, which combine to form the York. Rountree, *The Powhatan Indians of Virginia*, 118; E. Randolph Turner, "Native American Protohistoric Interactions in the Powhatan Core Area," in Rountree, ed., *Powhatan Foreign Relations*, 80–90.

7. Wayne E. Clark and Helen C. Rountree, "The Powhatans and the Maryland Mainland," in Rountree, ed., *Powhatan Foreign Relations*, 116. Indeed, Stephen R. Potter argues that the Patawomecks were an independent chiefdom rather than part of Powhatan's domain. Potter, *Commoners, Tribute, and Chiefs*, 179–80.

8. Turner, "Native American Protohistoric Interactions," 80. Jeffrey Hantman suggests that differences between the Monacans and the Mannahoacs were very slight and uses the term Monacan to refer to them jointly. Hantman, "Powhatan's Relations with the Piedmont Monacans," in Rountree, ed., *Powhatan Foreign Relations*, 95. See also J. Frederick Fausz, "Patterns of Anglo-Indian Aggression and Accommodation along the Mid-Atlantic coast, 1584–1634," in William W. Fitzhugh, ed., *Cultures in Contact: The Impact of European Contacts on Native American Cultural Institutions, A.D. 1000–1800* (Washington, D.C., 1985), 227–28.

9. Hantman, "Powhatan's Relations with the Piedmont Monacans," 104.

10. Archaeological data suggest that the cultural boundary between the coastal plain and the piedmont developed between AD 200 and 900. Turner, "Native American Protohistoric Interactions," 80–90.

11. For the identification of the Massawomecks as the Iroquois, see Potter, *Commoners, Tribute, and Chiefs*, 176–77. For another interpretation, see James F. Pendergast, "The Massawomeck: Raiders and Traders into the Chesapeake Bay in the Seventeenth Century," *Transactions of the American Philosophical Society* 81 (Philadelphia, 1991).

Matthew Dennis argues that the Iroquois, having formed a confederation with one another to promote peace among themselves during sixteenth century, sought to expand their "landscape of peace" until it encompassed their entire world. Dennis finds "little evidence that the Iroquois believed their vision would be promoted by warfare" until after the arrival of Europeans. Dennis, *Cultivating a Landscape of Peace: Iroquois-European Encounters in Seventeenth-Century America* (Ithaca, N.Y., 1993). Evidence from the perspective of Chesapeake Algonquians suggests that during the first decade of the seventeenth century, Iroquois raids had occurred long enough for Powhatans to describe them as a regular occurrence to the English. Strachey understood that the Patawomecks, Patuxents, Susquehannocks, and Tockwocks at the heads of the northern Chesapeake rivers were "contynually harrowed and frighted by them of whose cruelty the said people generally complayned." Strachey, *Historie*, 48, 107; John Smith, *The Proceedings and Accidents of the English Colonie in Virginia, [1606–1612] . . . 1612*, in Philip L Barbour, ed., *The Complete Works of Captain John Smith, 1580–1631* (Chapel Hill, N.C., 1986), 232; Henry Fleet, "A Brief Journal of a Voyage Made in the Bark 'Warwick,' to Virginia and Other Parts of the Continent of America," in Edward W. Neill, *The Founders of Maryland as Portrayed in Manuscripts, Provincial Records and Early Documents* (Albany, N.Y., 1876), 19–25.

12. Jeffrey Hantman notes that in the only English account about Monacans *from* a Monacan, Amoroleck told John Smith in 1608 that he knew of only three worlds; those of the Powhatans, the Monacans, and the Massawomecks. His account reinforced Powhatan descriptions of the Massawomecks as warlike: according to Amoro-

leck, "The Massawomecks did dwell upon a great water, and had many boats, and so many men that they made warre with all the world." Hantman, "Powhatan's Relations with the Piedmont Monacans," 101; Hantman, "Between Powhatan and Quirank: Reconstructing Monacan Culture and History in the Context of Jamestown," *American Anthropologist* 92 (1990): 679; Smith, *The Proceedings and Accidents of the English Colonie in Virginia,* in Barbour, ed., *The Complete Works,* 1:176.

13. Pocahontas was visiting Patawomeck friends north of the Potomac when she was captured by the English in 1613. Clark and Rountree, "The Powhatans and the Maryland Mainland," 116, 132; Ralph Hamor, *A True Discourse of the Present State of Virginia* (1615) (New York, 1971), 4.

14. Turner, "Native American Protohistoric Interactions," 76–77.

15. See William E. Myer, *Indian Trails of the Southeast* (1923) (Nashville, Tenn., 1971); Helen Hornbeck Tanner, "The Land and Water Communication Systems of the Southeastern Indians," in Peter H. Wood, Gregory A. Waselkov, and M. Thomas Hatley, eds., *Powhatan's Mantle: Indians in the Colonial Southeast* (Lincoln, Nebr., 1989), 6.

16. "Francis Magnel's Relation of the First Voyage and the Beginnings of the Jamestown Colony," 1 July 1610, in Philip Barbour, ed., *The Jamestown Voyages under the First Charter* (Cambridge, Eng., 1969), 1:154. Barbour suggests that by "West India" Magnel meant land west of the falls, but the existence of long-distance travel networks and Magnel's further statement that "these messengers say that those who are in India treat their natives very badly, and like slaves, and the English tell them that those people are very cruel and wicked, meaning the Spaniards" suggests that the Powhatans did in fact send messengers as far as the Gulf Coast, or that information was relayed to them from that distance. See also Tanner, "Land and Water Communication Systems," 17.

17. Thomas E. Davidson, "Relations between the Powhatans and the Eastern Shore," in Rountree, ed., *Powhatan Foreign Relations,* 137. Smith reported that "Their manner of trading is for copper, beades, and such like, for which they give such commodities as they have, as skins, fowle, fish, flesh, and their country corne. But their victuall is their chiefest riches." Smith, *A Map of Virginia,* in Barbour, ed., *The Complete Works,* 1:164–68.

18. Much of the copper in the Chesapeake probably came from Michigan's Keweenaw Peninsula in Lake Superior, where the only large quantities of native (pure rather than ore, and therefore requiring no smelting) copper in the world occur. Copper from Michigan is known to have traveled as far as Florida. Kiril Spiroff, "Sketch of Michigan's Geologic History," in *Our Rock Riches,* Bulletin of the Michigan State Geological Survey, vol. 1 (Lansing, Mich., 1964), 1; J. R. Van Pelt, "Boston and Keweenaw-An Etching in Copper," in ibid., 11, 12; John R. Halsey, "Miskwabik-Red Metal: The Roles Played by Michigan's Copper in Prehistoric North America" (Keweenaw County Historical Society, 1992), 2, 5; originally printed in *Michigan History Magazine,* 1983. There are small deposits of native copper in western Virginia and in New Jersey, but they are so small that they could have produced only beads, not sheets. Spiraff, "Sketch," 1; Turner, "Native American Protohistoric Interactions," 82, cites John Swanton, *The Indians of the Southeastern United States,* Bureau of American Ethnology Bulletin 137 (1946) (New York, 1969), 493. See also Quinn, ed., *The Roanoke Voyages 1584–1590,* 1:269–70.

19. Helen C. Rountree, "The Powhatans and Other Woodland Indians as Travelers," in Rountree, ed., *Powhatan Foreign Relations,* 33–35. A path led west and south-

west from the headwaters of the Rappahannock as well, but these headwaters were well west of Tsenacommacah's fall line western boundary and therefore did not provide access to western trade for coastal Algonquians.

20. Rountree, "Summary and Implications," in Rountree, ed., *Powhatan Foreign Relations*, 215–21; Clark and Rountree, "The Powhatans and the Maryland Mainland," 119; Smith, *Map*, Barbour, ed., *Complete Works*, 1:146–48, 150. See Turner, "Native American Protohistoric Interactions," 87–92 and Rountree, "Summary and Implications," 219–21 for discussion of the importance of trade patterns, Powhatan location, and ability to create regional monopolies on luxury goods for the evolution of Powhatan's political power.

21. Samuel Purchas, *Hakluytus Posthumus or Purchas His Pilgrimes* (1625) (Glasgow, 1904–6), 19:151–52; cited in Rountree, "The Powhatans as Travelers," 23.

22. Francis Jennings, "Susquehannock," in Trigger, ed., *Northeast*, 364.

23. Several historians, including Edmund S. Morgan and Neal Salisbury, have noted the degree to which John Smith regarded Hernán Cortés as an appropriate model, but few have seen that attention to Spanish histories extended beyond Smith. Morgan, *American Slavery, American Freedom*, 77; Salisbury, *Manitou and Providence: Indians, Europeans, and the Making of New England, 1500–1643* (Oxford and New York, 1982), 100.

24. Smith's *Generall Historie* in Barbour, ed., *Complete Works*, 2:299. Edmund Morgan points out that Smith here was paraphrasing Edward Waterhouse, *A Declaration of the State of the Colony and . . . a Relation of the Barbarous Massacre* (London, 1622), in Susan Myra Kingsbury, ed., *Records of the Virginia Company of London* (Washington, D.C., 1906–35), 3:541–79. Morgan, *American Slavery, American Freedom*, 77.

25. For a much expanded version of this argument, see April Lee Hatfield, "Spanish Colonization Literature, Powhatan Geographies, and English Perceptions of Tsenacommacah/Virginia," *The Journal of Southern History* 69 (2003): 245–82.

26. Strachey noted that the Powhatan (James) River "falleth from Rockes far west in a country inhabited by a Nation as aforesaid that they call *Monacan*; but where it cometh into our discovery it is *Powhatan*." About forty miles above the falls the river branched, the northern branch coming from "certayne steepe mountaynes, that are said to be impassable," the southern from "high Hills, a far off within the Land, from the toppes of which Hills the people say they see another Sea, and that the water is there salt, and the Journey to this Sea from the Falls by their accompt should be about 10 dayes, allowing according to a March some 14 or 16 myles a day." Strachey, *Historie*, 34–35, 41–42.

27. Strachey, *Historie*, 109–10.

28. Thomas E. Davidson, "Relations," 137. Davidson argues that the English inherited the Powhatans' role "in an already existing cross-bay trade network" with the Eastern Shore Algonquians. In the 1622 Anglo-Powhatan war the Eastern Shore tribes fought on the side of the English. Ibid., 149–50. For the First Anglo-Powhatan War, see J. Frederick Fausz, "'An Abundance of Blood Shed on Both Sides': England's First Indian War, 1609–1614," *VMHB* 98 (1990): 3–56.

29. Fausz, "The Powhatan Uprising," 550–51; J Frederick Fausz "Merging and Emerging Worlds: Anglo-Indian Interest Groups and the Development of the Seventeenth-Century Chesapeake," in Lois Green Carr, Philip D. Morgan, and Jean B. Russo, eds., *Colonial Chesapeake Society* (Chapel Hill, N.C., 1988), 54–57.

30. John Martin, "How Virginia may be Made a Royal Plantation," December 15, 1622, in Kingsbury, ed., *The Records of the Virginia Company of London*, 3:707–8.

31. William Waller Hening, ed. *The Statutes at Large; being a Collection of all the Laws of Virginia, from the First Session of the Legislature, in the Year 1619* (Richmond, Va., 1809), 1:57–58, 88.

32. John Smith, *A True Relation of such occurrences and accidents of note, as hath hapned in Virginia . . .* in Barbour, ed. *Complete Works*, 1:29.

33. John Smith, *The Proceedings of the English Colonie in Virginia, 1606–1612, 1612,* in Barbour, ed. *Complete Works*, 1:236.

34. Davidson, "Relations," 143–46, 150.

35. For John Smith's Monacan prisoner and guide Amoroleck, see Smith, *The Generall Historie of Virginia, New-England, and the Summer Iles* (1624), in Barbour, ed., *The Complete Works* 2:176–77.

36. He was with Christopher Newport and twenty others. At the town of Powhatan they had left "a mariner in pawn with the Indians for a guide of theirs." Smith, *A True Relation*, 1:27, 30–31.

37. Smith, *Map*, 150–51.

38. Strachey, *Historie*, 92.

39. Strachey, *Historie*, 105–7.

40. Smith, *Map*, 1:165–66. See also Strachey, *Historie*, 105–7. When Smith referred generically to "the Savages" he meant the Powhatans, illustrating their central position in the English perception of Indian political and social geographies.

41. Strachey described an apparent Monacan-Powhatan alliance: "Powhatan had manie enemies, especially in the westerly Countryes, before we made our Forts and habitacions so neere the Falls, but now the generall Cause hath united them." Strachey, *Historie*, 105–6. See also Hantman, "Powhatan's Relations with the Piedmont Monacans," 110.

42. Gregory A. Waselkov, "Indian Maps of the Colonial Southeast," in Wood et al., *Powhatan's Mantle*, 292. For examples of Potomac River Indians drawing such maps for Henry Fleet, see Fleet, "A Brief Journal," 29–30.

43. Waselkov, "Indian Maps of the Colonial Southeast," 292. In maps from the late seventeenth and early eighteenth centuries, Waselkov finds a "maze of paths and rivers carefully detailed and connecting many of the other map elements. . . . Rivers and trails, distinguished [from one another] only in the captions, merge to form communication networks that define the limits of mapped space, which is otherwise unbounded."

44. For a discussion of the distinction between the two kinds of Indian maps, see Gregory A. Waselkov, "Indian Maps of the Colonial Southeast: Archaeological Implications and Prospects," in G. Malcolm Lewis, ed., *Cartographic Encounters: Perspectives on Native American Mapmaking and Map Use* (Chicago, 1998), 206–7.

45. Barbara Belyea, "Inland Journeys, Native Maps," in Lewis, ed., *Cartographic Encounters*, 141–42.

46. Rountree, "The Powhatans as Travelers," 35.

47. The Virginia Assembly tried periodically to outlaw all trade with Indians or specific aspects of that trade, but by the 1630s had little ability to enforce such laws. See Paul Chrisler Phillips, *The Fur Trade* (Norman, Okla., 1961), 1:163–65.

48. For a discussion of Anacostan linguistic affiliation, see Clark and Rountree, "The Powhatans and the Maryland Mainland," 112n; Potter, *Commoners, Tribute, and Chiefs*, 13.

49. Fleet, "A Brief Journal," 22–25.

50. Fleet, "A Brief Journal," 22–25.

51. Fleet, "A Brief Journal," 27–28. Fleet understood the Massawomecks to have four chiefs, live in palisaded towns, and include over thirty thousand people. His brother's journey to the Massawomecks took seven days going and five days coming.

52. Fleet, "A Brief Journal," 29.

53. The other focus of English Virginia fur trading in the 1620s and 1630s was William Claiborne's trade with the Susquehannocks at the head of the Chesapeake Bay. Claiborne established trading posts at Palmer's Island at the mouth of the Susquehanna River and at Kent Island in the bay. From those locations, he traded with the Susquehannocks who controlled one of the three main precontact Indian travel routes out of the Chesapeake, the primarily waterborne trade route that via rivers and brief portages reached sources of thicker northern beaver pelts. For a discussion of Virginian William Claiborne's trade with the Susquehannocks, see Chapter 8 and Fausz, "Merging and Emerging Worlds."

54. Hening, ed., *Statutes*, 1:323–25.

55. Hening, ed., *Statutes*, 1:322–25. In the treaty, "Necotowance King of the Indians" acknowledged that he held "his kingdome from the King's Ma'tie of England," and "that his successors be appointed or confirmed by the King's Governours." The colony agreed "to protect him or them against any rebells or other enemies whatsoever."

56. Shortly after the end of the war, Anglo-Indian negotiations reveal a split in the Powhatan polity, which theretofore had dealt as a single entity with the colony. In 1649 the Virginia Assembly granted land to three Powhatan werowances separately, in response to "theire severall Petitions." During the second half of the seventeenth century there is little evidence of a unified Powhatan political organization. Helen C. Rountree, *Pocahontas's People: The Powhatans through Four Centuries* (Norman, Okla., 1990), 89–91. The Assembly Act is in Warren Billings, ed., *The Old Dominion in the Seventeenth Century: A Documentary History of Virginia, 1606–1689* (Chapel Hill, N.C., 1975), 229–30. Thomas Ludwell later noted, correctly or not, that the Powhatans "like to warr with each other and destroyed themselves more in a year than we can do it," suggesting that by the 1640's the English clearly wanted to supplant Tsenacommacah without preserving its original inhabitants. Rountree, *Pocahontas's People*, 103, cites Longleat vol. 73, Bath 65 ff 202–3. A division among the Powhatans may necessarily have resulted from the recognition, required by the treaty, that Virginia had supplanted Tsenacommacah.

57. Ben McCary, *Indians in Seventeenth-Century Virginia* (Charlottesville, Va., 1957), 81; Rountree, *Pocahontas's People*, 93–94. Rountree cites Charles City County, Records, 1655–65, 61, for information from the Weyanock werowance. Perhaps they were not Monacans, however. John Lederer wrote that in 1670 several Indians had told him that the Richahecrians lived "not far to the Westward of the Apalataean Mountains, are seated upon a Land, as they term it, of great Waves." John Lederer, *Discoveries of John Lederer with Unpublished Letters of and about Lederer to Governor John Winthrop, Jr.*, ed. William P. Cumming (Charlottesville, Va., 1958), 26.

58. James H. Merrell, *The Indians' New World: Catawbas and Their Neighbors from European Contact through the Era of Removal* (Chapel Hill, N.C., 1989), 49–91.

59. For a discussion of this trade from the perspective of the piedmont traders, see Merrell, *The Indians' New World*, 23–40.

60. The travel accounts all describe a trade for furs and deerskins, and do not mention slaves, though we know that Virginians were involved in Indian slave trading by at least the 1670s. See Merrell, *The Indians' New World*, 36–37; Joel W. Martin, "Southeastern Indians and the English Trade in Skins and Slaves," in Charles Hudson and Carmen Chaves Tesser, eds., *The Forgotten Centuries: Indians and Europeans in the American South, 1521–1704* (Athens, Ga., 1994), 304–24.

61. Wesley Frank Craven, *White, Red, and Black: The Seventeenth-Century Virginian* (Charlottesville, Va., 1971), 66.

62. Strachey, *Historie*, 56–57; Rountree, "The Powhatans as Travelers," 23.

63. Edward Bland, *The Discovery of New Brittaine*, printed in Alexander Salley, Jr., ed., *Narratives of Early Carolina, 1650–1708* (New York, 1911), 1–19. They also took four horses, suggesting that the paths were well traveled and maintained.

64. Bland in his account of their travels continually made note of "old Indian fields" between the towns, indicating that the paths led through inhabited or recently inhabited lands. Bland, *Discovery*, 12.

65. Bland, *Discovery*, 8–9.

66. Abraham Wood was present as burgess from Henrico at the Grant Assembly session during which the treaty was approved. Hening, ed., *Statutes*, 1:322. The treaty stipulated that whenever any of "Necotwoance and his people" came to trade or with a message for the governor, they had to report to Fort Royal, Fort Henry, or John Flood's house to receive badges allowing them to enter the colony. Ibid., 326–27.

67. Bland, *Discovery*, 9–10.

68. Bland, *Discovery*, 10–11.

69. The Meherrins are not known to have ever been under Powhatan jurisdiction, but they may have entertained him when he traveled to their towns. Bland, *Discovery*, 11.

70. Bland, *Discovery*, 11–12.

71. Bland, *Discovery*, 16–18.

72. Bland, *Discovery*, 18–19.

73. Bland, *Discovery*, 16–17.

74. Rountree, *Pocahontas's People*, 94; "Colonial Letters, &c." (Ludwell Papers), *VMHB* 5 (1897): 47–48; "Indians of Southern Virginia, 1650–1711: Depositions in the Virginia and North Carolina Boundary Case," *VMHB* 7 (1900): 350; 8 (1900): 2, 4, 5.

75. In his note to the reader, William Talbot acknowledged that the English relied on Indian geographical knowledge. To lend legitimacy to Lederer's descriptions, Talbot assured his audience that "All these I have compared with Indian Relations of those parts (though I never met with any Indian that had followed a Southwest-Course so far as this German) and finding them agree, I thought the Printing of these Papers was not injury to the Author, and might prove a Service to the Publick." Lederer, *Discoveries*, 3.

76. Lederer, *Discoveries*, 19–22. Lederer does not identify his guides further than the generic "Indians." At least one was Susquehannock.

77. Lederer, *Discoveries*, 20–21.

78. That a Susquehannock could guide him southwest from Virginia suggests a wide range of Susquehannock travels.

79. Lederer, *Discoveries*, 22–26.

80. There is disagreement over the location of this passage. See Alan Vance Brice-land, *Westward from Virginia: The Exploration of the Virginia-Carolina Frontier, 1650–1710* (Charlottesville, Va., 1987).

81. Lederer, *Discoveries*, 31–32. For a report that Lederer returned with Spanish coins, see Thomas Glover, *An Account of Virginia, Its Scituation, Temperature, Productions, Inhabitants and Their Manner of Planting and Ordering Tobacco* (1676) (Oxford, 1904), 10. James Merrell locates the Usheree at the Esaw town near the confluence of Sugar Creek and the Catawba River, what would become the center of Catawba in the eighteenth century. *The Indians' New World*, 47, 94.

82. This was where the Iroquois Massawomecks came down river to meet the Piscataways and Anacostans. Lederer, *Discoveries*, 38–39. For the Shenandoah path, see Myer, *Indian Trails*, 27.

83. After Pyancha, Abraham Wood, and Edward Bland returned from their trip, Wood continued to trade with Indians. The Virginia Assembly issued grants during the 1650s to several colonists, including Wood, to explore to the west and initiate trade contacts with Indians. Phillips, *The Fur Trade*, 166–67; Timothy Silver, *A New Face on the Countryside: Indians, Colonists, and Slaves in South Atlantic Forests, 1500–1800* (New York, 1990), 72.

84. Wood had been involved in other explorations as well. See Clarence Alvord and Lee Bidgood, *The First Explorations of the Trans-Allegheny Region by the Virginians, 1650–1674* (Cleveland, Ohio, 1912), 183. Alvord and Bidgood include John Clayton's transcript of Robert Fallam's journal, entitled *A Journal from Virginia, beyond the Apailachian mountains, in Sept. 1671*. Hantman includes Saponi among the Monacans. Hantman, "Powhatan's Relations with the Piedmont Monacans," 99.

85. Wood to Richards, August 22, 1674, in Alvord and Bidgood, *First Explorations*, 210–11.

86. Beverley, *The History and Present State of Virginia*, ed. Louis B. Wright (1705) (Chapel Hill, N.C., 1947), 191; R. P. Stephen Davis, Jr. and H. Trawick Ward, "The Occaneechi and Their Role as Middlemen in the Seventeenth-Century Virginia-North Carolina Trade Network," in R. P. Stephen Davis, Jr., Patrick C. Livingood, H. Trawick Ward, and Vincas P. Steponaitis, eds., *Excavating Occaneechi Town: Archaeology of an Eighteenth-Century Indian Village in North Carolina* (CD ROM) (Chapel Hill, N.C., 1998); McCary, *Indians in Seventeenth-Century Virginia*, 67.

87. Wood to Richards, *First Explorations*, 211–13.

88. Wood to Richards, *First Explorations*, 223–25.

89. For increased warfare in Iroquoia and Iroquois recruitment raids, see Jennings, *The Ambiguous Iroquois Empire*, 95–142; Dennis, *Cultivating a Landscape of Peace*, 213–56; Daniel K. Richter, *The Ordeal of the Longhouse: The Peoples of the Iroquois League in the Era of European Colonization* (Chapel Hill, N.C., 1992), 50–66, 144–49, 161–63.

90. Wilcomb E. Washburn, *The Governor and the Rebel: A History of Bacon's Rebellion in Virginia* (Chapel Hill, N.C., 1957), 29–30, cites Address of March 24, 1676, Longleat, vol. 77, fol. 66.

91. For Bacon's Indian slaves, see Richard Dunn, "Masters, Servants, and Slaves in the Colonial Chesapeake and the Caribbean," in David B. Quinn, ed., *Early Maryland in a Wider World* (Detroit, Mich., 1982), 250, citing inventory in CO 5/1371/219–250 PRO.

92. Marion Tinling, ed., *The Correspondence of the Three William Byrds of West-over, Virginia 1684–1776* (Charlottesville, Va., 1977), 1:3. Sarah Grendon, Thomas Stegge's widow, was a Bacon supporter as well. Susan Westbury, "Women in Bacon's Rebellion," in Virginia Bernhard, Betty Brandon, Elizabeth Fox-Genovese, and Theda Perdue, eds., *Southern Women: Histories and Identities* (Columbia, Mo., 1992), 38; cites Berkeley to Henry Coventry, July 1, 1676, Coventry Papers, vol. 77, fol. 144, Bath, Longleat.

93. Wilcomb Washburn dismissed Robert Beverley's assertion that the rebellion was caused by "the Instigation of Two or Three Traders only, who aim'd at a Monopoly of the *Indian* Trade . . ." because Beverley's father had been a strong supporter of Berkeley. Beverley may have been right about the importance of the Indian trade to Bacon's rebellion though for reasons slightly different from the ones he identified. While advantages over other English traders may have mattered, perhaps obliteration of the Occaneechees as middlemen mattered as much. Washburn, *The Governor and the Rebel*, 29, cites Beverley, *History of Virginia*, 74. See also Morgan, *American Slavery, American Freedom*, 215–70.

94. Byrd withdrew his support from Bacon once the rebels directed their attacks against fellow English Virginians. Byrd may also have been one of the colonels Durand of Dauphiné described in his *Voyages*, who led militia against Indians and had the conquered land surveyed for speculation. T. H. Breen, "A Changing Labor Force and Race Relations in Virginia 1660–1710," *Journal of Social History* 7 (1973): 15; cites Durand of Dauphiné, *Voyage d'un Francois Exile Pour le Religion . . .* (1687), ed. Gilbert Chinard (New York, 1934), 109, 179–80. Ian K. Steele notes that direct English access to southwestern trade was a result of Bacon's destruction of Occaneechee, but does not discuss it as a possible cause of the attack. *Warpaths: Invasions of North America* (New York, 1994), 56–57.

95. "Articles of Peace," *VMHB* 14 (1906): 289–96; Rountree, *Pocahontas's People*, 100; Martha W. McCartney, "Cockacoeske, Queen of Pamunkey: Diplomat and Suzeraine," in Wood et al., *Powhatan's Mantle*, 173–95.

96. While the treaties of the 1640s limited English control to former Powhatans, Bacon's desire to open up western lands to English trade and settlement meant he attacked both Powhatans and Siouans. The treaty following Bacon's Rebellion for the first time drew a tributary relationship between Virginia and Indians who had not been part of Tsenacommacah. On May 29, 1677, representatives of ten tribes signed: Pamunkey, Appamattuck, Weyanock, Nansemond, Nantaughtacund, Portabaccos, Nottoway, Meherrin, Monacan, and Saponi. In exchange for recognition of their landholdings, the Indians who signed acknowledged their dependence on the king of England and bound themselves to give notice of strange Indians on the frontier and assist the English against their enemies. Hening, ed., *Statutes*, 1:323–25; "Articles of Peace," *VMHB* 14 (1906): 289–96; McCary, *Indians in Seventeenth-Century Virginia*, 82–83.

97. Davis, et al., eds., *Excavating Occaneechi Town* (CD ROM), Figure 2.

98. Merrell, *The Indians' New World*, 37–48.

99. See Chapter 8.

100. Byrd's letters contain several references to "the traders being just now gone out" or the traders being "all out now." Byrd to Arthur North[?], March 8, 1686, in Tinling, *Correspondence*, 1:57; Byrd to Perry and Lane, March 8, 1686, in Tinling, *Correspondence*, 1:58.

101. Byrd to Perry and Lane, March 8, 1686, in Tinling, *Correspondence*, 1:58.

102. Byrd to Arthur North, June 5, 1685, in Tinling, *Correspondence*, 1:41.

103. Merrell, *The Indians' New World*, 29; cites Francis Nicholson to the Committee, January 26, 1690/1, CO 5/1306, 43 (LC trans); H. R. McIlwaine, ed., *Executive Journals of the Council of Colonial Virginia* (Richmond, Va., 1925–66), 1:254–55.

104. Rountree cites continued use of tributary guides during the 1690s. Rountree, *Pocahontas's People*, 103, cites Hening, *Statutes* 3:82–85.

105. Byrd to Thomas Grendon, April 29, 1684, in Tinling, *Correspondence*, 1:15–16.

106. Francis Jennings, "Indians and Frontiers in Seventeenth-Century Maryland," in Quinn, ed., *Early Maryland in a Wider World*, 216–41.

107. Byrd to Thomas Grendon, April 29, 1684, in Tinling, *Correspondence*, 1:15–16.

108. Byrd to Perry & Lane, June 16, 1688, in Tinling, *Correspondence*, 1:82.

109. Byrd to Daniel Horsmanden, August 8, 1690, in Tinling, *Correspondence*, 1:136; James H. Merrell, "'The Customes of Our Countrey' Indians and Colonists in Early America" in Bernard Bailyn and Philip Morgan, eds., *Strangers within the Realm* (Chapel Hill, N.C., 1991), 118–19.

110. See Chapter 8.

111. Other historians have noted that early English colonial settlements on the mainland functioned as islands. Peter Wood wrote that Carolina's early colonists worked to have "the surrounding native population assume, in effect, the confining function performed by the sea in the West Indies" for black slaves by encouraging Indians to capture and return runaways. See Peter H. Wood, *Black Majority*, 53; J. Frederick Fausz uses the imagery to describe Virginia's English settlements in relation to one another in 1621: "dispersed among dozens of seemingly safe plantation 'islands,'" surrounded by a "sea of native neighbors." Fausz, "Merging and Emerging Worlds," 51. Ian Steele argues that "Islands of people on the English Lesser Antilles were less isolated than those who lived on the North American sea of land." Steele, *The English Atlantic*, 119.

Chapter 2

1. For the tobacco trade to Europe, see Russell R. Menard, "The Tobacco Industry in the Chesapeake Colonies, 1617–1730: An Interpretation," *Research in Economic History* 5 (1980): 109–77; John J. McCusker and Russell R. Menard, *The Economy of British America, 1607–1789* (Chapel Hill, N.C., 1991), 117–43; and Jacob M. Price, *Tobacco in Atlantic Trade: The Chesapeake, London, and Glasgow, 1675–1775* (Brookfield, Vt., 1995), a collection of Price's articles dealing primarily with eighteenth-century transatlantic tobacco trade.

2. These numbers represent English imports of American colonial tobacco, in lieu of any direct evidence of Virginia tobacco production. McCusker and Menard, *The Economy of British America*, 120–21.

3. Philip Alexander Bruce paid more attention to Virginia's seventeenth-century intercolonial trade than have most historians since. *Economic History of Virginia*, passim.

4. September 23, 1639, Northampton County Court. Susie M. Ames, ed., *County*

Court Records of Accomack-Northampton, Virginia, 1632–1640 (Washington, D.C., 1954), 149–52. Brian had received sixteen or eighteen gallons of strong waters from Mr. Bushrod (perhaps Virginia intercolonial merchant Thomas Bushrod, who traded to New Netherland during the 1660s, by which point he had become a Quaker—see Chapter 5) for one thousand pounds of rolled tobacco. Brian also used some of the tobacco to buy himself a musket and five bushels of corn. To go to the Caribbean, he hired six men, who spent forty days on the ship's charge. Samuel Maverick, with whom Brian stayed at Noddles Island, and presumably drank the liquor, was a Massachusetts colonist and the agent at Noddles Island for the Newfoundland Governor David Kirke. The General Court of Massachusetts leased Noddles Island to Samuel Maverick. William B. Weeden, *Economic and Social History of New England 1620–1789* (Boston, 1890), 1:132–50

5. Lois Green Carr, "Diversification in the Colonial Chesapeake: Somerset County, Maryland, in Comparative Perspective," in Carr et al., eds., *Colonial Chesapeake Society*, 343–45; Menard, "Chesapeake Tobacco Industry." See also Lois Green Carr and Lorena S. Walsh, "Economic Diversification and Labor Organization in the Chesapeake, 1650–1820," in Stephen Innes, ed., *Work and Labor in Early America* (Chapel Hill, N.C., 1988), 144–88.

6. Carr, "Diversification in the Colonial Chesapeake," 344–45. Menard reports "substantial regional variations in tobacco prices [within the Chesapeake] . . . as early as the mid-1640s." "Chesapeake Tobacco Industry," 112.

7. The seventeenth century saw multiple short-term cycles of expansion, overproduction, and falling prices. Depressions occurred at the end of the 1620s, the end of the 1630s, the mid-1650s, and the mid-1660s, with periods of recovery in between. Particularly significant was the long period of stagnation in tobacco production that lasted from the mid 1680s to around 1715. Menard, "Chesapeake Tobacco Industry," 114, 123–24. Maryland historians have noted the diversification that occurred at the turn of the century in areas producing poor tobacco there, while those producing higher quality tobacco expanded their output. Menard, "Chesapeake Tobacco Industry," 154.

8. Cumulative evidence from court records indicate that trade to Barbados, Massachusetts, and New Netherland-New York were most important, as does anecdotal evidence, such as Governor Edmund Andros's 1696 report that Virginia traded to "New York Barbados and the islands and New England." C.O 5/1309, No. 16, cited in Morgan, *American Slavery, American Freedom*, 139n.

9. Susie M. Ames, *Studies of the Virginia Eastern Shore in the Seventeenth Century* (Richmond, Va., 1940), 52–53, 64–65. Eastern Shore gained a reputation for agricultural diversity by the 1670s. Ames, *Studies*, 53, citing Thomas Glover, *An Account of Virginia* (1676) (Oxford, 1904), 16.

Accomack county was established in 1634 and covered Virginia's entire Eastern Shore. In 1643 the assembly renamed it Northampton. In 1663 the assembly divided it, with Accomack to the north and Northampton to the south. Emily J. Salmon and Edward D. C. Campbell, Jr., eds., *The Hornbook of Virginia History*, 4th ed. (Richmond, Va., 1994), 159.

10. Early in the century Virginia and Bermuda depended on one another for necessities. George Sandys to John Ferrar, April 8, 1623, Newport News. In the spring of 1623, concerned with the possibility of famine in Virginia, the government sent a ship to Bermuda for supplies. W. Noel Sainsbury, ed., *Calendar of State Papers, Colonial Series (CSPC)* (London, 1860–1939), 1574–1660, 42–43, #27.

11. [October] 1618. *CSPC 1574–1660*, 19, #38.

12. *VMHB* 65 (1957): 466, quoted in Perry, *Formation of a Society on Virginia's Eastern Shore*, 147.

13. February 8, James City. *CSPC 1574–1660*, 175, #3; Governor Harvey to [Secretary of State Francis Windebank], July 14, 1634, Virginia. *CSPC 1574–1660*, 184, #22. During the first tobacco boom of the 1620s, Virginians produced very little except tobacco but used trade and force to acquire corn from Chesapeake Indians. They traded some of that to New England. By the mid-1630s, however (partly due to diversification that accompanied the falling prices of the late 1620s and early 1630s), some of the corn they traded was English grown.

14. In 1624 in an attempt to preserve an alliance with the Patawomecks, who had long provided the English with substantial amounts of corn, Governor Sir Francis Wyatt "thought fitt, for this present yeare to restreine all perticuler trade for Corne, within the Bay , and to appropriate that trade, only for the publique benefit of the Colony," suggesting that some corn acquired from Indians was already traded to Plymouth. Potter, *Commoners, Tribute, and Chiefs*, 187; Kingsbury, *Records of the Virginia Company of London*, 4:447.

15. One of the references was to a lading of one hundred barrels of corn. Nicholas White of Accomack wrote a will in 1639 because he was "Bound for a voyage to New England." Robert Custis in 1652 was "By the blessing of God bound to New England." Ames, *Studies*, 60–61, citing Northampton records. William Claiborne made an agreement in London to carry corn from Virginia to Boston in the *Africa*. Ames, *Studies*, 61, citing Edward D. Neill, *History of the Virginia Company of London* (Albany, N.Y., 1869), 408 and Hening, ed., *Statutes*, 1:227. During the early 1630s, Captain John Stone carried corn and cattle from Virginia to Boston. David Peterson (Pietersz) De Vries, *Voyages from Holland to America, AD 1632–1644*, trans. Henry C. Murphy (1853) (New York, 1971), 64.

16. Henry Fleet, "A Brief Journal," in Neill, ed., *Founders of Maryland*, 19–37.

17. Fleet, "A Brief Journal," 35.

18. For example, when Fleet tried to trade with the Massawomecks who rejected his goods, he noted that "They had two axes, such as Captain Kirk traded in Cannida, which he bought at Whits of Wapping, and there I bought mine, and think I had as good as he." According to Fleet, "These people delight not in toys, but in useful commodities." The Indians called themselves Mostikums, but Fleet believed that they were Hereckeenes (three days from the Mostikums and one of their confederate nations) and "with their own beaver, and what they get of those that do adjoin upon them, do drive a trade in Cannida, at the plantation," a fifteen-day trip from the Potomac. Fleet, "A Brief Journal," 30–31.

19. Edmund Morgan compiled these figures. While he was arguing for the significance of cattle for the whole colony, all his examples came from the Eastern Shore or the Southside, reflecting that in fact these two regions depended most on intercolonial trade and therefore provided the most striking presence of cattle and other intercolonial trade goods. Morgan, *American Slavery, American Freedom*, 138, citing Norfolk and Northampton records.

20. Ames, *Studies*, 55, citing Northampton records. Ames emphasized the number and importance of cattle evident in the Eastern Shore records. *Studies*, 56–57.

21. On May 17, 1641, for example, the Accomack court awarded an attachment

against 1,038 pounds of pork that surgeon John Stringer owed Humphery Edwards for beaver pelts. Susie M. Ames, ed., *County Court Records of Accomack-Northampton, Virginia 1640–1645* (Charlottesville, Va., 1973), 85, fol. 40.

22. Hening, *Statutes*, 1:227; Ames, *Studies*, 61; Weeden, *Economic and Social History of New England*, 126. The 1640 cattle shortages may have resulted from disease. In the 1670s, Virginia's cattle populations suffered two epidemics, the first of which destroyed over fifty thousand head of cattle (at a time when the human population was around 42,000). Menard, "The Tobacco Industry," 136.

23. Hening, ed., *Statutes*, 2:261–62; Ames, *Studies*, 64.

24. Hening, ed., *Statutes*, 2:338–39; Ames, *Studies*, 64.

25. Ames, ed., *Accomack-Northampton 1640–1645*, March 29, 1641, 76, fol. 36.

26. Ames, ed., *Accomack-Northampton 1640–1645*, July 6–8, 1641, 93–96, 44-fol. 46. The corn was already loaded onto a vessel bound for New England.

27. Captain John Manning of New Haven carried salt, wine, and bread to Virginia, where he traded for tobacco. Sugar and beaver may have also been in the boat. Charles J. Hoadly, ed., *Records of the Colony or Jurisdiction of New Haven, from May, 1653, to the Union* (Hartford, 1858), 2:68. March 26, 1654. On September 28, 1653, Michall Tainter (Taynter), master of New Haven merchant Isaac Allerton's ketch, left Barbados for Virginia to sell mackerel and strong beer belonging to Boston vintner Evan Thomas. *Suffolk Deeds Book* (Boston, 1883), 2:191. Allerton, who also was to go on the voyage, also engaged himself to sell some of Thomas's mackerel. *Suffolk Deeds Book*, 2:192.

In a reversal of the common pattern in which Virginians sent livestock to New England, in the 1650s Eastern Shore merchant Edmund Scarborough attempted to buy ten ewes from Boston merchant William Brenton, to be delivered to Scarborough in Rhode Island. Northampton County Court Order Book, 1654–1661, fol. 2, 45–47.

28. The same reporter described a great trade from Boston to Barbados with fish and other provisions, including fruit from Long Island. *CSPC 1661–1668*, 532, #1660. For an overview of New England's intercolonial trade, see Bernard Bailyn, *The New England Merchants in the Seventeenth Century* (Cambridge, Mass., 1955).

29. Steele, *The English Atlantic*, 296–97.

30. For example, in the 1690s New England merchant William Pepperell sent New England goods with New England shipmaster Samuel Adams to Accomack, Virginia, merchant William Anderson. Adams and Pepperell purchased pork and beef from Accomack planter Samuel Sandford and took it to Barbados. Ames, *Studies*, 63, cites Accomack Orders 1690–1697, 74.

31. Perry, *Formation of a Society on Virginia's Eastern Shore*, 148.

32. Russell Menard has found that cattle and grain prices in Maryland rose and fell with tobacco prices, reflecting demands created by increasing numbers of immigrants during tobacco booms. "Chesapeake Tobacco Industry," 124–25. Whether this was equally true throughout Maryland and also for those areas of Virginia that marketed some of their cattle to the Caribbean is unknown. Sugar prices fluctuated, likely affecting the prices that Caribbean planters could pay for mainland provisions. McCusker and Menard, *Economy of British America*, 125, 154–58.

33. Goods in estate inventories do not help us compare transatlantic, intercolonial, or intracolonial trade with any specificity because they cannot tell us what tobacco went to New Netherland and what tobacco to London, or what meat and grain served an internal Chesapeake market, and what went to other colonies.

34. John Hammond, "Leah and Rachel, or, the Two Fruitfull Sisters Virginia, and Mary-Land," in Peter Force, ed., *Tracts and Other Papers Relating Principally to the Origin, Settlement, and Progress of the Colonies of North America* (1844) (Gloucester, Mass., 1963), Tracts 3:9, 14, 19.

35. See C. R. Boxer, *The Dutch Seaborne Empire, 1600–1800* (New York, 1965). The Dutch also sent some European grain (which English Virginians preferred to the corn they produced themselves) to Virginia in exchange for tobacco. Before the sugar revolution in Barbados, Kiliaen van Rensselaer noted his preference for trading his grain to Virginia, because it was closer and produced better tobacco. A. J. F. van Laer, trans. and ed., *Van Rensselaer Bowiew Manuscripts* (Albany, 1908), 566. See also *CSPC 1574–1660*, 418, #26.

36. Dutch colonies in the Americas included New Netherland (1624–64 and briefly in 1674), Curaçao (1634–present), Pernambuco (1630–54), and Surinam (1667–1975). New Netherland gained control over New Sweden and the rest of Delaware Bay in 1655, after which it struggled with Maryland over that claim and the boundary between the colonies until the English conquered New Netherland in 1664.

37. Joyce D. Goodfriend, "Burghers and Blacks: The Evolution of a Slave Society at New Amsterdam," *New York History* 59 (1978): 136–37.

38. In 1631 Governor Sir John Harvey granted a commission to William Claiborne to trade with the Dutch. At midcentury, Captain William Whittington and Eastern Shore merchant William Kendall made a contract with Jacob L. van Sloot to ship tobacco to Manhattan. Ames, *Studies*, 47, citing Northampton Wills & Deeds, 1657–66, 33. Eastern Shore planter and merchant Colonel Argoll Yardley also traded tobacco to Peter Jacobson at Manhattan. When Yardley died, his wife Ann (born in the Netherlands) and her second husband, John Wilcox, maintained the relationship with Jacobson at least long enough to clear the accounts. Order Book 1658, January 29–October 28, 3.

39. Dennis J. Maika, "Commerce and Community: Manhattan Merchants in the Seventeenth Century" (Ph.D. diss, New York University, 1995), 31–32.

40. De Vries, *Voyages*, 112, 183; "A Perfect Description of Virginia," 1649, in Force, ed., *Tracts and Other Papers*, vol. 2.

41. John R. Pagan, "Dutch Maritime and Commercial Activity in Mid-Seventeenth-Century Virginia," *VMHB* 90 (1982): 491.

42. Bruce, *Economic History of Virginia*, 2:324, citing *Documents relating to the Colonial History of New York*, vol. 14, 77. Barbadians made similar efforts to ensure access to Dutch traders during the 1640s, not just to provide shipping during the English Civil War, but also because the Dutch controlled much of the transatlantic slave trade that Barbadian planters increasingly depended upon for labor as they began to make the transition from tobacco to sugar production.

43. Hening, ed., *Statutes*, 1:258.

44. In 1655 Edmund Scarborough petitioned the Dutch Council for permission to return to Virginia with slaves he had purchased in Manhattan. Ames, *Studies*, 49, citing Berthold Fernow, ed., *Documents Relative to the History of New York* (Albany, N.Y., 1877), 12:94.

45. H. R. McIlwaine and John P. Kennedy, eds., *Journals of the House of Burgesses of Virginia (JHB)*, 13 vols. (Richmond, Va., 1906–15), 1:74; discussed by Pagan, "Dutch Maritime and Commercial Activity," 493n.

46. McIlwaine, ed., *JHB 1619–1658*, 76.

47. John Pagan found complaints from Virginians that the acts disrupted shipping, but notes that illegal trade continued during the 1650s. "Dutch Maritime and Commercial Activity," 496–97. For evidence of Chesapeake-New Netherland trade relations in the 1650s and 1660s see Maika, "Commerce and Community," 112–25.

48. Wesley Frank Craven, *The Southern Colonies in the Seventeenth Century, 1607–1689* (Baton Rouge, La., 1949), 375–76. When England sent a military fleet to force Virginia royalists to submit to the new government in 1652, some observers reported that Dutch ships in the James River supported royalist Governor William Berkeley. Beverley, *History*, 63. The first Anglo-Dutch war did, however, create tensions between some Dutch and English colonists on the Eastern Shore. In 1653 the Northampton County justices "received a petition from the Dutchmen in generall (inhabitants of this county) wherein, they . . . complain[ed] of a ruinous violence, suddenly to be acted upon them to their utter ruin." They asked the governor and council to order, "not only they but the whole County (if not the whole Country) will be in danger of disturbance." "Northampton County Records," *VMHB* 5 (1897–98): 37, quoted in Pagan, "Dutch Maritime and Commercial Activity," 497.

49. Ames, *Studies*, 48–49.

50. Hening, ed., *Statutes*, 1:536–40; Pagan, "Dutch Maritime and Commercial Activity," 497. See also James A. Rawley, *The Transatlantic Slave Trade: A History* (New York, 1981), 86.

51. Pagan, "Dutch Maritime and Commercial Activity," 498–99; Ames, *Studies*, 49–50.

52. Dennis J. Maika, "Jacob Leisler's Chesapeake Trade," *de Halve Maen* 68 (1994): 11. According to Maika, "Trade between Manhattan and the Chesapeake continued uninterrupted after the English imperial government's intrusion into New York in 1664," though Cathy Matson argues that by that time the 1660 Navigation Act had already altered tobacco trade routes so that less Chesapeake tobacco went through New Netherland en route to Europe. Matson, *Merchants & Empire: Trading in Colonial New York* (Baltimore, 1998), 18.

53. On April 25, 1655, Richard Hincksman petitioned Oliver Cromwell that his ship *Rose of London* be allowed to proceed to Barbados with stranger mariners because he was unable to hire enough English seamen for the voyage. *CSPC 1574–1660*, 423, #42.

54. Clerks may have been responsible for the Anglicization, but Foxcroft's name is spelled consistently by multiple English clerks, suggesting that he himself was responsible. On February 12, 1674, Charles II wrote to all admirals and governors of foreign plantations that Isaac Foxcroft, master of ship *Carolus Secundus*, had come into the Kingdom on encouragement from the king's July 12, 1672, declaration in favor of the subjects of the United Provinces. *CSPC 1669–1674*, 553, #1219–20.

55. De Vries, *Voyages*, 63–64; Ames, *Accomack-Northampton, 1632–1640*, xxxvii, 22–23.

56. Ames, ed., *Accomack-Northampton 1632–1640*, xxxvii, citing Northampton Records. Charleton supported Edmund Scarborough's raids against Indians in 1651 and 1652.

57. Ames, ed., *Accomack-Northampton 1632–1640*, citing Northampton Orders Deeds and Wills, vol. 2, 41, fols. 196, 365. Ibid., xxxvii, citing *Encyclopedia of Virginia Biography* (New York, 1915), 1:207.

58. In January 1636 Eastern Shore planter Thomas Hunt traded tobacco to Mr. Richard Orchard for mackerel. January 4–5, 1636, Ames, ed., *Accomack-Northampton 1632–1640*, 46.

59. Charleton traded with New England from the early 1630s and later with New Netherland also. Ames, ed., *Accomack-Northampton 1640–1645*, xiii. Edmund Scarborough made many voyages to New Netherland both before and after the 1651 Navigation Act. His later trouble with Director-General Stuyvesant likely had more to do with the two men's personalities or Scarborough's attempts to avoid New Netherland duties than to England's Navigation Acts. Ames, *Studies*, 47. Scarborough traveled to Boston to trade in the 1650s. *Suffolk Deeds Book* (1880), 1:290–91.

60. Norfolk County, Wills and Deeds C, 1651–56, 116a, 107, 127–27a.

61. Samuel Maverick to Colonel Nicolls, Whitehall, [April] 1669. *CSPC 1669–1674*, 20, #59.

62. Edward Neill, *Virginia Carolorum* (Albany, N.Y., 1886), 131; Ames, *Studies*, 46.

63. For food shortages in Boston, see Darrett B. Rutman, *Winthrop's Boston: A Portrait of a Puritan Town, 1630–1649* (Chapel Hill, N.C., 1965), 63, 178.

64. Ames identifies Frances Pott, Argoll Yardley, William Roper, John Stringer, and Edmund Scarborough as Eastern Shore traders to Maryland. Ames, *Studies*, 62, citing *Archives of Maryland*, 10:45, 85–86, 191–92, 213, 312–13, 315–17, 449. For some of the commercial activities of Jacob Derickson and Seabrent Derickson, see *Archives of Maryland*, 10:162, 248, 333, 384. Marylander Colonel William Stevens of Somerset County had close Virginia ties and had a plantation in Virginia. Calvert and Cecil county merchants and merchants from the town of Oxford and other places appeared in Virginia and Maryland. Ames, *Studies*, 62, citing Accomack and Northampton records.

65. On May 28, 1667, John Renny received permission to transport cattle over the Pocomoke River into Maryland. Accomack County Virginia Order Book 1666 October 16–1670 January 26, Virginia Historical Society, Mss 3Ac275a, typescript by Susie May Ames, 1942–46, 68. On February 23, 1644, Accomack County planter Richard Hudson told the court that Daniel Duffeild had come into his house "to beate some Corne for the Marylanders." Ibid., 354–55.

66. Governor Harvey to Secretary Windebank, Virginia, December 16, 1634. *CSPC 1574–1660*, 193, #37.

67. Carr and Walsh, "Economic Diversification and Labor Organization," 152–53.

68. For a discussion of Barbados-Virginia commercial links beginning in the 1630s, see Bruce, *Economic History of Virginia*, 1:321, 460–61. On July 30, 1634, the Company of Providence Island gave instructions to Joseph Collins, the chief pilot and commander of the *(Long) Robert* of London, bound for Providence Island, to discharge passengers (likely in the Leeward Islands), take in salt at Tortuga, send the ketch immediately to Providence Island and Association, where he should deliver the company's letters, take on board any Africans bought on their account, and if inhabitants wanted to desert Association, ship them to Providence. He was then to go to the Mosquito Coast to deliver goods for the mainland and get freight for his return voyage. If he got salt from Tortuga, he should take it to Virginia to sell on his way home, and take anyone willing to go as servants from St. Christopher or Association to Providence. *CSPC 1574–1660*, 189, #24.

69. Early after Barbadians began to produce sugar, they requested permission

from the House of Lords to import over one hundred oxen from Virginia. Bruce, *Economic History of Virginia*, 1:298; cites Royal Hist. Mss. Commission 6th Report, appendix, 203.

70. Evidence of York County-Barbados trade, all from the 1670s and later, can be found in York County Deeds, Orders, Wills (DOW) 4, 282; DOW 6, 108, 112, 191, 431; DOW 10, 294.

71. In 1678, thirteen ships bound for Virginia cleared customs in Barbados. C.O. 1/44, ff. 246–66, cited in Morgan, *American Slavery, American Freedom*, 139n. In 1672 the ketch *Recovery* traded from Boston to Virginia, from Virginia to Barbados, back again to Virginia, and from there to England. It carried tobacco, pork, tar, and peas from Virginia to Barbados. Special Court Boston August 26, 1672. John F. Cronin, ed., *Records of the Court of Assistants of the Colony of the Massachusetts Bay 1630–1692*, vol. 3, 1642–73 (Boston, 1928), 246–47. William Fitzhugh sent 6,240 staves to Barbados in the 1680s. Bruce, *Economic History of Virginia*, 2:493.

72. For examples, see Norfolk County, Wills and Deeds C 1651–1656, 83a (1654); ibid., 89a (1654); Ames, *Studies*, 206 (1668); Accomack Order Book, 1666–70, 432 (1670); ibid., 451 (1670).

73. For examples, see Ames, *Studies*, 54, 62–64. Robert Pitt of Accomack County carried pork from other Accomack planters to trade for Barbados sugar in his ketch *Barbados*. On one voyage he carried thirteen barrels of pork to Barbados for Edmund Scarborough. Ibid., 63–64.

74. Armitage had brought two of the sides of bacon back to the Eastern Shore and only had to pay for those his crew had consumed plus the court costs. Accomack County Virginia Order Book, 1666–70, 92.

75. For a list of Barbadian merchants with large sales to Virginia during the second half of the seventeenth century, see Bruce, *Economic History of Virginia*, 2:328n.

76. Ames, *Studies*, 63, citing George Beer, *The Old Colonial System, 1660–1754* (1912) (New York, 1933), 1:83.

77. Willoughby to Secretary Williamson, February 10, 1673. *CSPC 1669–1674*, 464–65, #1029.

78. Steele, *The English Atlantic*, 285. Steele's tables contain other Barbados colonial entries and clearances from 1681–1738. That there were usually many more total entries than clearances suggests as well that entries were recorded more carefully.

79. Ames, *Studies*, 63; H.R. McIlwaine, ed., *Executive Journals of the Council of Virginia 1699–1705* (Richmond, 1927), 2:193. Virginians also acquired some salt from the Caribbean. On November 13, 1667, St. Christopher's residents, dispersed after French took over (on April 11, 1666), noted in a petition that the French takeover endangered all the islands and inconvenienced the mainland by "the want of salt made upon the island for New England and Virginia." *CSPC 1661–1668*, 517–18, #1629.

80. John Noble, ed., *Records of the Court of Assistants of the Colony of Massachusetts Bay 1630–1692*, vol. 3, 1642–73 (Boston, 1928), 246–47.

81. New England ships in London with goods from several other American colonies provide evidence of New England mariners' increasing role in carrying the goods of other colonies. *CSPC 1661–1668*, 430–31, #1337, #1343, December 3–4, 1666; New Haven Colony Court. Hoadly, *New Haven Colony Records*, 2:200 (1657), 316 (1659).

82. *CSPC 1669–1674*, 34, #89 [July] 1669; *CSPC 1669–1674*, 34, #91 [July] 1669. The proximity of Southside counties made overland transportation of cattle possible

and shortened the difficult voyage for those sent by ship. (The records of cattle trade I have seen have all been by ship.) On July 30, 1670, Henry Brayne wrote to [Sir Peter Colleton] from Nansemond River, Virginia, that he had drawn a bill of exchange payable on sight for £80 15s 6d for goods shipped and for furnishing his ship the *Carolina* with a supply for his plantation at Keyawah or Port Royal. He had acquired the goods from Richard Bennett, William Berkeley, and Thomas Godwin. *CSPC 1669–1674*, 77, #224.

83. *CSPC 1669–1674*, 87, #248. On September [9], 1670, for example, Joseph Dalton wrote from Albemarle Point to Ashley that "The people [are] in a very good plight, especially since provisions came from Virginia." *CSPC 1669–1674*, 91, #257. A ship had come from Virginia on August 23 with provisions and live cattle. In [September] 1670 John Locke wrote that the *Carolina* brought six months' provisions from Virginia. *CSPC 1669–1674*, 89, #252. See also ibid., 86, #246; 138–39 #347; 167 #428; 179–80, #471; 196–98, #493.

84. Joseph West and others wrote of the desperate need Carolina had for Virginia supplies. *CSPC 1669–1674*, 168, #430. See also *CSPC 1669–1674*, 182–83, #427; 184–87, #473.

85. *CSPC 1669–1674*, 211–12, #516.

86. Wood, *Black Majority*, 33–34.

87. The Northampton court recorded the letter on November 10, 1656. Northampton County Court Order Book, March 28, 1654–June 28, 1661, typescript by Susie May Ames, Virginia Historical Society Mss 3N8125a, folder 2, 68–69. In 1651 William Whittington of Northampton County, Virginia, appointed the Boston mariner William Strangidge his attorney to collect debts from shoemaker Angell Hollett. *Suffolk Deeds Book*, 1:145, 36.

88. All the Virginia men involved lived on the Eastern Shore, but Thorndike described them simply as "Virginians." November 10, 1656, Northampton County Court Order Book, 1654–55, fol. 2, 67.

89. Fayall, June 17, 1671. The witnesses had English names. The power of attorney was recorded in Boston, where two of the witnesses "Mr William Taylor & Jeremiah Cushin appeared before" the court on December 29, 1671 and testified that they were present when Nethway signed the letter of attorney. *Suffolk Deeds Book* (Boston, 1894), 7:271.

90. As early as 1628, Captain John Preen reported to the Privy Council that he had made four voyages to supply St. Christopher and Virginia with provisions. *CSPC 1574–1660*, 94, #58 [August] 1628. In the fall of 1653 ships left London bound for New England and Virginia; or Virginia and Barbados; or Virginia, Barbados, and Malaga. *CSPC 1574–1660*, 407, #11; ibid., 409, #12. In [1670] [French privateers] took an English ship, bound from Virginia to the English Caribbean, at Martinique. Antigua Governor William Byam to Barbados Governor William Lord Willoughby. *CSPC 1669–1674*, 204–5, #508. In 1673 Don Philip Hellen (alias FitzGerald), captain of a Spanish man-of-war, took English mariners in the *Humility* of London, as they sailed between Jamaica and Virginia. *CSPC 1669–1674*, 537, #1178, December 5, 1673.

91. Ames, *Studies*, 144–45; Ames, ed., *Accomack-Northampton 1632–1640*, xxxvii; 453–54, 240; "The Church in Lower Norfolk County" 82; Ames, *Studies*, 144, cites Accomack Wills V, 1673–76, 241; *CSPC 1669–1674*, 556–58, #1226, 602, #1335.

92. In 1649 boatwright John Godfrew bought eight hundred acres on the Eliza-

beth River in Lower Norfolk County, where his services would be convenient to any ships entering or leaving the bay. Despite the large size of his plantation, he continued to work as a boatwright, and was so identified five years later when he sold the plantation to planter Thomas Dadford. Norfolk County, Wills and Deeds C, 1651–56, January 16, 1653. See also Ames, ed., *Accomack-Northampton 1640–1645*, 394, 397–98. January 7, 1645.

93. Ames, *Studies*, 47.

94. Nell Marion Nugent, probably more familiar with Virginia headrights than any other scholar, thought "sea captains . . . especially active in the acquisition of land through the transportation of settlers." *Cavaliers and Pioneers: Abstracts of Virginia Land Patents and Grants* (1934) (Richmond, Va., 1977), 1:xxv. In fact, Henry Hartwell, James Blair, and Edward Chilton believed that ship masters abused the headright system, claiming headrights for their mariners who did not intend to remain in the colony, or for passengers who had paid their own transportation (and therefore claimed their own headrights). The system provided deserting seamen the opportunity to claim land rights, which some believed they did not deserve, not having paid for their own transportation (except by their labor). *Present State of Virginia and the College* (1697), 1615–18. Bruce, *Economic History of Virginia*, 1:519–21, makes the same argument, citing Virginia Land Patents I 1623–43, 559. Marcus Rediker argued that "Desertion was . . . an essential component of seafaring labor . . . [that] confirmed the 'free' in free wage labor." Mobility provided the greatest source of seamen's power in the early eighteenth century. *Between the Devil and the Deep Blue Sea: Merchant Seamen, Pirates, and the Anglo-American Maritime World, 1700–1750* (Cambridge, Eng., 1987), 105, 115.

95. Peter Earle, *Sailors: English Merchant Seamen, 1650–1775* (London, 1998), 176–77.

96. "A Perfect Description of Virginia," in Force, ed., *Tracts and Other Papers*, 2:5. James Perry found a probable 25 (and certain 15) merchants or mariners identified among first time landowners on the Eastern Shore in the early seventeenth century. *Formation of a Society on Virginia's Eastern Shore*, 156.

97. Ames, *Studies*, 65–66.

98. On October 24, 1654, Virginia planter Rowland Williams acknowledged owing Boston innholder Evan Thomas £22, presumably for staying at his inn, to be paid in good Virginia tobacco or English goods delivered at Boston. *Suffolk Deeds Book*, vol. 2 (1883), 191.

99. Ames, ed., *Accomack-Northampton 1640–1645*, xv–xvi; citing *Documents Relative to the Colonial History of New York* (Albany, N.Y., 1877), 12:94. Scarborough first served as a commissioner in October 1643. He had received legal training in England and represented Northampton in the March 1643 General Assembly. Elected speaker of General Assembly in November 1645, he was also sheriff of Northampton and surveyor general of Virginia from 1655 to 1671 (officially after 1666.) After the Restoration he may have received favor as the brother of Charles Scarborough, who was chief physician to Charles II. Sandra Lee Rux, "Edmund Scarburgh" (M.A. thesis, Trinity College, 1980), 61, cites Ralph T. Whitelaw, *Virginia's Eastern Shore: A History of Northampton and Accomack Counties* (Richmond, Va., 1951), 1:625.

100. Rux, "Edmund Scarburgh," 15–16.

101. Ames, ed., *Accomack-Northampton 1640–1645*, xv–xvi, citing *Proceedings of the Council of Maryland*. Scarborough had conflicts with Indians, Dutch, Quakers, Marylanders, and Puritans.

102. Rux, "Edmund Scarburgh," 25–26.

103. Ames, ed., *Accomack-Northampton, 1632–1640*, xxxvii.

104. Ames, ed., *Accomack-Northampton 1640–1645*, 81–83.

105. Ames, ed., *Accomack-Northampton 1640–1645*, 61. The inventory included a map, a plate, an asterlaine (probably astrolabe–precursor to sextant), a quadrant, a cross staff, two pair of compasses, a seaman's calendar, a bible, clothes, cloth, bedding, and skins.

106. For the growth of New England's shipping and shipbuilding industries, see Bailyn, *New England Merchants*, 82–101. For an example of Virginia ship work done in New England, see *Suffolk Deeds Book* (Boston, 1883), 2:101–2.

107. For example, in 1635 Dutch ship captain David Peter De Vries went to New Netherland "to make my ship tight, as it was extremely leaky, which I could not do in the English Virginias." In New Netherland he asked Director General Van Twiller to hire some carpenters for him, if possible, or if not, he would sail to New England to have the work on his ship done there. De Vries, *Voyages*, 108–9.

108. Marion V. Brewington, "Chesapeake Sailmaking," *Maryland Historical Magazine* 65 (1970): 138, cites Kingsbury, ed., *Records of the Virginia Company of London*, 4:144.

109. *CSPC 1574–1660*, 151, #54, May 27, 1632.

110. Ames, ed., *Accomack-Northampton 1640–1645*, 77–78. March 29, 1641.

111. Ames, ed., *Accomack-Northampton 1640–1645*, 355. February 23, 1644.

112. DeVries, *Voyages*, 188–89.

113. The Dutch trader David Peterson De Vries wrote that it could be difficult to get provisions in Virginia during the 1630s because, except for what they meant to market, "every one there only produced for himself," but he himself was able to acquire provisions and later mariners did not express similar complaints. De Vries, *Voyages*, 176–77. In 1667 shipmaster Robert Pitt bought 2,850 pounds of pork as provisions for his ship's company, as well as two seventy-gallon barrels of tar, a twenty-eight gallon barrel of tar, and fifty-four pounds of rope. Testimony of mariner John Tille, November 13, 1667. Accomack County, Order Book 1666–70, 136–38.

114. "A Perfect Description of Virginia," 109.

115. For more examples of shipbuilding and repairing, see Ames, ed., *Accomack-Northampton 1632–1640*, 122; Ames, *Studies*, 142–43; Accomack County, Order Book, 1666–70, 8; *CSPC 1661–1668*, 460, #1460, April 19, 1667; testimony of mariner John Tille, November 13, 1667. Accomack County, Order Book 1666–70, 136–38.

116. For an overview of colonial population growth and economic growth, see McCusker and Menard, *Economy of British America*, 51–88, 211–35.

Chapter 3

1. John Clayton, *The Reverend John Clayton: A Parson with a Scientific Mind*, ed. Edmund Berkeley and Dorothy Smith Berkeley (Charlottesville, Va., 1965), 53. For other examples, see James Horn, *Adapting to a New World: English Society in the Seventeenth-Century Chesapeake* (Chapel Hill, N.C. 1994), 140–41.

2. For additional discussion of Chesapeake geography and settlement, see Kevin

P. Kelly, "'In dispers'd Country Plantations': Settlement Patterns in Seventeenth-Century Surry County, Virginia," in Thad W. Tate and David L. Ammerman, eds., *The Chesapeake in the Seventeenth Century: Essays on Anglo-American Society and Politics* (New York, 1979), 183–205; and D. W. Meinig, *The Shaping of America: A Geographical Perspective on 500 Years of History*, vol. 1: *Atlantic America, 1492–1800* (New Haven, Conn., 1986), 144–60.

Historical geographer James O'Mara dismisses contemporaries' and historians' observations about the relationships between Virginia's waterways and lack of towns as physical environmental determinism but provides no alternative explanation for seventeenth-century dispersed settlement patterns. Obviously physical geography was not the only factor. The headright system and traders' and colonists' desires to avoid official scrutiny and custom duties also encouraged dispersed settlement and shipping, but they would not have been possible without the Chesapeake's unusual estuary system. See James O'Mara, *An Historical Geography of Urban System Development: Tidewater Virginia in the 18th Century*, Geographical Monographs (Downsview, Ontario, 1983), 13:3, 114–23.

3. "A Perfect Description of Virginia" (London, 1649), in Force, *Tracts and Other Papers*, vol. 2 (1836) (Gloucester, Mass., 1963), 3, 5.

4. Perry, *The Formation of a Society on Virginia's Eastern Shore*, 149; Bailyn, *New England Merchants*, 79; J. M. Sosin, *English America and the Restoration Monarchy of Charles II: Transatlantic Politics, Commerce, and Kinship* (Lincoln, Nebr., 1980), chap. 1.

5. Eighteenth-century accounts of seamen rolling half-ton tobacco hogsheads from barns to creeks navigable by shallops or flatboats, work they considered "unfit for men," likely described seventeenth-century practice as well. Earle, *Sailors*, 80; Arthur Pierce Middleton, *Tobacco Coast: A Maritime History of Chesapeake Bay in the Colonial Era* (1953) (Baltimore, Md., 1984), 282–83. For ships' long stays in the Chesapeake, see Steele, *The English Atlantic*, 42; James F. Shepherd and Gary M. Walton, *Shipping, Maritime Trade, and the Economic Development of Colonial North America* (Cambridge, Eng., 1972).

6. On January 18,1639, Governor John Harvey and the Virginia Council wrote to the Privy Council that they were "compelled to require masters of ships not to break bulk until they arrive at James City." W. Noel Sainsbury, ed., *Calendar of State Papers, Colonial Series (CSPC) 1574–1660* (London, 1860), 287–88, #5. On July 26, 1655, in obedience to the Act for the Regulation of Trade and of Establishing Ports & Places for Markets that the Assembly had passed on March 20, 1654, the Lower Norfolk court appointed two places in that country that it judged convenient. Each was to have a church or meeting place and a market. One day a week would be appointed as market day. Norfolk County, Wills & Deeds C, 1651–56 (Library of Virginia, microfilm), 161.

7. In 1705 Presbyterian minister Francis Mackemie described changes in Chesapeake marketing that came with the development of Norfolk as a port town in the early eighteenth century: "Norfolk Town at Elizabeth River . . . carry on a small Trade with the whole Bay . . . You may frequently buy at the three beginnings of Towns, at Williamsburg, Hampton & Norfolk, many things which strangers have no opportunity of having elsewhere at any rate; and at more modest Prices than are expected at Private Plantations." His statement also illustrates the highly personal nature of traditional Chesapeake trade, which made it somewhat more difficult for "strangers" than those with acquaintances. Francis Mackemie, "A Plain and Friendly Perswasive to the Inhab-

itants of Virginia and Maryland for Promoting Towns and Cohabitation," *VMHB* 4 (1897): 255–71.

8. At least early in the century, the term mariner did not carry connotations of social status and referred to any one involved in the sailing of ships. Masters and ship captains were of high status and served in various political offices. Although merchants may or may not have been mariners as well, many merchants traveled at least periodically with their cargoes to trade their merchandise directly and reinforce their economic and social contacts. Although individuals throughout the century combined the roles of planter and merchant (intercolonial and transatlantic), most of my examples involving ship captains (mariners) of high status are from before 1670. Thus, it is possible that at the end of the century it became less common for planters and colonial officials to also be mariners.

9. For an analysis of the role of common seamen in creating the Atlantic world, see Rediker, *Between the Devil and the Deep Blue Sea*, 10–76; Peter Linebaugh and Marcus Rediker, *The Many-Headed Hydra: Sailors, Slaves, Commoners, and the Hidden History of the Revolutionary Atlantic* (Boston, 2000).

10. Hinckley to Blathwayt, March 16, 1684, in "The Hinckley Papers," *Massachusetts Historical Society Collections*, 4th series 5, 123.

11. De Vries, *Voyages*, 29. De Vries wrote that he could not refuse because Martin Thysz from Zealand had put the Portuguese on shore at Nevis.

12. De Vries, *Voyages*, 30–33. They went to Swanendail at the mouth of Delaware Bay, a Dutch fort that Indians had destroyed in 1630. De Vries had been a patron of the settlement.

13. They met both "Armewamen" and "Minquas" (Susquehannocks), who were at war with one another. De Vries, *Voyages*, 41–43. They needed corn for their return to Holland and feared that they could not get it at New Amsterdam. De Vries, *Voyages*, 46–47.

14. De Vries, *Voyages*, 50–51.

15. De Vries, *Voyages*, 51–52.

16. Wesley N. Laing, "Cattle in Seventeenth-Century Virginia," *VMHB* 67 (1959): 153; "A Perfect Description of Virginia," 14–15.

17. De Vries, *Voyages*, 52–53.

18. De Vries, *Voyages*, 55.

19. De Vries, *Voyages*, 63–64.

20. See, for example, the 1654 case tried in New Haven in which Captain John Manning was accused of trading with the Dutch at Manhattan the previous winter and "so furnishing the enimies of the comonwealth of England wth provissions." Witnesses included members of Manning's international crew Thomas Burrett (English), Martine Notus (Dutch), and Lawrence Pollett (French). Hoadly, ed., *New Haven Colony Records*, 2:68. March 26, 1654.

21. De Vries, *Voyages*, 53.

22. De Vries, *Voyages*, 58.

23. De Vries, *Voyages*, 71–95. After establishing their Guiana colony, De Vries and some of the mariners left, perhaps intending to return with additional supplies. While in Kecoughtan, Virginia, the following spring, he learned that his Guiana colony "was broken up by the disorders of some English and seamen among them." The English, supposedly under the command of the Dutch, had without Dutch permission boarded

a Spanish ship come for water, killed the Spanish, and taken the ship as a prize. The Dutch seamen, despite ripening crops in the ground, agreed to abandon the Guiana colony, sail the boat to the Caribbean, and acknowledge the English as captains and themselves as servants, in return for a share of the booty from the Spanish ship. But when they reached the Caribbean, the English who had convinced them to sail sold the seamen as servants to planters. De Vries concluded that "The English are a villainous people, and would sell their own fathers for servants in the Islands," and that those who planted colonies should not include seamen ("scoundrels" in his eyes), except those needed to sail. De Vries, *Voyages*, 113.

24. De Vries, *Voyages*, 104–7. For a discussion of the English settlement on Tortuga (Association Island) and the 1635 Spanish attack on it and Providence Island, see Karen Ordahl Kupperman, *Providence Island, 1630–1641: The Other Puritan Colony* (Cambridge and New York, 1993), especially 197–98.

25. De Vries, *Voyages*, 108–9. At Point Comfort they met the London ship with the captive Governor Harvey on board, sent to England by his council and the people.

26. De Vries, *Voyages*, 111.

27. When he arrived in Virginia he found that he could not acquire his tobacco because there were too many English ships and too little tobacco as a result of "a great mortality that year" so he left for New Netherland on May 6. De Vries, *Voyages*, 113–14.

28. Frederick was secretary of the city of Amsterdam, and a manager of the West India Company. De Vries, *Voyages*, 121.

29. De Vries, *Voyages*, 126–28.

30. De Vries, *Voyages*, 148.

31. De Vries, *Voyages*, 176–77.

32. De Vries, *Voyages*, 180–81.

33. De Vries, *Voyages*, 181–83.

34. De Vries, *Voyages*, 183.

35. De Vries had failed to acquire tobacco during his 1635 voyage. De Vries, *Voyages*, 113–14.

36. De Vries, *Voyages*, 183.

37. De Vries, *Voyages*, 184–88

38. "A Perfect Description of Virginia" (London, 1649), in *Collections of the Massachusetts Historical Society* 2nd ser., 9 (1832), 105, 119.

39. Ames, ed., *Accomack-Northampton 1640–1645*, 378–79, July 28, 1644.

40. Ames, *Studies*, 69, cites a 1678 court case in Accomack County, Wills and Deeds, 1676–90, 139. Transatlantic shipping in the seventeenth-century Chesapeake was seasonal, with ships arriving in the late fall or early winter and leaving in the spring. This pattern changed dramatically at the end of the century, when ships began arriving in the spring and departing in the summer. Steele, *The English Atlantic*, 42.

41. Accomack County Order Book, 1666–70, 136–38.

42. Ames, ed., *Accomack-Northampton 1640–1645*, 45–46. The case did not involve an accusation that the crew had stolen the heifer, which would have provided a reason to use the ship's departure to date the event.

43. Norfolk County, Wills and Deeds C, 1651–56, 141.

44. Steele, *The English Atlantic*, 59; cites Isaac Norris to William Righton, 11 seventh month 1699, Historical Society of Pennsylvania, Isaac Norris Letterbook, 1699–1702, 72, 123.

45. The seamen alleged "that it was impossible to gain a passage in winter, and that the load being corn, was the more dangerous." Fleet, "A Brief Journal," 21. Corn's light weight perhaps made it a dangerous cargo in stormy conditions. The master and his mate, however, were both engaged for the delivery of Virginia corn to New England and so worked with Fleet "to persuade and encourage them to proceed." Ultimately, "with threats and fair persuasions," Fleet and the master prevailed.

46. Marcus Rediker argues that by the eighteenth century, Boston was popular among mariners, who thought it "a good town for 'frolicking,' not least because of its 'well rigged' young women." *Between the Devil and the Deep Blue Sea*, 65.

47. The connection between ordinaries and trade is evident in the 1668 Virginia law that restricted the number of ordinaries to two per county "unless in publick Places and great Roads [meaning ship roads, not overland roads], where necessary for the Accommodation of Travellers." *An Abridgement of the Laws In Force and Use in Her Majesty's Plantations* (London, 1704), 45.

48. Rediker, *Between the Devil and the Deep Blue Sea*, 153–204. For cross-race socializing in Virginia, see Morgan, *American Slavery, American Freedom*, 154–57, 311–12.

49. The author of "A Perfect Description of Virginia" claimed that Mathews owned forty slaves in 1648. "A Prefect Description of Virginia," 14–15.

50. November 28, 1642. Ames, ed., *Accomack-Northampton 1640–1645*, 221. See also ibid., 168. Testimony of John Dorman, May 9, 1642. Mr. William Burdett had purchased Warder's three years.

51. Some intercolonial traders acted as merchants and storekeepers between other settlers and intercolonial markets. Their stores then became additional congregating points. In November 1640 Peter Croper said that "coming into Stephen Charletons store" the previous January with his master Mr. Taylor's wheat, he received two bundles of trading cloth from Charleton. At least two other men, Edward Daniell and Mr. Cugley, were at the store when the transaction took place. Ames, ed., *Accomack-Northampton 1640–1645*, 51.

52. Ames, ed., *Accomack-Northampton 1640–1645*, August 31, 1643, 300–301. The carpenter asked six pounds of tobacco per ell (forty-five inches) of cloth, and Savage's servant offered him four but bought it for six on Berry's recommendation. The boatswain and cook, angry when they heard the rates, told the carpenter he could have sold the cloth for over twenty pounds of tobacco per ell.

53. Dankaerts, *Journal of Jaspar Dankaerts, 1679–1680*, Original Narratives of Early American History, ed. Bartlett Burleigh James and J. Franklin Jameson (New York, 1913), 135.

54. Deposition of John Martin, Norfolk County, Wills and Deeds C, 1651–56, 72.

55. Norfolk County, Wills and Deeds C, 1651–56, 72, January 16, 1654.

56. Deposition of Ed(ward) Lloyd, Norfolk County, Wills and Deeds C, 1651–56, 72a.

57. Deposition of Lemuell Mason, gentleman and justice, aged twenty-five. Norfolk County, Wills and Deeds C, 1651–56, 72, January 16, 1654.

58. The court ruled that a half-owner like Fassett, "haveing an imploymt: part" such as master, had greater power over the vessel than the other half owner. The court ordered Lambert to pay five thousand pounds of tobacco to Fassett "towards the repracon of his good name & creditt." Norfolk County, Wills and Deeds C, 1651–56, 72a,

January 16, 1654. Later during the same court session, Lambert sold the *Seahorse*, "fitted for ye Barbados," to Fassett. Ibid., 83, April 4, 1654, recorded April 16. The following week, Fassett made plans to deliver two thousand pounds of sugar to William Wescombe[?]. April 24, 1654, recorded October 18, 1654. Ibid., 103.

59. Norfolk County, Wills and Deeds C, 1651–56, 83, recorded April 16, 1654.

60. Ames, *Studies*, 49, citing Fernow, ed., *Documents Relative to the History of New York*, 12:94.

61. Dauphiné of Durand, *A Huguenot Exile in Virginia* (1687) (New York, 1934), 160.

62. Letter to Thomas Wentworth, Earl of Strafford, August 19, 1635, quoted in Neill, *Founders of Maryland*, 53.

63. *CSPC 1574–1660*, 79–80, #9.

64. York County, Deeds, Orders, Wills 2 (typescripts at the Colonial Williamsburg Research Foundation), August 26, 1661, #1311, 1329, 1349, 1350, 1351, 126–31. This case came to court just after the clerk recorded an order against Quakers.

65. August 31, 1643. Ames, ed., *Accomack-Northampton 1640–1645*, 301–6.

66. Ames, ed., *Accomack-Northampton 1640–1645*, 304. On their way up the Chesapeake, Ingle told the Virginians that they could thank Frank Yardley for their trip to Maryland because if the Yardleys had not affronted him, he would have stayed at Accomack with his ship.

67. Ames, ed., *Accomack-Northampton 1640–1645*, 304–5. Depositions of John Thompson, William Whittington, and George Vaux (gentleman).

68. *Records of the Court of Assistants of Massachusetts Bay 1630–1692*, vol. 2, 1630–44 (Boston, 1904), 25.

69. Hoadly, *New Haven Colony Records*, 2:227.

70. On April 26, 1655, Captain George Swanley complained to the Norfolk court that Mr. William Johnson came aboard his ship as a passenger for England and stayed on the ship for about sixteen weeks, eating from the ship's provisions that whole time, and had since deserted his intended voyage, but had not paid for the food he had eaten. Norfolk County, Wills and Deeds C, 1651–56, 140a. The court ordered Johnson to pay Swanley three hundred pounds of tobacco.

71. William Bradford, *History of Plymouth Plantation 1602–1646* in *Massachusetts Historical Society Collections*, 4th ser., 3 (Boston, 1856), 125–29.

72. Bradford, *History*, 127–28. "I must acknowledg my selfe many ways indebted, whose books I would have you thinke very well bestowed on him, who esteemeth them such juells. My host would not suffer me to remember (much less to begg) Mr Ainsworths elaborate worke upon ye 5 books of Moyses. Both his & Mr Robinsons doe highly comend the authors, as being most conversante in ye scripturs of all others. And what good (who knows) it may please God to worke by them, through my hands, (though most unworthy), who finds shuch high contente in them. Your unfained and firme freind, John Pory." August 28, 1622.

73. For discussion of the circulation of news in the Atlantic, see Steele, *The English Atlantic*, passim.

74. Steele's recognition of Virginia's distance in terms of travel time despite its being the "closest of the colonies to England economically" illustrates the difficulty of drawing precise conclusions about correlations between trade and communication. Steele, "Empire of Migrants and Consumers: Some Current Atlantic Approaches to the

History of Colonial Virginia," *VMHB* 99 (1991): 498, 512. Steele also points out, however, that in order to understand colonists' perceptions about their distance from England, we need to realize that travel times were improving (and therefore seemed good by colonists' point of reference if not ours), and that maritime travel from London to some colonial ports (Bridgetown, Barbados and Boston, Massachusetts) was so much more frequent than travel from London to some parts of the British Isles (County Clare and the Shetland Islands) that those colonial ports possessed greater access to London news. "Empire of Migrants and Consumers," 497. See also Steele, *The English Atlantic*, 6. Until Carolina developed exports for European markets, it lacked direct English shipping, and much of its communication with England took place by way of Virginia. For examples, see Joseph West to Lord Ashley, June 27, 1670, *CSPC 1669–1674*, 71, #203; Sayle and council at Ashley River to the Lords Proprietors, [September] 1670, *CSPC 1669–1674*, 85, #245 and Flor O Sullivan to [Lord Ashley], September 9, 1670, *CSPC 1669–1674*, 88, #250.

75. Fleet, "A Brief Journal," 24. On November 28, 1650, a license permitted inhabitants of New England to trade to Barbados, Virginia, Bermuda, and Antigua until July 31, 1651, despite the act of October 3, 1650, prohibiting such trade, because the distance was so great that New Englanders could not have certain knowledge of the earlier act. *CSPC 1574–1660*, 347, #28. See also Steele, *The English Atlantic*; Julius Scott, "The Common Wind: Currents of Afro-American Communication in the Era of the Haitian Revolution" (Ph.D. diss, Duke University, 1986).

76. "The Mather Papers," *Massachusetts Historical Society Collections*, 4th series 8, 199–200. Captain Higginson ("brother of Mr. Higgn of Salem") came to Virginia from London at the end of the previous October as commander of a new ship called the *America* and told his brother the news. "He saith that those [seamen] that have come to Virginia, doe generally complaine of there greate Taxes, & say that Cromwell sought the good of the Land."

77. Linebaugh and Rediker, *The Many-Headed Hydra*; Rediker, *Between the Devil and the Deep Blue Sea*.

78. On December 31, 1669, for example, Matthias Nicolls wrote from New York to Colonel Richard Nicolls, one of Grooms of the Bedchamber to the Duke of York, that Mr. Boone had arrived two or three days earlier by way of Virginia with news of his health and welfare. *CSPC 1669–1674*, 47, #133.

79. Durand of Dauphiné, *A Huguenot Exile in Virginia*, 172.

80. Northampton County Court Order Book, 1654–61, fol. 2, 45–47.

81. Northampton County Court Order Book, 1654–61, fol. 2, 29. A similar case appears in Northampton County Court Order Book, fol. 4, 32, 37–38.

82. The sale was recorded in the secretary's office in Jamestown and endorsed by the Northampton County Court on December 13, 1681. *Suffolk Deeds Book* (1902), 12:204. At least one of the witnesses, William Kendall, was a trader to New England. The documents were entered in Boston on May 12, 1682. Ibid., 205–6.

83. Ames, ed., *Accomack-Northampton 1640–1645*, 394, 397–98. January 7, 1645.

84. For a list of powers of attorney between Barbados and Virginia, see Bruce, *Economic History of Virginia*, 2:326–27.

85. Roggers admitted to the problem, but assured the court that his bread had improved. Hoadly, *New Haven Colony Records*, 2:142. The court issued a warning.

86. For an introduction to admiralty law and its application in American colo-

nies, see David R. Owen and Michael C. Tolley, *Courts of Admiralty in Colonial America: The Maryland Experience, 1634–1776* (Durham, N.C., 1995), esp. 1–19.

87. "Minutes of Council and General Court," *VMHB* 19 (1911): 134–36.

88. Sandra Lee Rux, "Edmund Scarburgh—A Biography" (M.A. thesis, Trinity College, 1980), 47, cites Fernow, ed., *Records of New Amsterdam*, 1:331–36. Galeanock is perhaps a mistranslation of Occohannock, the creek where Scarborough lived.

89. Morton Wagman, "Liberty in New Amsterdam: A Sailor's Life in Early New York," *New York History* 64 (1983): 113, cites Berthold Fernow, trans. and ed., *The Records of New Amsterdam from 1653 to 1674* (1897) (Baltimore, 1976), 2:428–29; 1:22.

90. Norfolk County, Wills and Deeds C, 1651–56, 159. The Antigua court also stipulated that Huffey and Selby would not pay rent for the vessel during its repairs. Ibid., 159–59a.

91. Norfolk County, Wills and Deeds C, 1651–56, 158a–59.

92. Huffey explained that Chichester's nonpayment had caused him great damage because by waiting for it he had lost his return to England that year. Chichester appealed the case to the governor and council and put in good security that he would appear the following October in Jamestown. Norfolk County, Wills and Deeds C, 1651–56, 160–61a. When intercolonial traders had to put in security, they needed to be able to rely on their connections and reputations to have others vouch for them like this.

93. Huffey had failed to pay for his use of the vessel and "by his many indirect, & illegal courses" had forced him on several other voyages, keeping the *Hopewell* out of its owners' hands for almost a year after the agreed date of return. Norfolk County, Wills and Deeds C, 1651–56, 159a–62. Commissioners included intercolonial traders Thomas Lambert, Francis Emperor, William Daynes, and Thomas Daynes.

94. Carpenter Henry Davis, seaman John Gelney, mate Aldred Follett, seaman Robert Viccary, seaman Thomas Lambert, and boatswain Richard Bott testified in the case. July 16, recorded July 20, 1655. Norfolk County, Wills and Deeds C, 1651–56, 162a.

95. For an extended discussion of such court cases and their legal implications, see April Lee Hatfield, "Mariners, Merchants, and Colonists in Seventeenth-Century English America," in Carole Shammas and Elizabeth Mancke, eds., *The Transatlantic Experience and British Imperial Visions, 1600–1800* (Baltimore, forthcoming). See also Owen and Tolley, *Courts of Admiralty in Colonial America:* Tolley's and Owen's Appendix A ("Case Studies") summarizes all maritime cases in Maryland's colonial courts. Those from the seventeenth century (237–77) provide multiple examples of Maryland courts ruling over colonial and English ships, merchants, and seamen, including ones from Virginia.

96. *Suffolk Deeds Book* (1888), 4:295.

97. Hoadly, *New Haven Colony Records*, 1:366. February 1, 1648.

98. Hoadly, *New Haven Colony Records*, 1:421. December 5, 1648.

99. Hoadly, *New Haven Colony Records*, 2:425. October 16, 1661.

100. The Massachusetts court similarly granted a divorce to Hope Ambrose in 1678. Her husband Samuel Ambrose had been gone four years and she too presented evidence from intercolonial travelers, William Timberleg and John Hunt, who had seen her husband in Jamaica, where he lived with another woman and boasted of his "carnall fellowship wth hir." *Records of the Court of Assistants*, 1:127.

101. The phrase is from A. J. R Russell-Wood, *A World on the Move: The Portuguese in Africa, Asia, and America 1415–1808* (New York, 1993).

Chapter 4

1. Thomas Baldreage of Virginia lived "in Potomack river over against Maryland." A Virginia widow who had gone to Barbados after her husband's death to settle an estate he had owned on the island carried the letter. "Westmoreland County Records," *WMQ* 1st ser., 15 (1906): 176–78.

2. Alfred D. Chandler estimated the number of white Barbadian emigrants (to all locations) in the seventeenth century at 30,000. "The Expansion of Barbados," *Journal of the Barbados Museum and Historical Society* 13 (1946): 106–7. Richard Dunn put the number at 10,000. *Sugar and Slaves: The Rise of the Planter Class in the English West Indies, 1674–1713* (New York, 1972), 112–13. Both are estimates for European emigrants only.

3. See Alison Games, *Migration and the Origins of the English Atlantic World*; James P. Horn, "Moving on the the New World: Migration and Out-migration in the Seventeenth-Century Chesapeake" in Peter Clark and David Souden, eds., *Migration and Society in Early Modern England* (Totowa, N.J., 1988), 172–212; Warren M. Billings, "The Transfer of English Law to Virginia, 1606–1650," in K. R. Andrews, N. P. Canny, and P. E. H. Hair, eds., *The Westward Enterprise: English Activities in Ireland, the Atlantic, and America 1480–1650* (Detroit, Mich., 1979), 221–34.

4. Alison Games found that of the 486 migrants to Massachusetts Bay from London in 1635, 61 percent remained in the in the colony and 39 percent moved on, most of them to other New England colonies. *Migration and the Origins of the English Atlantic World*, 170–71. Lorena S. Walsh found that 35–36 percent of free adult men left Charles County, Maryland, between 1660 and 1690. "Staying Put or Getting Out: Findings for Charles County, Maryland, 1650–1720," *WMQ* 3rd ser., 44 (1987): 89–103. Closer to sixty percent of servants left Charles County upon becoming free during the second half of the seventeenth century. Lorena S. Walsh, "Servitude and Opportunity in Charles County, Maryland, 1658–1705," in Aubrey C. Land, Lois Green Carr, and Edward C. Papenfuse, eds., *Law, Society, and Politics in Early Maryland* (Baltimore, 1977), 111–33. See also Horn, "Moving on in the New World," 172–212. Records allowing the calculation of persistence do not allow us to finding place of origin (colonial vs. European) for immigrants.

5. For enumeration of Virginia headright grants for each year from 1635 to 1699 see Craven, *White, Red, and Black*, 15. For estimates of Virginia and Maryland tithable populations, see Menard, "Chesapeake Tobacco Industry," 157–61. He lists 16,067 taxables in 1678, 16,534 in 1679, and 17,000 in 1680.

6. Observers throughout the second half of the seventeenth century reported high outmigration from Barbados. Our means for determining the increase in overall population from the increase in the numbers of taxables are imperfect. Multipliers for 1699 range from 1.86 for Northumberland to 3.3 for Norfolk. Menard, "Chesapeake Tobacco Industry," 116–17. Headright grants sometimes reflected older, rather than recent immigration of the individuals for whom rights were claimed. Nell Marion Nugent, *Cavaliers and Pioneers*, 1:xxiv–xxvi.

7. The first intercolonial migrations were between Virginia and Bermuda, which were established together by the Virginia Company. For a discussion of one such migration, and the significance of Bermudan experiences for English colonists who ultimately went to Virginia, see Linebaugh and Rediker, *The Many-Headed Hydra*,

8–35. In 1635 two ships brought 205 settlers from Bermuda to Virginia, adding to the 4,914 present already. W. Noel Sainsbury, ed., *Calendar of State Papers, Colonial Series (CSPC) 1574–1660* (London, 1860), 55, #201.

8. Horn, *Adapting to a New World*, 19–77; Games, *Migration and the Origins of the English Atlantic World*, 13–44.

9. *CSPC 1574–1660*, 95, #62; ibid., 27, #100–101.

10. Merrell, *The Indians' New World*, 24–27, 102–6.

11. Stephen Charleton's trips between the Chesapeake and New England facilitated the migrations of New Englanders to Virginia. In 1642, for example, the carpenter John Knight agreed to move from New England to Accomack County, Virginia, to build a house and a mill for Charleton. Charleton lived in Puritan Hungars parish. Knight's servant John Cuttings agreed to accompany Knight in exchange for his freedom. Ames, ed., *Accomack-Northampton 1640–1645*, 229–31.

12. Perry, *Formation of a Society on Virginia's Eastern Shore*, 160.

13. See Chapter 5; J. F. Bosher "Huguenot Merchants and the Protestant International in the Seventeenth Century" *WMQ* 3rd ser., 52 (1995): 77–102; David Hancock, *Citizens of the World: London Merchants and the Integration of the British Atlantic Community, 1735–1785* (Cambridge, Eng., 1995), 83–84, 139–42; Tolles, *Quakers and the Atlantic Culture*; Jacob M. Price, *Perry of London: A Family and a Firm on the Seaborne Frontier, 1615–1753* (Cambridge, Mass., 1992).

14. Barbadian Joseph Warden, for example, made his Rappahannock County, Virginia, trading partner John Morrah the godfather of his son Thomas. Morrah confirmed that relationship by willing his godson one thousand pounds of muscovado sugar. Bruce, *Economic History of Virginia*, 2:327n., cites Rappahannock County Records, 1677–82.

15. Ames, ed., *Accomack-Northampton 1640–1645*, 251–52. Pellham was Catholic, and one of the letters was addressed to Father Andrew White, so likely Cobbs was Catholic and intending to move to Maryland. Ames suggests Cobbs may have been the Jesuit Thomas Copley, but he moved to Maryland in 1637 and probably did not need such letters in 1642.

16. *CSPC 1661–1668*, 528, #1657. A copy of a list of people who left Barbados included twenty-four hundred to Virginia and Surinam between 1646 and 1658. Chandler, "The Expansion of Barbados," 106–36.

17. For the sugar revolution, see Dunn, *Sugar and Slaves*, 110–16, 152–54; McCusker and Menard, *Economy of British America*, 149–56. Although land always remained more accessible in the colonial Chesapeake than in Barbados, greater opportunities for landholding induced similar migration from Virginia and Maryland to Pennsylvania and other new colonies at the end of the seventeenth century. Virginia Governor Francis Nicholson wrote in 1695 that "many families, but especially young men" left for Pennsylvania because land was cheaper there. Horn, "Moving on the in the New World," 183. T. H. Breen, "A Changing Labor Force and Race Relations in Virginia, 1600–1710," *Journal of Social History* 7 (1973): 16; *CSPC 1693–1696*, 511.

18. "Considerations concerning the settlement of . . . Guiana." February 16, 1652, *CSPC 1574–1660*, 41, #373–374.

19. Willoughby suggested that those leaving Barbados "will not go to Jamaica as it is unhealthy and the land not good for planting." November 4, 1663 Lord Willoughby to the King, November 4, 1663, *CSPC 1661–1668*, 166–67, #578. In 1664

Thomas Modyford repeated his 1652 opinion, this time in encouraging migration to Jamaica, that Barbadoes "cannot last in a height of trade three years longer." *CSPC 1661–1668*, 180, #629.

20. Carl Bridenbaugh and Roberta Bridenbaugh, *No Peace beyond the Line: The English in the Caribbean, 1624–1690* (New York, 1972), 219.

21. Francis Sampson to his brother John Sampson, June 6, 1666, *CSPC 1661–1668*, 385, #1212. In a letter written June 11, Michael Smith wrote the same information from Nevis to London merchant Richard Chaundler: "Many have been sent for Virginia and New England and 2,000 old men, women, and children, have been sent to Nevis." *CSPC 1661–1668*, 387, #1214. See also ibid., 387 #1215. On August 24, 1671, after England regained the island, Governor Charles Wheler scheduled a court of claims for "all his Majesty's subject having any . . . property to any estate on the island." Expecting quick intercolonial and transatlantic communication, he gave those in England, Europe, Virginia, Jamaica, Carolina, Bermuda, and New England only three months to make their claims; those in Barbados and other Caribbean islands, one month. Sir Charles Wheler to Colonel Strode, Governor of Dover Castle, from Nevis, August 24, 1671. *CSPC 1669–1674*, 274, #658.

22. Bridenbaugh and Bridenbaugh, *No Peace beyond the Line*, 208.

23. For a 1650 example of Lownes' Barbados-Virginia trade, see Norfolk County, Wills and Deeds C, 1651–56, 89a.

24. Norfolk County, Wills and Deeds C, 1651–56, 28a, 46. Colonists received grants of fifty acres for every person they could claim to have transported into Virginia. Large land grants indicated that a planter had brought servants or slaves into the colony or had purchased them from outside the colony after his arrival there. Colonists sometimes received their grants years after the actual transportation. A single land grant could represent more than one immigration, and a single person was occasionally counted more than one time, though this was not the intent of the system. Nugent, *Cavaliers and Pioneers*, 1:xxiv–xxvi.

25. Norfolk County, Wills and Deeds C, 1651–56, 1–2, 28, 49, 51a, 89a. When intercolonial trader Virginia Captain Matthew Wood traveled, Lownes took care of his livestock.

26. Norfolk County, Wills and Deeds C, 1651–56, 41a.

27. The Council and Assembly of Nevis to Francis Lord Willoughby, "Governor of Barbados and the rest of the Caribbees," *CSPC 1661–1668*, 204–205, #731.

28. The western half of Lower Norfolk became Norfolk County in this division.

29. G. Andrews Moriarity, "The Emperour Family of Lower Norfolk County," *VMHB* 23 (1915): 417–20, 438–40. "The Church in Lower Norfolk County," *Lower Norfolk County Virginia Antiquary* 4 (1902): 83–86. Rutman and Rutman, *A Place in Time*, 147.

30. Moriarity, "The Emperour Family," 418, and Nugent, *Cavaliers and Pioneers*, 1:283, 343.

31. Sarah Emperor's first husband, gentleman Edward Oistin, received on of the largest early land grants in Barbados, one thousand acres in 1629. Oistin's Town and Oistin's Bay, in Christ Church parish, Barbados, were named for his family. Dunn, *Sugar and Slaves*, 51. Moriarity, "The Emperour Family," 418. Elizabeth Emperor Horbin perhaps married a brother of merchant and planter Joseph Horbin, who also owned extensive estates in Jamaica and South Carolina. Moriarity, "The Emperor Family," 418.

32. "The Church in Lower Norfolk County," 82.

33. "The Church in Lower Norfolk County," 83.

34. Alice Granberry Walter, *Captain Thomas Willoughby, 1601–1657: of England, Barbadoes, and Lower Norfolk County, Virginia: Some of His Descendants, 1601–1800* (Virginia Beach, Va., 1978), 3–12. See also Horn, *Adapting to a New World*, 392–93.

35. Moriarity, "The Emperour Family," 418. Emperor may have been fluent in Dutch because of Dutch background, the unusual surname reflecting Anglicization of a Dutch name. At least one known Dutch immigrant to the Chesapeake had the first name Emperor. Jeffrey A. Wyand and Florence L. Wyand, *Colonial Maryland Naturalizations* (Baltimore, 1986). The Emperors intermarried with the Dutch Moseley family in Lower Norfolk. Margery Wood Furguiele, *Genealogical Glimpses—Maternal* (Culpeper, Va., 1992), 199–213.

36. "The Church in Lower Norfolk County," 84.

37. Moriarity, "The Emperor Family," 418; *The Original Lists of Persons of Quality . . . 1600–1700* (1880) (Baltimore, 1962), 433, 418.

38. "The Church in Lower Norfolk County," 86, 438–39; Princess Anne County, Deed Book 1, part 1 (1691–1708), fol. 53 (Library of Virginia, Richmond, microfilm reel 2.); Princess Anne County, Deed Book 1, part 1 (1691–1708), fol. 155.

39. In his will (dated May 26, 1698, and proved July 20, 1711, in Princess Anne County), Francis Tully Emperor left all his property to his son, Francis. If Francis died, all his estates in Virginia were to go to the children of his brother Tully Emperor and his estates in Barbados to his wife's sister's children there. "The Church in Lower Norfolk County," 87.

40. Princess Anne County, Deed Book 1, part 1 (1691–1708), fol. 4–6.

41. Princess Anne County, Deed Book 1, part 1 (1691–1708), fol. 130.

42. Princess Anne County, Deed Book 1, part 1 (1691–1708), fol. 149.

43. Moriarity, "The Emperour Family," 438.

44. Elizabeth Emperor Horbin continued to live in Princess Anne County for at least two years after she wrote the will, which was proved November 4, 1695(6?). Princess Anne County, Deed Book 1, part 1 (1691–1708), fol. 130.

45. Princess Anne County, Deed Book 1, part 1 (1691–1708), fol. 149.

46. Moriarity, "The Emperour Family," 440.

47. Ann Emperor, first cousin of Francis Tully Emperor and Sarah Oistin Emperor, married John Walker at St. Michael's Parish, Barbados, on November 29, 1686. Walkes were regularly recorded as Walkers in Barbados and Virginia records. John Walke was brother of the Virginia merchant Thomas and the Barbadian merchant Jonathan. Moriarity, "The Emperour Family," 439–40. In September 1697 Francis Tully Emperor showed concern for the Walke family by selling 650 acres to Colonel Anthony Lawson, Mr. Edward Moseley, and William Moseley, executors of Thomas Walke's will, for them to hold for Anthony Walke, Thomas Walke's second son. Princess Anne County, Deed Book 1, part 1 (1691–1708), fol. 149. Anthony Lawson's daughter Mary married Thomas Walke in 1689. "Families of Lower Norfolk and Princess Anne Counties," *VMHB* 5 (1897): 139–40. Lawson also had contacts in Jamaica. In 1685 Jamaican William Dundas appointed him his attorney to collect debts in Lower Norfolk. Bruce, *Economic History of Virginia*, 2:328n., citing Lower Norfolk County, 1675–86.

48. Hillyard had bought the land from Thomas Chamberlaine, who had pur-

chased it from John Sandford. Princess Anne County, Deed Book 1, part 1 (1691–1708), fol. 12. I have not found evidence that Hillyard was related to Barbadian planter William Hilliard, who had grown wealthy producing cotton and tobacco and been one of the earliest successful sugar producers in the 1640s. Peter F. Campbell, *Some Early Barbadian History* (Barbados, 1993), 91–94, 135, 136. However, Virginia ship captain Hillyard was familiar with the island whether or not he was related to the Barbadian planter of the same name. Hillyard kept land in Princess Anne where he raised cattle, hogs, sheep, and horses on his Virginia plantation, where he owned at least one slave. Princess Anne County, Deed Book 1, part 1 (1691–1708), fol. 84. After he died in Barbados in 1694, one of the witnesses, Mr. Thomas Brown, went from Barbados to Virginia in July to certify that he had seen William Hillyard sign and seal that will. A second Barbadian witness, John Smith, traveled to Virginia the following spring. That two witnesses made the journey within a year of Hillyard's death reveals the frequency of travel between the colonies.

49. Urple C. Taylor and Pattie M. Grady, "Dr. John Robertson Walke of 'Physic Hill,' Chesterfield County, Va.: His Ancestors and Descendants" (Chesterfield, Va., 1987), in Barbados Archives, Lazaretto, St. Michael.

50. "Families of Lower Norfolk and Princess Anne Counties," 139–53.

51. He witnessed the will of slaveholder Thomas Downes on April 18, 1684. Recopied Deed Books, Barbados Archives, RB 6/40, 409–12.

52. Taylor and Grady, "Dr. John Robertson Walke;" Bruce, *Economic History of Virginia*, 2:328, citing Records of Lower Norfolk County, 1685–96, 194.

53. William Byrd to Jonathan Walke, May 29, 1689, in Tinling, ed., *Correspondence*, 1:104.

54. "Families of Lower Norfolk and Princess Anne Counties," 139–53.

55. Recopied Deed Books, Barbados Archives, RB 6/16, 184–86.

56. For other examples of Barbadian merchant family networks, see Norfolk County, Wills and Deeds C, 1651–56 (Library of Virginia, microfilm reel 44), 73. The three men instrumental in establishing Norfolk were Anthony Lawson, William Robinson, and William Moseley.

57. Accomack County Virginia Order Book 1666 October 16–1670 January 26, Virginia Historical Society, Mss 3Ac275a, typescript by Susie May Ames, 1942–46, 375. Ames, *Studies*, 47–48n. See also the naturalization and denization of other Dutch immigrants in "Proceedings of the House of Burgesses," *VMHB* 8 (1901): 391; *WMQ* 1st ser., 27 (1918–19): 136; "The Randolph Manuscript," *VMHB* 17 (1909): 243–45.

58. Edwin R. Purple, "Contributions to the History of the Ancient Families of New York, Varleth—Varlet—Varleet—Verlet—Verleth," *The New York Genealogical and Biographical Record* 9 (1878): 53–62, 113–25 and 10 (1879): 35–38. For citations on the Varlett family, I am indebted to Daphne Gentry for unpublished research notes on the life of Anna Varlett Hack Boot, compiled for the Library of Virginia.

59. Purple, "Contributions," 53–62. The three daughters who did not move to Virginia were Maria, Catherine, who married Francois de Bruyn of New Amsterdam, and Judith, who married Nicholas Bayard (the son of Samuel Bayard and Anna Stuyvesant Bayard Varlett), and survived, partly thanks to Peter Stuyvesant's intervention, a witchcraft accusation in Connecticut in the early 1660s. Carol F. Karlson, *The Devil in the Shape of a Woman: Witchcraft in Colonial New England* (New York, 1987), 25–26.

60. Nugent, *Cavaliers and Pioneers*, vol. 1 (1623–66), 265, 285, 412; Whitelaw, *Virginia's Eastern Shore*, 685–86. Hening, *Statutes*, 1:499; McIlwaine, ed., *JHB 1619–1658/9*, 112; *JHB, 1659/60–1693*, 10; *JHB 1659/60–1693*, 11; *JHB 1619–1658/9*, 131.

61. While in New Amsterdam in 1651 and again the following fall, she and merchant Augustine Herman were codefendants in several lawsuits, some instigated by her brother's brother-in-law, Governor Peter Stuyvesant. Purple, "Contributions,"54.

62. For a discussion of women's merchant activities in New Netherland, see Dennis Maika, "Commerce and Community: Manhattan Merchants in the Seventeenth Century" (Ph.D. diss., New York University, 1995), 206.

63. Northampton County Court Order Book, March 28, 1654–June 28, 1661, typescript by Susie May Ames, Virginia Historical Society Mss 3N8125a, fol. 1, 15; ibid., 6a.; Ames, *Studies*, 47–48, citing Northampton County, Wills and Deeds IX, 1657–1666, 27; Whitelaw, *Virginia's Eastern Shore*, 1:685–86.

64. The headrights included George Nicholas Hack, Sepherin Hack, An(n) Kathrine Hack, Domingo, a Negro, George, a Negro, Kathrine, a Negro, Ann, a Negro, Hendrick Volkerts, Rnick Gerrits, Bermon Nephrinninge, Giltielmus Varlee (Varlett?), Augustine Hermons, Barnard Rams, Augustine Rieters, Adrian Rams, Claus Gisbert, Brigitta Williams, and Cornelis Hendrickson. Northampton County Court Order Book, 1654–61, fol. 4, 32–34, April 5, 1659.

65. Matson, *Merchants and Empire*, 26.

66. Northampton County Court Order Books, 1654–61, fol. 2, 108–9.

67. Only three days after Herman received the Cecil County Bohemia Manor grant (see below), George Hack received a grant of eight hundred acres on the Sassafras River in the same county.

68. Purple, "Contributions," 54–57.

69. Northampton County Court Order Book, 1654–61, fol. 1, 39, March 5, 1655, recorded September 20.

70. Herman's public complaint may have ensured Stringer's payment. As a trader to New Netherland, Stringer's reputation with Herman was important. Northampton County Court Order Books, 1654–61, fol. 2, 108–9.

71. Northampton County Court Order Books, 1654–61, fol. 3, 13–15.

72. Northampton County Court Order Books, 1654–61, fol. 3, 11–12. John Custis' sister Ann married Argoll Yardley, the county justice who had argued with Richard Ingle. Perry, *Formation of a Society on Virginia's Eastern Shore*, 152.

73. Northampton County Court Order Books, 1654–61, fol. 3, 35–36. John Reyne, who packed Vaughn's tobacco, intended to go to New Netherland with it. Ibid., 10–15.

74. *Proceedings and Acts of the General Assembly of Maryland*, April 1666–June 1676, vol. 2 of *Archives of Maryland* (Baltimore, 1884), 144–45. *Proceedings of the Council of Maryland*, 1636–16, vol. 3 of *Archives of Maryland* (Baltimore, 1885), 398. Accomack County Deeds and Wills, 1664–71, 11. George Hack's inventory included ninety-six books in high German, Dutch, Latin, and English, putting it among the largest libraries of mid-seventeenth-century Virginia. Nugent, *Cavaliers and Pioneers*, vol. 1 (1623–66), 525. Though Anna had applied for Maryland denizenship, she apparently moved back to Virginia later that year and continued trading. On April 16, 1666, Anna Hack petitioned to be discharged from a judgement against her husband for transporting eleven head of cattle from Virginia to Maryland. [Accomack County] Deeds and Wills, 1663–66, 119–20. It seems likely, given her continued trade to New Netherland and her decision to have a new boat built, that her description of herself as poor may have reflected her attempt to avoid the fine rather than an actual inability to pay it.

75. Accomack County Order Book, 1666–70, 50, 89–91, July 16, 1667; Ames, *Studies*, 142–43; Accomack County Order Book, 1666–70, 90, May 27, 1667.

76. For Boot's activities as a Manhattan merchant, see Maika, "Commerce and Community," 94, 118, 124–25, 197, 340. Boot had traded between New Netherland and the Eastern shore for at least a decade, and moved to Gloucester County, Virginia, west of the Chesapeake Bay, and acquired Virginia denizenship in 1660. In the 1650s, when Boot was in Manhattan, the Holland-born Eastern Shore merchant John Custis (who had collected Augustine Herman's tobacco) served as Nicholas Boot's attorney to trade with Eastern Shore merchant William Kendall. Northampton County Court Order Books, 1654–61, fol. 3, 9, January 29, 1658; ibid., fol. 4, 55a, November 28, 1659. The Virginia Assembly required that he and his family constantly reside in Virginia for two years and after that to make Virginia their primary place of residence. McIlwaine, ed., *JHB 1659/60–1693*, 10. The assembly's loosening of residency requirements after the first two years may reflect their recognition that his occupation as merchant required mobility and that that mobility well served the colony as a whole. Boot's will was written January 9, 1668, proved April 8, 1668, and recorded April 18. [Accomack County] Deeds and Wills, 1664–71, 68. Nicholas was sometimes Claus. Boot also appears Boodt, Bout, Boat, Bootsen. Anna Varlett appears last in a commercial transaction in 1677. She had died by July 1685. *Archives of Maryland*, 2:144–45; Purple, "Contributions."

77. On January 25, 1671, Lydia Prichard testified that she had heard Anna say that she was "a widdow woman and had nobody to do her business for her" and so concluded to sell half of the sloop to Cornelius Vanhoofe for fifty-five hundred pounds of tobacco, but her subsequent instigation of successful suit against Vanhoofe reveals that she was anything but helpless in her widowhood. Accomack County Orders and Wills, 1671–73, 58, 20.

78. Accomack County Orders and Wills, 1671–73, 134. On November 19, 1672, the General Court ordered the Accomack County Court to rehear the case. H. R. McIlwaine, ed., *Minutes of the Council and General Court of Colonial Virginia 1622–1632, 1670–1676* (Richmond, Va., 1924), 320.

79. Anna Varlett also continued to increase her landholdings through headrights, sometimes by furthering the migration from New Netherland to the Eastern Shore. In the 1670s she received certificate for over 1,350 (and possibly over 2,250) acres in Virginia. January 16, 1672. Accomack County Orders and Wills, 1671–73, 48; Accomack County Wills, etc., 1673–76, 180; Nugent, *Cavaliers and Pioneers* (1666–95), 2:158. Her business activities apparently involved more than transporting the products of her plantations for imports from New Netherland. In 1668 in Accomack she commissioned John Richards to make her six spinning wheels and enough tables and cupboards to suggest her intent either to house employees or resell furniture. [Accomack County] Orders and Wills, 1671–73, 224.

80. In 1679 in New York, Herman's oldest son Ephraim Herman married Elizabeth Rodenburg, daughter of former Curaçao vice-director Lucas Rodenburg. Danckaerts, *Journal*, 80.

81. Maika, "Commerce and Community," 206; Martha Dickinson Shattuck, "A Civil Society: Court and Community in Beverwyck, New Netherland, 1652–1664" (Ph.D. diss., Boston University, 1993), 164.

82. Jean Jordan, "Women Merchants in Colonial New York," *New York History* 58 (1977): 418, cites Jacob Judd, "Margaret Hardenbrook Philpse," in Edward T. James, ed., *Notable American Women, 1607–1950: A Biographical Dictionary* (Cambridge, Mass., 1971), 3:61–62, and Mrs. John King Van Rensselaer, *The Goede Vrouw of Mana-*

ha-ta at Home and in Society, 1609–1760 (1898) (New York, 1972), 33–35. In 1679 Jaspar Dankaerts described a Dutch merchant in Albany as "one of the Dutch female traders, who understand the business so well." Ibid., 419; Dankaerts, *Journal*, 318.

83. Linda L. Sturtz notes that "The medieval 'custom of London' permitted women who engaged in business on their own account to operate as 'feme sole traders,' but that this remained an urban phenomenon. Sturtz found two eighteenth-century instances in which the Virginia House of Burgesses granted Virginia women the right to trade as de facto femes soles, in each case because their husbands had abandoned them. *Within Her Power: Propertied Women in Colonial Virginia* (New York, 2002), 66–68. Those cases are significantly different from that of Varlett, who traded independently while her husband was present. English merchants noted the difference between Dutch and English practice. Sir Josiah Child wrote in 1693 that English merchants commonly attempted to convert their estates to land before their death to prevent their widows, who in contrast to Dutch mercantile wives were ignorant about trade, from mismanaging their third of those estates. [Sir Josiah] Child, *A New Discourse of Trade* (London, 1693), 5 and Lawrence Stone and Jean Fawtier Stone, *An Open Elite? England, 1540–1880* (Oxford, 1984), cited in Sturtz, *Within Her Power*, 144.

84. Emphasis mine. Norfolk County, Wills and Deeds C, 1651–56, 24–25a, recorded November 10, 1652.

85. The naturalization record lists Garrett Vanswaringen born in Reensterdwan, Holland; Barbarah DeBarette born in Valenchene in the Low Countries when under Spanish rule; Elizabeth Vanswaringen daughter of Garrett and Barbarah born in New Amstel; and Zacharias Vanswaringen son of Garrett and Barbarah born in New Amstel. See Wyand and Wyand, *Colonial Maryland Naturalizations*, 5.

86. See, for example, the 1677 will of Doodes Minor and the 1694 will of his son Minor Doodes. "Minor Family," *WMQ* 1st ser., 8 (1899–1900): 196–200. For a discussion of the differences between English and Dutch inheritance and their use in New York after the English conquest of New Netherland, see David E. Narrett, "Dutch Customs of Inheritance, Women, and the Law in Colonial New York City," in William Pencak and Conrad Edick Wright, eds., *Authority and Resistance in Early New York* (New York, 1988), 27–55. See also Joyce Goodfriend, *Before the Melting Pot: Society and Culture in Colonial New York City, 1664–1730* (Princeton, N.J., 1992), 186.

87. Sturtz, *Within Her Power*, 49–51.

88. Endorsed June 28, 1666, "Mrs Ann Taft To the Honoble John Wintropp Esqre Govrnor of the Southern parts of New England." Winthrop Papers, n.p., Massachusetts Historical Society, Boston, microfilm reel 8.

89. Accomack County Order Book, 1666–70, 94–95, 261–62. For Vassall's Barbadian origins, see *VMHB* 12 (1905): 303.

90. The Jamaica Council ordered that Scarborough's executors, within the following twelve months, make clear that they really intended to settle the land "and comply with the bonds for bringing on their number of hands." If not, the land was to return to the king to be disposed of as the governor pleased. However, the executors instructed Vassall to send the slaves back (to Virginia?) and declared that they intended to desert the plantation. St Jago, Minutes of the Council of Jamaica, 1672, *CSPC 1669–1674*, 382, #881.

91. Some other intercolonial merchant families relied on women. In December 1654 Elizabeth Lloyd, wife of intercolonial trader Cornelius Lloyd of Elizabeth River in

Lower Norfolk, relied on her "trusty & well beloved frend Nicholas Hart of New England mrchant" to serve as her attorney there to receive all tobacco or money due to her and to sue on her behalf. Norfolk County, Wills and Deeds C, 1651–56, 109a, 119. See also *Suffolk Deeds Book* (1906), 14:261–62. August 20, 1696.

92. Only one record of tension between English and Dutch settlers survives: during the First Anglo-Dutch War in 1652, Dutch settlers complained of "a ruinous violence, suddenly to be acted upon them. In July 1653 the Virginia Assembly responded to the county court's request for help by sending the governor, secretary, and several councilors to Northampton "for the settlement of the peace of that county." Ames, *Studies*, 8–9, citing Northampton County Deeds and Wills, 1651–54, fol. 162, and Hening, ed., *Statutes*, 1:384.

93. Such a conclusion confirms the work of David Ormrod and J. F. Bosher about importance of Calvinist Protestantism to Atlantic trade. Ormrod, "The Atlantic Economy"; Bosher, "Huguenot Merchants and the Protestant International in the Seventeenth Century," *WMQ* 3rd ser., 52 (1995): 77–102. For a similar argument about Dutch New Yorkers, see A. G. Roeber, "'The Origin of Whatever Is Not English among Us': The Dutch-speaking and the German-speaking Peoples of Colonial British America," in Bailyn and Morgan, *Strangers within the Realm*, 220–83. Joyce Goodfriend offers a different interpretation. See *Before the Melting Pot*.

94. Migration from New England began as early as 1624, when Governor Sir Francis Wyatt and the Council of Virginia wrote to Henry, Earl of Southampton and the Council and Company of Virginia that "Widow Smaley when she arrives from New England shall find all lawful favour." *CSPC 1574–1660*, 70, #30.

95. See for example Reverend William Hubbard, "A General History of New England," *Massachusetts Historical Society Collections*, 2nd ser. 5 (1815) (Boston, 1848): 72–73.

96. Bradford, *History*, 151–53.

97. Bradford, *History*, 235–38.

98. John Oldham moved from Plymouth Colony to Virginia and back again. Bradford, *History*, 190–91.

99. Cronin, ed., *Records of the Court of Assistants*, 3:223–24.

100. Ames, ed., *Accomack-Northampton 1640–1645*, 234, January 3, 1643.

101. On May 7, 1662, after five years absence on his part, the Massachusetts Bay Governor and Council allowed her to sell his house and land in Salem to pay the debts for her support. Nathaniel B. Shurtleff, ed., *Records of the Governor and Company of Massachusetts Bay, Massachusetts Historical Society Collections*, vol. 4, part 2, 1661–74 (Boston, 1854), 47.

102. "Admissions to the town of Boston, 1670–1700," 58, 60. For another example, see ibid., 61.

103. Ames, ed., *Accomack-Northampton 1632–1640*, xxxi, citing Northampton County Orders, Deeds and Wills, 2:xlv, 363.

104. After Stone delivered the cattle and corn to Boston, Indians killed him on the Connecticut River in 1633. De Vries, *Voyages*, 64; Ames, ed., *Accomack-Northampton 1632–1640*, xxxi, citing Accomack-Northampton Records, 1:39.

105. Ames, *Studies*, 143; Ames, ed., *Accomack-Northampton*, 1632–1640, 11, 14.

106. Ames, ed., *Accomack-Northampton 1632–1640*, 206–12. John Stone's trade involved Henry Fleet and Eastern Shore Puritans Obedience Robins and William Clai-

borne as well as New Netherland. Ames, ed., *Accomack-Northampton 1632–1640*, 16–17. Ibid., xxxi. See also De Vries, *Voyages*, 64, 125–26; Ames, ed., *Accomack-Northampton, 1632–1640*, 23–24; William Bradford, *History of Plymouth*, ed. W. T. Davis (New York, 1908), 310–11; Ames, *Studies*, 61; Ames, ed., *Accomack-Northampton 1640–1645*, 20–21, 195.

107. Mary Catherine Wilheit, "Obedience Robins of Accomack: Seventeenth-Century Strategies for Success" (M.A. thesis, Texas A&M University, 1997).

108. Ames, ed., *Accomack-Northampton 1632–1640*, xxviii–xxxi.

109. Babette M. Levy, "Early Puritanism in the Southern and Island Colonies" *American Antiquarian Society Proceedings* 70 (1960): 142–43, citing Samuel Eliot Morison, *The Founding of Harvard* (Cambridge, Mass., 1935), 228–40. He owed his creditors over £1000.

110. Levy, "Early Puritanism," 144–47. Puritans John Rodgers and David Richardson preached at Hungars parish after Doughty left. Richardson moved to Somerset County, Maryland, after Berkeley discovered nonconformity on the Eastern Shore when he fled there during Bacon's Rebellion. Ibid., 147–48.

111. Levy, "Early Puritanism," 140–41.

112. Frederick William Gookin, *Daniel Gookin 1612–1687: Assistant and Major General of the Massachusetts Bay Colony. His Life and Letters and Some Account of his Ancestry* (Chicago, 1912), 58.

113. Gookin's headrights included the slave Jacob Warrow. Gookin, *Daniel Gookin*, 66–67.

114. Gookin, *Daniel Gookin*, 64.

115. Gookin, *Daniel Gookin*, 72, 73.

116. Gookin, *Daniel Gookin*, 75, citing John Winthrop, *The History of New England from 1630 to 1649*, ed. James Savage (1790) (New York, 1972), 2:432. Gookin traded to Maryland as well as to Virginia in his own vessels. Gookin, *Daniel Gookin*, 76, citing Edward D. Neill, *Terra Mariae, or, Threads of Maryland Colonial History* (Philadelphia, 1867), 123.

117. In 1655, Gookin shipped five people on Elias Parkman's voyage to Virginia and paid him in tobacco. Gookin, *Daniel Gookin*, 76–77.

118. Samuel Eliot Morison, "Virginians and Marylanders at Harvard College in the Seventeenth Century," *WMQ* 2nd ser., 13 (1933): 5. John Utie's father, Councilor Captain John Utie of York County, had helped Fleet obtain licence for trade from the Virginia Council, and Daniel Gookin had helped Fleet identify Indian trading partners. Fleet, "A Brief Voyage," 35; James F. Pendergast, "The Massawomeck: Raiders and Traders into the Chesapeake Bay in the Seventeenth Century," *Transactions of the American Philosophical Society* 81, part 2 (1991), 15.

119. Morison, "Virginians and Marylanders," 6–8.

120. Morison, "Virginians and Marylanders," 7.

121. Utie was among seventeen students who participated in a student revolt and subsequently did not have enough days to graduate. Morison, "Virginians and Marylanders," 4–5.

122. The Virginians who attended New Amsterdam's Greek and Latin school during the 1660s similarly broadened their world and formed relationships with classmates that facilitated later intercolonial business contacts. Maika, "Commerce and Community," 143.

123. *CSPC 1661–1668*, 161–62, #560.

124. *CSPC 1661–1668*, 303, #1005.

125. *CSPC 1669–1674*, 277–80, #664.

126. Some were frightened by the memory of the failed Cape Fear settlement, illustrating their willingness to learn from other colonial experiences. Brigs to Halstead, November 1671, *CSPC 1669–1674*, 280–81, #665.

127. *CSPC 1669–1671*, 324, #746. 1672.

128. Vassall moved to Virginia, where his daughter married Rappahannock merchant Nicholas Ware, with whom Vassall had carried on a Chesapeake-Caribbean trade while still in Barbados. *Tyler's Quarterly* 7 (1925): 46; "Virginia in 1639–40: Wyatt's Second Administration," *VMHB* 13 (1906): 379. Barbadian immigrant and Carolina Governor Sir John Yeamans also had family in southern Virginia. His nephew Joseph Woory represented Isle of Wight County in the House of Burgesses in 1684. See the discussion of Vassall, Ware, Yeamans, and Woory in Chapter 6.

129. *CSPC 1661–1668*, 506–7, #1601; 509, #1611.

130. Peter H. Wood, *Black Majority*, 30–31, citing Records of the Secretary of the Province, South Carolina Department of Archives and History (1675–95), 39–41 and A. S. Salley, ed., *Records of the Secretary of the Province and the Register of the Province of South Carolina, 1671–1675* (Columbia, S.C., 1944), 59, 66–69.

Chapter 5

1. Joan R. Gunderson, "The Search for Good Men: Recruiting Ministers in Colonial Virginia," *Historical Magazine of the Protestant Episcopal Church* 48 (1979): 453–64. Vestry independence in Virginia mitigated ties to England during the seventeenth century. Warren M. Billings, *Virginia's Viceroy: Their Majesties' Governor General: Francis Howard, Baron Howard of Effingham* (Fairfax, Va., 1991), 81; Edward L. Bond, *Damned Souls in a Tobacco Colony: Religion in Seventeenth-Century Virginia* (Macon, Ga., 2000), 211–14; Gunderson, "The Myth of the Independent Virginia Vestry," *Historical Magazine of the Protestant Episcopal Church* 44 (1975): 133–41.

2. James Horn, *Adapting to a New World*, 385.

3. Bond, *Damned Souls*, 240.

4. Peter G. Lake, "Calvinism and the English Church, 1570–1635," *Past and Present* 114 (1987): 32–76; Lake, "The Laudian Style: Order, Conformity and the Pursuit of Holiness in the 1630s," in Kenneth Fincham, ed., *The Early Stuart Church* (Stanford, Calif., 1993), 161–85; Lake, "A Charitable Christian Hatred: the Godly and their Enemies in the 1630s," in C. Durston and J. Eales, eds., *The Culture of English Puritanism, 1560–1700* (New York, 1996), 145–83. See also Anthony Milton, "The Church of England, Rome and the True Church: The Demise of a Jacobean Consensus," in Fincham, ed., *The Early Stuart Church*, 187–210; Peter Collinson, *The Religion of Protestants: The Church in English Society, 1559–1624* (Oxford, 1982); Lake, "Defining Puritanism–Again?" in F. Bremer, ed., *Puritanism: Transatlantic Perspectives on a Seventeenth-Century Anglo-American Faith* (Boston, 1993), 3–29; Judith Maltby, "'By this book': Parishioners, the Prayer Book and the Established Church," in Fincham, ed., *The Early Stuart Church*, 115–37; John Morrill, "The Religious Context of the

English Civil War," in Richard Cust and Ann Hughes, eds., *The English Civil War* (London and New York, 1997), 159–80; Nicholas Tyacke, "Puritanism, Arminianism and Counter-Revolution," in Cust and Hughes, eds., *The English Civil War*, 136–58.

5. Bond, *Damned Souls*, 140–45. Bond suggests that the presence of Indians may have mitigated differences between Puritans and Anglicans, but the absence of clergy seems a more likely explanation.

6. James Horn argues that "England's religious heterogeneity was transferred to the Chesapeake: Nonconformity in Virginia and Maryland was not an aberration." *Adapting to a New World*, 410–11. This chapter will argue that as the century progressed, intercolonial ties as well as transatlantic ones nurtured nonconformity in Virginia, while officials used their links to England to enforce Anglicanism on the colony.

7. Indeed, Frederick Tolles found that most of Philadelphia's "early Quaker merchants" came "from the other American colonies, where for a period of years they had had an opportunity to exercise their talents in mercantile pursuits." *Meeting House and Counting House: The Quaker Merchants of Colonial Philadelphia, 1682–1763* (Chapel Hill, N.C., 1948), 43. J. F. Bosher finds similar connection between religious and commercial networks for French Huguenot merchants in the last two decades of the seventeenth century, arguing that the Huguenot merchants formed part of a larger Protestant international merchant community based on both commerce and common religion. He claims that the "overseas business of Huguenot merchants flourished in the atmosphere of personal trust based on a common religion and carefully fostered relations of scattered families." Doing business with others of the same religion produced a sense of common purpose and responsibility that reduced the risk of fraud. See J. F. Bosher "Huguenot Merchants and the Protestant International in the Seventeenth Century," *WMQ* 3rd ser., 52 (1995): 77–102, quote, 78.

8. See Cynthia Jean Van Zandt, "Negotiating Settlement: Colonialism, Cultural Exchange, and Conflict in Early Colonial Atlantic North America, 1580–1660" (Ph.D. diss., University of Connecticut, 1998), 187–225. See also Van Zandt, "The Dutch Connection: Isaac Allerton and the Dynamics of English Cultural Anxiety in the *Gouden EEUW*," in Rosemarijn Hoefte and Johanna C. Kardux, eds., *Connecting Cultures: The Netherlands in Five Centuries of Transatlantic Exchange* (Amsterdam, 1994), 51–76

9. Walter S. Allerton, *A History of the Allerton Family in the United States, 1585–1885, and A Genealogy of the Descendants of Isaac Allerton* (New York, 1888), revised by Samuel Waters Allerton (Chicago, 1900), 13, 21–23.

10. For Loockerman's Chesapeake–New Netherland trade, see Dennis J. Maika, "Commerce and Community: Manhattan Merchants in the Seventeenth Century" (Ph.D. diss., New York University, 1995). On January 20, 1642, Allerton sold his yacht *Hope* to Loockermans and in 1643 Allerton and Loockermans received a grant in New Amsterdam for two lots on the Great Highway. Isaac J. Greenwood, "Allertons of New England and Virginia," *New England Historical and Genealogical Register* 44 (1890): 290–96. For his naturalization, see Wyand and Wyand, *Colonial Maryland Naturalizations*, 7.

11. On September 27, 1654, New Haven Governor John Davenport wrote that Mr. Allerton was then on a voyage to Virginia. Allerton, *History of the Allerton Family*, 24–25.

12. Greenwood, "Allertons," 292.

13. Allerton, *History of the Allerton Family*, 26.

14. Greenwood, "Allertons," 291; Allerton, *History of the Allerton Family*, 27. The will referred to specific debts (including one determined by arbitration of Augustine Herman) owed by and to Allerton, and general reference to "all my debts in Delaware Bay and Virginia . . . and in Barbadoes."

15. Allerton, *History of the Allerton Family*, 31.

16. Greenwood, "Allertons," 292.

17. The island in the Potomac between Washington, D.C., and Arlington, Virginia, now the National Park Service's Theodore Roosevelt Island, was called Barbados Island in the mid-seventeenth century, perhaps so named by an immigrant from the Caribbean.

18. Allerton, *History of the Allerton Family*, 32, citing *VMHB* 1 (1893), 199; Northumberland and Westmoreland records; Hening, *Statutes*, 2:257. Allerton was a Westmoreland County justice of the peace in 1677.

19. On June 10, 1691, Governor Francis Nicholson reported to London that Richard Lee, Isaac Allerton, and John Armistead, out of scruple of conscience, refused to take the oath and were left out of the Council. Allerton, *History of the Allerton Family*, 33.

20. Isaac and his first wife Elizabeth had three children. Their son Isaac, after accompanying his father to Virginia as a child, returned to New Haven as an adult. Allerton, *History of the Allerton Family*, 34.

21. Babette M Levy, "Early Puritanism in the Southern and Island Colonies," *American Antiquarian Society Proceedings* 70 (1960): 81–85. See also Kevin Butterfield, "Puritans and Religious Strife in the Early Chesapeake," *VMHB* 109 (2001): 5–36.

22. John Frederick Fausz, "The Powhatan Uprising of 1622: A Historical Study of Ethnocentrism and Cultural Conflict" (Ph.D. diss., The College of William and Mary, 1977), 296. The 1622 Indian attack ended the plans for the college at Henrico. Copland went instead to Bermuda, where in 1635 he was organizing a school. Copland wanted to build a missionary college from which men could be sent to convert Virginia Indians. See *Winthrop Papers* (Boston, 1929), 3:84–85; 5:96–97, 182–85; and Levy, "Early Puritanism," 175. Levy cites Edward D. Neill, *Memoir of Reverend Patrick Copland* (New York, 1871).

23. Levy, "Early Puritanism," 109–10.

24. Bosse moved from Virginia to New England in 1631. Kingsbury, ed., *Records of the Virginia Company of London*, 3:414. See also Levy, "Early Puritanism," 107.

25. Levy, "Early Puritanism," 108–9.

26. The letter, dated May 24, 1642, is reprinted in Jon Butler, "Two 1642 Letters from Virginia Puritans," *Massachusetts Historical Society Proceedings* 84 (1972): 99–109, quotes, 105–6.

27. Edmund Morgan, *American Slavery, American Freedom*, 412.

28. Nansemond Puritans to Christ Church Elders, May 24, 1642, in Butler, "Two 1642 Letters," 105.

29. Butler, "Two 1642 Letters," 105–9.

30. Butler, "Two 1642 Letters," 106, citing William Haller, *The Rise of Puritanism* (New York, 1938), and Christopher Hill, *Society and Puritanism in Pre-Revolutionary England* (New York, 1964), for examples.

31. Butler, "Two 1642 Letters," 108.

32. William Durand to John Davenport, July 15, 1642, in Butler, "Two 1642 Let-

ters," 107. Durand and the other Virginia Puritans who had written to New England believed that prayer connected the Virginians not only to Davenport but to New England Puritans in general. Durand explained to Davenport that the letter the parishioners had sent had been addressed generally rather than to any specific person "because the worke is great and of deepe consequence, wherein the more are interested, the more prayers and better successe is hoped for."

33. John Winthrop, *The History of New England from 1630 to 1649*, ed. James Savage (Boston, 1853), 2:94. Winthrop wrote of Bennett's arrival in a small pinnace and stated that the letters were openly read in Boston on a lecture day. The General Court approved of the elders' choice and "ordered that the governour should commend them to the governour and council of Virginia, which was done accordingly."

34. Winthrop, *History*, 2:94.

35. New England churches also sent material help to other colonies. On July 29, 1666, the Roxbury Church reported that "Divers strangers that came from Christopher's Island being in that necessitie & distress by sicknes lamenesse &c besides the prvision made for them by the Generall Court, the severall Churches contributed towards their relief." Boston Records Commission, Report 6, *A Report of the Record Commissioners, containing the Roxbury Land and Church Records* (Boston, 1881), 204.

36. Winthrop, *History*, 2:73, 74, 94, 95.

37. Winthrop, *History*, 2:115–16.

38. Winthrop, *History*, 2:115–16. This Puritan worship in private houses may have set the stage for Quaker popularity in the same areas.

39. John Winthrop, *Journal*, ed. James Kendall Hosmer, *Original Narratives of Early American History* (New York, 1908), 2:167–68; cited in Wilcomb E. Washburn, "Governor Berkeley and King Philip's War," *New England Quarterly* 30 (1957): 363–77, quote 363–64. For the Virginia Assembly's order that the ministers leave the colony, see Hening, *Statutes*, 1:277.

40. Edward Johnson, *The Wonder-Working Providence of Sion's Saviour in New England*, ed. J. Franklin Jameson, *Original Narratives of Early American History* (New York, 1910), book 3, 265–67; cited in Washburn, "Governor Berkeley," 365.

41. Winthrop, *Journal*, 2:168, cited in Washburn "Governor Berkeley," 364.

42. Levy, "Early Puritanism," 89.

43. Horn, *Adapting to a New World*, 399.

44. Levy, "Early Puritanism," 132–33; Daniel R. Randall, *A Puritan Colony in Maryland* (Baltimore, 1886), 17. Puritans in Nansemond County later said that they had been "invited and encouraged" by Stone to move to Maryland and that he had promised they would find religious liberty there. "Virginia & Maryland, or, the Lord Baltimore's Printed Case 1655," in Force, ed., *Tracts and Other Papers*, 2:28–29.

45. Harrison arrived in Elizabeth River in 1640. Horn, *Adapting to a New World*, 389.

46. *Winthrop Papers*, 5:434–40. See also Levy, "Early Puritanism," 126–27, citing Lower Norfolk County Orders, May 25, 1640.

47. Thomas Harrison to John Winthrop, November 2, 1646, in *Winthrop Papers*, 5:116–17.

48. Levy, "Early Puritanism," 127; Winthrop, *History*, 2:334; Johnson, *Wonder-Working Providence*, 351–53. American Puritans relied on one another and on their growing intercolonial networks for religious news from England as well as for prayers.

Both kinds of connections strengthened the bonds that tied Virginia Puritans to New Englanders. In another letter to Winthrop in the winter of 1648, this time from Nansemond, Harrison discusses with Winthrop news that had reached Virginia of toleration in England, reporting that "Parliament proceeds to settle the affaires of the Kingdome: That golden apple The ordinance for toleration, is now fairly fallen into the lap of the Saints."

49. *Winthrop Papers*, 5:212–13.

50. Sayle had received a grant from Parliament for the project. Longtime Puritan Atlantic world resident Patrick Copland, originally part of early Virginia Company plans, and now elder of the Puritan church in Bermuda, was among the group of seventy Bermudian migrants to Eleutheria. Winthrop, *History*, 2:407–9.

51. Durand may have preached using notes he had taken from sermons he had heard Davenport give in London. Horn, *Adapting to a New World*, 391; Levy, "Early Puritanism," 237; Philip Alexander Bruce, *Institutional History of Virginia in the Seventeenth Century* (New York, 1910), 1:257.

52. Levy, "Early Puritanism," 130.

53. Atherton to Winthrop, Jr., August 30, 1648 (received November 9), in *Winthrop Papers*, 5:273.

54. Adam Winthrop to John Winthrop, Jr., September 1, 1648, in *Winthrop Papers*, 5:277.

55. Winthrop, *History*, 2:334.

56. Lucy Downing to John Winthrop, Jr., at Pequot, Salem, December 17, [1648]. In *Winthrop Papers*, 5:290–91. In the fall of 1649 New Englanders still referred to Harrison as the minister of the Church at Virginia. Boston Record Commission, Report 9, *Boston Births, Baptisms, Marriages, and Deaths, 1630–1699* (Boston, 1883).

57. Levy, "Early Puritanism," 128–29, citing Edward D. Neill, "A Chapter in American Church History," *New Englander* (1879).

58. Norfolk County Reel 44 Wills & Deeds C 1651–56, 157a; Richard Beale Davis, "The Devil in Virginia in the Seventeenth Century," *VMHB* 65 (1957): 131–49; McIllwaine, *Minutes of the Council and General Court of Colonial Virginia*, 111–14; Bruce, *Institutional History*, 1:278–88.

59. Horn, *Adapting to a New World*, 393–94, citing Edward Papenfuse, *A Biographical Dictionary of the Maryland Legislature* (Baltimore, 1979), 1:290; 2:534, 574–75, 593–94, Lower Norfolk County, Wills & Deeds B, 1646–51, f. 88, 115, 129, 209, C (1651–55), f. 113–14, 117, 158, D (1656–66), f. 29. See also Levy, "Early Puritanism," 135.

60. Boston Records Commission, Report 6, *A Report of the Record Commissioners, containing the Roxbury Land and Church Records* (Boston, 1881), 87.

61. Levy, "Early Puritanism," 134.

62. In 1676, when William Berkeley fled to the Eastern Shore during Bacon's rebellion and realized the extent of nonconformity there, Anglican officials responded with attempts to enforce Anglican conformity.

63. Levy, "Early Puritanism," 140–41.

64. John Rosier, who served Bennett's Plantation in the early 1630s, was in Nansemond during the late 1630s, in York county in 1640, on the Eastern Shore in 1641, and in Northumberland County in 1650. Francis Bolton preached on the Eastern Shore before moving to Bennett's Plantation in 1623. Levy, "Early Puritanism," 140.

65. His preaching was noted as a memorable event in Eastern Shore court

records. For example, in May 1654, Sara Hinman, testifying to the Northampton County Court in a case completely unrelated to Drisius' presence in the region, noted time by referring to "The last Sabbath that Mr Drissius preached here." Northampton County Court Order Books, 1654–61, typescript by Susie May Ames, Virginia Historical Society Mss 3N8125a, fol. 1, 36–37. For a discussion of Drisius's Dutch contacts, see Levy, "Early Puritanism," 144.

66. Horn, *Adapting to a New World*, 398; Michael Graham, "Meetinghouse and Chapel: Religion and Community in Seventeenth-Century Maryland," in Carr et al., *Colonial Chesapeake Society*, 260.

67. For a discussion of Quaker travel in England's American colonies, see Frederick B. Tolles, *Quakers and the Atlantic Culture* (1947) (New York, 1960). For numbers, see ibid., 14.

68. Kenneth L. Carrol, "Elizabeth Harris, the Founder of American Quakerism," *Quaker History* 57 (1968): 96–111; Bruce, *Institutional History*, 1:225–26. According to Bruce, the Quaker sect was first heard of in England about 1647. See also Kenneth L. Carroll, "Quakerism on the Eastern Shore of Virginia," *VMHB* 74 (1966): 170–89.

69. Levy, "Early Puritanism," 150–51. Tolles provides examples of a typical trip, that of Christopher Holder who went to New England in 1656 and stayed until 1657 when he went to the Caribbean. He returned by Bermuda to Rhode Island and Massachusetts. He went from there to Virginia, returning in 1659 to Rhode Island and Massachusetts. In 1660 he returned to England. After that he made several more trips to America. An atypical trip was that of Mary Fisher, who went to Barbados in 1655, from there to Massachusetts in 1656, to England in 1657, to Nevis in 1658, to Constantinople in 1660, ending in Charleston, South Carolina. Tolles, *Quakers*, 26–27.

70. Bruce, *Institutional History*, 1:226. The legislature reacted quickly to Quaker missionary activities and in 1658 banned Quakers from Virginia. Hening, *Statutes*, 1:532–33.

71. Bruce, *Institutional History*, 1:226–27.

72. In 1683 he went from England to the Caribbean. Tolles, *Quakers*, 27.

73. Levy, "Early Puritanism," 150–51.

74. Governor Berkeley ordered county sheriffs to suppress Quaker meetings. During the mid- and late-1670s Henrico and Nansemond county officials persecuted Quakers. Levy, "Early Puritanism," 154–55.

75. Quoted in Horn, *Adapting to a New World*, 395, citing Lower Norfolk County, Wills and Deeds D (1656–66), f. 360–74, 380, 392, 396; John Bennett Boddie, *Seventeenth Century Isle of Wight County, Virginia* (Chicago, 1938), 113–14.

76. George Fox, *The Journal of George Fox*, ed. Norman Penney (Cambridge, England, 1911), 2:242.

77. Horn, *Adapting to a New World*, 396.

78. Hening, *Statutes*, 2:181–83; Bruce, *Institutional History*, 1:239.

79. In 1663, magistrates sentenced Mary Thompkins and Alice Ambrose to receive thirty-two lashes each and to be drawn to the pillory with a noose around their necks. Bruce, *Institutional History*, 1:240.

80. Bruce, *Institutional History*, 1:232, citing Northampton County Records, 1657–64, f. 82, 84.

81. Horn, *Adapting to a New World*, 396–97; Bruce, *Institutional History*, 1:240; Levy, "Early Puritanism," 396. There were limits to these Quakers' ability to hold their

offices, however. In 1663 the Virginia Assembly accused the Lower Norfolk County Burgess John Porter of being "loving to the Quakers" and expelled him from the House of Burgesses for refusing to take the burgess's oath, showing that not all those nonconformists who gained political influence during the Interregnum were able to maintain it after the Restoration. Horn, *Adapting to a New World*, 395.

82. Fox, *Journal*, 2:240, for descriptions of meetings in Potomac and Rappahannock.

83. Letter of George Rofe to Stephen Crisp. The letter is summarized in C. F. Smith, *Stephen Crisp and his Correspondents*, which is cited in Henry J. Cadbury "Intercolonial Solidarity of American Quakerism," *Pennsylvania Magazine of History and Biography* 60 (1936): 362–74; quote, 363.

84. Tolles, *Quakers*, 26.

85. Many of the Quaker ministers' journals are rich in narrative information about a variety of subjects, in particular the interactions between Indians and Europeans in Virginia and Maryland. Though several of them have been published, they have been underused, especially considering the dearth of this kind of detailed description for the seventeenth-century Chesapeake.

86. John Tompkins to William Ellis and Aaron Atkinson, December 1, 1697, in James Backhouse, *The Life and Correspondence of William and Allice Ellis* (London, 1849), 40–41.

87. See Fox's *Journal* and Epistles. For a discussion of Fox's concern with organization, see Cadbury, "Intercolonial Solidarity," 364.

88. Their meetings with slaves provoked serious concern among Barbadian elites. George Fox, *To the Ministers, Teachers, and Priests, (So called, and so Stileing your Selves) in Barbadoes* ([London], 1672).

89. John Stubbs, writing to England from Newport, Rhode Island, in August 1672, reported to George Fox's wife Margaret that her husband had gone to Maine and that "wee are not likely to see thy husband, till wee see him in Virginia." In the same letter, Stubbs told Margaret Fox that she could direct a letter to him "to Edward Man for Conveyance to us in Puttuxan River in Maryland, to James Preston there." Letter of John Stubbs to M. Fox, from Newport, Rhode Island June 14, 1672 in Fox, *Journal*, 2:217.

90. Fox, *Journal*, 2:240–41.

91. Fox, *Journal*, 2:244.

92. Fox, *Journal*, 2:233–34 .

93. See for example Fox, *Journal*, 2:235.

94. Meetings with public friends were attractive in part because they were different. Not only was Fox famous throughout the English colonial world, the meetings themselves were out of the ordinary and seem to have attracted many besides Quakers, though it is difficult to tell in what capacity non-Quakers came to the meetings. Fox reports all attendants as converts, but some were surely observers.

95. Tolles, *Quakers*, 26, quotes Thomas Jordan to George Fox, November 18, 1687, in *Journal of the Friends Historical Society* 33 (1936): 57.

96. For example, see the letter from John Stubbs to Margaret Fox, written from Rhode Island, April 19, 1672, printed in Fox, *Journal*, 2:205; and the letter of George Fox to Friends in London, written from Rhode Island the same day, in Fox, *Journal*, 2:210–11. See also *The Second part (or an Addittion to the Journall of G ffs Travailes in*

America in the year 1672 and "Fox's Epistles and Queryes," in Fox, *Journal*, 2:224–29, 235–37, 240, 244, 245n, 246.

97. Fox to Friends in London, Rhode Island, April 19, 1672, in Fox, *Journal*, 2:211.

98. Fox, *Journal*, 2:224–28.

99. See Fox, *Journal*, passim.

100. Fox, *Journal*, 2:240, 244.

101. Fox, *Journal*, 2:235.

102. Dankaerts, *Journal*, 156.

103. Fox, *Journal*, 2:245n, citing George Bishop, *New England Judged by the Spirit of the Lord* (London, 1703), 29 for quote.

104. Letter of John Stubbs to Margaret Fox, from Newport, Rhode Island, January 29, 1672, printed in Fox, *Journal*, 2:216–17. Jay was also Gay.

105. Fox, *Journal*, 2:239.

106. Cadbury, "Intercolonial Solidarity," 366, citing only MS at Swarthmore College.

107. Cadbury, "Intercolonial Solidarity," 366.

108. Tolles, *Quakers*, 26, quoting circular letter, "To ministering Friends" May 20, 1685, printed in *Pennsylvania Magazine of History and Biography* 29 (1905): 105–6.

109. He also asked to be remembered to Richard Bennett and Thomas Dewes, Virginians he had converted from Puritanism. Fox, *Journal*, 2:234n.

110. Fox, *Journal*, 2:246.

111. Levy, "Early Puritanism," 156, citing Lower Virginia Monthly Meeting Minutes.

112. While imprisoned in Virginia, he wrote letters, now in the Friends Library in London, to New England clergy. Fox, *Journal*, 2:231.

113. Fox, *Journal*, 2:235, citing William Edmundson, *A Journal of the Life, Travels, Sufferings, and Labour of Love . . . of . . . William Edmundson* (London, 1715), 59.

114. Fox, *Journal*, 2:223.

115. Fox, *Journal*, 2:221–22.

116. In 1657 George Fox wrote an epistle to "Friends beyond sea, that have Blacks and Indian Slaves." He and other Quakers sent circular letters to the American colonies. See for example, "The Books & Divine Epistles of Josiah Coale" (London, 1671), discussed in Tolles, *Quakers*, 32.

117. Stubbs to Fox, June 19, 1672, printed in Fox, *Journal*, 2:202–6.

118. Cadbury, "Intercolonial Solidarity," 367. Fox wrote an open letter at Elizabeth River in Lower Norfolk County which sixteen Lower Norfolk residents signed before sending it on to the Nansemond meeting. Levy, "Early Puritanism," 156.

119. Cadbury, "Intercolonial Solidarity," 363.

120. Cadbury, "Intercolonial Solidarity," 364, citing R. M. Jones, ed., *The Quakers in the American Colonies* (1911) (New York, 1962), 434. The plan was never realized.

121. Tolles, *Quakers*, 34.

122. Tolles, *Quakers*, 34.

123. Bruce, *Institutional History*, 2:244–45, provides examples of Quakers' establishing meeting houses during the following years. The Act of Toleration required that every Protestant sect which had seceded from Church of England present regular statements about where they held their services.

124. Bruce, *Institutional History*, 2:247–49, citing Henrico County Records, 1688–97, 192–93. The same proclamation is recorded in York County Records, 1690–94, 27.

125. Bond, *Damned Souls*, 215–20; Jon Butler, *Awash in a Sea of Faith: Christianizing the American People* (Cambridge, Mass., 1990), 42–43.

126. Bond, *Damned Souls*, 204–6, 231, 234.

127. *Collections of the Protestant Episcopal Historical Society* (New York, 1851–53), 1:xix, cited and quoted in Cadbury, "Intercolonial Solidarity," 368–69.

128. September 1, 1703. *Collections of the Protestant Episcopal Historical Society*, 1:xl-xli, quoted in Tolles, *Quakers and the Atlantic Culture*, 25.

129. Notwithstanding considerable evidence to the contrary, including Keith's report, Tolles argues that the development of family-based intercolonial commercial networks did not occur on any significant scale until the eighteenth century. Tolles, *Quakers*, 31. Hall, *Contested Boundaries*, offers an assessment similar to Tolles.

130. According to James Horn, "Neither in England nor in the colonies was the ideal of one church and one nation achieved. Increasingly after the Restoration, the Anglican church was one church among many." *Adapting to a New World*, 406.

131. Bond, *Damned Souls*, 238; Hening, *Statutes*, 3:170–71.

132. Quaker merchant networks flourished in the eighteenth century, using strengthened and increasingly integrated transatlantic and intercolonial trade connections.

Chapter 6

1. Alden T. Vaughan, "Blacks in Virginia: A Note on the First Decade," *WMQ* 3rd ser., 29 (1972): 474–78; Kathleen M. Brown, *Good Wives, Nasty Wenches, & Anxious Patriarchs: Gender, Race, and Power in Colonial Virginia* (Chapel Hill, N.C., 1996), 108–9.

2. For English attitudes toward Africans, see Winthrop D. Jordan, *White over Black: American Attitudes toward the Negro, 1550–1812* (Chapel Hill, N.C., 1968); *WMQ* 3rd ser., 59 (1997): "Constructing Race."

3. Peter H. Wood notes English South Carolinians' adoption of the word pickaninny from the Portuguese. *Black Majority*, 174. In the 1640s Richard Ligon identified the word pickaninny as one that enslaved women in Barbados used for their own children and that English colonists learned from those women. *A True & Exact History of the Island of Barbadoes* (1657) (London, 1970), 48.

4. Vaughan, "Blacks in Virginia," 474–78. The names of Africans which appeared in the census were: Angelo, John Pedro, Antoney, Isabell, William (the son of Antoney and Isabell), Antonio, and Mary.

5. Robert Rich to Nathaniel Rich, February 22, 1618, in Vernon A. Ives, ed., *The Rich Papers: Letters from Bermuda, 1615–1646: Eyewitness Accounts Sent by the Early Colonists to Sir Nathaniel Rich* (Toronto, 1984), 59, quoted in Virginia Bernhard, "Beyond the Chesapeake: The Contrasting Status of Blacks in Bermuda, 1616–1663," *The Journal of Social History* 59 (1988): 548–49.

6. Morgan, *American Slavery, American Freedom*, 123–30; Warren M. Billings, "The Law of Servants and Slaves in Seventeenth-Century Virginia," *VMHB* 99 (1991): 45–62.

7. A 1625 shipmaster refused to carry servants to Virginia where, he claimed, they

"were sold heere upp and downe like horses." Morgan, *American Slavery, American Freedom*, 129.

8. For slaves' origins, see especially Philip D. Morgan, *Slave Counterpoint: Black Culture in the Eighteenth-Century Chesapeake* (Chapel Hill, N.C., 1998), 2–3; Morgan, *American Slavery, American Freedom*, 303–6; Ira Berlin, *Many Thousands Gone: The First Two Centuries of Slavery in North America* (Cambridge, Mass., 1998), 39. For work on African ties, see Lorena S. Walsh, *From Calabar to Carter's Grove: The History of a Virginia Slave Community* (Charlottesville, Va., 1997), esp. 56–113; Ira Berlin, "From Creole to African: Atlantic Creoles and the Origins of African-American Society in Mainland North America," *WMQ* 3rd ser., 53 (1996): 251–88; John Thornton, "The African Experience of the '20 and Odd Negroes' Arriving in Virginia in 1619," *WMQ* 3rd ser., 47 (1990): 477–502; Thornton, "African Dimensions of the Stono Rebellion," *American Historical Review* 96 (1991): 1101–13. For the mobility of English colonists, see Games, *Migration and the Origins of the English Atlantic World*.

9. Alison Games, "'The Sanctuarye of our rebell negroes': The Atlantic Context of Local Resistance on Providence Island, 1630–1641," *Slavery and Abolition* 19 (1998): 1–21.

10. See Chapter 3.

11. Games, "'The Sanctuarye of our rebell negroes'," 10–11.

12. Joyce D. Goodfriend, "Burghers and Blacks: The Evolution of a Slave Society at New Amsterdam," *New York History* 59 (1978): 137, citing Directors to Stuyvesant, April 11, 1661, E. B. O'Callaghan, *Voyages of the Slavers St. John and Arms of Amsterdam, 1659, 1663* (Albany, N.Y., 1867), 183–86.

13. In 1645 George Downing revealed that within three years of Barbados' first sugar production, planters regarded English servants as a means to acquiring slaves. He wrote that anyone aspiring to become a Barbadian sugar planter needed English servants "for so therby you shall be able to doe somthing upon a plantation, and in short tim be able with good husbandry to procure Negroes (the life of the place) out of the encrease of your owne plantation." Carl Bridenbaugh and Roberta Bridenbaugh, *No Peace beyond the Line: The English in the Caribbean, 1624–1690* (New York, 1972), 117, quoting *Winthrop Papers*, 5:43–44.

14. Games, "The Sanctuarye of our rebell negroes'," 18, n 5.

15. David Barry Gaspar, "With a Rod of Iron: Barbados Slave Laws as a Model for Jamaica, South Carolina, and Antigua, 1661–1697," in Darlene Clark Hine and Jacqeline McLeod, eds., *Crossing Boundaries: Comparative History of Black People in Diaspora* (Bloomington, Ind., 1999), 343–66; Wood, *Black Majority*, 3–34; Dunn, *Sugar and Slaves*, 111–16; Richard Dunn, "The English Sugar Islands and the Founding of South Carolina," *South Carolina Historical Magazine* 72 (1971): 81–93. See also Winthrop D. Jordan, "The Influence of the West Indies on the Origins of New England Slavery," *WMQ* 3rd ser., 18 (1961): 243–50.

16. Ira Berlin, "Time, Space, and the Evolution of Afro-American Society on British Mainland North America," *American Historical Review* 85 (1980): 69–71.

17. Blacks made up more than half of Virginia's agricultural labor force by 1690. Russell Menard, "From Servants to Slaves: The Transformation of the Chesapeake Labor System," *Southern Studies* 16 (1977): 362. Barbados made the same transition in the 1640s and 1650s. See Dunn, *Sugar and Slaves*, 226. Fewer servants immigrated because social conditions in England were improving while at the same time Virginia

acquired a bad reputation and the establishment of other colonies offered migrating servants other choices. These factors reduced the supply of indentured servants to the Chesapeake before their numbers were replaced by an increase in the supply African slaves, suggesting that change in planter preference had little to do with the transition. Menard, "From Servants to Slaves," 373–82. Prices for indentured servants rose to the point that slave prices (forced down by West Indian planters) could compete with them. The increasing affordability of slaves was enhanced by the fact that mortality rates in Virginia fell to the point that a planter could be reasonably sure that a slave would live longer than the average term of indenture for servants, thereby justifying the payment of higher initial prices for slaves. In addition, growing social problems with freed indentured servants may have discouraged planters from choosing to bring more to Virginia. The social problems also inspired planters to buy excess land, creating an artificial shortage to discourage further servants from choosing Virginia. See Morgan, *American Slavery, American Freedom*, 271–315; Allan Kulikoff, *Tobacco and Slaves: The Development of Southern Cultures in the Chesapeake: 1680–1800* (Chapel Hill, N.C., 1986), 3–44. High slave prices and low tobacco prices did not allow Virginia planters to purchase Africans in large numbers until the late 1670s. Virginia planters had tried to encourage the slave trade between the 1640s and the 1660s by exempting the Dutch from the ten shilling export duty on tobacco exchanged for Africans. James A. Rawley, *The Transatlantic Slave Trade*, 86.

18. For the best summary of these debates, see Alden T. Vaughan, "The Origins Debate: Slavery and Racism in Seventeenth-Century Virginia," *VMHB* 97 (1989): 311–54. A historiographical preoccupation with tracing the origins of Virginia slavery (as the "first" of the future United States to adopt slavery and therefore a key to understanding the origins of U.S. slavery) began with Oscar and Mary Handlin in 1950 and depended on an anachronistic division between the seventeenth-century Caribbean and mainland colonies that obscured the connections between slavery in Virginia and other parts of the Atlantic world. Oscar Handlin and Mary F. Handlin, "Origins of the Southern Labor System," *WMQ* 3rd ser., 7 (1950): 199–222.

19. Philip Morgan's *Slave Counterpoint*, Edmund S. Morgan's *American Slavery, American Freedom*, and Allan Kulikoff's *Tobacco and Slaves* provide important analyses of slavery in colonial Virginia. However, none fully examines the connections between Virginia planters and slaveholders elsewhere. J. Douglas Deal more explicitly rejects the notion of outside influences on Chesapeake slavery. Deal, *Race and Class in Colonial Virginia: Indians, Englishmen, and Africans on the Eastern Shore during the Seventeenth Century* (New York, 1993), 175. Evidence that an Atlantic context shaped Virginia slavery is, indeed, more difficult to piece together than is evidence for the influence of Barbadian slavery on Carolina or Jamaica slavery, but it nonetheless exists. In fact, the evidence for the significance of a broad Atlantic context influencing Chesapeake slavery suggests that historians of slavery in Jamaica and Carolina think beyond Barbados to consider a more complicated circulation of ideas, practices, and legal influences in the late seventeenth-century Atlantic world, rather than a simple borrowing from Barbados.

20. These apparently were shipped by Barbadian merchants without any previous arrangements with particular buyers in Virginia. Philip Alexander Bruce, *Economic History of Virginia*, 2:2, 84, 325, citing Records of Lower Norfolk County, 1646–51, fol. 115, 105. Records also include consignments restricted to slaves. Bruce cites Records of

Rappahannock County, 1656–64, 274 and Records of Lower Norfolk County, 1666–75, 23.

21. For dates of servant and slave supplies, see Menard, "From Servants to Slaves," 363.

22. See esp. Morgan, *American Slavery, American Freedom*, 108–30, 295–315; Billings, "The Law of Servants and Slaves," 45–62.

23. Vincent T. Harlow, *A History of Barbados, 1625–1685* (1926) (New York, 1969), 340; W. Noel Sainsbury, ed., *Calendar of State Papers, Colonial (CSPC) 1661–1668* (London, 1890), 528, #1657. The information appears in the following statement: "At least 12,000 former landholders and tradesmen have gone off, . . . Between 1643 and 1647 to New England, 1,200; to Trinidado and Tobago, 600; between 1646 and 1658 to Virginia and Surinam, 2,400; between 1650 and 1652 to Guadaloupe, Martinique, Mariegilante, Grenada, Tobago, and Curazoa, 1,600; with Colonel Venables to Hispaniola and since to Jamaica, 3,300."

24. Hilary Beckles, *A History of Barbados: From Amerindian Settlement to Nation-State* (Cambridge, Eng., 1990), 27; Dunn, *Sugar and Slaves*, 111.

25. Atkins's list is printed in John Camden Hotten, ed., *The Original List of Persons of Quality . . . 1600–1700* (1880) (Baltimore, 1962) and discussed by Dunn, who defines large scale planters as those with more than sixty slaves. A total of 175 such planters lived on the island in 1679. *Sugar and Slaves*, 96, 110.

26. The immigrants from Barbados to Carolina, like other Caribbean-mainland migrants, included a wide variety of people, including large-scale planters and small farmers, merchants, artisans, servants, and slaves. An impressive number of wealthy planters came to Carolina, bringing with them gangs of African slaves. Some less wealthy whites also often brought one or two black slaves each. The migration therefore lodged a significant number of slaves in Carolina in the 1680s, before the rice boom. White Barbadians quickly came into power in Carolina. Between 1669 and 1737, eleven of the twenty-three governors had lived in the Caribbean or were the sons of Caribbean migrants. See Dunn, *Sugar and Slaves*, 111–15 and Wood, *Black Majority*, 13–34.

27. Population estimates for the two colonies are 39,900 (Virginia) and 6,600 (Carolina, with 1,200 of that South Carolina) in 1680, 49,300 (Virginia) and 11,500 (Carolina, 3,900 of that South Carolina) in 1690, and 64,000 (Virginia) and 16,400 (Carolina, 5,700 of that South Carolina) in 1700. McCusker and Menard, *Economy of British America*, 136, 172.

28. Indeed, Maryland governor Thomas Notley was a Barbadian immigrant and among the largest slaveowners in Maryland.

29. For population figures see Morgan, *American Slavery, American Freedom*, 404, 420–23.

30. *CSPC 1685–1688*, 128, #503: "Minutes of Council of Barbados."

31. For another example of the Emperors' bringing slaves to Virginia (in 1671), see G. Andrews Moriarity, "The Emperour Family of Lower Norfolk County," *VMHB* 21 (1912): 417–20; continued in *VMHB* 23 (1915): 438–40.

32. The Emperors were close friends with William Robinson, possibly the same William Robinson who sat on the House of Burgesses and the Committee of Propositions and Grievances which drafted Virginia's first slave code of 1705. H. R. McIlwaine, ed., *Journal of the House of Burgesses of Virginia (JHB), 1702–1712*, viii, 132. The Emperor

family had close ties to several other prominent Virginians, to whom they could have supplied information about slavery and access to slaves through their links as traders with slaveholding Barbadian merchant family members, and perhaps through their Dutch connections. Several Emperor wills mention close ties to Tully Robinson of Accomack County, who sat in the House of Burgesses in 1699, 1700–1702, and 1703–5. McIlwaine, ed., *JHB, 1695–1702*, x, xi, *1702–1712*, vii, viii, 132. Tully Emperor, the brother of Francis Tully Emperor, had a daughter Mary who married Edward Moseley of Lynnhaven Parish, member of the House of Burgesses for Princess Anne County in the sessions of 1703–5 and 1705–6 (when Virginia's first comprehensive slave code was written). McIlwaine, *JHB 1702–1712*, vii; *1705–1706*, viii. This network of Barbadian immigrants and Virginia officeholders presented multiple opportunities for Barbadian ideas about slavery to spread through the Chesapeake.

33. In the spring of 1694 Francis Tully Emperor sold "one young negro woman slave about fifteen or sixteen years of age called by name Edee," to Richard Williamson, planter, of Lynnhaven Parish, Norfolk County. Princess Anne microfilm reel 2, f. 53.

34. Norfolk County Reel 44 Wills & Deeds C 1651–56, 27–27a.

35. Norfolk County Reel 44 Wills & Deeds C 1651–56, 34a, 39.

36. Nugent, *Cavaliers and Pioneers*, 1:xxiv–xxvi.

37. "Notes and Queries," *VMHB* 1 (1893): 201–2; McIlwaine, ed., *JHB 1659/60–1693*, ix.

38. In 1644 Captain James Holdip, who had traveled to Pernambuco, Brazil to bring back sugar cane (or perhaps received some from a Dutch ship), gave Henry's relative Thomas Applewhite, already a wealthy planter, fifty acres and canes to plant the land in exchange for twenty-five servants. Dunn, *Sugar and Slaves*, 62, cites Richard Pares, *Merchants and Planters* (Cambridge, Eng., 1960), 53; William Duke, *Some Memoirs of the First Settlement of the Island of Barbados* (1741).

39. He was also both merchant and planter. Mary Applewhite Norris, *A History of the Ancestors and Descendants of Robert Council Applewhite and Viola Felt* (Delco, N.C., 1956), 3.

40. Hotten, ed., *Original Lists*, 350, 400; James C. Brandow, *Omitted Chapters from Hotten's Original Lists of Persons of Quality* (Baltimore, 1982), 57. Henry Applewhite received £25 in 1701 as compensation for a runaway slave whom the colony had executed. Hilary Beckles, *White Servitude and Black Slavery in Barbados, 1627–1715* (Knoxville, Tenn., 1989), 105.

41. Norris, *Ancestors and Descendants*, 3; McIlwaine, ed., *JHB 1659/60–1693*, xi–xiv.

42. "Isle of Wight County Records," *WMQ* 1st ser., 7 (1899): 225, 302. On May 12, 1669 Moore was granted fourteen hundred acres of land. His brother Thomas Moore received a grant for twenty-four hundred acres on May 10, 1670, making them substantial landholders. For transport of servant see Hotten, *Original Lists*, 339. This transport might suggest that he maintained an estate in Barbados, but he does not appear in the Barbados census of 1679/80.

43. "Historical and Genealogical Notes and Queries," *VMHB* 8 (1901): 328.

44. "Isle of Wight County Records," 268, 258.

45. McIlwaine, ed., *JHB, 1659/60–1693*, vi.

46. Dunn, *Sugar and Slaves*, 114; *Tyler's Quarterly* 7 (1925): 46, asserts that John Yeamans "was represented in Isle of Wight" by Joseph Woory. The Yeamans family

was established in Barbados by 1638, which makes it likely that Woory or his parents had been in Barbados. See Dunn, *Sugar and Slaves*, 58.

47. Dunn, *Sugar and Slaves*, 115; "Historical and Genealogical Notes and Queries," *WMQ* 1st ser., 6 (1897): 121–32.

48. The census lists a total of 224 acres, sixty-three slaves, and three servants held in several counties by Elizabeth Yeamons, Lady Willoughby Yeamans, and Dame Willoughby Yeamans. Lady Yeamans was involved in a dispute with two other women for 719 acres. That all Yeamans' property in Barbados was held by women (perhaps one woman) may have resulted from the men's migrations to the mainland. The choice to maintain Barbadian family estates may have resulted from recognition that Barbadian connections could provide resources valuable to success in other colonies. See Hotten, *Original Lists*, 507, 472; and Brandow, *Omitted Chapters*, 48, 76.

49. William Byrd to Jonathan Walke, May 29, 1689, in Tinling, ed., *Correspondence*, 104.

50. Ligon, *History of Barbadoes*, 113.

51. Many Virginia planters joined the West Indian lobby in opposing the company's monopoly. Rawley, *The Transatlantic Slave Trade*, 160.

52. For a discussion of the economic prominence of the English Caribbean in the seventeenth century see McCusker and Menard, *Economy of British America*, 144–68.

53. Bruce, *Economic History of Virginia*, 1:321, 460–61.

54. Even in the few regions where local trade centers developed, commerce could provide contacts with slave societies. For example, Norfolk became a trade center for forest products and livestock, most of which went to the Caribbean. Meinig, *Atlantic America*, 154.

55. Elizabeth Donnan, ed., *Documents Illustrative of the Slave Trade to America* (Washington, D.C., 1930), 4:89.

56. Seymour to Board of Trade, November 18, 1708, quoted in Menard, "From Servants to Slaves," 366. Lorena S. Walsh calls the notion that most seventeenth-century Chesapeake slaves came from the Caribbean a "myth," arguing that intercolonial slave trade cannot account for the numbers of slaves in the Chesapeake by the end of the century. While contemporary observers pointed to the start of the eighteenth century for the change in Chesapeake slave origins, I, like much recent secondary literature, place the shift in the late 1670s or early 1680s. Furthermore, I am less interested in the precise date of the shift in origins than I am in considering the relative impact of creole and African slaves on early Virginia society. Walsh, "The Chesapeake Slave Trade: Regional Patterns, African Origins, and Some Implications," *WMQ* 3rd ser., 58 (2001): 144.

57. Some Virginia connections to the Royal African Company affected the development of Chesapeake slavery. Virginia planters sometimes invested their tobacco profits elsewhere, some in the lucrative slave trade to the West Indies. Several members of the Berkeley family, relatives of Governor Sir William Berkeley, held stock in the Royal African Company. These people gained connections in the Caribbean-directed trade that they could use to encourage a Chesapeake slave trade that would benefit their own plantations. "A List of the Royal Adventurers of England Trading to Africa, 1667," in Donnan, *Documents Illustrative of the Slave Trade*, 4:169–72. That Berkeley's brother-in-law, John Culpeper, lived for a time in Barbados is also possible. See Fairfax Harrison, "The Proprietors of the Northern Neck: Chapters of Culpeper Genealogy," *VMHB* 33 (1925): 350.

58. The Royal Adventurers Trading into Africa, founded in 1663 and reorganized as the Royal African Company in 1672, represented England's attempts to monopolize the increasingly lucrative slave trade to its American colonies, but did not have the support of West Indian planters or legislatures. Colonial governments, composed primarily of planters, worried more about their own profits than English law and generally favored a free competitive slave trade to reduce prices. Competition from interlopers and demands of the economically and politically powerful planters forced the company to bring larger supplies than it wished to deliver. This practice drove prices down, something the Royal African Company would have avoided had it been able to restrict supply. The results affected all English colonies in the Americas, including Virginia. Donnan, *Documents Illustrative of the Slave Trade*, 1:169n. David W. Galenson, *Traders, Planters, and Slaves: Market Behavior in Early English America* (Cambridge, Eng., 1986), 13–17.

59. In the early eighteenth century, Governor Alexander Spotswood observed that interlopers traded most to the Eastern Shore and lower James River, where the topography allowed them to avoid observation. Bruce, *Economic History of Virginia*, 2:328–29, citing *Official Letters of Governor Spotswood*, Virginia Historical Society Publication.

60. Galenson, *Traders, Planters, and Slaves*, 14–16

61. Richard Hall, ed., *Acts Passed in Barbados, from 1643 to 1762, Inclusive* (London, 1764), 41.

62. Galenson, *Traders, Planters, and Slaves*, 16–20.

63. Galenson, *Traders, Planters, and Slaves*, 22.

64. Such may have been the case for Captain George Pattison, who, during the mid-1670s, sold on his own account a cargo of "severall blacks or negros" from Barbados in Accomack County. Pattison was captain of the ship *Industry*. Testimony of Hugh Welburne, November 21, 1676, in the case of Thomas Cox *vs.* George Pattison. Ms. in Borthwick Institute of Historical Research, R. As 19/20, cited in Deal, *Race and Class in Colonial Virginia*, 192–93, n. 17.

65. For the Royal African Company's suspicions, see Galenson, *Traders, Planters, and Slaves*, 16–20.

66. "Notes from the Records of York County," *Tyler's Quarterly* 7 (1926): 210.

67. In 1668 John Keele traveled from Virginia to Barbados to purchase sugar from Nathaniel Cooke. Bruce, *Economic History of Virginia*, 2:325–26, citing Records of Lower Norfolk County, 1666–75, 41. Bruce also provides several examples of people living in or visiting Virginia who possessed power of attorney for Barbadian merchants to collect debts. See *Economic History of Virginia*, 2:326–27.

68. Lothrop Withington, "Virginia Gleanings in England," *VMHB* 12 (1905): 297–312.

69. "Virginia in 1639–40: Wyatt's Second Administration," *VMHB* 13 (1906): 379. In 1704 Nicholas Ware owned 718 acres in King and Queen County. "Virginia Quit Rent Rolls, 1704," *VMHB* 32 (1924): 157, 144–58.

70. William Byrd to Jonathan Walke, May 29, 1689, in Tinling, ed., *Correspondence*, 104.

71. William Byrd to Perry & Lane, March 29, 1685, in Tinling, ed., *Correspondence*, 31.

72. William Byrd to Sadler and Thomas, February 10, 1686, in Tinling, ed., *Corre-*

spondence, 50–51. He purchased some Barbadian slaves from London merchants who traded to multiple English colonies. In 1684 he wrote to London merchants Micajah Perry and Thomas Lane (whose letters to him generally came "via Barbados [and] New England") that "If you send the pinke to Barbadoes on our account I would have by her 5 or 6 Negro's between 12 & 24 years old about 1000 gallons rum 3 or 4000 pounds of sugar (muscovado) & abou[t] 200 pounds ginger." Byrd to Perry & Lane, December 30, 1684, Tinling, ed., *Correspondence*, 29, 9.

73. Muscovado sugar was cheaper and considered of poorer quality than white sugar. There was little demand for it in Europe but the mainland colonists bought substantial quantities. The white sugar Byrd purchased was a luxury in Virginia, and probably for use in his own household.

74. "Letters of William Byrd, First," *VMHB* 26 (1918): 125, 126.

75. William Byrd to London merchants Perry and Lane, June 21, 1684, in Tinling, ed., *Correspondence*, 25; and William Byrd to Thomas Grendon, June 21, 1684, in ibid., 23. Kennon served as burgess for Henrico in 1685 and 1686. Pleasants, elected in 1693, refused as a Quaker to take an allegiance oath and therefore lost his seat to William Randolph. Ibid., 23n.

76. Tinling, ed., *Correspondence*, 25, 50–51, 104.

77. Steele, *The English Atlantic*, 44.

78. Virginia planters also sometimes got a share in contracts for deliveries from Africa primarily to planters in Barbados. See Wesley Frank Craven, *White, Red, and Black*, 94; Kenneth G. Davies, *The Royal African Company* (London, 1957), 294–95; Donnan, ed., *Documents Illustrative of the Slave Trade*, 4:59; and Bruce, *Economic History of Virginia*, 2:83–84.

79. George Downing to John Winthrop, Jr., August 26, 1645, quoted in Dunn, *Sugar and Slaves*, 68. By 1700, English Island planters had purchased a total of more than 250,000 African slaves. *Sugar and Slaves*, 224.

80. Beckles, *History of Barbados*, 22–23.

81. *Great Newes from the Barbados* (London, 1676), 5–8, cited in Dunn, *Sugar and Slaves*, 85. Such descriptions abounded. Observers reported that "The Masters, for the most part, live at the height of Pleasure," and "in all Affluence of Pleasure and Delight." Bridenbaugh, *No Peace beyond the Line*, 374.

82. Craven, *White, Red, and Black*, 94; Bruce, *Economic History of Virginia*, 2:347.

83. Very few library inventories survive and those we do have seldom include all titles, so the single record of Ligon's *History of Barbadoes* may represent other copies of the book. Louis B. Wright, *The First Gentlemen of Virginia: Intellectual Qualities of the Early Colonial Ruling Class* (San Marino, Calif., 1940), 117–19, 201.

84. John Bennett Bodie, "Lygon of Madresfield, Worcester, England and Henrico, Virginia," *WMQ* 2nd ser., 16 (1936): 289–315, esp. 307–10, 315. Thomas Ligon named his first son William, perhaps after Berkeley, and his second Richard. If he named his second son after his brother (their father was named Thomas), the naming may have indicated continued closeness between the two siblings until Richard's death in 1662.

85. Willoughby was a member of the Lower Norfolk County Court, the Virginia House of Burgesses, and the Council of Virginia. Walter, *Captain Thomas Willoughby*, 3–12. Thomas Middleton (or his father) was a close neighbor of Thomas Modyford and Richard Ligon in Barbados. A ship of his accompanied Ligon and Modyford on part

of their voyage from England to Barbados. Campbell, *Some Early Barbadian History*, 134.

86. The feasts included "botargo" from Virginia, "the best" he "ever tasted." Ligon, *History of Barbadoes*, 37–38.

87. Ligon, *History of Barbadoes*, 108–13.

88. Ligon, *History of Barbadoes*, 43.

89. Ligon, *History of Barbadoes*, 46.

90. Ligon, *History of Barbadoes*, 48–54, 82.

91. Ligon, *History of Barbadoes*, 46, 52, 113, 105, 53.

92. Ligon, *History of Barbadoes*, 43.

93. Ligon, *History of Barbadoes*, 44, 37–38.

94. Ligon, *History of Barbadoes*, 44–46.

95. Members of House of Burgesses with known connections to Barbados or Barbadians included Thomas Mathew of Stafford County in 1676; William Byrd of Henrico County in 1677, 1679, 1680–82, and 1696–97, and of King and Queen County in 1702/3–5 and 1705–6; Henry Applewhite of Isle of Wight County in 1684, 1685–86, 1688, and 1691–92; Joseph Woory of Isle of Wight County in 1684; Tully Robinson of Accomack County in 1699, 1700–2, and 1702/3–5; and Edward Moseley of Princess Anne County in 1700–2, 1702/3–5, and 1705–6.

The Virginia Assembly passed legislation concerning slavery in the sessions of 1680–82 (when William Byrd was a member), 1691–92 (when Henry Applewhite was a member), 1699 (when Tully Robinson was a member), and 1705–6 (when William Byrd and Edward Moseley were members). William Robinson was a burgess for Lower Norfolk County in 1684 and 1685–86, Norfolk County in 1691–92 (when laws dealing with slavery were passed) and 1695–96, and for Richmond County in 1702/3–5 and 1705–6. He was on the Committee of Propositions and Grievances in the session of 1705–6, which drafted the 1705 slave code. Also on that committee was Christopher Robinson of Middlesex County. For lists of Virginia Burgesses, see McIlwaine, ed., *JHB 1677–1682*, ix–x; *1684–1688*, xi–xiv; *1691–1692*, xi–xiv; *1696–1697*, viii; *1699*, x; *1700–1702*, xi; *1702–1706*, vii–viii. The members of the Committee of Propositions and Grievances for 1705–6 is in *1702–6*, 132. Barbadian Colonel Guy Molesworth, banished for suspicion of leading a 1647 servant uprising on the island, settled in Virginia, where in 1660 he was a member of the assembly. Tonia M. Compton, " 'To Make Their Owne Termes': Servant Rebelliousness and the Transition to Slavery in Seventeenth-Century Barbados and Virginia" (M.A. thesis, Texas A&M University, 2001), 51, citing Nicholas Darnell Davis, *Pages from the Early History of Barbados* (Barbados, 1900), 2.

96. See especially Kathleen Brown, *Good Wives, Nasty Wenches*; and Holly Brewer, "Entailing Aristocracy in Colonial Virginia: 'Ancient Feudal Restraints' and Revolutionary Reform," *WMQ* 3rd ser., 54 (1997): 307–46.

97. For the relationship between English and Virginia servant law, see Billings, "The Law of Servants and Slaves," 45–62.

98. "The Lucas Manuscript Volumes in the Barbados Public Library," *Journal of the Barbados Museum and Historical Society* 10 (1942): 16, cites Appendix no. 1.

99. I have used a copy of the 1688 version, which according to Dunn "mainly echoed the provisions and language of 1661, with greater emphasis on the wickedness of the Negro 'Disorder, Rapines and Inhumanities to which they are naturally prone and inclined.' " *Sugar and Slaves*, 239, 242. Hall, ed., *Acts Passed in Barbados*, 113. See also Gaspar, "With a Rod of Iron."

100. The libraries of Richard Lee II (1715 inventory) and William Byrd II (probably 1744) both contained copies of W. Rawlin's *Laws of Barbados* (1699). Byrd also owned a 1683 or 1684 version of the *Laws of Jamaica* and Lee several copies (the earliest 1699) of *Acts and Laws of His Majesties Province of Massachusetts*, all indicating an early eighteenth-century (and perhaps late seventeenth-century) Virginia interest in other colony's laws. William Hamilton Bryson, *Census of Law Books in Colonial Virginia* (Charlottesville, Va., 1978), 25–26, citing John Spencer Bassett, *The Writings of Col. William Byrd* (New York, 1901), and L. B. Wright, "Richard Lee II, a Belated Elizabethan in Virginia," *Huntington Library Quarterly* 2 (1938): 1–35.

101. Quoted in Dunn, *Sugar and Slaves*, 245.

102. There is little evidence of any borrowing from Spanish law, even in Jamaica. David Barry Gaspar, "'Rigid and Inclement': Origins of the Jamaica Slave Laws of the Seventeenth Century," in Christopher L. Tomlins and Bruce H. Mann, eds., *The Many Legalities of Early America* (Chapel Hill, N.C., 2001), 85. English slaveholders likely rejected Spanish law because it was unsatisfactory (rather than unknown) to them. Spanish American slave law, inherited from laws applying to slaves in Spain, generally protected slaves from abuses of their owners, ensured certain religious and social rights, and limited their owners' power over them in comparison to the laws that English American legislators would develop. Alan Watson argues that "If England had undergone a Reception of Roman law [as did Spain, France, Portugal, and the Netherlands], then in English America there would have been fewer restrictions on masters freeing their slaves; there would have been more slaves freed; there would have been more blacks with access to money and property; and freed blacks would have been accepted as citizens." *Slave Law in the Americas* (Athens, Ga., 1989), xii.

103. Thomas D. Morris argues that "English law . . . provided the legal categories into which blacks as property could be placed. There was no need to adopt statutes to cover this; the common law of property already did, and it allowed wide authority to those who possessed property to use it as they pleased." *Southern Slavery and the Law, 1619–1860* (Chapel Hill, N.C., 1996), 42. While Morris is correct that English colonial legislators applied English property law to slaves, their fluctuating definitions of slaves as real estate or chattel indicate uncertainty about exactly how to apply that law, and the common decisions they ultimately reached indicate intercolonial communication.

104. William M. Wiecek, "The Statutory Law of Slavery and Race in the Thirteen Mainland Colonies of British America," *WMQ* 3rd ser. 34 (1977): 264. For the definition of servants as temporary chattel in England and Virginia, see Billings, "The Law of Servants and Slaves," 47–51.

105. Hall, ed., *Acts Passed in Barbados*, 64.

106. Hall, ed., *Acts Passed in Barbados*, 65.

107. Eugene Sirmans argues that Barbados maintained these legal definitions as long as slavery existed on the island, but see discussion of 1709 act below. M. Eugene Sirmans, "The Legal Status of the Slave in South Carolina, 1670–1740," *Journal of Southern History* 28 (1962): 463. One of the concerns was that slaves not be separated from estates, since that would render the land useless to the inheritor. Hall, ed., *Acts Passed in Barbados*, 64.

108. Hening, ed., *Statutes*, 2:288.

109. Hening, ed., *Statutes*, 3:333–34.

110. Thomas D. Morris also concludes that Virginia's 1705 decision that "Slaves

were 'real estate' and descended as such" followed the Barbados law. *Southern Slavery and the Law*, 66.

111. The Bermuda Assembly, the first English colonial legislature to enact a law specifically about slaves, referred in 1623 to slaves as vassals, indicating that some English colonists may have perceived slaves as tied to the land (in a way servants were not) long before Barbados and Virginia evidence reveals such a perception. Bernhard, "Beyond the Chesapeake," 553.

112. Brewer, "Entailing Aristocracy," 338–41.

113. Hall, ed., *Acts Passed in Barbados*, 188–201.

114. Hall, ed., *Acts Passed in Barbados*, 194–95.

115. Hall, ed., *Acts Passed in Barbados*, 196.

116. Hall, ed., *Acts Passed in Barbados*, 196–97.

117. Warren Billings, *The Old Dominion in the Seventeenth Century: A Documentary History of Virginia, 1606–1689* (Chapel Hill, N.C., 1975), 167.

118. Hening, ed., *Statutes*, 2:170.

119. Dunn, *Sugar and Slaves*, 245. See also Samuel Baldwin to Lords of Trade and Plantations, [June 14], 1680, *CSPC 1677–1680*, 551, # 1391.

120. "An Act for the Better Ordering and Governing of Negroes," September 27, 1661, C.O. 30/2, cited in Gaspar, "'Rigid and Inclement'," 91; Bradley J. Nicholson, "Legal Borrowing and the Origins of Slave Law in the British Colonies," *American Journal of Legal History* 38 (1994): 51.

121. Nicholson, "Legal Borrowing," 42–43; Watson, *Slave Law in the Americas*, 66; see also Gaspar, "'Rigid and Inclement'"; Wilcomb E. Washburn, "Law and Authority in Colonial Virginia," in George Athan Billias, ed., *Law and Authority in Colonial America* (Barre, Mass., 1965), 116–35; Billings, "Transfer of English Law to Virginia"; Morris, *Southern Slavery and the Law*, 17–21, 37–45, 62–67.

122. Dunn, *Sugar and Slaves*, 239–42. Hall, ed., *Acts Passed in Barbados*, 113.

123. Hening, ed., *Statutes*, 2:481.

124. The Bermuda Assembly also instituted a system of passes in 1663, forbade trade between whites and slaves, and outlawed the "evill events of Negroes, Molattoes or Musteses walking abroad on nights and meeting together, Notwithstanding many Proclamations made for restraint." They outlawed marriage between blacks and "his Maiesties ffree borne subiects" and required that blacks whose masters freed them (who might "count themselves ffree" but were "not free") leave the colony within one year or be enslaved to the colony. Bernhard, "Beyond the Chesapeake," 562–63.

125. Virginia officials believed they discovered "a Negro Plott" to kill all the English subjects of Virginia in the Northern Neck in 1680, a "discovery" likely more frightening because of the knowledge of actual uprisings elsewhere. Morgan, *Slave Counterpoint*, 20–21. For dates of revolts in Barbados see Dunn, *Sugar and Slaves*, 257–58.

126. Dunn, *Sugar and Slaves*, 260.

127. Slaves' participation in Bacon's Rebellion may have created some of Virginia legislators' fears. In the first half of the 1680s, Virginia's political leaders thought they detected "an evil spiritt at Worke, who governed in our Time of Anarchy." Virginia laborers' resentment over declining opportunities and tightening discipline may have found encouragement in the sharing of experiences (and resultant anger) among members of laboring population throughout the Atlantic, accounting for the similar timing

of feared rebellions and the conditions that produced legislation attempting to prevent rebellions. Quoted in T. H. Breen, "A Changing Labor Force and Race Relations in Virginia 1660–1710," *Journal of Social History* 7 (1973): 13. See also Linebaugh and Rediker, *The Many-Headed Hydra*.

128. Hall, ed., *Acts Passed in Barbados*, 114, 185; Hening, ed., *Statutes*, 3:103, 451. Barbados decriminalized a master's killing of his slave in 1661. Virginia did the same in 1669. Other colonies attributed this law to Barbados. Nicholson, "Legal Borrowing," 53, cites Barbados 1661 Slave Code, Clause 20 and Hening, ed., *Statutes*, 2:270.

129. Brown, *Good Wives, Nasty Wenches*; Morgan, "'Some Could Suckle over Their Shoulder': Male Travelers, Female Bodies, and the Gendering of Racial Ideology, 1500–1770," *WMQ*, 3rd ser., 54 (1997): 167–92.

130. Brown, *Good Wives, Nasty Wenches*, 115–20; Hilary Beckles, *Natural Rebels: A Social History of Enslaved Black Women in Barbados* (New Brunswick, N.J., 1989).

131. Dunn, *Sugar and Slaves*, 228; Beckles, *Natural Rebels*, 8.

132. Brown, *Good Wives, Nasty Wenches*, 195–97.

133. Hall, ed., *Acts Passed in Barbados*, Brown, *Good Wives, Nasty Wenches*, esp. 107–36. See also Terrence W. Epperson, "'To Fix a Perpetual Brand': The Social Construction of Race in Virginia, 1675–1750" (Ph.D. diss., Temple University, 1991).

134. Fox, *To the Ministers, Teachers, and Priests*.

135. Gaspar, "'Rigid and Inclement'," 93.

136. Beckles, *White Servitude and Black Slavery*, 112.

137. Princess Anne County, Deed Book 1, part 1 (1691–1708), fol. 149

138. A comparison of housing patterns might prove fruitful as well. In Barbados, by the time of Richard Ligon's visit to the island between 1647 and 1650, before the time of the large-scale migrations to Virginia and elsewhere, Barbadian slaveowners and Barbadian slaves lived in separate dwellings. Ligon, *History of Barbados*, 48; Jerome S. Handler and Frederick W. Lange, *Plantation Slavery in Barbados: An Archaeological and Historical Investigation* (Cambridge, Mass., 1978), 95–97. During the early seventeenth century in Virginia, indentured servants and masters tended to live in the same house. During the 1670s and 1680s, there was increasing separation between living quarters. Historical archaeologist James Deetz attributes this shift to rising tensions between masters and servants after the 1660s and argues that the model was in place before the major influx of slaves directly from Africa at the end of the seventeenth century. However, the change could also have been influenced by the immigration of Barbadian slaveholders and slaves in the 1670s and 1680s. See James Deetz, "American Historical Archeology: Methods and Results," *Science*, 239 (1988): 366; Deetz's argument is based on Dell Upton, *Three Centuries of Maryland Architecture* (Annapolis, Md., 1982), 44–57. See Morgan, *American Slavery, American Freedom*, 235–92, for a discussion of the rising tensions between masters and indentured servants.

139. In 1730 when Bermuda legislators reduced a fine for killing a slave, they noted their borrowing by citing that "our prudent neighbors in America as Barbados &c have thought fitt" to do so. Nicholson, "Legal Borrowing," 52, cites Michael Craton, *Sinews of Empire: A Short History of British Slavery* (Garden City, N.Y., 1974), 172n, Bermuda Act of 1730.

140. Lorena S. Walsh has recently criticized earlier estimates that 20 to 40 percent of Chesapeake slaves came from the Caribbean through the second decade of the eighteenth century. While I suspect she is correct that percentages were lower, the purchase of Caribbean slaves continued, and the roles of those slaves continued to differ from

the roles of Africans. Walsh, "The Chesapeake Slave Trade." For works that suggest a continued high percentage of Caribbean slaves in the early eighteenth-century Chesapeake, see Craven, *White, Red, and Black*, 94; Philip D. Curtin, *The Atlantic Slave Trade: A Census* (Madison, Wisc., 1969), 143–45; Walter Minchinton, Celia King, and Peter Waite, eds., *Virginia Slave-Trade Statistics 1698–1775* (Richmond, Va., 1984); Herbert S. Klein, "Slaves and Shipping in Eighteenth-Century Virginia," *Journal of Interdisciplinary History* 5 (1975): 384–85.

141. Walsh, *From Calabar to Carter's Grove*; Thornton, "African Dimensions of the Stono Rebellion."

142. Elaine Breslaw provides a provocative example of the kinds of important new questions that arise when one considers the possible paths that Atlantic creoles took and the possible impact of their prior experiences on their later behavior. Breslaw postulates that Tituba, slave of Reverend Samuel Parris, had been a Brazilian Indian enslaved among Africans in Barbados and that the knowledge she took from her life in those places was crucial to the events that precipitated the Salem witch hunts. *Tituba, Reluctant Witch of Salem: Devilish Indians and Puritan Fantasies* (New York, 1996).

143. T. H. Breen found that no Virginia masters complained that they had difficulty communicating with slaves until the 1690s, suggesting that the increasing numbers of enslaved Africans who arrived after the mid-1670s did not overwhelm the creole black population, and learned English relatively quickly or primarily from creole slaves rather than their masters. "A Changing Labor Force," 17. Eighteenth-century Georgia Trustees explicitly instructed colonists to purchase creole slaves born in Carolina "or at least has learned the English language and how to work" before purchasing Africans, "because nothing can be accomplished with the new ones without the encouragement and example of the old Negroes." Samuel Urlsperer, ed., *Detailed Reports on the Salzburger Emigrants who Settled in America* (Athens, Ga., 1968–81), 14:233.

144. See Sidney W. Mintz and Richard Price, *The Birth of African-American Culture: An Anthropological Perspective* (1976) (Boston, 1992), 42–51. See also T. H. Breen on the importance of "charter generations." "Creative Adaptations: Peoples and Cultures," in Jack P. Greene and J. R. Pole, *Colonial British America: Essays in the New History of the Early Modern Era* (Baltimore, 1984), 215–21.

For works that posit an eighteenth-century development of African-American culture in the Chesapeake see Kulikoff, *Tobacco and Slaves* and "The Origins of Afro-American Society in Tidewater Maryland and Virginia, 1700–1790," *WMQ* 3rd ser., 35 (1978): 226–59; Jean Butenhoff Lee, "The Problem of the Slave Community in the Eighteenth-Century Chesapeake," *WMQ* 3rd ser., 43 (1986): 333–61; and Russell R. Menard, "The Maryland Slave Population, 1658–1730: A Demographic Profile of Blacks in Four Counties," *WMQ*, 3rd ser., 32 (1975): 29–54.

145. Ira Berlin, "From Creole to African," 53, 251–88.

146. Slaves from Spanish and Portuguese colonies, which, judging from names in headright lists, continued through the seventeenth century, may not have spoken English upon arrival, but brought previous experiences of slavery and possessed a greater ability than Africans to negotiate (and perhaps influence) their lives as slaves in English Virginia. See Craven, *White, Red, and Black*, 84–85 and Bruce, *Economic History of Virginia*, 2:86–87.

147. In 1655 the planter William Jones complained that a former servant of his, the tanner Thomas Bethel, told his Indian servants that Jones "was mynded to send

them to the Barbadoes." Jones worried that this threat would scare them into running away and so took Bethel to court. Deal, *Race and Class in Colonial Virginia*, 50, citing Northampton County Deeds and Wills, 1654–55, fol. 113.

148. Phillip J. Schwartz suggests that slaves' African legal heritage also shaped their reactions to their encounter with Virginia law. *Slave Laws in Virginia* (Athens, Ga., 1996), esp. 13–33.

149. Nugent, *Cavaliers and Pioneers*, 2:241–42; Bruce *Economic History of Virginia*, 2:86 (citing Records of Lancaster County 1690–1709, 26); and Craven, *White, Red, and Black*, 94. Craven refers to the "repeated use" of the name Barbados Mary in headright lists for the second half of the seventeenth century. *White, Red, and Black*, 94.

150. Bridenbaugh, *No Peace beyond the Line*, 350.

151. Quoted in Morgan, *Slave Counterpoint*, 20–21. Maryland planters complained similarly of the "continual concourse of Negroes on Sabboth and holy days meeting in great numbers" and described slaves "Drunke on the Lords Day beating their Negro Drums by which they call considerable Numbers of Negroes together in some Certaine places." Francis Nicholson, when governor of Maryland, asserted that for slaves to visit one another thirty or forty miles away was "common practice." Menard, "The Maryland Slave Population," 37; cites *Maryland Archives* 38, 48; Somerset County Judicials, 1707–11, 1, Hall of Records; Nicholson to the Board of Trade, August 20, 1698, *Maryland Archives* 23, 498.

152. Durand of Dauphiné, *A Huguenot Exile in Virginia*, 105.

153. Mintz and Price, *The Birth of African-American Culture*, 43. Some Virginia slaves came to the Chesapeake via the Dutch entrepôt of Curaçao (where Virginians traveled to trade in the 1640s). Bruce, *Economic History of Virginia*, 2:324, citing *Documents Relating to the Colonial History of New York*, 14:77.

154. See Breen and Innes, *"Myne Owne Ground": Race & Freedom on Virginia's Eastern Shore, 1640–1676* (New York, 1980), 71–72. J. Douglas Deal doubts Breen and Innes' conclusions, thinking their evidence insufficient. Deal, *Race and Class in Colonial Virginia*, 165, citing Nugent, *Cavaliers and Pioneers*, 1:328; Land Patent Book 4, 35, Library of Virginia; Donnan, ed., *Documents Illustrative of the Slave Trade*, 3:414, 449; and Northampton Deeds 1651–54, fol. 204. That Scarborough's daughters later claimed those 41 Africans among 70 headrights in March 1656 suggests that they did in fact arrive.

155. Deal, *Race and Class in Colonial Virginia*, 175.

156. Deal, *Race and Class in Colonial Virginia*, 166; cites Northampton County Orders 1657–64, 198; Whitelaw, *Virginia's Eastern Shore*, 180–86.

157. See Chapter 4 and Goodfriend, "Burghers and Blacks," 143–44. In the 1650s a Miss Verlett bought eight "seasoned" Caribbean slaves from Geurt Tyssen in New Amsterdam. Matson, *Merchants and Empire*, 76. George Hack's headrights in 1659 included George Nicholas Hack, Sepherin Hack, An[n] Kathrine Hack, Domingo, a Negro, George, a Negro, Kathrine, a Negro, Ann, a Negro, Hendrick Volkerts, Rnick Gerrits, Bermon Nephrinninge, Giltielmus Varlee (Varlett?), Augustine Hermons, Barnard Rams, Augustine Rieters, Adrian Rams, Claus Gisbert, Brigitta Williams, and Cornelis Hendrickson. Northampton County Court Order Book, 1654–61, fol. 4, 32–34, April 5, 1659. Domingo, likely an Atlantic creole given his Iberian name, was apparently the only slave on the list whom George and Anna had not named after themselves.

158. In 1679, Jaspar Dankaerts met an ill Augustine Herman at Bohemia Manor

where, according to Dankaerts, "There was not a Christian man, as they term it, to serve him; nobody but negroes." Dankaerts, *Journal*, 115.

159. Deal, *Race and Class in Colonial Virginia*, 339.

160. Goodfriend, *Before the Melting Pot*, 112–13. Philipse wrote that "It is by negroes that I find my cheivest Proffitt. All other trade I only look upon as by the by."

161. Ames, Northampton County, Virginia Court Order Books, 1654–61, 75. Dutch Eastern Shore merchant Simon Overzee was also a slaveowner. The St. Mary's County, Maryland, court acquitted him of murdering his slave Antonio in 1659. Lois Green Carr, "Sources of Political Stability and Upheaval in Seventeenth-Century Maryland," *Maryland Historical Magazome* 79 (1984): 50; Gary Wheeler Stone, "St. John's: Archaeological Questions and Answers," *Maryland Historical Magazine* 69 (1974): 157–58.

162. For the relationship between gender and race in shaping patriarchy in Virginia, see Brown, *Good Wives, Nasty Wenches*, passim. For further Dutch slaveownership in Virginia, see "Minor Family," *WMQ*, 1st ser., 8 (1899–1900): 198.

163. Deal, *Race and Class in Colonial Virginia*, 325; citing Neill, *Virginia Carolorum*, 131n, 142n, 413; Harlow, *History of Barbados*, 18–19; *CSPC 1574–1660*, 313; Northampton County 1640–45, 98; Northampton County Deeds and Wills 1645–51, 39. Jerome Hawley was one of the seventeen men "of good birth and qualitie" among Maryland's first colonists. Lois Green Carr, Russell R. Menard, and Lorena S. Walsh, *Robert Cole's World: Agriculture and Society in Early Maryland* (Chapel Hill, N.C., 1991), 9.

164. In his 1646 land grant, Hawley claimed headrights for three slaves—Tony, Philip, and Mingo. Mingo and Philip were in Virginia by 1644 and 1645, and all three may have come with him in his initial migration from Barbados. Hawley, who was heavily indebted, put up his slaves as security for debts to Captain William Stone (as attorney of London merchant Samuel Chandler) in 1644 and to J. Stronger in 1647. Deal, *Race and Class in Colonial Virginia*, 325–26.

165. W. Jeffrey Bolster, *Black Jacks: African American Seamen in the Age of Sail* (Cambridge, Mass., 1997).

166. Deal suggests that Cane's name may have come from former service (as a servant or slave) to the Boston merchant Robert Keayne. Deal also notes that Cane's deposition describes his loading tobacco of the Eastern Shore merchant and planter Stephen Charleton. While doing so, Deal notes, Cane probably met some of Charleton's slaves and those of his neighbor Richard Vaughan, and perhaps made personal contacts that later brought him to the Eastern Shore permanently. Contacts with free blacks such as Philip Mongon probably exerted even greater influence on Cane's decision. Deal, *Race and Class in Colonial Virginia*, 317, citing Tommy Hamm, "The American Slave Trade with Africa, 1620–1807" (Ph.D. diss., Indiana University, 1975), 17–21.

167. Deal, *Race and Class in Colonial Virginia*, 324, citing Accomack County Orders and Wills 1671–73, 95.

168. At midcentury, ship masters from Barbados sold slaves to Lower Norfolk planters. Presumably they could have sold them for higher prices to wealthier tobacco planters farther up the James River. However, Barbadian ship masters were likely to know planters in Lower Norfolk and have other intercolonial trade there, making it more convenient for them to sell any slaves they had brought in that (poorer) region of the Chesapeake. Bruce, *Economic History of Virginia*, 2:324–25, citing Records of Lower Norfolk County, 1646–51, f.p. 115, 205.

169. "A Perfect Description of Virginia" (London, 1649), in *Collections of the Massachusetts Historical Society* 2nd ser., 9 (1832): 105, 119.

170. Lorena Walsh has found that in seventeenth-century Charles County, Maryland, quarters with black slaves had more cattle than those with only white servants. This relationship may stem not so much from a recognized ability of Africans with cattle as from the fact that those planters with larger numbers of cattle likely traded to the Caribbean and therefore could buy slaves more easily than planters producing only tobacco. Walsh, "Charles County, Maryland" (Ph.D. diss., Michigan State University, 1977); Morgan, *Slave Counterpoint*, 5. Joyce Goodfriend notes that the West India Company in 1657 planned that its slaves learn "Trades as carpentering, bricklaying, blacksmithing and others . . . as it was formerly done in Brazil and now is in Guinea and other Colonies of the Company." "Burghers and Blacks," 131. Dutch openness to enslaved artisans might have encouraged Virginia masters such as Edmund Scarborough and Samuel Mathews to employ slaves rather than servants in these trades. For Scarborough's shoe production, see Sandra Lee Rux, "Edmund Scarborough—A Biography" (M.A. thesis, Trinity College, 1980), 45–46, 51–53.

171. Russell Menard suggests that contrary the appearance of colony-wide statistics, the purchase of large numbers of African slaves by tobacco producing counties did not come at a time of contracting tobacco production. Rather, in the Western Shore counties, tobacco productions proceeded apace, while the Eastern Shore and Southside counties diversified even more than they had in earlier decades. "From Servants to Slaves," 386.

Chapter 7

1. Sainsbury, ed., *Calendar of State Papers, Colonial (CSPC) 1574–1660*, 313, #71; 479–80, #3.

2. *CSPC 1574–1660*, 340, #16. On June 3, 1650, the Virginia Council included Governor Sir William Berkeley, John West, Sir William Davenant, Samuel Mathews, Nathaniel Littleton, Henry Brown, William Brocas, Richard Bennett, Thomas Willoughby, Argoll Yardley, Thomas Petus, Humphrey Heggenson, William Claiborne, George Ludlow, Richard Townsend, Thomas Stegg, and Ralph Wormeley. Of these, Berkeley, West, Mathews, Littleton, Bennett, Willoughby, Yardley, Heggenson, Claiborne, and Wormeley had recorded intercolonial connections.

3. Berkeley to Nicolls, July 7, 1665, Virginia Historical Society, Richmond, Mss. 10: no. 131.

4. Samuel Sewell almanac entry, August 24, 1680, *Sewall Papers*, 1 (1674–1700), in *Massachusetts Historical Society Collections* 5th ser. 5 (1878): 48–49.

5. Effingham to Philadelphia Pelham Howard, July 8, 1684, Warren M. Billings, ed., *The Papers of Francis Howard Baron Howard of Effingham, 1643–1695* (Richmond, Va., 1989), 134–35.

6. Effingham to Blathwayt, February 13, 1685, Billings, ed., *Papers of Effingham*, 179–80.

7. Quoted in Steele, *The English Atlantic*, 103.

8. For example, on December 3, 1666, Sir Thomas Langton wrote that because no

ship was bound directly for New England the letter would come by way of Virginia and that it should take only ten days to travel from Virginia to New England. *CSPC 1661–1668*, 1338, #429.

9. As early as 1638, in New England, London officials sought to regulate and facilitate intercolonial communications by establishing a colonial post office that would be responsible for keeping a register of all persons going to or coming from New England, with every passenger receiving a ticket "as at Barbados." *CSPC 1574–1660*, 275, #113. Officials never succeeded in establishing a colony-wide post office during the seventeenth century. On June 1, 1663, Charles II wrote to Barbados Governor Francis Lord Willoughby describing the complaints of daily inconveniences "through defect of a sure way of intelligence," especially from Virginia, New England, Jamaica, Barbados, and other parts of America. To remedy this problem, Charles ordered Willoughby to establish a public office or offices for receipt of all letters and postage and to take care that a constant correspondence be maintained with all parts of English America and that private persons be forbidden to carry letters or packets. *CSPC 1661–1668*, 135, #463.

10. "Virginia in 1637," *VMHB* 9 (1902): 176–77.

11. Minutes of the Council and Assembly of Barbadoes, December 18, 1662, *CSPC 1661–1668*, 116–17, #392.

12. Berkeley to Secretary of State Sir Henry Bennet, Earl of Arlington, June 12, 1669, *CSPC 1669–1674*, 27, #73.

13. Effingham to Philadelphia Pelham Howard, July 8, 1684, Billings, ed., *Papers of Effingham*, 133–36.

14. Goodfriend, *Before the Melting Pot*, 61.

15. Others included Thomas Ludwell, Major General Robert Smith, Captain Joseph Bridger, Captain Peter Jennings, and Thomas Ballard. July 12, 1666, *CSPC 1661–1668*, 395, #1237. See also *CSPC 1661–1669*, 423, #1306 (November 8, 1666), and 432, #1348 (December 11, 1666).

16. Matthew Cradock to [John Endicott]. Shurtleff, ed., *Records*, 1:383–85.

17. March 22, 1638, *CSPC 1574–1660*, 266, #90.

18. Berkeley (or the governors he appointed) were to appoint as well "six fitting persons to be a Council to each." *CSPC 1661–1668*, 159, #555. The Lords Proprietors of Carolina also instructed Berkeley in relation to "the settling and planting some part of the province of Carolina," *CSPC 1661–1668*, 159–60, #556. On September 8, 1663, they gave him power to settle two governors in case "those who are for liberty of conscience may desire a Governor whom those of the other side of the river may not like, the design being to encourage all sorts of persons to plant." *CSPC 1661–1668*, 160, #557. The following day the Lords Proprietors wrote to Barbadians Colonel Thomas Modyford and Peter Colleton that they were sending two letters with a copy of the charter and proposals touching on the settlement of Carolina, adding that "if any argument be made concerning the charge of discovery, it will be answered what the Proprietors have done from Virginia." *CSPC 1661–1668*, 161, #559.

19. September 9, 1663, *CSPC 1661–1668*, 161–62, #560.

20. *Suffolk Deeds Book* (Boston, 1903), 13:180–81

21. A 1648 Virginia promoter noted that "Governour Sir William, caused half a bushel of Rice (which he had procured) to be sowen, and it prospered gallantly, and he had fifteen bushels of it, excellent good Rice . . . and we doubt not in a short time to have Rice so plentiful as to afford it at 2d a pound if not cheaper, for we perceive

the ground and Climate is very proper for it as our Negroes affirme, which in their Country is most of their food, and very healthful for our bodies." "A Perfect Description of Virginia" (London, 1649), in Force, *Tracts and Other Papers*, 2:14.

22. September 1, 1671, *CSPC 1669–1674*, 255, #612.

23. *CSPC 1669–1674*, 52, #141; ibid., 195, #489.

24. *CSPC 1669–1674*, 196, # 492.

25. *CSPC 1669–1674*, 260, #630.

26. [September], 1670, note in handwriting of John Locke of provisions at Ashley River. *CSPC 1669–1674*, 89, #252.

27. May 1, 1671, *CSPC 1669–1674*, 211, #516.

28. Barbados required that anyone leaving notify officials three weeks before departing, obtain a ticket, and provide security for dependents they left on the island. Dunn, *Sugar and Slaves*, 110.

29. Peter Stuyvesant to Richard Bennett, May 30, 1653, in Charles T. Gehring, ed., *Correspondence, 1647–1653*, New Netherland Documents Series, vol. 11 (Syracuse, N.Y., 2000), 206.

30. *CSPC 1669–1671*, 64, #178.

31. See, for example, the dispute that Virginia Governor Francis, Baron Howard of Effingham described in the summer of 1684 over Captain Thomas Smith's ship the *Constant*. Effingham to Sir Leoline Jenkins, June 17, 1684, in Billings, ed., *Papers of Effingham*, 117.

32. *Briefe Relation of the late Horrid Rebellion acted in the Island of Barbados* (London, 1650), quoted in Bridenbaugh and Bridenbaugh, *No Peace beyond the Line*, 23.

33. Cecil Headlam, ed., *Calendar of State Papers, Colonial Series, 1701* (London, 1901), 651–52, # 1042.

34. Shurteff, ed., *Records of Massachusetts Bay*, 4:428–429.

35. Hoadly, ed., *New Haven Colony Records*, 1:169. Hart claimed that Catchman owed him debts.

36. Cynthia Van Zandt, "Negotiating Settlement: Colonialism, Cultural Exchange, and Conflict in Early Colonial Atlantic North America, 1580–1660" (Ph.D. diss, University of Connecticut, 1998), 260–61.

37. In 1696 Richard Kellam, Jr., sued John Fog for transporting a woman servant of Kellam's across the Bay to the Potomac River and selling her there. Ames, *Studies*, 81, citing Accomack County Orders, 1690–97, 231–32.

38. Ames, ed., *Accomack-Northampton 1640–1645* (Charlottesville, Va., 1973), 276–77.

39. May 28, 1645, Ames, ed., *Accomack-Northampton 1640–1645*, 440.

40. Noble, ed., *Records of the Court of Assistants*, 2:59. In 1680 John Brice and William Lane both traveled on foot from Maryland to Milford, where they stayed with John Wing. The court feared that they were either runaways or Roman Catholics. "Admissions to the town of Boston, 1670–1700," *Boston Records Commission* 10 (1886): 55–82, April 27, 1680. New England servants sometimes attempted to escape to Virginia. On June 14, 1631, the Massachusetts Court of Assistants ordered that Phillip Swaddon be whipped for running away from his master Robert Seely and trying to go to Virginia. Noble, ed., *Records of the Court of Assistants*, 2:16.

41. Accomack County Virginia Order Book, 1666–70, Virginia Historical Society, Mss. 3Ac275a, typescript by Susie May Ames, 1942–46, 92–94. William Alchurch and

some of the others caught two of Scarborough's horses and sneaked to Pungoteage at night where they opened a storehouse, stole sails, bread, and meat belonging to Captain Pitts, and took it to Craddock Creek. On the night of June 15, Tarr, Wells, Davis, Mackmayon, Michell, and Micave took clothing, a gun, and other supplies and left for Craddock Creek, where Captain Bowman had left a boat ready in the water, his oars by his door, and his house open with provisions in it. Tarr, Wells, Michell, and Davis had these things in their possession when arrested. On Scarborough's petition, the Accomack court sentenced the returned runaways to make up their own time plus that of all those still absent, the costs of pursuing them, and the cost of the goods they had taken that had not been returned. Ames discusses the case in *Studies*, 89.

42. Accomack County Order Book, 1666–70, 97–98. The plans involved John Bloxam, Henry Chancee, William Court, Robert Hodge, Robert Parker, John Parker, John James Wells, Mr. Brown's two men (?) and Stephen, and Mr. West's Patrick, Abraham, John Tizard, John Tarr, (?) Hodrington, Miles Grace, and William Alchurch.

43. Ames, ed., *Accomack-Northampton 1632–1640*, 120–21.

44. Ames, *Studies*, 75, cites Accomack Wills, 1673–76, 296.

45. Council Minutes, July 5, 1692, McIlwaine, ed., *Executive Journals*, 1:262.

46. Ames, *Studies*, citing Accomack Wills and Orders, 1682–97, 93.

47. Franklin Bowditch Dexter, ed., *New Haven Town Records, 1649–1769* (New Haven, Conn., 1917), 2:275.

48. Accomack County Order Book, 1666–70, 223–24. Joanna sought refuge with intercolonial trader Ann Taft. Taft's trading partner merchant Edmund Scarborough served as Joanna's doctor and prepared the case against Smith. Rux, "Edmund Scarburgh," 79–80, cites Minutes of Council and General Court. For a discussion of this case, see Irmina Wawrzyczek, "The Women of Accomack Versus Henry Smith," *VMHB* 105 (1997): 5–26.

49. Ames, *Studies*, 88, citing Northampton County Orders and Wills, 1698–1710. See ibid., 189, 375 for similar cases involving North Carolina and New England.

50. Order Concerning Nathaniel Bacon, Massachusetts Historical Society Photostat from Massachusetts Archives (Boston), n.p.

51. Boston Town Records, June 29, 1678, *Boston Record Commission Report 7* (Boston, 1881), 121–22.

52. Ames, *Accomack-Northampton 1640–1645*, 313–17.

53. Accomack County Order Book, 1666–70, 54–55.

54. Accomack County Order Book, 1666–70, 104.

55. See Chapter 1 for discussion of Fleet's and Claiborne's activities trading with Indians in the northern Chesapeake.

56. J. Frederick Fausz, "Merging and Emerging Worlds: Anglo-Indian Interest Groups and the Development of the Seventeenth-Century Chesapeake" in Lois Green Carr, Philip D. Morgan, and Jean B. Russo, eds., *Colonial Chesapeake Society* (Chapel Hill, N.C., 1988), 75–84. When Dutch merchant David Peterson De Vries described the Chesapeake Bay, he explained that on Kent Island "many of them reside, under one Captain Klaver's government, who carried on there a great trade in peltries." De Vries, *Voyages*, 53–54.

57. Emphasis mine. The "Relation" implied that the Indians were alarmed because Claiborne spread a rumor that six ships had come "with a power of Spaniards." "Relation of the Successful Beginnings of Lord Baltimore's Plantation in Maryland," in Neill, *Founders of Maryland*, 38.

58. For more on Claiborne's relationship with the Susquehannocks and with Maryland, see Fausz "Merging and Emerging Worlds," 47–91. Sir John Wolstenholme and other Virginia planters joined Captain William Claiborne in petitioning the Privy Council that because they had spent a great deal of their own money to settle Kent Island, now within Lord Baltimore's patent, they might enjoy free trade and Baltimore might settle elsewhere. *CSPC 1574–1660*, 172, #87. Fleet convinced Calvert that Claiborne was inciting Maryland Indians to resist. On June 20, 1634, Claiborne met with the chief of the Patuxents in the presence of the governor's brother George Calvert (who lived and died in Virginia), Sir John Winter's brother Frederick, other Marylanders, and the Virginians John Utie and Samuel Mathews. The Patuxent chief denied that Claiborne had incited him against the Marylanders, saying that Fleet was a liar. Neill, *Founders of Maryland*, 49–50.

59. The other trader was Charles Harmon. Neill, *Founders of Maryland*, 51.

60. Neill, *Founders of Maryland*, 52; Fausz, "Merging and Emerging Worlds," 71–72.

61. Ames, ed., *Accomack-Northampton 1640–1645*, 170, 377.

62. Neill, *Founders of Maryland*, 11.

63. Neill, *Founders of Maryland*, 17.

64. Neill, *Founders of Maryland*, 17–18.

65. Neill, *Founders of Maryland*, 18, citing an 1860 Survey Map of the Potomac.

66. *CSPC 1669–1674*, 52, #142.

67. Merrell, *The Indians' New World*, 52–55, 68–77.

68. January 26, 1691, McIlwaine, ed., *Executive Journals 1680–1699*, 147.

69. McIlwaine, ed., *Executive Journals 1680–1699*, 157–58.

Chapter 8

1. Andrews, *Colonial Period*, vol. 4; Sosin, *English America and the Restoration Monarchy of Charles II*; J. M. Sosin, *English America and the Revolution of 1688: Royal Administration and the Structure of Provincial Government* (Lincoln, Neb., 1982); Wesley Frank Craven, *The Colonies in Transition, 1660–1713* (New York, 1968); Michael Garibaldi Hall, *Edward Randolph and the American Colonies, 1676–1703* (Chapel Hill, N.C., 1960); Ian K. Steele, *Politics of Colonial Policy: The Board of Trade in Colonial Administration, 1696–1720* (Oxford, 1968); Alison Gilbert Olson, *Making the Empire Work: London and American Interest Groups, 1690–1790* (Cambridge, Mass., 1992); Stephen Saunders Webb, *The Governors-General: The English Army and the Definition of the Empire, 1569–1681* (Chapel Hill, N.C., 1979). Considerable argument exists over the relative primacy of military, political, and commercial goals in shaping English colonial policy during the second half of the seventeenth century. See especially Richard Johnson, "The Imperial Webb: The Thesis of Garrison government in Early America Considered," *WMQ* 3rd ser., 43 (1986): 408–30; Webb, "The Data and Theory of Restoration Government," *WMQ* 3rd ser., 43 (1986): 431–59; "Governors or Generals?: A Note on Martial Law and the Revolution of 1689 in English America," *WMQ* 3rd ser., 46 (1989): 304–14. While Webb is correct to point to royal dependence on international warfare and military personnel to maintain English authority in America, his military emphasis

goes too far in downplaying the significance of commerce. Trade shaped Atlantic webs of communication and therefore the configuration of England's growing empire. While the Crown did exercise military control over its colonies, its ultimate concern was to funnel economic benefits of increasing Atlantic commerce to England, protecting those revenues from foreign competitors as well as (to some degree) from its own colonists.

2. "Speech of Sir William Berkeley, and Declaration of the Assembly, March, 1651," *VMHB* 1 (1893): 75–76.

3. September 26, 1651, Sainsbury, ed., *Calendar of State Papers, Colonial Series (CSPC), 1574–1660* (London, 1860), 360–61, #36. An earlier attempt to foster intercolonial conformity at mid-century centered on events of the English Civil War, Interregnum, and Restoration.

4. Steele, *The English Atlantic*, 118–20, 229–50. See also Steele, *Politics of Colonial Policy*; Webb, *The Governors-General*; Webb, *1676: The End of American Independence* (New York, 1984).

5. "Colonel Quary's Memorial to the Lords Commissioners of Trade and Plantations, on the State of the American Colonies," *Massachusetts Historical Society Collections* 3rd ser., 7 (1838): 222–47.

6. See Chapter 1.

7. Washburn, *The Governor and the Rebel*, 19–20.

8. Colonists elsewhere reached similar conclusions about Indians and colonial borders. On July 8, 1663, John Clarke (on behalf of the inhabitants of Rhode Island) described the history of the colony, noting that the colony could not legally "invade the natives within the bounds of other colonies without the consent of said colonies, nor for other colonies to invade the natives of other inhabitants within the bounds hereafter mentioned . . . without the consent of the Governor and Company of said colony." *CSPC 1661–1668*, 148, #512.

9. Sandra Lee Rux, "Edmund Scarborough—A Biography" (M.A. thesis, Trinity College, 1980), 33, cites Northampton County Court Records, 4:130.

10. The Susquehannocks had been Virginia trader William Claiborne's link to the northern fur trade during the early seventeenth century, until Maryland declared war on the Susquehannocks and prevented the Susquehannocks and Virginians from trading with one another. After the 1630s, the Susquehannocks traded primarily with the Swedes and Dutch in New Sweden and the parts of New Netherland that became English Delaware. From New York the Iroquois Five Nations fought the Hurons and their allies over control of the fur trade in the first half of the seventeenth century. The Five Nations beat and scattered the Hurons in the late 1640s and then turned on the Hurons' trading partners and allies, including the Susquehannocks. They failed to conquer the Susquehannocks but continued to fight with them for decades. Jennings, *The Ambiguous Iroquois Empire*, 98–112.

11. For example, in 1660 an Oneida war party attacked Maryland Piscataways "for being friends" to Maryland and the Susquehannocks. Maryland declared war on the Five Nations, who were allied with New York. Jennings, *Ambiguous Iroquois Empire*, 127.

12. Jennings, "Susquehannock," in Bruce Trigger, ed., *Northeast*, vol. 15 of Sturtevant, ed., *Handbook of North American Indians* (Washington, D.C., 1978), 365.

13. Jennings, *Ambiguous Iroquois Empire*, 140–42.

14. Washburn, *The Governor and the Rebel*, 21.

15. Indeed, Francis Jennings argues that Maryland had to help Virginia fight the Susquehannocks to avoid Virginia's conquering the Susquehannocks on their land in Maryland and then claiming Maryland land by rights of conquest. Jennings, *Ambiguous Iroquois Empire*, 146. Maryland, however, would have needed to participate to ensure Virginia would respect the boundary in the future with regard to incursions such as this, without necessarily fearing Virginia would try to annex Maryland territory.

16. Washington's first cousin, also John Washington, moved from Barbados to Surry County, Virginia.

17. Washburn, *The Governor and the Rebel*, 21–24.

18. Jennings, *Ambiguous Iroquois Empire*, 145–47; Morgan, *American Slavery, American Freedom*, 250–51.

19. For an exploration of the possibility that more mobile Atlantic residents possessed less strong allegiance to particular visions of individual colonies (using Isaac Allerton, Jr.,'s father as an example), see Cynthia Van Zandt, "The Dutch Connection: Isaac Allerton and the Dynamics of English Cultural Anxiety in the *Gouden EEUW*," in Rosemarijn Hoefte and Johanna C. Kardux, eds., *Connecting Cultures: The Netherlands in Five Centuries of Transatlantic Exchange* (Amsterdam, 1994), 51–76

20. Wilcomb Washburn, "Governor Berkeley and King Philip's War," *New England Quarterly* 30 (1957): 363–77, quote, 366–67, citing contemporary copy of letter from Berkeley to [Ludwell], February 16, [1676], library of the Marquis of Bath at Longleat, Wilts, England, the Henry Coventry Papers, 78, fol. 56. Washburn edited a copy which is at the Library of Congress.

21. Address to Charles II from the Virginia Assembly, March 24, 1676. Washburn, "Governor Berkeley and King Philip's War," 368–70, citing Longleat, LXXVII, fols. 66–67. The Susquehannock War likewise scared New Englanders, who expressed similar fears of long distance Indian alliances and strategies.

22. Berkeley to Ludwell, quoted in Washburn, "Governor Berkeley," 371, citing PRO C.O. 1/36, no. 37.

23. Berkeley to Secretary Joseph Williamson, quoted in Washburn, "Governor Berkeley," 374–75, citing C.O. 1/36, no. 36.

24. One of the primary goals of Iroquois warfare in the Chesapeake and farther south was assimilation, which would increase the numbers of the Iroquois and therefore strengthen them for fighting on other fronts. The Susquehannocks were especially desirable because of their reputation as skillful fighters. Additionally, there were still personal accounts to settle from their decades-long war. However, the Iroquois apparently were quite willing to accept Susquehannock assimilation initiated by Andros and achieved through treaties rather than through their own warfare.

25. Jennings, *Ambiguous Iroquois Empire*, 149–52.

26. Jennings, *Ambiguous Iroquois Empire*, 155–57.

27. Jennings, *Ambiguous Iroquois Empire*, xvii.

28. Jennings, *Ambiguous Iroquois Empire*, 159, 164.

29. The Iroquois required Chesapeake Indians' presence at treaty negotiations in order to include them in any settlement. Jennings, *Ambiguous Iroquois Empire*, 169. Iroquois traditional use of the paths south through the Shenandoah Valley facilitated Iroquois and Susquehannock attacks.

30. Jennings, *Ambiguous Iroquois Empire*, 215–16, citing Paul A. W. Wallace, *Indians in Pennsylvania* (Harrisburg, Pa., 1961), chaps. 14 and 15.

31. Penn to Effingham, June 8, 1684, Billings, ed., *Papers of Effingham*, 112–13.

32. Billings, ed., *Papers of Effingham*, 145n; Robert Livingston, *The Livingston Indian Records 1666–1723*, ed. Lawrence H. Leder (Gettysburg, Pa., 1956), 71–74.

33. Effingham to Philadelphia Pelham Howard, July 8, 1684, Billings, ed., *Papers of Effingham*, 133–36.

34. *Livingston Indian Records*, 71–73; Jennings, *Ambiguous Iroquois Empire*, 180.

35. Jennings, *Ambiguous Iroquois Empire*, 181–82.

36. They were to go by July 10, 1685. The council added, probably unnecessarily, that it would "be for ye Countries Interest, that Presents be made from this Government, and our Indians, to such Indians, as they goe to treat with, being a Custome amongst all nations of Indians, as ye tye and pledge for the performance of Articles of Peace." May 7, 1685, McIlwaine, ed., *Executive Journals 1680–1699*, 70–72.

37. Effingham to William Penn, July 9, 1687, Billings, ed., *Papers of Effingham*, 314.

38. Byrd to Effingham, June 10, 1689, Billings, ed., *Papers of Effingham*, 416–17.

39. McIlwaine, ed., *Executive Journals 1680–1699*, 103–5.

40. Stephen Saunders Webb, *Lord Churchill's Coup: The Anglo-American Empire and the Glorious Revolution Reconsidered* (New York, 1995), 198.

41. For the impact of King William's War on the Iroquois, see Richter, *Ordeal of the Longhouse*, 162–89.

42. In 1668 (?) Captain Robinson proposed to the King that Newfoundland should be well supported because the French would be bad neighbors to his Majesty's flourishing plantations in New England, New York, and Virginia. *CSPC 1661–1668*, 559, #1731.

43. The council was, however, careful about news. In 1691 it ordered that if anyone received "by Letters, or heare any strange News which may tend to the disturbance of the Peace of this Government, that they doe not presume to publish the same, but with the first Conveniency repaire to the next Justice of the Peace, and acquaint him therewith who is to Act therein according to Law." February 20, 1691, McIlwaine, ed., *Executive Journals 1680–1699*, 160–61.

44. For dates see Salmon and Campbell, eds., *Hornbook of Virginia History*, 104.

45. As Virginia's lieutenant governor, Nicholson traveled to New York in 1700 where he met with New York Governor Bellomont and Pennsylvania Governor William Penn. Steele, *The English Atlantic*, 127, cites CO 5/1289 21–25, Penn to the Board of Trade, 13 December 1700.

46. McIlwaine, ed., *Executive Journals 1680–1699*, 111.

47. The council also ordered the interpreters to tell the Virginia Indians "to be very Vigilent" in watching for "the Approach of any Forreigne Indyans." They were immediately to tell the closest militia officer if they heard of any. June 4, 1690, McIlwaine, ed., *Executive Journals 1680–1699*, 116–17. A year later, on May 18, 1691, the same fears persisted. See ibid., 182.

48. June 5, 1690, McIlwaine, ed., *Executive Journals 1680–1699*, 118; July 24, 1690, ibid., 120. In August Nicholson also interviewed George Lindsey, a soldier who had served in New York and had come to Virginia, about the situation in New York. From Lindsey's report Nicholson concluded that New York was in serious need of help, and sent Lindsey to London to give his account there. August 16, 1690, ibid., 128–33.

49. Isaac Allerton, Jr., was exempted from the next council meeting because he was commander of the Potomac militia. December 9, 1690, McIlwaine, ed., *Executive Journals 1680–1699*, 138–40.

50. January 15, 1691, McIlwaine, ed., *Executive Journals 1680–1699*, 140–46. For an analysis of Leisler's Rebellion in its Atlantic context, see John M. Murrin, "The Menacing Shadow of Louis XIV and the Rage of Jacob Leisler: The Constitutional Ordeal of Seventeenth-Century New York" (1990), in Stanley N. Katz, John M. Murrin, and Douglas Greenburg, *Colonial America: Essays in Politics and Social Development*, 5th ed. (New York, 2001), 380–418.

51. February 20, 1691, McIlwaine, ed., *Executive Journals 1680–1699*, 160–61.

52. January 15, 1691, McIlwaine, ed., *Executive Journals 1680–1699*, 140–46. Eyewitnesses John Swindall (a soldier who had been among the troops in New England's failed expedition to Canada the previous August), John Callaford, and Bartholomew Greene described the events to the Virginia Assembly. Greene's testimony included his observation that "Leisler and ye power of Boston, are at difference having as I heard little Correspondence together." January 26, 1691, ibid., 149–52.

53. April 19, 1692, McIlwaine, ed., *Executive Journals 1680–1699*, 238. Apparently the news was good because the following November the Council ordered the rangers to recess for the winter, as was usual. November 1, 1692, ibid., 272.

54. June 23–24, 1692, McIlwaine, ed., *Executive Journals 1680–1699*, 253–54. The councilors reiterated the safety need for "a friendly Correspondence . . . with the Inhabitants of Maryland which will be of great use in these times."

55. In March 1693 the Stafford militia commander George Mason wrote to the council that the Piscataway Indians had been coming over the Potomac from Maryland and that because it scared the colonists in Stafford he had asked the werowance of the Piscataways "that neither his nor any other Indians should come on our Side of the River till further Order from his Excelly," but the Council decided that the 1691 act for free trade with Indians permitted Piscataways to cross the river. March 17, 1693, McIlwaine, ed., *Executive Journals 1680–1699*, 278–79.

56. McIlwaine, ed., *Executive Journals 1680–1699*, 92–94.

57. McIlwaine, ed., *JHB 1659/60–1693*, 298 (May 1, 1688), 393 (April 13, 1693), 488–91 (November 11, 1693).

58. At the same meeting the councilors read a letter from Maryland Governor Lionel Copley saying that after reading the treaties of New York with the Five Nations, he would not send any money to New York until Virginia did. Nicholson was to write to Copley to tell him that Virginia, "knowing it to be their Duties to their Mas to give all Needfull Assistance to any of the Neighbouring Governments," had recently sent "one hundred & odd pounds" sterling to New York and "and have now Ordered one hundred pounds more to be sent them." July 6, 1692, McIlwaine, ed., *Executive Journals 1680–1699*, 259.

59. "Quary's Memorial," 231–32.

60. In the summer of 1693, New York Lieutenant Governor Benjamin Fletcher and his Council asked Andros to appoint a commissioner from Virginia to go to New York in October, to decide with other commissioners from New England, Maryland, and Pennsylvania, on quotas of men and money, "for the defence of their Maj[es]t[y']s Frontier, Garrisons att Albany during the present Warr." The Council sent Captain Miles Cary. September 1, 1693, McIlwaine, ed., *Executive Journals 1680–1699*, 296; July 18, 1694, ibid., 315.

61. If the Virginia rangers saw any indication that "any Forreign Indians" or French were approaching, the commanders were to inform immediately the closest militia officer who could then raise the militia. January 15, 1691, McIlwaine, ed., *Executive Journals 1680–1699*, 140–46.

62. March 7, 1691, McIlwaine, ed., *Executive Journals 1680–1699*, 162.

63. June 24, 1692, McIlwaine, ed., *Executive Journals 1680–1699*, 254–55. In 1669 (?) Nicolls wrote that in New York "every man, on his request, has liberty to trade for furs." *CSPC 1669–1674*, 49, #137.

64. Carl Bridenbaugh, *Cities in the Wilderness: The First Century of Urban Life in America, 1625–1742* (1938) (New York, 1964), 193.

65. January 15, 1698, McIlwaine, ed., *Executive Journals 1680–1699*, 377. The packets for other colonies traveled by way of Virginia; in March John Chyles requested payment for having been sent express to Maryland and New York "with his Majesties packets to those govts." March 9, 1698, Ibid., 379.

66. March 1698 (?), McIlwaine, ed., *Executive Journals 1680–1699*, 409.

67. June 22, 1699, McIlwaine, ed., *Executive Journals 1680–1699*, 459.

68. "Quary's Memorial," 231–32.

69. "Quary's Memorial," 231–34.

70. "Quary's Memorial," 232–34.

71. "Quary's Memorial," 232–34.

72. "Representation of Mr Byrd Concerning Proprietary Governments Anno 1700 [i.e., 1699]," in Louis B. Wright, ed., *An Essay upon the Government of the English Plantations on the Continent of America (1701)* (San Marino, 1945) (New York, 1972), 58–63; Carole Shammas, "Benjamin Harrison III and the Authorship of *An Essay upon the Government of the English Plantations on the Continent of America*," *VMHB* 84 (1976): 166–73.

Conclusion

1. For example, see "Petition of Divers Merchants and Others," "Virginia in 1652–53," *VMHB* 17 (1909): 357. Samuel Mathews (son of De Vries's acquaintance), acting as "Agent for the inhabitants of Virginia," was the primary signer.

2. As David Peterson De Vries's experiences illustrate, before 1650 even international disputes over territorial claims were of little concern to many colonists. See De Vries, *Voyages*.

3. See Russell Menard, "From Servants to Slaves: The Transformation of the Chesapeake Labor System," *Southern Studies* 16 (1977): 386.

4. Cary Carson, Norman F. Barka, William M. Kelso, Garry Wheller Stone, and Dell Upton, "Impermanent Architecture in the Southern American Colonies," in Robert Blair St. George, ed., *Material Life in America, 1600–1860* (Boston, 1988), 145.

5. See, for example, Morgan, *American Slavery, American Freedom*, 138.

6. Cynthia Van Zandt examines conflicts between William Bradford and Isaac Allerton, Sr., to argue that individuals such as Allerton, who traveled regularly in the Atlantic World, held property and offices in multiple colonies, and resisted strict one-colony allegiance requirements, were more common than historiography suggests, in

part because that historiography depends to such a great extent on men like Bradford, prolific writers who found Allerton's mobility and flexibility subversive and thus worked to define such peripatetic lives as aberrant. "The Dutch Connection: Isaac Allerton and the Dynamics of English Cultural Anxiety in the *Gouden EEUW*," in Rosemarijn Hoefte and Johanna C. Kardux, eds., *Connecting Cultures: The Netherlands in Five Centuries of Transatlantic Exchange* (Amsterdam, 1994), 51–76; Van Zandt, "Negotiating Settlement: Colonialism, Cultural Exchange, and Conflict in Early Colonial Atlantic North America, 1580–1660" (Ph.D. diss., University of Connecticut, 1998), 187–229.

7. This generalization may apply less in the Chesapeake than to other colonies because the lack of port towns in seventeenth-century Virginia made it difficult for customs officers to control trade.

8. Philip Alexander Bruce, *Economic History of Virginia*, 2:328n., cites Records of Lower Norfolk County, 1675–86, 292.

9. "Colonel Quarry's Memorial to the Lords Commissioners of Trade and Plantations, On the State of the American Colonies," *Massachusetts Historical Society Collections* 3rd ser., 7 (1838): 232–34.

10. Sandra Lee Rux, "Edmund Scarburgh—A Biography" (M.A. thesis, Trinity College, 1980), 15–16, 36–39.

11. Intercolonial Virginians also took prominent roles in the controversy over the establishment of Maryland, in part because of its effect on Indian trade in the northern Chesapeake and in part because of their vehement opposition as Puritans to the establishment of a neighboring Catholic colony. Among some Virginians, Maryland's Catholicism elicited fears of French and Indian or Spanish and Indian attacks on Virginia

12. For example, news of Leisler's 1689 Rebellion in New York reached Virginia via colonial American trade routes. Virginia's relationship to Iroquoia via precontact trade routes, in other words its location in the North American world, made the news pertinent. The impact of the Glorious Revolution on the English Atlantic and Anglo-French warfare within the larger Atlantic world provided the contexts necessary to make sense of the rebellion and the dangers it caused. When Virginia was asked, as a colony, to aid New York with money and soldiers in the decade of Anglo-French warfare that followed, it was as a colony that it resisted or complied.

13. Ian K. Steele attributes the growing efficiency of Chesapeake trade largely to the doubling of merchant seamen's wages that accompanied the generation of war beginning in 1689. *The English Atlantic*, 42.

14. Kevin P. Kelly argues that in Surry County, Virginia, isolation became more of a problem as the colonial population increased and could no longer confine its settlement to the James and its tributaries, which provided easy transportation, and thus at in the 1680s and 1690s built a network of roads. "'In dispers'd Country Plantations': Settlement Patterns in Seventeenth-Century Surry County, Virginia," in Thad W. Tate and David L. Ammerman, eds., *The Chesapeake in the Seventeenth Century: Essays on Anglo-American Society and Politics* (New York, 1989), 203.

15. Lorena S. Walsh, "The Chesapeake Slave Trade: Regional Patterns, African Origins, and Some Implications," *WMQ* 3rd ser., 58 (2001), 139–69; Morgan, *Slave Counterpoint*, 58–85.

Index

Acknowledgments

Over the course of writing this book, I have accumulated many debts to individuals and institutions. Financial support came from the Virginia Historical Society and the Center for the Study of New England History at the Massachusetts Historical Society (in the form of Andrew W. Mellon Fellowships), the Institute for Atlantic History, Culture, and Society (now the Global Institute for Culture, Power, and History) at Johns Hopkins University, District 9 of the National Society of Colonial Dames of America, the Jamestown Society, the Johns Hopkins University, and Texas A&M University. I received invaluable help from the staffs of the Library of Virginia, the Virginia Historical Society, the Massachusetts Historical Society, the Barbados Archives, and the Colonial Williamsburg Foundation. At Colonial Williamsburg, Ann Smart Martin, Julie Richter, Antoinette van Zelm, and Jennifer Jones made my research trips as enjoyable as they were profitable.

My most important debts are to friends, colleagues, and teachers for encouragement and criticism. At the University of Oregon, Matthew Dennis encouraged me to pursue this project, and his confidence in its importance has helped me to complete it. I was lucky at Johns Hopkins to have Jack Greene as advisor. His high standards for scholarship and his insistence on precise and logical argument have made this a better book and me a better historian. Robert Haskett, Quintard Taylor, Michel-Rolph Trouillot, and Franklin Knight also provided help at the early stages of formulating the project. The members of Jack Greene's ongoing research seminar were patient with my drafts and incisive with their criticism. In particular, I would like to thank James Baird, Nuran Çinlar, Carla Gerona, Rina Palumbo, Karin Wulf, and Natalie Zacek. Ann Little provided hospitality in Boston and generously sent me New Haven references. Pedro Welch introduced me to Barbados and the Barbados Archives. Tom Dunlap, Alan Kulikoff, and Daniel Vickers each read chapters, helping me think through questions of geographic, migration, and maritime history respectively. Max Edelson, Alison Games, Craig Hatfield, Carol Higham, James Horn, and Harold Livesay have generously read entire drafts of the revised manuscript. Each has made significant improvements. The History Department at Texas A&M University has provided me with time and resources to revise the manuscript and a stimulating intellectual environment in which to do so. At the University of Pennsylvania Press, Robert Lockhart read multiple revisions with great care as he helped transform the manuscript into a book. Judy Mattson manually corrected a formatting problem on very short notice. Michael Means at International Mapping Associates drew the maps. Many others have sent citations and references, listened to developing ideas, and asked important questions. Jon Maxwell has had faith in me and this project from the beginning.